Ireland's Great Famine, Britain's Great Failure

Ireland's Great Famine, Britain's Great Failure

William H. A. Williams

FIRST HILL BOOKS
An imprint of Wimbledon Publishing Company

This edition first published in UK and USA 2023
by FIRST HILL BOOKS
75–76 Blackfriars Road, London SE1 8HA, UK
or PO Box 9779, London SW19 7ZG, UK
and
244 Madison Ave #116, New York, NY 10016, USA

First published in the UK and USA by Anthem Press in 2022

Copyright © William H. A. Williams 2023

The author asserts the moral right to be identified as the author of this work.

All rights reserved. Without limiting the rights under copyright reserved above,
no part of this publication may be reproduced, stored or introduced into
a retrieval system, or transmitted, in any form or by any means
(electronic, mechanical, photocopying, recording or otherwise),
without the prior written permission of both the copyright
owner and the above publisher of this book.

British Library Cataloguing-in-Publication Data
A catalogue record for this book is available from the British Library.

Library of Congress Control Number: 2023935807

ISBN-13: 978-1-83998-969-8 (Pbk)
ISBN-10: 1-83998-969-6 (Pbk)

Cover Image: Bridget O'Donnell and children. She appeared in the Illustrated
London News, December 29, 1849, page 404. Image courtesy of the IU Libraries

This title is also available as an e-book.

To my grandchildren, Evie and Ziggy

CONTENTS

List of Figures		ix
Preface		xiii
Introduction		1

Part One   Culture, Religion and Politics in the Pre-Famine Decades

Chapter One	The Colonial Background	9
Chapter Two	From Stereotypes to Narrative: The Making of the Irish Other	15
Chapter Three	Politics and Religion in the Age of Daniel O'Connell	25
Chapter Four	Morality and Economics in the Age of Atonement	35

Part Two   The Rise and Fall of the Ireland's Potato Economy

Chapter Five	Poverty and Inequality: The Economic Background	47
Chapter Six	People, Land and Potatoes	59
Chapter Seven	*Phytophthora infestans* and the Collapse of the Potato Economy	89

Part Three   The Famine Years

Chapter Eight	The Arrival of the Potato Blight: 1845–46	103
Chapter Nine	The First Phase of the Famine: Black '46–'47	123
Chapter Ten	A False Dawn: 1847–48	167
Chapter Eleven	The Return of the Blight: 1848–49	195
Chapter Twelve	Years of Evictions: 1849–52	215

Part Four   The Post-Famine Years

Chapter Thirteen   Post-Famine Dreams and Irish Realities in the 1850s   233

Chapter Fourteen   In the Famine's Wake   249

Conclusion   277

Bibliography   291

Index   309

FIGURES

1. "The Irish Ogre Fattening on the Finest Pisantry," *Punch*, July 8, 1843 — 33
2. "The Real Potato Blight of Ireland," *Punch*, December 14, 1845 — 107
3. "The Cork Society of Friends' Soup Kitchen," *Illustrated London News*, January 16, 1847 — 150
4. "M. Soyer Model Soup Kitchen," *Illustrated London News*, April 17, 1847 — 152
5. "A View in Achill," *Illustrated London News*, March 3, 1844 — 160
6. "Scalpeen," *Illustrated London News*, December 15, 1849 — 206
7. "The Scalp of Brian O'Conner, Near Kilrush Union-House," *Illustrated London News*, December 22, 1849 — 207
8. "Conditions in Ireland," *Illustrated London News* — 219
9. "Conditions in Ireland," continued, *Illustrated London News* — 220
10. "Miss Kennedy Distribution Clothing at Kilrush," *Illustrated London News*, December 22, 1849 — 221
11. "Village of Moyeen," *Illustrated London News*, December 22, 1849 — 222
12. "Searching for Potatoes in a Stubble Field," *Illustrated London News*, December 22, 1849 — 223
13. O'Donnell. "Bridget O'Donnell and Children" *Illustrated London News*, December 22, 1849 — 224

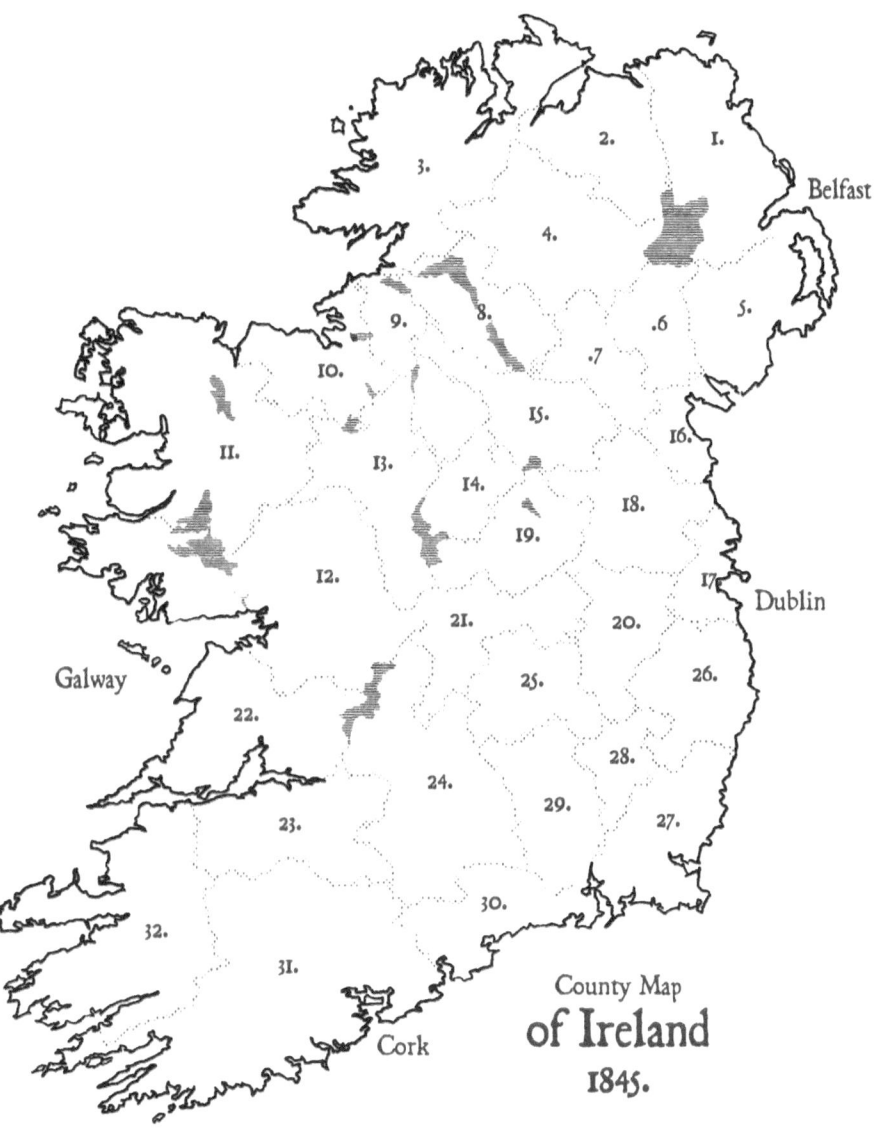

KEY TO THE COUNTY MAP OF IRELAND

1. ANTRIM
2. LONDONDERRY
3. DONEGAL
4. TYRONE
5. DOWN
6. ARMAGH
7. MONAGHAN
8. FERMANAGH
9. LEITRIM
10. SLIGO
11. MAYO
12. GALWAY
13. ROSCOMMON
14. LONGFORD
15. CAVAN
16. LOUTH
17. DUBLIN
18. MEATH
19. WESTMEATH
20. KILDARE
21. KINGS COUNTY (renamed OFFALY)
22. CLARE
23. LIMERICK
24. TIPPERARY
25. QUEENS COUNTY (renamed LAOIS)
26. WICKLOW
27. WEXFORD
28. CARLOW
29. KILKENNY
30. WATERFORD
31. CORK
32. KERRY

Map 1

PREFACE

My interest in the Irish Famine should have begun when I was a member of the Department of Modern History at University College, Dublin (UCD), in the late 1960s and early 1970s. As the visiting American historian, I was excused from dealing with Irish topics in the department's fortnightly honors tutorial system. However, I quickly learned that without some knowledge of Irish history, I would be left out of much of the conversations in the snug at Hartigan's Pub on Lower Leeson Street, the off-campus headquarters of UCD's male historians. Unlike many American academics at the time, Irish historians talked about their profession. Of course, in Ireland history can easily become family history and family history can sometimes drift into gossip—a confusing mixture for the visiting, clueless Yank. So as not to be left completely adrift, I opted to swat up some of the set topics in Irish history normally assigned in the honors tutorials. Oddly enough, the Famine was not one of them. At the time, there were only a few books available on the subject, and I recall little conversation, academic or otherwise, about that singular, cataclysmic event. I eventually realized that most of my Irish colleagues, all excellent historians, belonged to the "revisionist" generation, dedicated to writing "professional" Irish history drained of the old nationalist emotions and biases that had collected around the Famine. Although several of the university's leading historians had edited an important volume of essays (*The Great Famine: Studies in Irish History, 1845–52*, edited by Edwards and Williams), the topic did not seem a compelling one.[1]

Therefore, my interest in and knowledge of the Irish Famine developed only gradually after I left Ireland and began teaching courses on Irish history in Germany and the United States. Then, in 1997, in recognition of the sesquicentennial of "Black '47," I organized a series of public lectures on the Famine held at the Union Institute where I taught in Cincinnati, Ohio. While preparing my own talk, I suggested to my wife, Leslie A. Williams, that, as an art historian, she might provide an analysis of the period engravings that had appeared in *Illustrated London News* and *Punch*. She did, and eventually published the results.[2] After the lectures, I had expected that we would both return to our original research interests; I to my Irish travel accounts, and she to Victorian genre paintings. However, Leslie could not let go of the Famine. Or, perhaps, the Famine would not let go of her. Although we both shared a Pennsylvania–German background, unlike

---

1. For several relevant discussions on revisionism and other aspects of historical scholarship in Ireland, see the essays in Brady's *Interpreting Irish History: The Debate on Historical Revisionism*.
2. Leslie A. Williams, "Irish Identity and the *Illustrated London News*, 1845–1851: Famine and Depopulation."

me, my wife had Irish ancestry. A great-great grandfather had come over in the 1840s, eventually becoming a captain in the Union army (we still have his papers and sword). So, perhaps a certain outrage built up as she extended her research from illustrations to texts and from magazines to the coverage of the Famine by the major British newspapers. A book began to emerge with the working title "Killing Remarks." Unfortunately, before she could put the finishing touches on the manuscript she was diagnosed with cancer and died in 2001. I had promised her that I would edit her work for publication. Her book, *Daniel O'Connell, the British Press, and the Irish Famine: Killing Remarks*, appeared in 2003.

With Leslie's book published, I was now able to write up my research on Irish travelogues and early tourism. I eventually published *Tourism, Landscape, and the Irish Character: British Travel Writers in Pre-Famine Ireland* in 2008 and *Creating Irish Tourism: The First Century, 1750–1850* in 2010. Both books touched on Famine-related topics, and I now found that I, too, could not let go of the subject. Although I knew enough about the event to be impressed by its complexity, I still lacked a clear sense of how all of the pieces— geography and ecology, land ownership and land use, potato monoculture, demographic factors, British attitudes toward the Irish, as well as religious, political and economic issues—fitted together. My reading of systems theorist Gregory Bateson encouraged me to try to understand the *systemic* relations that link all these elements. My focus on that linkage is one of the things that I hope distinguishes this work from other general histories of the Famine.

In writing this book, I have drawn upon my extensive reading in Irish travel accounts written before, during and just after the Famine. In addition, I have also extended my wife's research on the British press with my own investigations of newspaper, periodical and other contemporary accounts. Fortunately, since the mid-1990s, there has been a considerable increase in the amount of scholarship dedicated to the Famine, most of it produced by Irish historians. While I have not been able read everything that has been published, I am a grateful beneficiary of much of this recent work.

As with my previous books, I would like to thank my friend Cincinnati poet Kevin McHugh for his invaluable editorial aid and advice. And, as always, all flaws and errors are distinctly my own.

I am also indebted to the Hamilton County Public Library System and Ohio Links for helping to get materials to a more than senior historian who no longer drives.

It has been 175 years since the massive potato failure of 1846. While I have tried to produce a work of sound scholarship based on extensive research, this book is intended for the broader audience for whom interest in the Irish Famine continues to grow.

Cincinnati, Ohio, 2021

INTRODUCTION

Writing this introduction during the second year of the novel coronavirus pandemic has been an odd experience. *Phytophthoras infestans*, the potato fungus that launched the Irish Famine in the 1840s, and COVID-19 might seem to have little in common, except for one thing: their considerable powers to disrupt societies, thereby exposing structural and cultural weaknesses. By the middle of 2021 only a few countries can be said to have managed the coronavirus virus effectively. Most others have struggled with the competing and seemingly incompatible demands of politics, economics, individual desires and public health. Faced with the sudden loss of the potato, something similar could be said of much of Europe in the mid-1840s. Some nations coped fairly well; some did not. In only one part of one country, the United Kingdom of Great Britain and Ireland, did the government's failure to meet the considerable challenge presented by the blight prove devastating. What happened in Ireland stands out as a unique and terrible event in the history of modern Europe. This book explores the reasons why.

The series of events known collectively as the Great Irish Famine resulted from the complex interaction of ecological, economic, social, political, and cultural factors involving both Ireland and Great Britain. Faced with the complexities of the situation, Christopher Morash has suggested that "the Irish Famine is an event that eludes definition. There is no single, clear consensus as to what constituted the Famine."[1] Many of its basic features—crop failure, excess mortality rates, hunger, disease, emigration, public works, soup kitchens—had all appeared before during previous Irish subsistence crises, although never on such a scale and for such a duration. In fact, it is even uncertain when the Famine began and ended. There has been a general tendency to date the crisis according to the appearance and eventual fading of *P. infestans* between 1845 and 1852. Coupling the Famine to the blight can be confusing, however. Although Ireland teetered on the brink of disaster in 1845, the year the blight first appeared, the country did not experience famine conditions. The partial destruction of that fall's potato crop caused hardship but not starvation. Nevertheless, weakened and vulnerable, many thousands died when the blight returned in 1846 on a much more virulent scale, wiping out almost all the tubers. By the fall of 1847, however, with a sharp reduction in potato cultivation, the blight seemed to be on the wane only to return in strength in the following year. The mortality rates of 1849 almost matched those of "Black '47." By 1850 the blight had receded in much of Ireland. Yet, it hung on in parts of the western Ireland through 1852.

---

1. Morash, *Writing the Irish Famine*, 2.

Even after that, Ireland's mortality rates and workhouse occupancies continued to run well above pre-Famine levels past the middle of the decade.

Another problem concerns historical labeling. The fact that the disaster involved much more than potatoes and blight is suggested by some of the names given to the event. In a sense, the catastrophe should be called "the Great British Famine," involving as it did a constituent country within the United Kingdom with relief efforts directed from London. This would at least establish the proper perspective within which to gauge responsibility for the tragedy. The more customary terms—the "Irish Famine," the "Great Irish Famine," or the "Irish Potato Famine"—threaten to place the event in too narrow a context. Even the word "famine" itself can be confusing, encouraging misleading assumptions regarding cause and effect. Many people assume that famines, when not caused by acts of war, are simply the results of environmental disruptions—drought, floods, insect infestation, or rampant plant disease—which destroy basic food supplies. Such explanations, however, threaten to mask the social, economic, and political factors that can often turn an "act of nature" into a famine. In 1861 the Irish nationalist leader John Mitchel famously tried to uncouple the Famine from *P. infestans* and the potato when he wrote: "The Almighty, indeed, sent the potato blight, but the English created the famine."[2] Few historians have been willing to follow Mitchel all the way down the road to implied genocide. He was, nevertheless, among the first to state that the crisis was not just a matter of too many people and too little food. Other factors were very much in play. Therefore, some commentators have preferred the term "The Great Hunger" (from the Gaelic *An Gorta Mór*), which Cecil Woodham-Smith used as the title for her 1962 groundbreaking study. That phrase encodes no misleading explanations; it begs no questions regarding cause and effect. It simply states a massive fact, which demands an explanation, one that reveals where the role of nature ends and that of human responsibility begins. Nevertheless, for the sake of custom and convenience, I refer throughout the text to "the Famine," while recognizing that the term has long been and remains rightly contested.

In some quarters there is even confusion regarding the identity of the Famine's victims. It was not, as it is popularly believed, the "Irish *people*" who starved or were driven into exile. Rather, the victims belonged to an economic class—the Irish *poor*. As John R. Butterly and Jack Shepherd maintain, "famine is first and foremost a problem of poverty and inequality." They quote one scholar to the effect that "famine is the *endpoint* of a lengthy process in which people in increasing numbers lose their access to food."[3] If the Irish Famine was an endpoint, however, where then was its beginning?

With so many factors contributing to the disaster, the closest one might come to tracing its origins lies in the introduction of an alien tuber into the colonial structure of landownership and management as it had evolved in Ireland by the late seventeenth century. Under those circumstances, the potato acted as an invasive species. It "took

---

2. Mitchel, *Last Conquest of Ireland (Perhaps)*, 219.
3. Butterly and Shepherd, *Hunger: The Biology and Politics of Starvation*, 37; quote, 29. Italics in original.

over," in the sense that it allowed for the reorganization of Irish agriculture around a monoculture. The result was a potato economy in which several million people, dependent upon a single prolific and highly nutritious source of food, provided the cheap labor upon which the country's important agricultural export trade depended. The destruction of the country's potato crop resulted, therefore, in more than a sudden huge loss of food. It also triggered the rapid collapse of the potato economy itself. Along with widespread hunger, this meant extensive unemployment and a drying up of rents, which in turn encouraged landlords to evict impecunious tenants. Moreover, as the potato economy broke down, the dynamics of the crisis shifted rapidly from the loss of the potato to the response of the British government.

In 1996, John Major, then prime minister of Great Britain, fearing political backlash on all sides, rejected a proposed memorial service commemorating the Irish Famine. A year later, however, during the sesquicentennial of "Black '47," his successor, Tony Blair, did acknowledge some British responsibility for the catastrophe. Yet, Blair was only partially correct when he stated: "Those who governed in London at the time failed their people through standing by while a crop failure turned into a massive human tragedy."[4] Britain's failure, however, cannot be described as "standing by" while thousands starved. The British government did, in fact, struggle to cope with an unprecedented challenge, deploying massive administrative machinery in response. However, continued large-scale social dislocation, high rates of mortality, evictions, and emigration can all be traced to the government's failure to clearly prioritize the demands of a vast humanitarian challenge while simultaneously following other, conflicting goals. Humanitarian demands became mixed with adherence to a narrow, moralistic version of laissez faire capitalism, to an insistence on minimizing any drain on the imperial treasury, and to an overwhelming desire to put an end to Ireland's potato monoculture by restructuring the country's agriculture. And always in the background there hovered a deep strain of the anti-Irish suspicion and prejudice endemic in British culture.

The seeds of Britain's failure, indeed, for the entire catastrophe, lie in the historical contexts within which the disaster unfolded. Through its narrow, deadly aperture, the Famine pulled and twisted together many of the strands of cultural, economic, and political tensions that had long shaped relations between Ireland and Great Britain. Some of these strands reach far back into history of the two islands. Trying to trace them all is akin to pealing the layers of an onion. While both activities may involve the shedding of a few tears, the onion will run out layers before Irish history runs out of years. Nevertheless, the Famine cannot be understood absent certain key factors that drove it and defined Britain's response to it. Part One of this study, "Culture, Religion and Politics in the Pre-Famine Decades," therefore, investigates a series of interlocking contexts that would ultimately shape the disaster. To set the stage, Chapter One, "The Colonial Background," provides a very brief summary of almost 700 years of Ireland's colonial history. Chapter

---

4. Quoted in Kinealy, "'The Famine Killed Everything: Living with the Memory of the Great Hunger," 11. For John Major, see https://www.irishtimes.com/news/politics/ex-british-pm-john-major-shelved-famine-commemoration-1.4137492. (February 10, 2020.)

Two, "From Stereotypes to Narrative: The Making of the Irish Other," focuses on how, over time, the British created out of that colonial experience a narrative about Ireland largely based upon negative stereotypes of the Irish people. At their worst mendacious and rebellious, at their best charming but feckless, the Irish were depicted as unable to manage their own affairs. As part of this narrative, British and Anglo-Irish travel writers even conjured up a "moral geography," which revealed how the alleged flaws in the Irish character were made visible in the country's landscape. Chapter Three, "Politics and Religion in the Age of Daniel O'Connell," explores how O'Connell's successful campaign for Catholic Emancipation, the Protestant reaction to it, and then his subsequent attempt to repeal the Act of Union combined to produce a negative political atmosphere on both sides of the Irish Sea. Chapter Four, "Morality and Economics in the Age of Atonement," briefly considers how liberal laissez-faire economics and evangelical moralism combined to influence the British government's famine policies. The Poor Laws receive particular attention since they became the principal mechanism for famine relief.

Part Two is titled "The Rise and Fall of Ireland's Potato Economy." Chapter Five, "Poverty and Inequality: The Economic Background," briefly summarizes the state of the Irish economy on the eve of the Famine. Chapter Six, "Land, People and Potatoes," presents a detailed investigation of the complex systemic interactions among land use, population pressures, and monoculture that produced Ireland's potato economy. Chapter Seven, "A Long Farwell to the White Potato: *Phytophthora Infestans* and the Collapse of the Potato Economy," considers whether the blight was the result of a freak accident of nature or the inevitable outcome of an unsustainable system that pushed too many people to the brink of survival. While rejecting the argument for inevitability, this chapter, drawing upon aspects of systems theory, maintains that Ireland's land/people/potatoes system incorporated a bias for disaster, which, once triggered by the arrival of the blight, led to inescapable calamity.

As noted above, the impact of the blight varied from year to year. Up until 1850 at least, the size and nature of each fall's potato harvest helped influence conditions for the following year. Therefore, Part Three: "The Famine Years," is structured around the annual *harvest* cycle (fall to fall) instead of focusing on each calendar year. Thus, Chapter Eight, "The Arrival of the Potato Blight, 1845–46," investigates the confusion surrounding the initial appearance of the disease, noting how responses to it fitted into preexisting British narratives about Ireland. This chapter also discusses Tory prime minister Robert Peel's response to the blight. Chapter Nine, "Black '46–47,'" covers the results of the nearly complete devastation of the potato harvest of 1846 and the new Whig government's response led by Prime Minister Lord John Russell. After launching a massive and highly problematic public works program, the government organized a successful attempt to feed one-third of the nation in the summer of 1847. This temporary approach was superseded by the Amended Poor Law Act that reduced feeding the hungry to merely one of several competing policy goals. Chapter Ten, "A False Dawn, 1847–48," shows how a healthier but appallingly small potato crop proved as devastating as the previous year's almost total destruction of a much larger yield. Chapter Eleven, "The Return of the Blight, 1848–49," reveals how a powerful revival of the disease virtually cancelled out a modest increase in potato cultivation. Mortality rates in many parts of Ireland matched or surpassed those of "Black '47," generally assumed to be the worst calendar year of the Famine. Chapter Twelve, "Years of Evictions, 1849–52," finds the blight increasingly confined to the western part of the country, where, however, the crisis was intensified by a rising tide of evictions, as the results of the potato economy's collapse continued to reverberate through the region. Throughout all the chapters in Part Three, there are discussions of key recurring topics, such as mortality rates, workhouse conditions, the role of private charity, the varying impacts of government policies, the changing patterns of emigration, and the government's decision to use the crisis to restructure rural Ireland.

Part Four: "The Post-Famine Years" reviews the consequences of the disaster. Chapter Thirteen concerns "Post-Famine Dreams and Irish Realities." Focusing on the 1850s, it first considers the failure of evangelical Protestant attempts to use the crisis to establish "the Second Reformation" (briefly discussed in Chapter Three). The rest of this chapter investigates the outcome of British efforts to restructure Irish agriculture in the wake of the Encumbered Estates Act of 1849. The act had been intended to force incompetent and indebted Irish landlords to sell out to an anticipated influx of English and Scottish investors and farmers. Using English "high-farming" techniques, these new "colonizers" were to transform the west of Ireland into a veritable garden, replacing Irish bogs with bountiful farms. These hopes figure in a series of promotional books aimed at attracting British interest in Irish agriculture. However, the realities of topography, climate, rising labor costs, falling grain prices, and the growing appeal of grazing gradually put an end to such dreams.

Just as the Famine twisted together many strands from the past, it also diffused its influences widely into the future. Chapter Fourteen, "In the Famine's Wake," summarizes some of the disaster's immediate and long-term influences upon Irish agriculture and land use, demographics and family structure, emigration and the diaspora, religion, language, and politics.

The "Conclusion" reviews the nature of Britain's great failure. It considers what alternative policies the government might have adopted, while acknowledging that there was no simple, easy solution to the crisis. Unfortunately, in the absence of strong, imaginative leadership, the government pursued too many conflicting goals and failed to find a workable approach that might have placed humanitarian concerns over the demands of private property, economic and social restructuring, and imperial budgets. The chapter ends by discussing the genocide issue, offering alternative approaches to judging British failures.

Part One

CULTURE, RELIGION AND POLITICS IN THE PRE-FAMINE DECADES

Chapter One

THE COLONIAL BACKGROUND

In 1845 the late potato blight crossed the Atlantic from America and struck Europe. Its impact varied from country to country, depending on the importance of the potato in a region's economy and diet and how effectively various governments dealt with its loss. Hardship was widespread and starvations occurred in a few places. By 1847 the crisis was generally over, except in Ireland. With varying degrees of intensity, the blight, along with extreme social dislocation, lingered on for six years. The census of 1851 revealed that Ireland had lost around one and a half million people to death and immigration, although the actual figure was probably closer to two million. Why had a serious but temporary crisis on the Continent become a disaster in Ireland? Many people believe that the answer lies somewhere in Ireland's long history of British colonialism. This idea that the Famine was somehow the end point of a long and steady march from the first English incursion into Ireland in 1169 to the tragic potato dependency of the 1840s is breathtaking in its sweeping simplicity. Yet, in trying to explain the Famine, the long colonial relationship between Britain and Ireland certainly mattered, although the ways in which it mattered requires some investigation. And, while the Famine cannot be explained without reference to Ireland's colonial past, neither can it be fully understood by reference to it alone. Therefore, while this chapter provides a very brief summary of Ireland's colonial background, subsequent chapters in this section introduce several other key cultural, political and economic factors that strongly influenced and shaped Britain's response to the Famine.

From a Colonial Kingdom to the United Kingdom

Poets like to depict Ireland as the last bit of Europe reaching out into the Atlantic toward wherever the next parish might be. If geography adhered to the logic of poetry, then the island's history might have been very different. As it is, a much larger island, dominated by England, intrudes between Ireland and the Continent, and, despite waves of invasions by Angles, Saxons, Danes and Normans, England is not Europe, as recent events have been at pains to point out. Nonetheless, as the bastard child of aggression, it was perhaps inevitable that, a century after the arrival of Williams the Conqueror, England would cast covetous eyes on the smaller isle to the west. If colonialism is a sin, then Ireland was the occasion for England's original transgression.

True, the Norman-Welsh knights who invaded Ireland in 1169 were there at the invitation of Diarmait Mac Murchada, the Irish king of Leinster, who, amid the seemingly endless struggles between the island's petty kingdoms, had managed to lose both his lands and his wife. Admittedly, she was someone else's wife when Diarmait "abducted" her, but this did not stop the deposed king from seeking aid from a more powerful monarch, King Henry II of England. Having more land-hungry knights than he knew what to do with, Henry obliged his Irish client and dispatched Strongbow, the Earl of Pembrooke, to Wexford. A few years later, Henry himself landed with a larger force and proclaimed himself Lord of Ireland. This was easier said than done, however. Although the English conquest of Ireland had begun, it would take another four and a half centuries to complete.

Superior military organization and arms enabled the invaders to take over Ireland's seaports and much of its more fertile lands. However, large portions of the island remained in the hands of the Gaelic nobility, defined by the English as "savages" occupying the "wilderness" areas beyond the walled towns and cultivated fields of the "civilized" settlers.[1] Colonialist propaganda aside, however, as time passed many of the settlers began to go native—to a degree. Living in their scattered castles far from England and royal control, they adopted the Gaelic language and some of the customs of the Irish. They even married into Gaelic families. Gradually, these somewhat Gaelicized English evolved into the Anglo-Irish, neither quite the one thing nor the other. Not fully accepted as English in England, they were not, in their own eyes, part of the "wylde Irish." True, they occasionally allied themselves with their Gaelic neighbors to try to circumvent the authority of England. Yet at the same time, they continued to proclaim their loyalty to the king. This was more than mere lip service. It was through the Crown that the settlers and their Anglo-Irish descendants held title to the lands that had been seized from the Irish. (As for the Irish, unless they swore fealty to the king, they were regarded as rebels and their lands open for the taking.) While the Anglo-Irish needed the king, however, he needed them, no matter how Gaelicized they might become. The limited extent to which the king's writ ran beyond Dublin and its surrounding counties—the so-called Pale—depended upon what cooperation he could get from his Anglo-Irish lords.

Much was made of the colonizing rhetoric based on the supposed contrast between the "King's Peace," as represented by lands under English control, and the alleged anarchy of the areas held by the "wylde Irish" rebels and "outlaws." The fact was, however, that any inherent instability in Ireland was exacerbated by instability in England. Throughout the Middle Ages, the seemingly endless struggles over the English Crown found echoes in battlefields in Ireland. It was only with the arrival of the first Tudor monarch, Henry VII, that things began to change. Before England could complete the conquest of the island, the king decided that he needed greater control over his Anglo-Irish subjects and their parliament in Dublin. Therefore, to rein in the Irish parliament, the king decided to clarify the island's colonial status. Operating through his deputy Edward Poynings in 1494, Henry forced the Dublin parliament to agree that it could meet only at his pleasure and only take up legislation that he had preapproved. His successor, Henry VIII, went further, and in 1542 had Ireland declared a kingdom with himself as its monarch. After an experiment in trying to rule Ireland through Anglo-Irish deputies ended

---

1. For a detailed account of this early colonial propaganda see Montaño, *The Roots of English Colonialism in Ireland*.

in a failed rebellion, Henry combined the task of extending his direct authority over the Anglo-Irish living beyond the Pale while pushing for the conquest of those parts of his colonial kingdom still in Irish hands. This was not fully accomplished until the end of the reign of Elizabeth I half a century later. The defeat of Hugh O'Neill of Ulster at the battle of Kinsale in 1603, and the subsequent abandonment of Ireland by the Irish nobility (the "Flight of the Earls"), marked the collapse of the last remaining Gaelic polity. Lands that had until then resisted royal authority were now open for settlement from Great Britain. Both Henry VIII and Elizabeth I had attempted plantation schemes but with little success. However, with O'Neill's defeat the new Stewart monarch, James I, instituted a vast settlement program for Ulster. Loyal Protestants were brought in from Scotland and England to take over land formerly in Irish hands. Despite recurring rebellions and war, immigration from the larger island continued throughout the seventeenth century. By 1700, 27 percent of the Ireland's population was of Scottish and English origin or descent. Other minorities included Welsh, French Huguenots and German Palatines.[2]

Ireland was not just an unusual mix of people. It was a mix of faiths as well. Back in 1534, Henry VIII, much in need of a divorce and a new queen who could give him a male heir, had declared himself head of the Christian church in England and Ireland. While the Irish were scornful, the Anglo-Irish were appalled. They were now torn between their loyalty to the Crown and their devotion to Roman Catholicism. Thanks to the Henrician Reformation, religion eventually became a more powerful factor than ethnic origin in dividing Ireland. Although the vast majority of the country's population remained Roman Catholic, most of those arriving during the seventeenth century adhered to some sort of Protestantism: Anglican or Presbyterian with a scattering of other Dissenters. While many of the Anglo-Irish remained Catholic, concern for their land titles kept them loyal to a British Crown that often treated them as pawns in the game of colonial politics. The game went against the Anglo-Irish Catholics, however, when the Puritan Parliamentarians in England overthrew and executed King Charles I in 1649. Cromwell's subsequent incursion into Ireland to put down the royalist Catholic Confederacy resulted in the loss of many lives and a transfer of Catholic lands into Protestant hands.

Although the restoration of the monarchy under Charles II in 1660 did little for the Catholic cause in Ireland, the eventual ascension to the throne by his brother, James II, in 1685 seemed to offer genuine hope: James was a Roman Catholic. This was too much for British Protestants, however, who drove him from the throne in 1690. What was hailed in Britain as a largely peaceful "Glorious Revolution" was neither peaceful nor glorious in Ireland where James fled to raise an army. After two years of warfare, James's Catholic forces were defeated, and more land moved from Catholic to Protestant ownership. In the wake of the exile of 12,000 Irish officers and men (the "Wild Geese") to the Continent in 1691, only 14 percent of Irish land remained in Catholic hands.[3] Even that number was destined to dwindle. The victorious Protestants used the Irish Parliament

---

2. Cullen, *The Emergence of Modern Ireland, 1600–1900*, 15.
3. Dickson, *New Foundations Ireland, 1660–1800*, 47.

to enact a series of Penal Laws designed to destroy the last vestiges of Catholic cultural, economic and political power in Ireland. The Catholic Church was suppressed. Its adherents could not hold public office nor serve as military officers. And if a Catholic landed family wished to pass on intact its estate to a single inheritor, it had to convert to Anglicanism. Since land represented power and wealth, few of the old remaining Anglo-Irish Catholic families could hold out. By the end of the eighteenth century, therefore, Catholics owned only about 5 percent of the land in Ireland. Most of the remaining land was in the hands of the new Protestant Ascendancy. Of course, throughout Europe most land was owned and controlled by an aristocratic class. In Ireland, however, only some of the Ascendancy had deep roots in the country. Others had families going back only a few generations, while some were English who had newly acquired their lands. Thus, as a ruling class, the Ascendancy differed from the majority of Irish people, Catholic and Dissenters, in language, culture, religion and history. Some of Ireland's landowning aristocracy were also alienated from the land itself. Long years of instability had encouraged some of them to extract whatever wealth they could from their estates. This frequently meant the deforestation of the old oak forests; the shift from pastorage to growing grain; and, under certain circumstances, farming for rents rather than for crops.

Accepted neither as Irish by the majority of the population nor as English in Britain, Ireland's Anglo-Irish aristocracy sought to reassert and update its identity during the eighteenth century. This was partly a matter of economic self-interest. The aristocracy used its control of the Irish Parliament to push back against London's attempts to control Ireland's trade and to limit competition from its manufactures. In 1782 the Dublin Parliament severely restricted the scope of Poynings's old law that had given the Crown control over its meetings and agendas. It was able to do this because the politics of colonialism had always run on a two-way street in Ireland. As noted above, the Irish ruling class had been dependent upon England for security, but for its part Britain depended upon the Anglo-Irish for the day-to-day running of Ireland. This became critical when, as the British colonies in North America moved from protest to revolution, Britain had to take troops out of Ireland for action abroad. Imbued with the spirit of self-assertion and "patriotism" wafting back across the Atlantic from America, the Anglo-Irish aristocracy enthusiastically took on the defense of Ireland. In 1778 they formed a militia, the Irish Volunteers, which within a few years had evolved into a political organization agitating for the removal of all limits to the powers of the Irish Parliament and for a general reform of the Irish political system.

There were limits, however, to how far the Ascendancy and its Volunteer movement could allow the spirit of reform and a nascent sense of national identity pull them. Middle-class Catholics and Protestants began to demand the end of the Penal Laws and access to full civil rights. The British government, simultaneously waging war with its rebellious American colonies and with France, was anxious to keep the peace in Ireland. It pressured the Dublin Parliament to repeal most of the remaining Penal Laws. One obstacle remained, however: Catholic Emancipation, the granting of full civil rights to Roman Catholics. Had the Anglican Ascendancy seen its way to accommodating these demands, the history of Ireland might have been different. As it was, the Ascendancy's gentlemanly reform movement found itself on the defensive in the face of demands for radical political and economic changes emanating from the middle classes in Dublin and Belfast. In 1791 the radicals, inspired as much by revolution in France as in America, formed the United Irishmen. Once it became clear that their demands would not be met, the United Irishmen sent envoys to France to seek support for a rising. A French invasion fleet did head for Bantry Bay in 1796. Fortunately for the unprepared British, a fortuitous gale, the so-called "Protestant Wind", scattered the French fleet before it could land troops on Irish soil. The British government, having already proscribed the United Irishmen, now moved against the group before it could take further action. A violent sweep of terror through Ulster in 1797 broke up the largely Protestant branch in the North. The following year, 1798, the southern branch of the United Irishmen, allied with the Defenders, groups of small Catholic farmers, took to the field. Without aid from the North, however, they were eventually defeated. A second French invasion force, landing in Mayo a few months later, arrived too late and was eventually forced to surrender. Doomed by a lack of coordination, the Rising of '98 nonetheless established a modern sense of nationalism in the Irish psyche.

As Great Britain approached the new century, it had to survey the wreckage of the old one. It had lost most of its North American colonies. It was still at war with France. And its colonial kingdom across the Irish Sea had once again proven internally unstable and a backdoor to invasion. Worse, the Anglo-Irish aristocracy, whose task it had long been to rule the island as a proxy for British interests, had proven utterly incapable of managing the affairs and keeping the peace. Having garnered for its Parliament as much control over Ireland as it could ever hope to enjoy, the Ascendency had nonetheless failed to govern, even in its own best interests. Unwilling to embrace judicious and timely reforms, especially Catholic Emancipation, it had also failed to prevent large-scale violence.[4]

Previous British governments had occasionally floated the idea of extending direct rule by the Imperial Parliament over Ireland. With the loss of the thirteen American colonies, each of which had their own separate legislature, Ireland reverted to what it had always been—an anomaly: a separate colonial kingdom with its own parliament. There was no longer anything like it within the empire. Prime Minister William Pitt decided that Ireland had to become a part of an expanded United Kingdom.[5] The parliament in Dublin's College Green would be abolished. Ireland would lose its status as a separate kingdom and would be incorporated into union with England, Wales and Scotland. A reduced number of Irish members, one hundred, all Anglicans, would sit in the House of Commons in London, where they would, of course, be very much a minority. Although the parliament in Dublin had to agree to all this, it initially refused. Only some members of the Ascendency had been sufficiently frightened by recent events to accept Great Britain's decision. For those lacking in enthusiasm, however, monies and titles flowed from London to Dublin Castle, and then over to the Irish MPs in College Green. The Irish Parliament finally abolished itself in 1800 with the new Union set to come into existence the following year. Shaken by the recent rebellion and comforted

---

4. See Richardson, "Political Anglicanism in Ireland, 1692–1801," 66.
5. See Bartlett, "'An Union for Empire':," 51, 53–54.

with bribes, the Ascendency committed political suicide, relegating to London the task of protecting its status as a privileged Anglican minority.

Having supposedly become an integral part of the United Kingdom, Ireland 's colonial relationship to Britain was changed but not ended. In terms of governance Ireland was still a colonial anomaly. For example, the Irish executive, consisting of a lord lieutenant or viceroy, along with his chief secretary and staff, remained in Dublin Castle to oversee Ireland's day-to-day affairs. Unique within the United Kingdom, the retention of the Irish executive signaled that, although a part of the Union, Ireland remained in a special category requiring some degree of direct imperial supervision.

As for that other bastion of colonial rule, the old parliament in Dublin, its demise is rife with ironies. While its abolition may have deprived the Ascendency of a political voice, it also left Ireland itself voiceless and powerless. Vociferous in its efforts, if not always successful, the Irish Parliament had tried to protect the island's nonagricultural sector from British competition. Now, in its absence, the former kingdom was completely open to British economic domination. In most parts of Ireland manufacturing and commercial activities dwindled, leaving most people dependent upon agriculture for their livelihood. And, of course, when the Famine struck, Ireland had no political institution to plead its case. It is not obvious, therefore, that the ending of its status as a colonial kingdom left Ireland in a better place.

To gage the primary impact of colonialism, it is necessary to look beyond political structures, economics and even issues involving control of the land—the supplanting of a Gaelic by an Anglo-Irish aristocracy. It is important to investigate how the colonial experience shaped the attitudes the British developed toward Ireland and the Irish and how those ideas infused almost every aspect of the relationship between the two islands.

Chapter Two

FROM STEREOTYPES TO NARRATIVE: THE MAKING OF THE IRISH OTHER

Peasants, Potatoes and Poverty

Among Great Britain's most enduring inventions that grew out of the colonial experience are a series of stereotypes of Ireland and the Irish, which so distorted reality that it became difficult for Britons themselves to understand their relationship to the other island and its inhabitants. Was it based on shared citizenship? Or was the relationship that of Protestant to Catholic, superior to inferior, parent to child, colonizer to colonized or all the above? In the process of seeking answers, British stereotypes combined to form a narrative of Irish backwardness, incompetence and inferiority that was destined to color Britain's responses to the Famine.

While stereotypical depictions of the Irish varied, one element remained constant. From the shapeless "caubeen" on his head, to the rags that half-clothed his body, to his bare feet, and, by extension, to his wretched cabin with its resident pig and manure pile, "Paddy" appeared to most Britons as the very embodiment of poverty. In fact, during the nineteenth century, the impression grew that poverty in Ireland was *uniquely* Irish, supposedly worse than anything to be found in even the vilest of Britain's industrial slums.[1]

Then there was the Irishman's diet, seen as a glaring example, if not the cause, of his dire condition. Deploying a classic example of food bias, the British assumed, wrongly, that the potato was nutritionally inferior to grain (on which English workers supposedly thrived). It was, moreover, seen as the cause of Paddy's economic, social and moral degradation. In Britain the work of harrowing, sowing, winnowing, harvesting, threshing and processing grain defined how "proper" food moved from field to mill to table. The potato's direct journey from soil to pot, however, required few intermediate steps and no processing whatever. Potato cultivation itself seemed too simple and effortless. Apparently, Paddy just stuck a piece of a pratie into the ground and then lay back to await the harvest, by which time the pot would be boiling, ready to receive its toil-free bounty. It did not help that the Irish called their potato patches "lazy beds," a term the British deemed all too appropriate.[2] Although they had some notion of the potato's nutritional value, even Anglo-Irish authors Anna and Samuel Carter Hall argued in the 1840s

---

1. See William H. A. Williams, *Tourism, Landscape, and the Irish Character*, 110–14.
2. Austin Bourke suggests that "lazy bed" may have been derived from the French word *laisser* (to leave) implying that once the potatoes were planted in their ridges they could be left alone; see *"A Visitation of God?" The Potato and the Great Irish Famine*, 66. For British anti-potato bias see 16–26; see also de Nie, *The Eternal Paddy*, 130–32.

that "the ease" with which the potato could be grown "has been the cause of evil." At the start of the Famine, Scottish-born Elizabeth Smith, mistress of the modest Baltiboys estate in County Wicklow, wrote that it would be a good thing if the potatoes disappeared altogether, since they "encouraged idleness, pauper marriage and dirty habits."[3]

Rags, tumble-down cabins, inferior food, lazy habits—the lesson seemed obvious. While individual hardship might be due to unfortunate happenstance, the poverty of a nation surely revealed an indolent, shiftless and careless people. Thus, Irish poverty had to be the product of Irish character.[4] Not that British observers were wrong in decrying Irish poverty. It was real enough and deep. For example, there was some truth in the oft-repeated contention that the castoff garments of English and Scottish beggars were routinely baled and shipped to Dublin and Cork to clothe the Irish poor.[5] Poverty even became part of the tourist experience in Ireland. Sites of poverty—the slums of Ireland's few cities, the decrepit cabins along the roads into which visitors felt free to stick their heads, the beggars who swarmed tourist locations—all became as much a part of the Irish Tour as the Lakes of Killarney and the Giant's Causeway.[6]

Nevertheless, British observers managed to exaggerate the extent of Irish poverty. The tourists gaze, so easily focused on the Irish poor, sought in vain for occupants of the next-higher rungs on Ireland's socioeconomic ladder. Trained from birth to recognize the fine gradations of class in their own society, Britons were unsettled by the apparent lack of a visible class structure in rural Ireland. Naval surgeon Thomas Reid, visiting Ireland in 1822, discerned only two classes: "The rich and the poor. [...] There is no middle class, no connecting link, nothing like a yeomanry."[7] Yet, not all Irish who looked poor were poor. Less likely to share the Protestant belief that outward appearances might reflect signs of inward grace, many middling Roman Catholic farmers did not choose to invest in clothing and housing. Historian Louis M. Cullen argues that they were more likely to put their money into cattle or dowries and education for their children. Most visitors did not realize that the farmer who stuffed rags in his broken windows and who wore a threadbare coat might be a man of sixty cows, able to occasionally lend money to his improvident landlord. One observer noted that even some wealthy farmers tended "to live well but dirty," roofing their cabins with thatch rather than with more fashionable slate.[8] Irishman Patrick Knight, visiting Ballycorey, County Clare, in 1836, admitted that, although many of the farms there bore themarks of *"outside* poverty," their occupants were not necessarily poor. Their houses offered "little cleanliness, or apparent comfort because they shunned luxuries and comforts." Instead, the "whole thought seems to be in

---

3. James and Ó Maitiú. *The Wicklow World of Elizabeth Smith: 1840–1850*, 64. See Hall, *Ireland: Its Scenery and Character &etc.*, 1:82.
4. See William H. A. Williams, *Tourism, Landscape, and the Irish Character*, 117–21.
5. Ibid., 94–95. See also Scally, *The End of Hidden Ireland*, 32, 180.
6. See William H. A. Williams, *Creating Irish Tourism*, 175–82.
7. Reid, *Travels in Ireland in the Year of 1822*, 337.
8. Quoted in Reilly, *The Irish Land Agent, 1830–60*, 27. See also Cullen, "Man, Landscape and Roads: The Changing Eighteenth Century," 125–26; William H. A. Williams, *Tourism, Landscape and the Irish Character*, 107–14.

the rearing and tending of cattle." Spending the night in the house of a man who had a hundred head of black cattle and two hundred of sheep, Knight noted: "There was not a single chair or stool in his house but one three-legged one,—no bed but rushes,—no vessel for boiling their meals but one, nor any for drinking milk out of but one." Knight's man of a hundred cows was probably part of what Kevin Whelan has identified as Ireland's "invisible" rural middle class. Accustomed to keeping a low profile and forgoing conspicuous consumption, this largely Catholic, rural middle class remained invisible to most British visitors.[9]

British stereotypes of the Irish were more complex than the fixation on poverty might suggest, however. The Irish were occasionally credited with certain likable, even admirable, traits, although some British observers managed to find even these dubious. For example, Paddy's often amusing loquaciousness made him suspect to those Britons who claimed to value Saxon sincerity and truth above what they took to be Hibernian flattery, hyperbole and entertainment. Although some visitors admitted that the Irish peasant could be generous and helpful, Paddy nonetheless seemed *too* willing to abandon his work to accompany any lady or gentleman who hailed him. Many British visitors admired Paddy's simplicity, hospitality, sentimentality and loyalty, along with his love of music and poetry. However, according to Edward G. Lengel, British Victorians regarded these as "feminine" traits. Compared to Paddy, the more "masculine" English countryman might seem bearish, self-regarding and even sullen. Yet, he was a steady worker who got the job done. Likable as he might appear, Paddy did not seem steady, nor, to British eyes, did he ever seem to get the job done. And this was the problem. British observers concluded that, on inspection, even the Irishman's apparent strengths turned out to be weaknesses.[10]

Such suspicions had their origins in the common colonial clash between metropolitan "modernity" and traditional modes of life on the periphery. As Murry G. H. Pittock observes, on one level Britons were occasionally pleased to view the Welsh and Scottish "Celts" as emblematic of a sentimentalized, "romantic backwardness," representing the customs of a bygone era left bobbing quaintly in wake of the modern age.[11] When it came to Ireland, however, few customs seemed merely quaint. Irish funerals, especially the wakes punctuated by loud wailing (the famous "Irish cry"), struck British tourists as bizarre. Equally mystifying were the formalized "faction fights," mostly stick combat with shillelaghs, that often accompanied fairs. Also confusing to Protestant observers were the frequent pilgrimages on saints' days, which the Irish called "making the pattern." While uneasy with the rounds of popish prayers, British visitors were horrified at the drinking,

---

9. See Whelan, *The Tree of Liberty*, 27–-31, 51. For Knight, see his *Erris in the "Irish Highlands" and "The Atlantic Railway,"* 104.
10. See William H. A. Williams, *Tourism, Landscape, and the Irish Character*, 122–26. See also Lengel, *The Irish Through British Eyes*, 165:
11. Pittock, *Celtic Identity and the British Image*, 37–38; See also Williams, *Tourism, Landscape, and the Irish Character*, 71.

dancing and wild celebrations that usually concluded these events. Such mixture of the sacred and the profane appeared to be signs of a backward, premodern society.[12]

Religious, Moral and Racial Geographies

It was, moreover, strange and disturbing for British tourists to wander around a part of their kingdom in which Roman Catholics represented such a vast and vital majority. Deploying what might be called the "Protestant gaze," the visitors were surprised and even shocked at encountering evidence of Catholicism's reemergence in Ireland after long years of suppression under the Penal Laws. Some observers, visiting popular pilgrimage sites, even claimed to discern a confessional landscape. In the 1830s Rev. Caesar Otway, an evangelical, Anglo-Irish writer, visited Station Island in Lough Derg, County Donegal. He declared the site, long known as St. Patrick's Purgatory, "the very landscape of desolation [...] of such a degrading character, that [...] I said to myself, 'I am already in purgatory.'" It was, he wrote, the vision of a "monstrous birth of a degraded and dreary superstition."[13] The Protestant gaze also fixed on remnants of Catholic Ireland's "dark," "superstitious" past, as represented by its many ecclesiastical ruins. Rev. Otway was particularly sensitive in this regard. Referring to well-known monastic sites, he lamented: "What a dreary vale is Glendalough, what a lonely isle is Inniscaltra, what a hideous place is Patrick's Purgatory, what a desolate spot is Clonmacnois." As Luke Gibbons has noted, "moldering abbeys and monasteries," along with ruined castles and graveyards, were "familiar stage-prompts of the gothic *mise-an-scene*."[14] As such, these Romantic tropes turned Ireland's historical landscape into a visual record of Protestantism's triumph over a "blighted" religious past. Contemplating the ruins of Muckross Abbey at Killarney, Rev. Isaac Weld could not view such sites with "their long dismal isles—their dark and narrow cells, without drawing a comparison favorable to ourselves between the gloomy and bigoted notions of monkery and the more enlightened opinions of the modern day."[15]

In addition to Ireland's confessional landscapes, British visitors discovered moral ones as well. Believing that Nature's agricultural bounty should accompany her aesthetic triumphs, they were shocked to find extreme poverty inhabiting picturesque landscapes. As Lady Henrietta Chatterton wrote, Ireland too frequently presented "a picture of distress where all nature seemed to rejoice; a mass of wretchedness amid the perfection of beauty." Rev. John East, traveling during the Famine, lamented that "it was mortifying and humbling to one's human nature to revert from the glorious things of the Creator's

---

12. See Ó Giolláin, "The Pattern"; Ó Crualaoich, "The 'Merry Wake.'" For tourist reactions to funerals, patterns and faction fighting see Williams, *Tourism, Landscape, and the Irish Character*, 42–45, 72–79.
13. Otway, *Sketches in Ireland*, 148–50. For confessional landscapes see A. Williams, *Tourism, Landscape, and the Irish Character*, 48–50.
14. Gibbon, *Gaelic Gothic* 11; Otway, *Tour of Connaught*, 71; see also 72.
15. Weld, *Illustrations of the Scenery of Killarney and the Surrounding Country*, 21. For tourist reactions to Irish ruins and graveyards see Williams, *Tourism, Landscape, and the Irish Character*, 32–47.

earth [...] to the mean and grovelling and *scarcely human things* of one's own race."[16] And then there were the bogs, which, to many Victorians, represented wasteland begging to be drained and put to use. Only Paddy's sloth and his landlord's apathy, they concluded, stood as barriers to the march of agricultural progress.

Indeed, when it came to agriculture, many Britons had very definite ideas regarding the appearance of good farmland. Familiar with the rich, arable lands of the "Home Counties" around London, they were accustomed to encountering a landscape transformed by modern crop rotation into an orderly system of fields enclosed by stout stone walls and flowering hedgerows. England's "enclosure movement" had produced the British ideal of agrarian landscape—pretty but also productive. The well-tended fields, the landlord's manor house, the village with its church (Anglican, of course) combined the aesthetics of the picturesque with symbols of good order, progress and agricultural bounty. This quintessentially English landscape formed the template against which Irish agrarian tracts were measured and usually found wanting.[17] The enclosure movement had, of course, reached many of Ireland's richer farmlands. Yet, even on the best estates and farms visitors found Ireland's hedgerows inferior to those in Surrey. Irish plow lines seemed crooked, and everything wanted weeding, untidy signs of moral laxity. In the west of Ireland, where pasturage was on the increase, the resulting large fields struck British eyes as empty and unstructured. Worse, the surrounding small upland farms, not to mention the pratie patches of the cottiers, seemed cluttered and uncared for. Every aspect of rural Ireland seemed to mock British ideals of hard work and good husbandry. The Irish agrarian landscape simply did not look right to eyes trained to respond to the aesthetics and socioeconomic structure of the English countryside. Looking at Ireland and thinking of England, the visitors interpreted the differences in moral terms. Ireland's agricultural landscape suggested the moral laxity of a whole people.[18] There was an exception, however: Ulster.

Two Ulsters, in fact, coexisted in the British mind. One was the historic nine-county province that constituted the northern part of Ireland. A kind of geographical and economic microcosm of the whole island, this Ulster contained hilly land and dramatic seascapes, fertile glens and boggy mountains, prosperous farms and areas crowded with rural poverty. One-fifth of the province was wasteland with one-third covered in lakes. In some townlands in Monaghan, population density ranged between 600 and 1,300 people per square mile.[19] Such concentrations were typical of much of southern and western Ulster through which runs Ireland's drumlin belt, a landscape made up of swarms of small hills rising out of intervening lakes and bogs. Thanks to a widespread proto-industry centered on linen production, much of this region was packed with numerous farming–weaving–spinning families. With the decline of cottage industry

---

16. East, *Notes and Glimpses of Ireland*, 65; italics added; Chatterton, *Rambles in the South of Ireland in the Year 1838*, 1:97.
17. See Williams, *Tourism, Landscape, and the Irish Character*, 138–41.
18. Ibid., 142–46.
19. Duffy, "The Famine in County Monaghan," 171. For wasteland and lakes see Smyth, "The Province of Ulster and the Great Famine," 417, 418.

in the 1830s, however, many parts of the drumlin areas were about as poor as anywhere else in Ireland. However, farms to the north and east were often larger and enjoyed better soil. And it was these, largely Protestant, more prosperous areas, mentally detached from the provinces' bog lands and poor farms, that formed the nucleus of what the British came to call "Ulster."[20]

To British imaginations this carefully edited version of Ulster looked more English than Irish. In fact, to some visitors this truncated Ulster did not look Irish at all. Touring the more prosperous northern and eastern areas of the province in 1834, Henry D. Inglis, announced that "Ulster" had nothing in common with the rest of Ireland. "There is, in fact, no trace of an Irish population among any class." Traveling from Newry to Armagh, William Makepeace Thackeray rejoiced in the "well-tilled fields, neat farmhouses." Compared to the rest of Ireland, "people and landscape everywhere have a plane, hearty and flourishing look."[21] It was the industrializing city of Belfast, however, that seemed the least "Irish" place in Ireland. Scottish visitor Robert Graham marveled at the "hustle and bustle" of Belfast. On entering the city, he was astounded "to find myself so suddenly *out of Ireland*." Samuel Carter and Anna Hall claimed that Belfast "is in Ireland, but not of it." In Leitch Ritchie's opinion, while Belfast was the third largest city in Ireland, it was the *first* city from "a moral point of view."[22]

The British thus created an abbreviated "Ulster" that included only what they wanted to see and excluded large areas of poverty and privation. The result was an Ulster made up of the best, the most Protestant parts of the province, which, of course, seemed most like Britain. This "Ulster" became a moral model that shamed the rest of Ireland, peopled by the "real" Irish—the Catholics. "Ulster" was, therefore, both an exemplar and a reproach to the rest of the country.[23] Ireland, the model implied, could grow and prosper only to the extent that it became less Irish.

Although religion was a powerful factor in shaping British attitudes toward Ireland, by the 1830s many Britons, nevertheless, found expressions of overt sectarian prejudice somewhat embarrassing. Therefore, relatively few observers wanted to ascribe the supposed superiority of Ulster to Protestantism. What, then, could account for its seeming unique position? Inglis, a Scot, struggled with this question. He denied that religion accounted for Ulster prosperity "to any great degree." However, when crossing from Donegal into County Londonderry near Strabane, he suddenly thought himself "among a different *race* of men." Visiting Ulster a year later, Dr. James Johnson claimed that north of the line between Drogheda and Ballyshannon (which roughly traces the drumlin belt) "one could clearly perceive the predominance of Scoto-Britannic over Celto-Milesian"

---

20. For the drumlin belt and contrasting areas see William H. A. Williams, *Tourism, Landscape, and the Irish Character*, 147–51, 153.
21. Thackeray, *Irish Sketchbook*, 257. Inglis, *A Journey throughout Ireland, during the Spring, Summer and Autumn of 1834*, 2:250, 2:328.
22. Ritchie, *Ireland, Picturesque and Romantic*, 2:54; Graham, *A Scottish Whig in Ireland*, 232, italics added; Carter and Hall, *Ireland: Its Scenery and Character & etc.*, 3:24.
23. For an extended discussion of "moral" Ulster, see Williams, *Tourism, Landscape, and the Irish Character*, 147–61.

qualities among the people. Other observers settled for more familiar, if no more accurate, terms such as "Scots," "Saxons" and "Celts." Whatever one called them, to Johnson these groups were *"aliens to each other,* in blood, language and religion!"[24] Others might have added the word "character." An article in the *News of the World* in October 1845 contrasted the apparent economic success of Belfast to the poverty of Galway in the west of Ireland. The "energetic and industrious character of one population ensures prosperity, and the apathetic indifference of the other brings about decay." The "Celtic race" in Galway displayed "their capacity of long endurance, their easy tractability of disposition, and their contentment with almost any lot. [...] virtues which the English people have not. [...] And it is the very "virtue" of the poor Celtic peasant which tend to his destruction and wretchedness." Since he would not help himself, "the poor, uneducated, contented Irish peasant must not only be taught civilized habits, but forced into them."[25]

In this pre-Darwin era neither the term nor the concept of "race" had yet taken on an insistent biological definition. The word represented, as Michael de Nie has suggested, "a metalanguage in Anglo-Saxon discourse, a vehicle for expressing multiple anxieties and preconceptions," concerning culture, religion and class.[26] As used in the 1830s and early 1840s, "race" frequently stood for national character, combining "nurture"—customs, habits, religion—along with "nature." This mixture is apparent in Thackeray's description of what he regarded as the "typical," presumably Protestant, Ulster residents: "The people's faces are sharp and neat, not broad, lazy and knowing-looking, like that of many a shambling Diogenes who may be seen lounging before his cabin in Cork or Kerry. [...] The [Ulster] people speak with a Scotch twang, and as I fancied, much more simply and to the point." Instead of putting Ulster's uniqueness down to religion, however, Thackeray preferred the idea of "Scotchism," by which he meant "thrift, prudence, perseverance, boldness and common sense." If he was thinking of Protestantism, he did not say.[27]

The indeterminate role of biology did not hinder the Victorian pastime of ranking "races" from superior to inferior, relegating the most "savage" peoples to the bottom of the heap. By the eve of the Famine the British could claim considerable colonial experience among some of the "inferior" and "barbarous" groups of the non-white world. This did not prevent British stereotypes from consigning the Irish peasantry to those supposedly beyond the boundaries of civilization. With his pig, his rags and barely thatched cabin Paddy seemed worse off than Africans, North American Indians or the natives of Micronesia. Trying to sketch a typical Irish cabin, Thackeray declared that "a Hottentot Kraal has more comfort in it." To Thomas Carlyle the sight of the beggars in Kildare town suggested a village in Dohomey. And inevitably, the Irish peasants' cabins with their thatched, high-pitched roofs brought to mind American Indian wigwams. To

---

24. Johnson, *A Tour of Ireland with Meditations and Reflections*, 327, italics original. See also Inglis, 2:213–14. For "race of men" see 2:188.
25. *News of the World*, October 19, 1845, 3a.
26. De Nie, *The Eternal Paddy*, 5.
27. Thackeray, *Irish Sketchbook*, 259.

some extent these were literary tropes, and, in some cases, were mixed in with more sympathetic and occasionally insightful observations. Nevertheless, by the eve of the Famine such language was taking on a life of its own, threatening to turn Paddy into a truly disturbing figure: a white, European, Christian *savage*, not only beyond the pale of civilization, but perhaps beyond humanity itself. Contemplating Irish poverty, surgeon Thomas Reid wondered, "how it was possible for *human beings* to exist in such circumstances?"[28]

Such comments suggest how easy it was for fear and detestation of poverty to hover on the edge of racism. The American writer Marilynne Robinson has called attention to the connection between poverty and racism. In nineteenth-century Britain, poverty represented a permanent social condition. The poor constituted an unchanging class, their status defined and governed by the Poor Laws. As such, they represented, in Robinson's words, a "virtual race, not simply people who had fallen upon hard times. The marks of poverty were a stigma comparable in some of their effects to the marks of race under slavery or Jim Crow or apartheid."[29] Once the stigma of poverty became deeply attached to a particular people, such as the Irish, the road to racism was open.

The Narrative of the Irish Other

In discussing the formation of modern British national identity, Linda Colley suggests that people "decide who they are by reference to who and what they are not."[30] In other words, they try to define themselves vis-à-vis "the Other." Commenting on the role of Catholic France as Britain's dominant Other in the eighteenth century, Colley notes, "Britishness was imposed over an array of internal differences in response to contact with the Other, and above all in response to conflict with the Other." However, while the French Other emerged out of Britain's long struggle with France, there was still the somewhat older Other, the "Celts," against whom an English and then a British identity continued to evolve. True, as a sense of Britishness took shape, any Welsh, Scots or Irish who wished could share in that identity without relinquishing their Celtic background—provided it was sufficiently quaint, picturesque and nonthreatening. As Murry G. H. Pittock suggests, there was a desire among Britons to marginalize their Celtic fringe into a condition of "mere ethno-cultural tribalism."[31] The Scottish Highlander in his invented kilt and kit became a Romantic adjunct to the realm a generation *after* his grandfather's defeat at the Battle of Culloden in 1746.

This never completely worked with the Irish, however. There was no way the British could sentimentalize the United Irishman's Rising of 1798 as a colorful example of "local patriotism." Nor could ragged Pat be embraced as an example of merely quaint, local color. In addition, Daniel O'Connell's campaigns for Catholic Emancipation and

---

28. Reid, *Travels in Ireland in the Year 1822*, 187, italics original; Thackeray, *Irish Sketchbook*, 89; Carlyle, *Reminiscences of My Irish Journey in 1849*, 70.
29. Robinson, "Which Way to the City on the Hill," *New York Review of Books*, 66:12 (July 18, 2019), 43.
30. Colley, *Britons: Forginag a Nation, 1707-1837*, 6.
31. Pittock, *Celtic Identity and the British Image*, 23, 49.

the Repeal of the Act of Union seemed to make Ireland more, rather than less, alien to Protestant, imperial Britain. The stronger the sense of Britishness became, the more alien the Irish appeared. In Pittock's words, "retrogressive alienization of all Irish who displayed difference prevented comprehension of the Irish situation and led to successive crises at the end of the eighteenth and throughout the nineteenth century."[32] With the final defeat of Napoleon, the Irish resumed their traditional role as Britain's Other, or at least its Near Other, albeit under altered circumstances. Thanks to the Act of Union, tensions between Great Britain and Ireland became internalized as imagined struggles between unity versus disunity, order versus chaos, a British "Us" versus an Irish "Them."

This was not just a process of demarcation (we do this; they do that) as much as it was one of definition (this makes us British; that makes them Irish). Within the moralistic universe of Victorian Britain, Paddy served as a convenient repository for those traits the British most feared in themselves. "Irish" traits threatened the maintenance of a society turned inside-out by industrialization, urbanization, technological progress and a rapid expansion of wealth inequality. The British could not afford to tolerate in themselves the behavior they posited in the stereotypical Irishman—improvident, easygoing, careless, lazy, pugnacious, overly fond of the drink—traits that threatened to undermine a social and economic system that itself was full of tensions and contradictions. Such behaviors challenged Britons' sense of control, faith in rational progress and maintenance of the discipline that held together Great Britain's new moralistic, capitalistic culture. As Leslie A. Williams argues, "Any Irish trait could easily generate its British opposite, which would always be superior or positive in comparison to the Irish." And the reverse was also true; the traits most admired by the British were generally assumed to be lacking in the Irish. As Michael de Nie states, "The Irish were the mirror opposite of the British," although, he adds, "they were still a reflection." Nonetheless, as de Nie suggests, whatever hopes Britons had that Paddy might be anglicized and brought to the British side of the mirror were eventually shattered.[33] The Famine was a major factor in this disappointment.

By assuming that the Irish were inherently inferior, many British observers avoided inquiring too deeply into the political and economic circumstances in which Irish poverty seemed to flourish. Their Irish narrative shielded many Britons from acknowledging the harsh realities of the legacy of colonialism in Ireland and the economic costs of the imposition of agrarian capitalism on a society dominated by landlords. The narrative also implied that, left to their own devices, the Irish were incapable to managing their own affairs. It would take the firm hand of Britain, guided by its supposed superior values and modern ideas, to sort things out and set Ireland upon the road of progress. Whatever happened in Ireland, including the Famine, would be filtered through this narrative. Well before the arrival of the potato blight, however, British attitudes would be tested by events in Ireland stemming from the conflation of religion, politics and nationalism.

---

32. Pittock, *Celtic Identity and the British Image*, 52–53.
33. de Nie, *The Eternal Paddy*, 269; also 23, 119. Leslie A. Williams, *Daniel O'Connell, the British Press and the Irish Famine*, 360. For an extended discussion of the British/Irish dichotomy based on Gregory Bateson's theories about cultural redundancy see 344–65.

Chapter Three

POLITICS AND RELIGION IN THE AGE OF DANIEL O'CONNELL

The United Kingdom and Catholic Emancipation

Once the British government had determined to abolish the Irish Parliament and incorporate the island into the Union, it had also decided to repeal the last of the Penal Laws and grant Roman Catholics full citizenship. During the Rising of '98, the Catholic Church had proved loyal to the Crown. Many Catholics had served in the ranks of the Yeomen in suppressing the rebellion. Consequently, there were those in the government who felt that Catholic Emancipation would help guarantee the tranquility of Ireland under the Union. However, not only were Irish Protestants still steadfastly opposed to such a move, many Britons, including King George III, regarded the measure as a threat to what they considered the Kingdom's Protestant identity.[1] After centuries of resisting Catholic foes at home and abroad, Britons, including many Scots, Welsh and some Irish, came to identify themselves as members of a Protestant nation. By the eighteenth century, Britons had, in Linda Colley's words, "defined themselves as Protestants struggling for survival against the world's foremost Catholic power"—France. In fact, during the almost constant warfare with France, Britons came to see themselves as "a chosen people struggling towards the light, a bulwark against the depredations of [the Catholic] Antichrist."[2] The target of this aggressive, paranoid Protestant identity was not limited to France. Once the issue of Catholic Emancipation was raised, anti-Catholic sentiment shifted from the Continent toward the sister island that had just joined the United Kingdom.

When, therefore, Prime Minister William Pitt the Younger tried to pass a Catholic reform bill in the wake of the Act of Union, he failed. Although Pitt resigned, negotiations with the Catholic hierarchy in Ireland eventually produced what seemed a workable approach. Roman Catholics would receive full political rights; in return the British government would be granted a veto over episcopal appointments within the Kingdom's Catholic hierarchy. Then, something unexpected happened. In 1808, lay Catholic opposition, led by a young Irish barrister named Daniel O'Connell, pressured the Irish bishops to reject the government's proposed veto.[3] In addition to giving voice to the religious

---

1. Colley, *Britons: Forging of the Nation, 1707–1830*, 340.
2. Ibid., 6. See also 18, 23. 25, 30.
3. Larkin, *The Pastoral Role of the Roman Catholic Church in Pre-Famine Ireland, 1750–1850*, 87–92. For attempts to find a compromise in "Denominational Nomination" see 266–67.

pride of middle-class Catholics, O'Connell's aggressive stance also injected an element of Irish nationalism into the debate. When the government refused to consider Catholic relief without the veto, O'Connell made it clear that Ireland's Catholics would no longer simply request Emancipation; they would demand it.

O'Connell prepared for an unprecedented political fight by organizing a well-financed campaign of agitation. With the support of most of Ireland's Catholic hierarchy, he took over the staid, upper-class Catholic Association and turned it into what was perhaps the world's first political machine. Lacking the usual backing of a wealthy aristocratic patron, O'Connell reorganized the association's finances around a "Catholic Rent," based on dues graduated down to the level of the peasantry—a farthing a week, a penny a month. The funding was organized at the parish level, where members were mobilized for a series of mass meetings held around the country. Through such measures, O'Connell and his movement played a key role in inventing the politics of mass democracy.[4]

Keen to avoid any suggestion that his agitation would lead to armed insurrection, O'Connell embraced a strategy of nonviolent confrontation. He planned to stir up the country through a series of mass meetings, building tensions until the government would be forced to capitulate. The moment arrived in 1828 when O'Connell stood for a parliamentary seat in County Clare. He won, but in order to assume his seat he had to take the Oath of Supremacy, a remnant of the old Penal Laws, which involved abjuring the power of the Roman Catholic Church. O'Connell refused. The election was run again, and again he won, and again he refused to take the oath. With opinion in Ireland raised to a fever pitch, this was the moment for which O'Connell had planned. Even in the best of times, Ireland was hardly tranquil. The Catholic Emancipation campaign had played out amid a rising tide of agrarian unrest. Thus, with O'Connell having raised Irish expectations to a high level, neither the Tory prime minister, the Anglo-Irish Duke of Wellington, nor his leader in the House of Commons, Robert Peel, could be sure of what would happen if the government continued to block Catholic Emancipation. After considering the situation, they blinked. The Oath of Supremacy was revoked. In 1829 "The Liberator," as O'Connell was now called, entered Parliament where he would command a small group of Irish MPs.[5]

Those Britons harboring strong anti-Catholic, anti-Irish sentiments were appalled. For them, Catholic Emancipation played into the British narrative that saw the Irish as a volatile, unruly people, easily led by their priests in league with an unscrupulous, powerful demagogue. With political cartoons gaining in popularity, O'Connell provided a face for anti-Irish sentiment in Britain. Even among the more liberal-minded who agreed that Catholic Emancipation was an overdue necessity, many were still uneasy about O'Connell's methods. Rousing the Catholic masses to intimidate the government

---

4. Whelan, *The Bible War in Ireland*, 193–94.
5. Even after the Oath of Supremacy was removed, Roman Catholics seeking to enter Parliament had to take a new oath by which they abjured any intention to subvert the established Church of England and the government. They also had to swear to maintain the Protestant nature of the constitution. See Yates, *The Religious Condition of Ireland, 1770–1850*, 47–48.

was disturbing enough. Worse, thanks to the Act of Union, the doors of the Imperial Parliament were suddenly thrown open to Irish politics and Irish agitation. From that point on, Irish issues, which would eventually include the Famine, would play out on the British stage.

Evangelicals, the Second Reformation and the Catholic Response

Despite misgivings, however, many Britons eventually accepted Catholic Emancipation, believing that religious intolerance had no place in a modern, enlightened age. However, what was an important secularizing step within Britain proved to be a highly controversial sectarian one in Ireland. The effectiveness with which the Roman Catholic hierarchy had swung its Church's organizational structure behind O'Connell disturbed many within Ireland's Protestant minority. Moreover, the populist nature of O'Connell's movement—the union of priests, people and politicians working together at the grassroots level—shook the foundations of the Ascendancy's political conservatism. The resulting reaction created what R. F. Foster has called "a distinctly Protestant political culture."[6]

Protestantism in Ireland was, in fact, facing a crisis that had been building for a long time. By the latter half of the eighteenth century, the Anglican Church's anomalous situation had become too obvious to ignore. Despite the Penal Laws, the established church had failed to attract even a significant minority of Irish citizens into its fold. Roman Catholics, as well as Presbyterians and other Dissenters, showed little inclination to join. Thus, the Protestant aristocracy and its church had become, in the words of Neil Yates, "a compromise ascendancy." Sitting at the pinnacle of Irish society, they commanded no allegiance from most of the population. Eventually, a sort of sectarian stalemate emerged. Starting around 1770, Ireland's three main religious groups entered a five-decade period represented by limited, informal cooperation and even minimal toleration. However, during the 1820s, roiled in part by the struggle over Catholic Emancipation, Ireland's religious atmosphere changed radically.[7] On the one hand, while their church rejuvenated and expanded its organization, Roman Catholics began to assert their long-frustrated desire for political and social power. On the other hand, the disappearance of the Irish Parliament and its House of Lords had robbed the Anglican bishops of much of their political influence. At the same time, an emergent, aggressive evangelical movement within the Church of Ireland began a push to succeed where mainstream Anglicanism had failed: to convert Ireland's Roman Catholics to Protestantism. By the 1820s radical voices within all denominations were assailing the status quo. Protestant evangelicals were among the most vociferous.

Evangelicalism, which first emerged in England and Wales during the eighteenth century, had been inspired by pietistic movements on the Continent. In contrast to the cold formality of the Anglican Church, evangelicals stressed a more emotional approach to religion based on personal conversion and a close, literal reading of the Scriptures.

---

6. Foster, *Modern Ireland: 1600–1972*, 302.
7. Yates, *The Religious Condition of Ireland, 1770–1850*, xix–xx.

They sought to spread their highly personal approach to Protestant Christianity through preaching, as well as by distributing Bibles and religious tracts. Although some liberal-minded British evangelicals had supported Catholic Emancipation, many Irish evangelicals had been deeply opposed to it. Shocked and angered by O'Connell's success, they redoubled their efforts to promote the Protestant cause.[8] They responded to a resurgent Catholic majority by launching what they called "the Second Reformation." With the Bible as their principal weapon, their goal was to convert the Irish Catholic masses to "true" Protestant Christianity. During the first few decades of the nineteenth century, several hundred thousand Bibles and Testaments were distributed by groups such as the London Hibernian Bible Society and the Dublin-based Hibernian Bible Society. This spiritual drive combined easily with a desire to ensure social control by promoting Protestant social and economic values along with Protestant theology.[9]

For a time, the Second Reformation collided with grassroots, anti-Protestant millennialism centered on the writings of Charles Walmsely, an eighteenth-century English Catholic bishop who wrote under the penname of Signore Pastorini. Predicting the imminent destruction of Protestantism, the "Prophecies of Pastorini" swept through the southwest of Ireland in the early 1820s, often as an adjunct to agrarian agitation. While the Pastorini fervor appears to have died amid famine conditions in 1822, anti-Protestant millennialist sentiment helped to fuel popular support for O'Connell's emancipation movement, even while the Liberator struggled to publicly separate himself from the taint of sectarianism.[10]

Sectarian tensions in Ireland were already high when they erupted over educational issues. Many of Ireland's Catholics desired some sort of education for their children. In 1811, Dublin's Kildare Place Society, a Protestant organization with access to government funds, initiated nonsectarian classes for the poor. For a time, there was a quiet Roman Catholic acquiescence in the program. At one point, Daniel O'Connell became a member of the society's board of governors. However, around 1815 some Irish evangelicals took Napoleon's defeat at Waterloo as a providential sign and, thus encouraged, became more assertive in their proselytizing. Consequently, the Kildare Place Society's schools became more controversial. Growing Catholic opposition finally prompted the government to intervene. The Kildare Place schools eventually lost their government financial support. The issue was finally put on a path toward resolution when a system for national education was established in 1831. By 1837 the national Board of Education had created separate, publicly funded schools run either by Catholics or Protestants. This measure, however, effectively undercut one of the main thrusts of the evangelical campaign to entice Catholics away from their Church.[11]

---

8. Irene Whelan, *Bible War in Ireland*, 153, 155, 175–76. For a detailed account of one part of this movement, see Akenson, *Discovering the End of Time*.
9. Irene Whelan, 72–73.
10. Donnelly, Jr., *The Land and the People of Nineteenth-Century Cork*, 131, 145–46. For the connection of Pastorini to agrarian agitation see 7, 9–10, 119–49. For the role of the "Prophecies" in sectarian tensions see also Irene Whelan, 141–46.
11. Irene Whelan, 234-35; Yates, *The Religious Condition of Ireland, 1770–1850*, 56–59.

By then, however, Ireland's contending religious factions were already engaged in other battles, such as the "Tithe Wars." In addition to supporting their own clergy, Irish Catholics had to pay tithes to the established Protestant Church of Ireland. The 1820s experienced often violent resistance to what Catholics saw as a religious tax. Finally, the Tithe Act of 1838 mandated that landlords, rather than tenant farmers, would pay the tax, which was, of course, eventually folded into increased rents. However, Catholics were at least spared the indignity of having to openly support a clergy whose spiritual power they did not recognize. And, although they retained income from the tithe, the Church of Ireland lost an opportunity to openly assert its unique position as Ireland's established church.[12]

By the mid-1830s, some within the Irish evangelical fold felt that they were losing ground in their push for the Second Reformation. First, Catholic Emancipation had become a reality. Then the Tithe War ended in a distinctly unsatisfactory compromise. At around the same time, the Church of Ireland had lost its state-supported monopoly on education and on certain social services. Some evangelicals, however, still committed to aggressive proselytism, shifted their focus to the Gaelic-speaking Catholic masses in the west of Ireland. There Irish was a spoken rather than a written language. So, instead of teaching the peasantry to read either Irish or English, Protestant missionaries found it easier to hire Irish-speaking individuals who could read Gaelic translations of the Scriptures to the people in their own homes. Inevitably, the Catholic clergy came to view the use of the Irish language in a religious context as a Trojan Horse harboring Protestant heresy.[13]

Attempts to convert Catholics in the west of Ireland were organized by key Anglican bishops and their clergy, who in turn received cooperation from sympathetic landlords and their wives. Evangelizing efforts were supported by organizations such as the Protestant Colonization Society, founded in 1830. To protect converts who embraced Protestantism, several missions were established in the west of Ireland. Supported by donors in Britain and in Ireland, most of these institutions were small. However, a few larger "colonies" on the Dingle Peninsula in Kerry and on Achill Island in Mayo attracted a good deal of attention. Although offering schooling for children, instruction in modern farming techniques for men and domestic industry for women, the missions were essentially proselytizing beachheads, and, as in the case of Achill, they generated a good deal of hostility within the local Catholic community.[14] Unfortunately, during times of subsistence crises, evangelical attempts at relief sometimes became caught up in sectarian tensions. It was during the 1830s that the derisive term "souper" was first applied to converts accused of exchanging their Catholic faith for Protestant gifts of free food (soup) and clothing. Therefore, when the potato blight arrived in 1845 the ground was already

---

12. Yates, *The Religious Condition of Ireland, 1770–1850*, 50–51.
13. Ó Tuathaigh, *I mBéal an Bháis: The Great Famine and the Language Shift in Nineteenth-Century Ireland*, 21.
14. Yates, *The Religious Condition of Ireland, 1770–1850*, 272–75. See also Irene Whelan, 252–53; 256–60; Ní Ghoibúin, *Dugort, Achill Island, 1831–1861*; Patricia Byrne, *The Preacher and the Prelate*.

prepared in parts of western Ireland, especially in Connemara, for a bitter heightening of the Bible wars amidst widespread suffering and starvation. In this environment, the terms "souper" and "souperism" would become part of the Famine legacy.[15]

Inevitably, sectarian confrontations in Ireland—Catholic Emancipation, the Tithe War, conflicts over education, evangelical missionary efforts—did little to engender British confidence in the stability, much less civility, of Irish society. At the same time, evangelical attacks on Catholicism, coupled with a moralistic critique of the Irish character, fitted easily into the British narrative about Ireland and the Irish. Given his popish superstitions and mendacious poverty, "Paddy" hardly represented the kind of civilization for which the United Kingdom was supposed to stand. Thus, thanks in part to the "Bible wars" and the counter reassertion of Catholic power, the impact of anti-Catholicism on British opinions about the Irish, can, in the words of Irene Whelan, "hardly be overestimated."[16] Inevitably, sectarian issues would become caught up in the public discourse surrounding the Famine.

Daniel O'Connell and the Repeal Campaign

The resurgence of Irish nationalism proved another factor influencing British attitudes during the pre-Famine decades. Defeated in its revolutionary form in 1798, nationalism reemerged as a constitutional issue when Daniel O'Connell, newly seated in Parliament, demanded the repeal of the Act of Union and the reestablishment of an Irish legislature in Dublin. Having recently expanded the Union, however, the British had little interest in altering it, especially on the heels of Catholic Emancipation. When Parliament refused to even study the issue in 1834, the Liberator decided to put Repeal on temporary hold and to devote himself to building more political support. He sought an alliance with the Whigs in hopes of gaining some meaningful reforms for Ireland. In 1835, as part of the so-called Litchfield House Compact, O'Connell agreed to swing his parliamentary faction behind a reformist minority Whig administration under Lord Melbourne. The Whigs did address some important Irish issues, such as tithes and education, as well as police and local government reform, not always to the Liberator's satisfaction. Pragmatic as he was, O'Connell began to realize that his alliance with the Whigs could only produce limited results while risking the loss of political support at home.[17] So, when Melbourne's government was replaced by the Tories led by Robert Peel in 1841, O'Connell reinvested in his original conviction that the only way to help Ireland was to restore the Irish Parliament.

The Liberator, of course, knew what to do. He easily revived the structures and tactics that had served him so well in the struggle for Catholic Emancipation. He established a Repeal Association modeled on the earlier Catholic Association, with mass meetings and membership dues extending down into the peasantry. Since most Irishmen could

---

15. Irene Whelan, 256.
16. Ibid., 271.
17. McDowell, "Ireland on the Eve of the Famine," 74–75.

not vote and would not benefit directly from the return of an Irish parliament, only by accentuating an enhanced concept of Irish nationhood could the Liberator galvanize the masses and bring maximum pressure on the British government. Such a move, however, implied defining Ireland as a nation, and therein lay a problem. O'Connell never clearly elucidated his concept of an Irish nation. Sometimes it seemed more a means rather than an end. He desired a regenerated Ireland, Catholic but also liberal, endowed with some of the trappings of self-government. Beyond that, the actual details involved in "Repeal" remained wonderfully ambiguous, clearly open to negotiation. The question was, would O'Connell's reliance on rhetoric rather than substance retain the loyalty of his younger followers, who were already breathing the heady air of romantic nationalism sweeping through the Continent?[18]

As O'Connell's Repeal campaign progressed, action was added to rhetoric, and Ireland began to take on the appearance, at least, of a nation on the march. His mass outdoor assemblies, complete with converging processions, temperance brass bands and cavalcades of horsemen, were so large that the press dubbed them "monster meetings." O'Connell began to hold these huge gatherings at historic venues, such Tara, ancient seat of the High Kings of Ireland. And although he constantly reiterated his loyalty to the Queen and reaffirmed the nonviolent nature of his movement, his speeches seemed to reawaken the dormant power of Irish nationalism among his supporters. At the Tara meeting on August 15, 1843, he was presented with a "Repeal Cap," a tasseled hat that incorporated certain designs copied from of an ancient crown recently recovered from an Irish bog. When campaigning in Dublin, the Liberator, resplendent in his new headgear, took to presiding over Repeal processions from the top of a great triumphal car.[19]

O'Connell was sure that the strategy he had developed during the Emancipation campaign would work again: organize Ireland, bring the country to a fever pitch, create a moment of crisis and, thus, force the government to capitulate or at least negotiate. However, repealing the Act of Union presented a very different kind of challenge. Emancipation, which had involved civil rights and religious toleration, had attracted significant support in Britain. And, while it had constitutional implications, Emancipation did not seriously challenge the structure of the United Kingdom. On the other hand, by the 1840s the Union had assumed an almost sacred aura in the eyes of many Britons, who saw their country as the seat of a mighty worldwide empire. Would not the return of an Irish parliament to Dublin be the first step toward a demand for ultimate independence for Ireland? Britons thought that any attempt to weaken, much less break apart, the Union would surely cripple both Kingdom and empire.

And then there was the question of trust. Could Ireland again be allowed even a modicum of self-government? It was true that, except for Robert Emmet's abortive rising in 1803, there had been no further attempts at revolution since 1798. Nevertheless, to

---

18. Nowlan, "The Political Background," 132. See also Foster, *Modern Ireland: 1600–1972,* 308–9.
19. For O'Connell's Repeal Cap see Leslie A. Williams, *Daniel O'Connell, the British Press and the Irish Famine,* 87–88. O'Connell's triumphal car, first used in 1832, was a three-tiered conveyance topped by a chair large enough to suggest a throne; see 89, 99n9.

many Britons, Ireland, even under the Union, hardly seemed a peaceful place. In addition to the continued undercurrent of agrarian unrest, there had been seemingly endless sectarian tensions. Moreover, despite a very limited franchise, the expansion of Catholic political power, no matter how gradual, meant that a restored Irish Parliament would eventually fall into Catholic hands. Then there were the methods O'Connell used in both of his campaigns—the mobilization of mass support among Irish Catholics with the help of the Church. Add it all up, and, as R. F. Foster has suggested, the concept of an Irish nation, however defined, appeared as a Catholic idea to many Britons, while the Union seemed a Protestant one.[20]

Having designated 1843 as the "Year of Repeal," O'Connell held a series of mass meetings throughout the spring and summer, ratcheting up rhetoric that to suspicious ears seemed to carry overtones of rebellion. Enthusiasm and tensions increased, leading to what was intended to be the largest of all monster meetings scheduled for October 8 at Clontarf on the outskirts of Dublin, As the site of a battle at which the forces of Brian Boru, High King of Ireland, defeated the Dublin Danes in 1014, Clontarf easily appealed to the Irish nationalist imagination. Nearing panic, Robert Peel's Tory government banned the meeting and mobilized the army in and around Dublin. O'Connell now faced the real possibility of large-scale violence if he stuck to his plan. This time the Liberator blinked; he cancelled the Clontarf meeting.[21] The crisis melted away—almost.

Not satisfied with its victory, the government proceeded to arrest O'Connell and some of his lieutenants on charges of conspiracy to commit treason. At the subsequent state trial in January 1844, O'Connell and his confederates were found guilty by a jury packed with Protestants, and, while the case was on appeal to the House of Lords, the Repeal leaders were remanded to Richmond Prison in Dublin. O'Connell won his appeal and was freed on September 7. By this time the techniques of mass politics were sufficiently advanced to encourage the Liberator to return to Richmond Prison the next day and, riding atop his great triumphal car, lead an enormous and carefully staged procession through the streets of Dublin. When it passed the imposing structure on College Green that had once housed the old Irish Parliament, O'Connell stopped his car, rose and pointed dramatically to the building.[22] It was a grand, theatrical gesture, and the crowd loved it. But it was without meaning. The government's ill-considered and futile attempt to punish him had momentarily eclipsed the fact that O'Connell's bluff had been called and that he had lost the Repeal battle.

With no viable fallback position, O'Connell found it increasingly difficult to hold his Repeal organization together. Rifts, in fact, had already appeared within its ranks. In 1842 a group of Irish intellectuals and writers, including Thomas Davis, Charles Gavin Duffy and John Blake Dillon, founded *The Nation*, one of the most exciting Irish journals of its day. It sought to translate cultural nationalism into a political and even social movement.

---

20. See Foster, 316–17.
21. MacDonagh, *The Emancipist: Daniel O'Connell, 1830–1847*, 239.
22. *Illustrated London News* depicted the moment in a dramatic and highly detailed engraving; v (1844), 164. See Leslie A. Williams, *Daniel O'Connell, the British Press and the Irish Famine*, 89.

An unflattering British view of O'Connell's Repeal campaign.

Figure 1 "The Irish Ogre Fattening on the Finest Pisantry," *Punch*, July 8, 1843

Those nationalist-minded Protestant and Catholic middle-class intellectuals whom the journal attracted eventually became known as "Young Ireland." Despite O'Connell's acquittal, they understood very clearly that his nonviolent tactics, when pushed to the limit, had failed. As a result, many within *The Nation* group refused to rule out revolutionary action. During the Famine, O'Connell's Repeal Association would eventually split on this issue.

O'Connell's stock was also at low ebb in Britain. While he had never been liked by the Tories, he had once enjoyed some goodwill among the Whigs because of his support for a variety of liberal causes. He had championed the abolition of slavery and lent his backing to electoral reform. He supported most laissez-faire policies, including the abolition of protectionism. Simultaneously, he embraced middle-class concerns about the rights of private property, leading him to oppose labor organizations, as well as the Factory Acts intended to regulate working conditions.[23] Nevertheless, his critics were angry about his continued calls for Repeal and his often-vituperative rhetoric aimed at Britain. This shift in British attitudes can be seen in the treatment of O'Connell by the satirical journal *Punch* between 1843 and 1844 (see Figure 1). Like most of the British press, the editorial board

---

23. For O'Connell's liberalism, see Macintyre, *The Liberator*, 165; Nowlan, *The Politics of Repeal*, 5–6, 7, 49; Ó Tuathaigh, *Ireland before the Famine: 1798–1848*, 162.

of *Punch*, which included the writer William Makepeace Thackeray, had been strongly opposed to the repeal of the Union. The magazine not only attacked O'Connell's campaign but deployed its talented cartoonists to ridicule the Liberator himself. By 1845 the magazine's caricatures of O'Connell began to change. Up until his release from prison, his features in most of *Punch*'s cartoons had been no more distorted than those of other victims of the magazine's caricaturists. By 1845, however, the drawings lengthened the distance between O'Connell's nose and his upper lip, suggesting simian features. More significantly, around the same time, depictions of O'Connell's peasant supporters also begin to take on a distinctly simian cast. The racist depictions of Paddy as ape man that would proliferate in British and American political cartoons after 1860 were already beginning to emerge on the eve of the Famine.[24]

The problem was not just that *Punch*, along with much of the British press, derided O'Connell. The magazine's self-appointed task was, after all, to torment politicians. O'Connell, however, was more than a politician. He stood not only for a party but for a nation. It was, therefore, almost inevitable that in attacking Daniel O'Connell, the British press ended up attacking the Irish people. As a result, many Britons may have found it difficult to separate their increasing dislike of "the Liberator" from their feelings about the Irish themselves. Coming on the eve of the Famine, British reaction to O'Connell's Repeal movement reflected increased suspicion and annoyance regarding Ireland at a time when the country would need all the help and understanding from Britons that it could muster. Unfortunately, when the blight destroyed Ireland's potato crop in the fall of 1846, many in Britain refused to believe that the Irish were really starving. Such reports fitted into a narrative of Irish hyperbole and mendacity, a narrative which, although easily associated with O'Connell and his followers, had roots deep in Britain's colonial history with Ireland. As suggested earlier, however, that history is only one factor in accounting for Britain's response to the Famine. Economics, ideology and class are also essential to understanding the crisis.

---

24. For *Punch* cartoons of O'Connell, see Leslie A. Williams, *Daniel O'Connell, the British Press and the Irish Famine*, 55–65, 92, 96, 148, 176 and 225. For the cartoons of the Irish peasant see 94, 148, and 159. The author suggests that the simianization of the features of O'Connell's peasant supporters began in *Punch* cartoons between 1842 and 1843; 64–65. For simian-featured peasants *during* the Famine see Donnelly, *Great Irish Potato Famine*, 120, 128 and 129. For the changes in British cartoon images of the Irish from the 1840s to the 1860s see Curtis, Jr., *Apes and Angels*, 31–33, 98–100.

Chapter Four

MORALITY AND ECONOMICS IN THE AGE OF ATONEMENT

The Middle Class, Evangelicalism and Christian Economics

Although the Whig government that would determine British policy during the Famine contained more than its share of titled aristocrats, its policies were strongly influenced by the demands of the recently enfranchised British middle class, which, ironically, owed a debt to Daniel O'Connell. England's ancient restrictive franchise had long limited middle-class participation in politics. However, O' Connell's innovations in mass politics provided a model for mobilizing British public opinion to demand electoral reform. Just as the Liberator had marshaled the Irish peasantry behind his causes, British middle-class supporters of franchise reform organized support down to the street level, without, of course, entertaining the slightest intention of extending the vote to tradesmen and workers. The Whigs eventually took up the cause, and England's first Reform Bill was passed in 1832. While the bill did increase middle-class representation, the political ramifications would not fully manifest themselves until the Famine. Nevertheless, the economic ideals of liberalism, first espoused by Adam Smith in *The Wealth of Nations* in 1776—limited government, low taxes, open competition, and free trade—formed the backbone of middle-class adherence to political economy. And although politics remained a game for rich men, it was not one that, in the words of S. J. Connolly, they "could play with reference to themselves alone [...] [They] found it necessary to take some account of a newly awakened popular opinion."[1] Thus, in 1838, under the banner of the Anti-Corn Law League, middle-class reformers would again deploy O'Connellite tactics to launch an aggressive campaign to end protectionism in the grain trade.

Along with liberalism, evangelicalism also played an important role in molding British public opinion. British evangelicalism was a highly personal form of Christianity involved in seeking God through prayer and Scripture. However, it also contained a strong social component as well. God was to guide one's daily actions in all things, public as well as private. This combination of personal piety and worldly involvement invited individuals to assume responsibility for the well-being of society, as well as the state of their own souls. Evangelicals were supposed to pursue policies that would enhance the moral development of the whole of society. (If, in the process, the nation also advanced economically, then so much the better.) British evangelicals shared with their Irish brethren concerns about modes of Protestant worship and a hostility toward Catholicism. However, while

---

1. Connolly, "The Great Famine and Irish Politics," 36.

Irish evangelicals felt themselves embattled at home, their brethren in Britain saw threats on a broader scale. By the 1790s British evangelicals found the world an uncertain, even dangerous place. The French Revolution had sent shock waves through Great Britain. It not only threatened the Kingdom's security; the moral order itself seemed to have been violated.[2] Yet, it was not just revolutions and wars abroad that disturbed evangelicals. At home, radicalism and the social dislocation produced by industrialization caused evangelicals like William Wilberforce to see the world "as in a state of alienation from God, as lost in depravity and guilt." How was man "to escape from the wrath to come?" he asked.[3] The early nineteenth century became, therefore, not only an "Age of Improvement," advancing to the drumbeat of the "March of Progress," but, in Boyd Hilton words, also an "Age of Atonement."[4] In response, evangelicals sought greater control over their society.

Evangelicalism in Great Britain, therefore, pushed beyond the church door and elbowed its way into the country's cultural, social, political and economic life. In part, this reflected a widespread reactionary shift, the result of Britain's almost hysterical response to the French Revolution. Yet, according to Gerald Newman, at its heart evangelicalism was, in a moral sense, revolutionary. Its goal, in Newman's words, was to "transform, nationalize, level and make uniform their country's institutions."[5] Evangelism sought to instill a national sense of discipline and seriousness into British life that included a dedication to work, public piety, obedience and an acute consciousness of status. In this sense, moral reform sought to redirect Britain from its essentially rural past, dominated by the culture of the landed aristocracy and gentry, toward the mores of the urban, middle-class, commercial and industrial country it was becoming.[6] Political moralism was, therefore, nothing less than the bourgeoisie's attempt to shift power from the aristocracy to itself. By the 1830s, this drive for moral reform had found its political voice in the liberal campaigns to abolish slavery, to enact electoral reform and to repeal agricultural protection represented by the Corn Laws, as well as to oppose worker's attempts to organize.

When it came to charity, liberal suspicion of the working class combined with evangelical theology. The salvation of a hungry man's soul was at least as important as the state of his stomach, if not more so. Some evangelicals opposed what they called "paternalism"— a sentimental intervention in society to merely ameliorate human suffering.[7] Since they believed that God bestowed suffering for a purpose, there had to be good reasons for interfering with divine will. Providentialism, the belief that all things happen according to God's will, was, therefore, an important part of the evangelical mindset. This allowed many evangelicals to combine the potentially contradictory elements of Smithian laissez-faire principles, Malthusian demographics and Benthamite utilitarianism. For example,

---

2. For evangelical reaction to the French Revolution see Newman, *The Rise of English Nationalism*, 82, 234–36.
3. Quoted in Hilton, *Age of Atonement*, 4.
4. Ibid., 3.
5. Newman, *The Rise of English Nationalism*, 235.
6. Ibid., 236.
7. Hilton, *Age of Atonement*, 207.

evangelicals embraced Adam Smith's emphasis on individualism and his desire to keep government out of the economy. They reasoned that, because God's plans were revealed in the unfolding of events, governmental interference in society should be kept to a minimum. However, they shared with the secular-minded Bentham the idea that government might, under certain circumstances, intervene to improve society. Thus, on some issues, they were occasionally willing to support what might today be called social engineering, provided it led to moral, as well as humanitarian, ends.[8]

This mixing of moralism with financial matters can be seen in what was sometimes called Christian economics, which regarded the marketplace as a moral educator, as well as an economic engine. Market competition instilled within individuals a conscience based on self-denial, hard work and the avoidance of temptation. Thus, inequality was not only a social and economic necessity; it also served to rein in pleasure-seeking among the lower orders and to encourage self-discipline at all levels of society.[9] As Geoffrey Russell Searle suggests, "Distinctions in social rank and wealth [...] were said to fit in with God's plans, because they stimulated competition by appealing to the ambitious and by providing work-incentives to the laboring poor, which in turn led to the development of meritorious traits of character."[10] Embracing the virtues of prudence, self-denial and hard work offered what Richard D. Altick calls "an escape clause" from the grim determinism of God's "benevolent" scarcity. And, of course, sometimes hard work and thrift really did pay off. Therefore, in Peter Gray's view, the more optimistic and moralistic adherents of Christian economics believed in "a retributive yet beneficent providence with a resolutely non-Malthusian confidence in rapid economic progress and in the utility of state intervention to attain clearly defined moral ends."[11]

The combination of providential morality and liberal economics fitted comfortably into Great Britain's emerging capitalist society. It also provided the framework and vocabulary needed to meet the challenges of industrialization and rapid economic expansion. In this respect, evangelicals exerted an influence beyond their numbers, establishing what Boyd Hilton has called a "moral hegemony over public life." However, as moral reform spread beyond the ranks of the evangelicals and throughout British society, it became less dependent upon formal religious ties. One did not have to be pious to embrace the moralistic qualities that seemed to make British society work and prosper.[12] Piety did not have to walk hand in hand with Mammon. However, sometimes Mammon's desire to save money, make a profit and discipline the workers ran conveniently in tandem with evangelical goals. This combination may be seen in the philosophy behind England's

---

8. Ibid., 6–7, 15–16, 206–7. See also Himmelfarb, *The Idea of Poverty*, 167.
9. Hilton, *Age of Atonement*, 32.
10. Searle, *Morality and the Market in Victorian Britain*, 10. For Christian economics see Gray, *Famine, Land and Politics*, 14–16.
11. Gray, "'Potatoes and Providence,' British Government Responses to the Great Famine," 77. For Christian economics see 76–78. For the benevolence of scarcity and the "escape clause" see Altick, *Victorian People and Ideas*, 127, 170–71.
12. Newman, *The Rise of English Nationalism*, 238. For quote see Hilton, *The Age of Atonement*, 219.

New Poor Law, which, when extended to Ireland, was destined to play a dominant role in the Irish Famine.

The New English Poor Law of 1834

With its combination of divine retribution, utilitarian optimism and capitalist discipline, Victorian England's approach to welfare bears the imprint of evangelical "class moralism."[13] While those living in abject poverty could not be allowed to suffer, it was not enough just to feed and clothe them. They had to be cared for in ways that did least harm to their moral capacities. Because no one should be tempted to live off welfare, charity, no matter how well intentioned, could not be allowed to encourage the lax and sinful habits, which had probably produced hardship in the first place.[14] Nor could charity be allowed to blunt the need to discipline low-wage workers who had not yet learned to work to the rhythm of factory bell and machine, to follow orders or to live within their meager means. When such people failed to measure up and needed help, the subsequent burden to the taxpayers had to be minimized.

England's old Poor Law harkened back to the Elizabethan era when care for the destitute depended upon a local, parish-based system of support. Originally designed at a time when England could expect to occasionally experience famine conditions, the Poor Law evolved into an all-purpose welfare system. The "deserving poor," unable to maintain themselves on their own resources because of age, infirmity or absolute impoverishment, were generally granted what became known of as "outdoor" relief, which allowed them to continue living on their own. This was offered as a right to the truly needy. Over time, however, the classic questions that invariably haunt modern welfare eventually arose: how to define "need" and "deserving," and how to discourage lazy individuals from a life of public dependency? Also, what of those able to work but unable to find employment? While the Elizabethan Poor Law condemned able-bodied "sturdy beggars" who were capable of working, allowances were gradually made to support some of the unemployed poor. Yet, as Britain's population increased, technological innovations and changes in agriculture unsettled long-established patterns of employment. Many people lost trades or access to land. The resulting increase in the numbers of poor exerted a corresponding upward pressure on taxes. Eventually, it seemed as if an urbanizing, industrializing England could no longer afford its old welfare system.

There were other problems as well. As the Elizabethan Poor Law had been parish-based, individuals could be relieved only in the parish where they had been born. But what if an applicant had to travel in search of work? Might not the Poor Law threaten individual mobility and initiative? Moreover, while relief was a right, it was also a stigma, conflating the *poor* with the status of the *poorest*—the paupers. In a society becoming increasingly enamored with individualism, it seemed that the Poor Law threatened to rob the poorer part of society of self-respect and enterprise. Finally, any system that

---
13. See Hilton, *The Age of Atonement*, 242, 244.
14. Searle, *Morality and the Market in Victorian Britain*, 14.

might supplement the livelihood of the working poor threatened to undercut the low wages offered by employers, who felt they were already being taxed enough to support the indigent.[15]

By the late eighteenth century, the Poor Laws had become the center of debates about morality and economics as expressed in the competing philosophies of Adam Smith and Rev. Thomas Malthus. In his 1798 book, *An Essay on the Principle of Population*, Malthus set forth his demographic theories with mathematical precision. He argued that populations, advancing geometrically, would always push ahead of the food supply, which could only grow arithmetically. At best, there would always be people verging on starvation and seeking welfare. At worst, there would be famines and wars. Malthus eventually softened his dour prognosis, slightly, with the idea of "moral restraint." He argued that the mere threat of starvation could act as a "check" on those careless, carnal appetites that led to unsupportable procreation among the poor. However, this slender reed of hope appeared problematic to many middle-class evangelicals, who preferred to offer the poor more positive incentives for improvement instead of threats of famine.[16]

Adam Smith had a somewhat sunnier vision. Unlike Malthus, he did not fear a rising population. In fact, he embraced it as a sign of prosperity, provided individuals were free to take advantage of the opportunities created by an unregulated market in an expanding economy. The Poor Law, however, threatened to distort the labor market. It might tempt those who able to work to leave the labor force and become unproductive drones. Worse, the system threatened to demoralize those poor who found themselves tainted by association with pauperism. And that was the crux of the problem. "Poor" and "pauper" did not define the same people. Somehow, the working poor had to be separated from the truly destitute. If the Poor Laws were to be reformed instead of abolished, then the concept of poverty had to be disconnected from that of destitution and the distinction enshrined in law and practice.[17]

To accomplish this, reformers looked to an already existing institution—the workhouse. Under the old Poor Law, the workhouse had been used to offer "indoor" relief for those without domiciles of their own. Under the new law passed in 1834, it was to provide the mechanism for separating the poor from the paupers. The new workhouse was intended to suggest, physically and psychologically, a prison-like environment, complete with harsh discipline and punishments. Thus, under the Benthamite "all-or-nothing" principle, applicants had to be willing to give themselves and their families over entirely to the workhouse regime. Once inside the workhouse, families were separated. The food was sufficient but dull; the clothing coarse; the required work repetitive and demeaning.[18] Although relief was granted as a right, inmates who decide to leave forfeited any further claims to that right. There would be no re-admittance. Thus, the pauper had a right to

---

15. See Himmelfarb, *The Idea of Poverty*, 149, 154–55.
16. Hilton, *The Age of Atonement*, 76–78. For Malthus see Searle, *Morality and the Market in Victorian Britain*, 10, 11.
17. Himmelfarb, *The Idea of Poverty*, 160–61.
18. Mahoney, *Grim Bastilles of Despair*, 13. For "all or nothing" see Nally, *Human Encumbrances*, 103.

housing, food and clothing, but under conditions so onerous that only the truly destitute and unemployable would apply. In this way, the specter of life in the workhouse provided "the test" for admittance. Only those who found life on the streets "less eligible"—less comfortable, less appealing—than existence in the workhouse would seek admittance. "The test," enshrined in the New Poor Law for England and Wales, was intended as a check on moral hazard. However, since the workhouse was not mandated for all Poor Law Unions, only a minority of England's indigent were actually forced to knock on its doors. Although by 1839 the workhouses had absorbed 98,000 paupers, 560,000 were still sustained through outdoor relief.[19]

The New English Poor Law seemed a workable fit, joining the culture of moralism to a newly emergent industrial capitalism. Indeed, the workhouse perfectly complimented the factory. It provided guaranteed basic support for those unable to survive within the realm of work and low wages. At the same time, the threat of this punitive, dehumanizing alternative for the laboring poor meant that employers would never lack workers scrambling for jobs at the lowest pay. Whatever its merits or demerits, however, no one in 1834 could have imagined that England's new welfare model, once extended and adapted to Ireland, would become the primary engine of famine relief.

The Irish Poor Law of 1838—"the most harsh […] and unkind friend"

The idea of a poor law for Ireland had been knocking around government circles for decades. However, once the New English Poor Law was in place, fear that Irish paupers would flood into Britain made finding some response to Ireland's poverty imperative.[20] This posed a serious question, however: to what extent could the English model, intended for an industrializing society, work for one that was predominantly agrarian and very poor? In 1833, a year before England's New Poor Law was finally enacted, the Whig government appointed a Royal Commission to inquire into the feasibility of a similar approach for Ireland. Richard Whately, Anglican Archbishop of Dublin, was appointed to head the commission. Whately, an Englishman with limited experience in Ireland, was, nevertheless, an economist as well as a theologian. He sent commissioners around the country to gather information, and his half-million-word report produced a broad survey of conditions in Ireland. Reviewing the results, Whatley became convinced that an English-style Poor Law could never work in the face of widespread Irish poverty. He estimated that over half-a-million laborers with 1,800,000 dependents were out of work for 30 weeks of the year. The total, 2,385,000, was, in fact, close to the one-third of the Irish population dependent on the potato.[21] Instead of focusing on how to manage the Irish poor, therefore, Whately suggested ways by which they might be made less poor.

---

19. Altick, *Victorian People and Ideas*, 123; Crossman, *The Poor Law in Ireland 1838–1948*, 10.
20. Crossman, *The Poor Law in Ireland 1838–1948*, 3. The author points out that although Ireland had no statutory poor relief system prior to the Poor Law, it did have a variety of public and private welfare institutions, mostly for the sick; 3–5.
21. Mac Atasney, *"This Dreadful Visitation:" The Famine; in Lurgan/Portadown*, 2–3: Crossman, *The Poor Law in Ireland 1838–1948*, 7.

What they needed, he insisted, was work. Therefore, he recommended establishing agricultural schools, along with a "Board of Improvement" that would encourage landlords to hire poor workers to drain and enclose the bogs. Whately also recommended publicly assisted emigration to reduce the size of what appeared to be a redundant labor force. None of these suggestions were new, but they did at least attempt to address some of the underlying problems of Irish poverty. Unfortunately, these recommendations looked to the long, rather than the short, term and promised to be rather expensive.[22]

Unsurprisingly, the government was not pleased with Whately's report. George Cornewall Lewis, a Whig civil servant, was taxed with writing an executive memorandum to the report. Rejecting the commission's recommendations, Lewis insisted that Ireland could benefit from a Poor Law with a workhouse "test." However, he argued against extending outdoor relief to Ireland, fearing that Irish poverty would drain away the country's wealth. The real point of an Irish poor law based entirely on the workhouse, he suggested, did not lay in how many people might be relieved. As Lewis explained, "it was not so much that the peasantry will be *actually* relieved, as that they feel that they *may be* relieved [...] the prospect of relief will give them security." Thus, the spirit of agrarian violence would be lanced "by opening the doors of the workhouse to all, although few might be admitted to it." Without explaining exactly how, Lewis was convinced that such a welfare system would somehow lead to more employment and "to the creation of a class of labourers independent of their potato ground."[23]

Apparently, Lewis, like other proponents of an Irish Poor Law, believed that landlords, faced with the threat of higher taxes to support workhouse paupers, might prefer to hire peasants for cash wages instead of paying them in potatoes. By the same token, the peasants might accept a system that suggested (but did not promise) that they might not starve if deprived of a "little taste of land" on which to grow their praties. Of course, such arguments bypassed Whately's wide-ranging and expensive schemes for emigration and agricultural improvement.[24] They also ignored one important fact. In rural England and Wales, only the able-bodied poor were forced to seek relief in the workhouses. As noted above, even under the New Poor Law those truly unable to fend for themselves were still entitled to outdoor relief. In Ireland, however, there would be no outdoor relief for anyone. Those seeking help, able-bodied or incapacitated, would have to submit to the "test," surrender their independence and enter the workhouse. Thus, what was a promise to the British poor looked more like a threat to the Irish.[25]

With Whately's report shelved, the home secretary, Lord John Russell, gave the job of devising an Irish Poor Law to George Nicholls, who had already served as a commissioner for England's New Poor Law. After a lightning tour of Ireland, Nicholls' duly announced that a poor law, carefully adapted to the peculiarities of Ireland, would eventually work

---

22. For a summary of the Commission's recommendations see McDowell, "Ireland on the Eve of the Famine," 43–44; For Whately's plans see Nally, *Human Encumbrances*, 105–6.
23. Lewis, *On Local Disturbances in Ireland and on the Irish Church Question*, 331, italics original.
24. McDowell, "Ireland on the Eve of the Famine," 45–46.
25. See Mokyr, *Why Ireland Starved*, 290.

its wonders. It would not only reduce beggary. It would also facilitate a shift to agrarian wage labor, as well as diminish the flow of paupers across the Irish Sea seeking relief in England. Best of all, an Irish Poor Law would make Irish property—the taxpayers—responsible for Irish poverty, a concept that would eventually be copper-fastened to relief policy during the Famine.[26]

Nicholls, strongly influenced by Benthamite principles, imagined a link between state welfare and social engineering. By bringing some order to what Nicholls took to be the social chaos of rural Ireland, the Irish Poor Law would attract investments and encourage efficient farming, resulting in greater production and more employment. Moreover, Nicholls believed that it would promote "general wellbeing because it will be accompanied by improvements in the habits of the whole class [of the peasantry]."[27] Others hoped that the Poor Law would bring about a clearer demarcation of classes in Ireland. Visiting the country in 1837, Scottish writer Leitch Ritchie complained that there seemed to be no intervening class between the poor and the gentry. Observing Irish peasants at work, he could discern "no sturdy, surly yeoman, as in England, distinguished from his labourers both by the respectability of his dress, and his air of command. […] [In Ireland] We see but a group of ill-clad men, boys and women—all of the same rank." Ritchie hoped that an Irish Poor Law would change all that by creating what he called "the wanting classes. […] It will give the lower orders the habit of attending to and thinking about, their own wants; instead of looking as hitherto, with more than childish helplessness, for some political miracle. […] [U]ntil Irish society is broken into the small *selfish* circles of England, it will be impossible to operate upon it with advantage."[28] Consequently, well before the Famine, Ireland's Poor Law system became linked to ideas for restructuring the country's agrarian society. This helps explain why, once the disaster struck, some people in Britain viewed the Famine as a great opportunity.

Given the way that England dealt with its own poor, it was not likely to be more generous with Ireland's paupers. When the Irish Poor Law was adopted in 1838, it provided even less protection for the destitute than had the English original. As noted above, while the English New Poor Law continued to offer outdoor relief, in Ireland it was banned. Moreover, while English paupers had a right to relief, their Irish counterparts did not. They could be turned away if a workhouse was full. This suited a government that felt it could not build nearly enough workhouses to accommodate all of Ireland's paupers.

Daniel O'Connell opposed the Irish Poor Law, not because of its lack of generosity, but because it violated his personal combination of liberal and religious doctrines. The proposed bill, he felt, would threaten individual self-reliance and undercut familial responsibilities and communitarian charity.[29] Other critics maintained the long-standing argument that a Poor Law would never work in Ireland because of the vast extent of Irish poverty. Its "less eligibility" test, intended to limit workhouse occupancy in England,

---

26. See Woodham-Smith, *The Great Hunger: Ireland, 1845–49*, 37.
27. Nally, *Human Encumbrances*, 113. See also Mahoney, *Grim Bastilles of Despair*, 13.
28. Ritchie, *Ireland, Picturesque and Romantic*, 1:75, 2:32, italics original.
29. Leslie A. Williams, *Daniel O'Connell, the British Press and the Irish Famine*, 29–31.

might not have the same effect in Ireland, as Jonathan Binns suggested in 1836. Visiting there as an agricultural assistant to Whately's Poor Law Commission, Binns was amazed at the extent and depth of Irish poverty. He therefore questioned whether a Poor Law could ever work in such an environment. "In England, a workhouse may *easily* be made less agreeable [...] than a labourer's home; in Ireland [...] what sort of habitation can you put [the Irishman] in, that will not be infinitely superior to his damp, dark cabin? [...] And how is he to be *fed* in a workhouse, in a manner *inferior* to his ordinary mode of subsistence?"[30] Binns need not have worried, however. Prior to the Famine, even many of Ireland's beggars preferred life on the road or among their families and neighbors to the atmosphere of incarceration that defined the new workhouses. In fact, Ireland's workhouses were planned and built on the assumption that most of Ireland's paupers would never come knocking. And this, to Nicholls, was the whole purpose of the "test." "I wish to see the poorhouse looked to with dread by our laboring classes." While Poor Law relief would not let the poor starve, it would be, nonetheless, "a hard taskmaster [...] the most harsh and unkind friend they can apply to."[31]

Under the 1838 Irish Poor Law, the country was divided into 130 "unions," created by combining existing administrative parishes. Each union had a board of guardians, consisting of elected members drawn from the local upper and middle class, along with government-appointed ex-officio members. The local boards reported to the Poor Law Commission in Dublin, which in turn was responsible to its parent organization in London. The board of guardians had the onerous task of "striking" or setting the cess or tax rate, based on property valuations. Since the guardians were taxing themselves and their neighbors, striking the rates became a highly contentious affair, especially during the Famine. Tenant farmers who had to pay their own taxes were a continual source of resistance. So unpopular was the very idea of Poor Law rates in Ireland that, even before the Famine forced steep increases in taxation, rate collectors sometimes needed police protection.[32]

The board's first task was to build a workhouse complex designed to house a community of paupers, as well as a union's officials and their employees. Anxious to speed the process along, Nicholls saw to it that one man, George Wilkinson, supplied all architectural plans. His standard designs included offices, dormitories, dining areas, school rooms, kitchens, laundries, indoor and outdoor work areas, cells for the mentally ill and an infirmary. An extra-mural pauper's graveyard was often close by.[33] Because of Ireland's contentious religious history, there were no chapels. Dining areas would do for Sunday services; Protestants first shift, Catholics second. The entire workhouse complex was enclosed within high walls. If anything kept a poor Irishman or woman from applying for admittance to the workhouse, it was the shame and horror of ending their days behind those walls. By 1842 most of the structures, 122 out of 130, were up and

---

30. Binns, *Miseries and Beauties of Ireland*, 2:441, italics original.
31. For quote see Mac Atasney, *"This Dreadful Visitation:" The Famine; in Lurgan/Portadown*, 6.
32. Ó Cathaoir, "The Workhouse during the Great Famine," 221–22.
33. For Wilkinson and his designs see Mahoney, *Grim Bastilles of Despair*, 15–27.

running, a rather remarkable feat of organization and construction within a span of seven years. Of course, such haste often left shoddy work in its wake.[34]

As noted above, England's New Poor Law had been partly inspired by the idea of disciplining the country's industrial workers, who, faced with the indignities of the workhouse, might chose to work for the lowest wages. In Ireland, however, the workhouse suggested a different economic and social agenda. While many Irish landlords disliked the Poor Law because it would raise taxes, others saw it an excuse for evicting unwanted tenants. The point was not lost on some of the tenantry, who, on the Devonshire estate in Kings County, tried to prevent the building of the local workhouse. As one observer at the time suggested, with the threat of Poor Law rates, the landowners were more interested in removing poverty than in relieving it.[35]

England's old Elizabethan Poor Law system had been established within the shadows of bygone famines. By the time of the passage of the New Poor Law Act, however, England had largely lost its fear of such threats.[36] In Ireland, however, subsistence crises occurred regularly. Therefore, George Nicholls, the designer of the Irish Poor Law, tried to make it very clear that, in the event of famine, "where the land has ceased to be reproductive [...] a Poor Law will no longer be operative [...] to the extent adequate to meet such an emergency."[37] In fact, in the few years before the Great Famine, relief efforts during times of food shortages were scrupulously kept separate from the operations of the Irish Poor Law system. When the potato blight appeared in 1845, many Poor Law officials wanted to maintain the separation between normal poor relief and general want. Unfortunately, Nicholls' warnings were forgotten, and Ireland's Poor Law quickly became the de facto principal mechanism for supplying famine relief.[38] During the crisis, a correspondent of *The Times* noted that the workhouse test could be effective only when conditions inside might be considered worse than conditions outside. "It must cease to be a test at all when there is no option but to accept it [relief] or die."[39]

---

34. Ó Cathaoir, "The Workhouse during the Great Famine," 221.
35. Reilly, *The Irish Land Agent, 1830–60*, 60. For removing poverty see 73.
36. For link between the Elizabethan Poor Law and famines see O'Sullivan and Lucking, "The Famine World Wide: The Irish Famine and the Development of Famine Policy and Famine Theory," 199.
37. For quote see Kinealy, *The Great Calamity: The Irish Famine, 1845–52*, 231. See also Nicholls, *A History of the Irish Poor Law: In Connexon with the Condition of the People*, 309; Christine Kinealy, "The Role of the Poor Law During the Famine," 107, 108., 177.
38. Kinealy, "The Role of the Poor Law during the Famine," 107, 108. See also Crossman, *The Poor Law in Ireland 1838–1948*, 19.
39. *The Times*, July 5, 1849.

Part Two

THE RISE AND FALL OF THE IRELAND'S POTATO ECONOMY

Chapter Five
POVERTY AND INEQUALITY: THE ECONOMIC BACKGROUND

Manufacturing and Deindustrialization in Pre-Famine Ireland

During the eighteenth century, Britain was converting itself into the world's first industrial society through a series of interconnecting mini "revolutions" in mining and manufacturing technology, finance, agriculture and transportation. Meanwhile, although Ireland's economy was growing, it was weak or lacking in many of those threshold elements that ushered in Britain's transformation. For example, in the wake of the Act of Union, Irish investment capital often found more attractive opportunities on the other side of the Irish Sea. This left Irish banks, increasingly dominated by London, too weak to take significant risks in internal investment. It did not help that, instead of investing in Ireland's agricultural resources, many landowners spent immense sums, often borrowed, in building country houses and landscaping their estates.[1] Ireland also lacked an abundance of the kinds of raw materials essential to industrialization. Most of the country's mining activity was economically marginal. The country's few copper mines, although among Europe's oldest, were of only intermittent importance. The island's coal deposits were small, and, except for a few fields in Ulster, were geologically eroded, rendering them inferior in quality and often difficult to exploit. Scottish and Welsh coal imported into Dublin and Belfast was often cheaper than the domestic product.[2] Ireland's one great natural resource, its oak forests, was largely depleted by 1800, sacrificed to building materials and to numerous small, estate-based iron works that produced only low-grade ore.[3]

Ireland did enjoy a relatively good road system, which it continued to expand into the 1840s. However, the quality of the roads, remarked upon by many tourists, was due in part to the absence of the kind of heavy traffic that left many English roads deeply rutted. And while two canals linked Dublin to the River Shannon system, only 70 miles of railway track, most of it centering on Belfast and Dublin, had been laid by 1845.[4]

---

1. Mokyr, *Why Ireland Starved*, 185–86. See also Macdonagh, "The Economy and Society, 1830–45," 231.
2. Ó Gráda, *Ireland: A New Economic History, 1780–1939*, 315, 317; Rynne, *Industrial Ireland, 1750–1930*, 82, 93, 141–42. See also Aalen, *Man and Landscape in Ireland*, 198.
3. For estate forestry see Neeson, *A History of Irish Forestry*, 91–114. Colin Rynne points out that only a few larger Irish foundries, established in 1820s and 1830s, played an important role in serving Ireland's domestic needs Industrial Ireland; 271–76.
4. Macdonagh, 229. For road quality see Rynne, *Industrial Ireland, 1750–1930*, 311. See also William H. A. Williams, *Creating Irish Tourism: The First Century, 1750–1850*, 12–14.

The real impact of steam transportation on pre-Famine Ireland originated on the other side of the Irish Sea. England's railroads brought goods to its seaports, and steamships carried them to Belfast, Dublin and Cork, helping to further erode Irish manufacture in the process. The rapid expansion of Ireland's railroads after 1845 only tied Ireland more closely to the British economy.[5]

Textiles represented the one area where Ireland did seem to have a potentially strong manufacturing base even before the Act of Union. While the British Parliament occasionally tried to suppress competition from Irish textiles, the Irish Parliament, having found its voice by the latter part of the eighteenth century, tried to support Irish manufacturing with protective tariffs and subsidies.[6] For a time, it even seemed that the manufacturing balance between Britain and Ireland was shifting in the latter's favor. Several factors changed the situation, however. First, around 1800, breakthroughs in manufacturing technology enabled Britain to capitalize on the economies of scale, making its factory-made goods cheaper. At the same time, the Act of Union extended Great Britain's common market, based on free-trade policies, to Ireland. As a result, whatever protection the old Irish Parliament had provided to the country's manufactures gradually evaporated. The last Irish custom duties levied on goods imported from Britain were abolished in 1824. By then the country had also lost its own currency. Within little more than two decades after 1800, Ireland had become a small economy completely open to powerful overseas economic forces far beyond its control.[7]

Even if Ireland could have protected its home industries, its economy might then have been hobbled by high prices and possibly by inferior goods.[8] Regardless, without protection, Irish woolens declined in the face of British competition, along with iron mongering and tanning. The fate of the Irish cotton industry was more complicated. An early adapter of the spinning jenny, the cotton industry took off in the 1780s, not only in Belfast but also in parts of southern Ireland. Although the number of failed firms does not speak well for Irish business acumen, up until around 1810 Irish cotton manufacturing employed thousands of workers. The southern mills produced coarse cloth largely for the domestic market. While seemingly secure, however, Irish manufacturers failed to follow the English in investing in the newest technology. Absent Irish tariffs and with the arrival of steam on the Irish Sea after 1820, most of the cotton mills in southern Ireland collapsed. The story was different in Belfast. The city produced finer grades of cotton cloth, and for a while its cotton industry overshadowed linen manufacturing. With the advent of "wet" spinning technology, however, there were larger profits to be made in linen. Cotton did not so much collapse in Ulster as it was pushed into the background

---

5. Aalen, *Man and Landscape in Ireland*, 156.
6. Kevin J. James, *Handloom Weavers in Ulster's Linen Industry*, 20; Ó Gráda, *Ireland: A New Economic History, 1780–1939*, 292-95.
7. Mokyr, *Why Ireland Starved*, 279.
8. Ibid., 279, 289. For late eighteenth-century Ireland's terms of trade and the pros and cons regarding the loss of Irish protection see Ó Gráda, *Ireland: A New Economic History, 1780–1939*, 306–7.

by linen production, suggesting that Ireland could expand only one textile industry at a time.[9]

From the vantage point of Belfast, Ireland's linen industry thrived. Visiting the city around 1840, William Makepeace Thackeray described the "fine night-exhibition" created by the city's "huge spinning mills [...] of which the thousand windows are lighted up at nightfall."[10] Thackeray, however, seemed unaware that Belfast's industrial success came at the expense of other parts of Ireland. From the late eighteenth century to the end of the Napoleonic Wars, Irish linen had been produced by cottage-based weaving and spinning families throughout much of Ulster and the northern parts of Leinster and Connaught. As early as the 1780s, one-fifth of the adult male workforce in Ulster was employed in linen weaving, while an even greater number of women were engaged in spinning. Although women may have earned only a pittance from spinning, that, combined with their traditional market role in selling eggs, poultry and garden produce, often contributed to the difference between a family's comfortable survival and penury. In fact, farmer/weaving/spinning families enjoyed twice the income of the average cottiers and laborers, even though many occupied poor-quality land.[11]

At its height in 1820, this decentralized linen industry supported 70,000 cottage weavers and their families in Ulster alone. Landlords there encouraged linen production because it promised good rents, sometimes 25 percent above the average, from small holdings on generally inferior soil. Regarding farmer-weavers as dependable sources of rent, a petty landlord might supply one cottage with a year's worth of flax while providing a loom for another. In such cases the families ended up essentially working for their landlord.[12] It was the potato, however, that held the system together. Growing potatoes allowed these families to devote much of the income from linen, as well as oats and barley, to paying the rent. Peter Solar notes that the cultivation of potatoes, flax and the production of linen complemented each other, since the peak activities associated with each came at different times of the year.[13] This combination of proto industries with potato cultivation may have contributed to the spike in population growth from 1732 to 1821. Much of that increase, ranging from 300 to 600 percent, was situated along the drumlin belt in western Ulster, and northern Leinster and Connacht. As previously noted, this area, with its mix of cottage manufacturing and farming, constituted one of the most densely populated rural areas in Europe.[14]

---

9. Mokyr, *Why Ireland Starved*, 176–77. For Irish cotton industry see Ó Gráda, *Ireland: A New Economic History, 1780–1939*, 274–81.
10. Thackeray, *Irish Sketchbook*, 264, 265.
11. For women see Nolan, "The Great Famine and Women's Immigration from Ireland," 64. For the spread of the linen cottage industry see Kevin Whelan, "The Modern Landscape: From Plantation to Present," 76–77. For distribution of linen production see maps on 78, 79.
12. Doyle, *Charles Powell Leslie II's Estates at Glaslough, County Monaghan, 1800–1841*, 39,48. See also Duffy, "Mapping the Famine in Monaghan," 442.
13. Solar, "The Potato Famine in Europe," 116. See also Kevin J. James, *Handloom Weavers in Ulster's Linen Industry*, 19.
14. See map, figure 2, in J. Smyth, "'Mapping the People.' The Growth and Distribution of the People,'" 15.

With the end of the Napoleonic Wars, however, cottage-based linen production went into a rapid decline. In Kings County, for example, linen output, which had been valued at £50,000 in 1760, had fallen to £20,000 in 1816. The decline continued irreversibly, putting more pressure on the land and, therefore, rents, as former weaving families had to rely entirely on farming.[15] Then, between 1820 and 1830 Ireland's decentralized cottage-based linen production suffered two dramatic setbacks. First, cheap factory-made cotton fabric, much of it of English manufacture, eroded the market for the coarser Irish linen yarn and weave made outside of eastern Ulster. Second, with the adoption of "wet" spinning technology to Irish factories after 1825, the cottage-spun skeins of linen yearn produced by the cottage-weaver's wives and daughters lost market share, resulting in a serious drop in income for thousands of families in the west. Not only did women lose part of their earning potential, but also their husbands had to weave with factory-made yean, purchased at prices set by the merchants. This, as Gerard Mac Atasney points out, amounted to a new "putting out system," which cut into a family's income and independence.[16] On the other hand, manufactured yearn was easier to work with, allowing women and even children to take over a family's weaving duties. In parts of County Monaghan, families did not so much abandon linen as change their involvement with it. With women often replacing men at the looms, there was less spinning and more farming, along with a greater involvement in the growing and processing flax.[17] In other areas, however, especially in the west, handloom weaving simply fled much of the countryside to become concentrated in Belfast and its hinterland. Consequently, linen manufacture in the western Ireland collapsed. In 1817, County Mayo had boasted five linen markets, the one in Westport attracting 4,000 to 5,000 people annually. However, whereas buyers paid £81,640 for Mayo linen cloth in 1816, only a few thousand pounds' worth were purchased in 1840.[18]

Strictly speaking, deindustrialization in Ireland was, therefore, more a regional rather than a national phenomenon. Eastern Ulster's gain in the concentration of linen production resulted in a significant loss elsewhere, leaving former western cottage producers far from markets and employment opportunities. Unfortunately, the decline of nonagricultural employment was greatest in those western areas where population growth was highest and the land quality was poorest. On the Continent, when proto industries declined, other growth areas often took up the slack in employment opportunities. This did not occur in Ireland outside of Belfast. When cottage industries failed, there was nothing to take their place, except farming and potato dependence.[19]

---

15. Reilly, *The Irish Land Agent, 1830–60*, 27.
16. Mac Atasney, *"This Dreadful Visitation": The Famine; in Lurgan/Portadown*, 94-95. For the adoption of "wet" spinning, see Kevin J. James, *Handloom Weavers in Ulster's Linen Industry*, 29–30.
17. Doyle, *Charles Powell Leslie II's Estates at Glaslough, County Monaghan, 1800–1841*, 15–16, 18.
18. For linen production in Mayo see Ó Gráda, *Ireland: A New Economic History, 1780–1939*, 282, 284. For collapse of linen in Mayo see Jordan, *Land and Popular Politics in Ireland*, 64. For the concentration of handloom weaving and the role of women see Kevin J. James, *Handloom Weavers in Ulster's Linen Industry*, 32–35; for competition from cotton see 30.
19. For the situation in Ulster and Connaught see Smyth, "The Province of Connaught and the Great Famine," 281. See also Kinealy and Parkhill, "Introduction" to *The Famine in Ulster*,

The sharp economic slowdown following the end of the Napoleonic Wars, accompanied by widespread deindustrialization, had a detrimental effect upon Ireland's social structure. Absent general industrial growth and in the face of a rural depression, Ireland's cities and towns stagnated, despite continued population growth. T. W. Freeman has calculated that only 20.2 percent of Ireland's pre-Famine population lived in towns containing twenty houses or more. In Connaught, the figure was only 10.3 percent. The town of Frebane in King's County provides an example of Ireland's skewed population dynamics. While the town grew by 7.19 percent between 1831 and 1841, the surrounding rural area grew by 23.36 percent. Nationwide, out of a total population of over 8 million in 1841, less than 500,000 lived in Ireland's eight largest cities and towns. Of these, Dublin counted only a quarter million and Belfast, still a relatively young city, only 75,000. Such figures pale when compared to England's burgeoning industrial centers.[20]

Those who lost work, whether from the demise of small, local mills and factories or from collapsing cottage industries, faced a simple choice: survive within the agricultural sector or emigrate. Displaced Irish workers seeking nonagricultural employment had to leave the island. Between 1831 and 1841, as many as 367,000 Irish embarked from ports in Ireland and Britain. Others settled in the larger island. The census of 1841 revealed 419,256 Irish-born living in Britain. This emigration may be one of the reasons why Ireland remained under-industrialized. Not only did potential workers leave the island but British manufacturers had no need to go to Ireland in search of cheap labor. Cheap Irish labor came to them.[21] Former industrial workers who did not choose to emigrate became totally dependent upon agriculture. By 1845, six out of every seven Irish people lived in rural areas.[22] The better off managed to rent small tracts of land. Many others became conacre farmers or cottiers. Virtually all of Ireland's poor became increasingly dependent upon the potato for their principal food. By seriously diminishing non-agrarian opportunities for employment, the deindustrialization of Ireland helped to increase the size of a potato-dependent population greatly at risk in the event of a massive crop failure.

Agriculture

For most of its history, pasturage had dominated Irish agriculture. Toward the late eighteenth century, however, a shift toward grain cultivation occurred, as prices rose in response to the wars with France. In 1784 the Irish Parliament passed an act that provided

---

2–3; Parkhill, "The Famine in County Londonderry," 151–52. For deindustrialization see Ó Gráda, *Ireland: A New Economic History, 1780–1939*, 306-13. For comparison between Ireland and European manufacturing see Mokyr, *Why Ireland Starved*, 282.
20. Freeman, "Land and People, circa 1841," 249. For the population of Irish cities see Macdonagh, "The Economy and Society, 1830–45," 231. For Frebane see Sheil, *Falling into Wretchedness: Ferbane in the Late 1830s*, 16.
21. Mokyr, *Why Ireland Starved*, 256–59, 282–83. For emigration data see Freeman, "Land and People, circa 1841," 261.
22. Mokyr, *Why Ireland Starved*, 16.

subsidies to expand Irish grain production and export. During the period between 1790 and 1815, the price of wheat in Dublin rose 61 percent.[23] Wheat, however, is not an ideal crop for a damp country with uncertain harvest weather—thus the expression, "*saving the harvest.*" Nevertheless, thanks to the boom in prices, Irish grain acreage—oats and barley, as well as wheat—expanded dramatically, altering the nature of an agricultural system now driven by a guaranteed market in Great Britain.[24]

As grain exports grew, it became correspondingly advantageous for owners of good arable Irish land to adopt the same techniques of enclosure and crop rotation that were revolutionizing English agriculture. So, beginning in the late eighteenth century, the enclosure of estate lands expanded in Ireland, but only in certain areas and under special circumstances. As Louis M. Cullen suggests, the complex business of consolidating small, scattered holdings into larger, coherent field systems was the work of resident rather than an absentee proprietors. Moreover, enclosure was profitable only on the best arable lands of Leinster and eastern parts of Ulster and in Munster.[25] Fortunately for the landowners and their major tenants, Irish labor was cheap. Cottiers received small plots of land on which they could erect a cabin and grow some potatoes. They paid their rent by working for the landlord according to seasonal demand. This system made it relatively easy for very poor people to have a certain degree of independence. They could marry, set up households and raise children. Unfortunately, they also remained trapped in poverty. Testifying before the Poor Law Inquiry just prior to the Famine, Rev. Justin McNamara described the situation of many laborers around Kinsale: "Though there are not many destitute in the strict sense of the word, there is an immense number in a most wretched condition, they have food, but of a bad kind, and of an insufficient quantity." Regarding their housing, he went on to say, "commonly a whole family, sometimes two or three families live in one room," under leaking roofs and without bedding other than rotten straw.[26]

As noted above, the postwar depression dealt Ireland a heavy blow. Between 1815 and 1816 grain prices fell between 40 and 60 percent with sharp losses in livestock as well.[27] At the same time, poor harvests in 1816 and in 1822 resulted in famine conditions in parts of the country. All this, when Ireland had to absorb the return to civilian life of thousands of demobilized soldiers. Nevertheless, the postwar decline in grain prices might have been worse, or, at least, have lasted longer, had Britain's landed aristocrats not sought to protect the Kingdom's grain market, an important source of their income. The protectionist Corn Laws of 1815 were intended to keep foreign grain out of the United Kingdom, thus guaranteeing relatively high prices for domestic crops. Thanks

---

23. Green, "Agriculture." 91.
24. For the role of agricultural exports in the Irish economy and politics in the eighteenth century see Dickson, *New Foundations Ireland*, 110–11, 116, 132.
25. For geographical concentration of large farms that lent themselves to enclosure see Kevin Whelan, The Modern Landscape 74–75, figure 23 on p. 76. For landlords' role in enclosure see Cullen, *The Emergence of Modern Ireland, 1600–1900*, 48. For regional patterns of enclosure see Aalen and Whelan, "Fields," 136–43.
26. See Flanagan, *The Great Famine in Kinsale*, 17.
27. Donnelly,, *The Land and the People of Nineteenth-Century Cork*, 24.

to the Act of Union, Irish grain producers enjoyed open access to the British market. Consequently, after the post-1815 deflation, Irish agricultural prices eventually regained some lost ground. In fact, those parts of the Irish economy tied into the export of grain, as well as livestock and other agricultural products, eventually returned to growth. As Cormac Ó Gráda suggests, this meant a rise in Ireland's aggregate income. Yet, the benefits did not trickle down to the lower third of the nation, whose cheap labor made it possible. Most of the laborers' meager income went into securing food and rent money.[28]

While the immediate postwar decline in grain prices did little to ease the population's pressure on the land, it did begin to change the nature of that pressure. While the years between 1760 and 1820 had witnessed an expansion of Irish grain production, that trend began to slowly reverse itself during the postwar period. Land was gradually moving out of tillage and back into pasturage. Large tracts in counties such as Tipperary and Galway were given over to cattle fattening. While commercial dairying had been dominant throughout much of Munster since the eighteenth century, the introduction of steamships on the Irish Sea encouraged a shift toward export cattle during the 1820s.[29]

Because it cut into the availability of tillage land, poor farmers and cottiers believed that any movement toward grazing threatened their livelihoods. Worse, the grazier, requiring fewer laborers than the farmer, was a poor employer. Instead of laborers, pasturage required grassland purged of small farms. As Kevin Whelan has noted, "given its extensive mode of land use, the grazier economy created a barren landscape with its attenuated social structure and only rudimentary settlement forms."[30] Moreover, transforming land from cultivation to grazing forced the expanding population of small farmers into the marginal uplands bordering the rich pastures. Even where land remained under cultivation, landlords might evict small farmers to create larger, more profitable holdings. Or large plots of prime land were taken out of cultivation and turned into carefully landscaped parklands that graced the estates of the Anglo-Irish aristocracy. Cormac Ó Gráda estimates that around 70,000 parks enclosed between 0.8 and 0.9 million acres, mostly fertile land that could have supported up to 100,000 small farmers.[31] Thus, landlords, seeking to maximize their incomes by consolidating their holdings, either for landscaping, pasturage or large-scale tillage, threatened to increase the poverty of those living at the other end of the economic spectrum. As early as 1814, the Bogs Commission, visiting County Roscommon, found that semi-bog lands on the edges of large grazing areas or improved estates were already crowded with displaced poor. Nevertheless, the county's population continued to grow by 20 percent between 1821 and 1841, much of the increase being among the poor. By 1841, 89.6 percent of Roscommon's dwellings

---

28. Gráda, *The Great Irish Famine*, 20–21. Ó Gráda sees the Irish economy continuing to grow after 1815, but at diminishing rates; *Ireland: A New Economic History*, 159–60, 162.
29. For the movement from tillage to pasturage see Aalen, *Man and Landscape in Ireland*, 154–55; Kevin Whelan, "The Modern Landscape," 72–73. Cormac Ó Gráda cautions, however, that the shift from tillage to grazing did not really accelerate until after the Famine. See Ó Gráda, "Poverty, Population and Agriculture," 130.
30. Kevin Whelan, "The Modern Landscape," 73.
31. Gráda, *Ireland: A New Economic History*, 125–26.

consisted of one- to four-room mud cabins. During the Famine, the county would lose 31 percent of its population, the highest loss of any county.[32]

Agrarian Resistance

While larger, consolidated farms might have offered more employment opportunities, Irish peasants feared that losing access to land meant a loss of status, as well as some control over their food supply. Leases offered some protection. Once they ran out, however, the landlord could evict small tenants and rent the land to someone else, consolidate it into larger tracts or shift it from tillage to pasturage. Under such circumstances even conacre farmers, who never enjoyed leases, might find that there was less land available for yearly rental. It is not surprising then that resistance to landlords' attempts to "improve" (restructure) their holdings rose sharply during the pre-Famine decades. As discontent increased, the small tenants formed secret societies, which, depending on time and place, went by a variety of names: Whiteboys, Blackfeet, Terry Alts, Caravats, Molly Maguires, Rockites, or Ribbonmen.[33] (Although each group was different, the term "Whiteboys" is used here generically to refer to agrarian resistance organizations.) Such groups, some originating in the eighteenth century and attracting mostly Catholics, carried out campaigns of intimidation and violence intended to enforce "traditional" wages and prices and to discourage landlord initiatives that threatened small farmers and laborers. Those tempted to take over land made available through evictions were often threatened or beaten and their cabins burned.

During the Famine, John Arthur Roebuck, a Radical MP, tried to explain the underlying causes of agrarian violence in Ireland:

> It is because the population always felt and distinctly understood that their holding a portion of land was absolutely necessary for their very existence. They felt that the law had not been their protector; therefore was it that they had recourse to that system of self-protection to which they had been driven by dire necessity; the very exigency of their situation had driven them to assassination.

Hyperbole aside, Roebuck was correct in concluding that most of Ireland's secret agrarian societies existed for one purpose: "to maintain the poor man in his wretched holding."[34] Regardless of justification, Whiteboy-type pressures may have limited landlord activity. The wave of evictions that followed in the wake of the crash of grain prices in 1815 was to some extent checked by the secret societies. As George Poulett Scrope

---

32. Mary Kelly, "The Famine in County Roscommon," 308–9.
33. The Ribbonmen were a network of secret societies divided between Ulster and Leinster branches, with ties to Scotland, England and America, where they were frequently known as the Molly Maguires and had links to the Ancient order of Hibernians. Jennifer Kelly, *The Downfall of Hagan: Sligo Ribbonmen in 1842*, 11; Mac Suibhne, *The End of Outrage*, 65, 66.
34. Quoted in *The Observer*, March 22, 1847 (2). According to Peter Gray, Roebuck once called Irish landlords "slaveholders with white slaves"; *Famine, Land and Politics*, 275.

observed in 1834, "But for the salutary dread of the Whiteboy Association, ejectment [eviction] would desolate Ireland and decimate her population." Compared to evictions, Scrope suggested, "the Whiteboy system" was "perhaps the lesser evil of the two."[35]

Several factors contributed to the rise in agrarian violence in the decades leading up to the Famine. First, as suggested earlier, there was the economic depression combined with bad weather following the Napoleonic Wars. Terence Dooley suggests that between 1815 and 1816 the landlords' attempts to maintain rents in the face of falling agricultural prices created a "time bomb" that threatened to pit them against middlemen and large tenant farmers on the one hand and aggrieved smallholders, cottiers and laborers on the other.[36] Agrarian unrest increased during the late teens and early 1820s, partly in response to the spread of a popular millenarian enthusiasm tied to the anti-Protestant, revanchist "Prophesies of Pastorini." As mentioned earlier, this movement swept through the Catholic population, poor and better off, in parts of the western midlands, Munster and sections of Connaught. In response, landlords and agents in Kings County formed a protective Protestant Association.[37] The "Pastorini" movement quickly subsided, but sectarian tensions resurfaced with the Tithe Wars and, continuously fueled by Protestant proselytism, were never fully absent from agrarian protest movements. Indeed, Whiteboy-type groups often mixed nationalist and anti-Protestant sentiments with economic and class issues.[38] While the more violent protest movements of the early 1820s declined, agrarian discontent and unrest continued, especially in areas hit by the decline in the textile industry or where the transition from tillage to grazing was strongest. As the commercialization of Irish agriculture became more intense, many landlords, who had once treated their tenants with some indulgence, now began to pursue stricter management policies. As they did, levels of unrest increased. Although most reported incidents did not involve actual violence, during the 1830s and the 1840s the Irish crime rate appears to have risen as fast as the population.[39]

Many of the agrarian resistance groups were founded on what James S. Donnelly, Jr. calls "the ethics of localism," leading them to defend what were thought of as customary rights. Such demands represented more than the archaic burden of "tradition." They were practical, indeed, desperate attempts on the part of the poor to defend themselves in the face of rising rents and scarcity of land. Balanced on the edge of survival, small farmers and laborers championed a "moral economy," one that opposed any

---

35. Quoted in Salaman, *The History and Social Influence of the Potato*, 283. For an example of tenant resistance see Sheil, *Falling into Wretchedness*, 23, 26, 38–46.
36. Dooley, *The Big House and Landed Estates of Ireland*, 24, 25.
37. For the Protestant Association see Reilly, *The Irish Land Agent*, 32. For "Pastorini" and agrarian agitation see Donnelly, "Millennialism and Sectarianism in the Rockite Movement of 1821–1824," 108–110.
38. Donnelly, *The Land and the People of Nineteenth-Century Cork*, 86–88, 342–45.
39. For data see Tuathaigh, *Ireland before the Famine: 1798–1848*, 165–66. For rise in crime rate see Mokyr, *Why Ireland Starved*, 137. For peasant resistance to "modernization" see Clark and Donnelly, "General Introduction," to their *Irish Peasants: Violence & Political Unrest, 1780–1914*, 5–10. In the same volume also see the authors' "Introduction: The Tradition of Violence," 28–29.

attempts to alter existing arrangements between landlord and tenant.[40] Therefore, in addition to attempting to block land consolidation, Whiteboyism also sought to prevent rent increases beyond customary levels. It was not just landowners and middlemen who might feel the Whiteboys' wrath. Any farmer, whatever his status, who had land to rent could become a target. In northern Tipperary, for example, 61 percent of the victims of agrarian resistance were farmers and only 10 percent landed gentry.[41] The high number of farmers among the victims of agrarian violence may also reflect Whiteboy attempts to regulate wages. As capitalism challenged the traditional structures of Irish agrarian society, the Whiteboy-type organizations sought to reassert customary rights over those of private property. It is little wonder that Cornewall Lewis called the secret societies "a vast trades union for the protection of the Irish peasantry."[42] Faced with what sometimes appeared to be a quasi-revolutionary situation, the British government responded by reorganizing the police force and issuing an endless string of Coercion Acts intended to enforce the peace.

It was not only those at the very bottom of the economic ladder who were involved in agrarian unrest. While the strength of the secret organizations lay in the small farms, the leadership seems to have come from tradesmen in the towns.[43] Moreover, between the poor and those middle-class farmers who were part of the market economy, there lay what is sometimes called "the middle peasantry." They were small farmers who were sometimes part of the agrarian labor force. As population pressure drove up rents and landlords pursued consolidation, the position of this middle group became increasingly precarious.[44] Finally, there was a growing class rift within the Catholic community. Some Whiteboy groups pressured Catholic priests, as well as Protestant ministers, to reduce fees charged for weddings, baptisms and funerals. More significantly, communal strains grew as the priests came to identify with the growing Catholic middle class represented by businessmen and strong farmers.[45]

Tenants' fears of eviction or rent increases were so widespread and deep that any attempts by a landlord or his agent to increase agricultural productivity by altering existing arrangements were viewed with suspicion. Even new varieties of plows brought in from Scotland or the Continent were occasionally sabotaged.[46] As a result, even though attempts at land consolidation were widespread, especially in the south and west, the resulting atmosphere of violence and intimidation may have limited landlords' efforts to

---

40. See Scally, *The End of Hidden Ireland*, 33–35. For "ethics of localism" see Donnelly, *The Land and the People of Nineteenth-Century Cork*, 88–91. For customary rights see Huggins, *Social Conflict in Pre-Famine Ireland*, 14; Foster, *Modern Ireland: 1600–1972*, 293–94.
41. Grace, *The Great Famine in Nenagh Poor Law Union, County Tipperary*, 185.
42. For quote see Foster, *Modern Ireland: 1600–1972*, 294.
43. James S. Donnelly, Jr. points out the influence of town-based Ribbonmen in Muster on the essentially rural Rockite movement; *The Land and the People of Nineteenth-Century Cork*, 20–23, 100–3.
44. For "middle peasantry" see Clark and Donnelly, "General Introduction," 7–8, 17.
45. Huggins, *Social Conflict in Pre-Famine Ireland*, 34. 60, 72, 117. See also Connolly, *Priests and People in Pre-Famine Ireland, 1780–1785*, 228–29; Kevin Whelan, *The Tree of Liberty*, 52–53.
46. Reilly, *The Irish Land Agent*, 55, 70.

initiate change. One land agent in County Cork explained that, while he was anxious to get rid of cottiers and small holders, long experience had taught him "the necessity of doing so in a manner least objectionable to the habits & prejudices of the people." This "necessity" often added to the cost of "improvement." Instead of just evicting unwanted tenants, some landlords found it prudent to buy them out by forgiving arears in rent, assisting with emigration or facilitating resettlement on undeveloped land. The latter was more common in the west where there was much uncultivated, subprime land. In Ulster, where there was less land available, assisted emigration may have been more prevalent.[47]

Landlords faced other potential obstacles to "improvement," such as the quality of the soil and the cost of drainage, as well as the scarcity of fertilizer. In the era before chemical fertilizers, restoring nitrogen to the soil was primarily an organic process involving animal or plant manure. However, much of Ireland's manure was tied up in the production of potatoes. Large, well-run farms could produce their own nitrogen-fixing green crops, such as clover, which also provided fodder for livestock, thus eliminating the need for fallow pastures. However, such techniques of "new husbandry" or "high farming" required knowledge, experience, oversight and discipline. Moreover, the application of such sophisticated approaches could not be made piecemeal. Their adoption had to be all part of a single process. In addition, essential activities, such as extensive draining, required some capital investment and risk, an off-putting prospect given the restless and unstable condition of the Irish countryside. Certainly, the impression, deeply embedded in the Irish narrative, of Ireland as a violent country did little to encourage investment from the outside.[48]

Although its economy gradually resumed a slow growth after the recession of 1815–1820, Ireland seems to have been economically stagnant during the five years preceding the Famine. Unable to reestablish and expand its manufacturing base beyond Belfast, or to extensively modernize its agriculture sector, Ireland remained a poor country by most standards of the day, especially those relating to the stability of a country's food supply. Joel Mokyr suggests that, within the European context, "The severity and frequency of subsistence crises […] became a central factor in the measurement of poverty, and the elimination of these crises from the European scene is an indication of the disappearance of poverty by this absolute definition." Unfortunately, Ireland would prove a tragic exception to the European norm.[49]

---

47. Mokyr, *Why Ireland Starved*, 131–34, 141; Gráda, *Ireland: A New Economic History*, 164. For land agent's quote see Donnelly, *The Land and the People of Nineteenth-Century Cork*, 53.
48. For "New Husbandry" in Ireland see Mokyr, *Why Ireland Starved*, 166–67. The author suggests that one factor that hindered land reclamation was that bringing additional arable land into production would have required fertilizer, most of which was already dedicated to existing fields, 174.
49. Mokyr, *Why Ireland Starved*, 15. Concerning Ireland's Pre-Famine economic growth see Ó Gráda, *Ireland: A New Economic History*, 166–67.

Chapter Six

PEOPLE, LAND AND POTATOES

By the eve of the Famine, approximately one-third of Ireland's population consisted of small tenant farmers and agricultural laborers. They lived primarily on potatoes that they grew themselves or received as wages for agricultural work. What little cash they saw came from occasional wages or from surplus produce or livestock they might sell. Most of this money went to their landlords for rent. Yet, these apparently marginal people and their potatoes were the foundation of the country's market-driven agrarian sector. It was their incredibly cheap labor, along with their remarkably high rents, that undergird Ireland's potato economy. The Famine was, therefore, the result of a double catastrophe, linked by the arrival of the potato blight. In wiping out the food supply of almost one-third of the Irish population in 1846, the blight not only introduced widespread famine conditions. It also set in motion the dissolution of the country's potato economy, a complex, nonlinear, social, economic and ecological system involving demography, patterns of land ownership and land use, and a potato-based monoculture. However, while the potato blight *triggered* both famine and its economic results, it should not be considered the *cause* of either catastrophe. One will not, for example, understand the toppling of a house of cards simply by focusing on the bump that triggered its failure, which ultimately lay in its precarious, unstable structure. Similarly, the failure of the potato economy lay in its fatally flawed structure, the result of the interaction among population pressures, land use and potato dependency—the subject of this chapter.

Population Growth: A Malthusian Case?

Approaching the area around Bantry Bay in 1827, the Anglo-Irish writer Rev. Caesar Otway had a grim epiphany. He beheld

> bare, desolate [...] rocky elevations, or bare gloomy moors, crowded with miserable huts, a population evidently and fearfully increasing, amid difficulties and privations [...] insufficient to check its monstrous progress; and I had read Malthus's convincing but gloomy book; and, war, pestilence and famine [...] rose up in necessary association, as summoned to feast on and make prey in future, of this teeming population.[1]

It was only late in the eighteenth century that observers began to take serious notice of the Ireland's rapidly expanding population. At mid-century, thanks in part to the

---

1. Otway, *Sketches in Ireland*, 275.

terrible famine of 1740–41, the population appeared to have stabilized at around 2.2–2.3 million. By 1790, however, that number had doubled to over 4 million and continued to grow. Between 1750 and 1845 Ireland's population more than tripled. Only Finland, Hungary and England rivaled or surpassed Ireland's demographic explosion. England's rise was, of course, fueled by industrialization; Ireland's was fueled primarily by potatoes.[2]

By the time Rev. Otway visited Bantry Bay, Ireland's demographic explosion was evident for all to see. It was, therefore, natural that Otway's mind turned to the grim prognostications of Rev. Thomas Malthus, whose theory that population would always surge ahead of food production continued to haunt speculations about demographic growth. Of course, Malthus' *An Essay on the Principle of Population* (1798), had been mainly concerned with Great Britain. Thanks to industrial technology and agricultural innovation, however, Britain's rapidly expanding population bypassed his projections of demographic disaster, and by the time he considered Ireland, he had slightly modified his thinking. He believed it might be possible that Ireland's population might check its growth before facing the ultimate sanction of famine.[3] Indeed, something like a Malthusian check may have been already at work in Ireland by the early decades of the new century. Although the population continued to grow until the Famine, the *rate* of growth peaked at around 1820 and then slowed. As discussed earlier, the end of the Napoleonic wars in 1815 brought a drop in agricultural prices and a temporary contraction of the Irish economy. That slump triggered a decline in the Irish marriage rates and a rise in emigration. Cormac Ó Gráda suggests that the departure of many young males inhibited marriage and, subsequently, birth rates, cutting by half Ireland's rate of natural increase.[4] Between 1815 and 1845 some 1.5 million Irish left the island. T. W. Freeman reports that in a single decade, between 1831 and 1841, 403,463 Irish emigrated from ports in Ireland and Britain.[5] Emigration rates varied, however, from one region to another. In the east, where landless agricultural workers had limited opportunities for employment, the emigrant's path drew tens of thousands each year. Out-migration was also high in the heavily populated drumlin belt of southern and western Ulster and in parts of north Leinster, areas that saw the erosion of cottage industries in the 1830s. In the west, however, where population growth was highest, emigration rates were lower. In fact, emigration did not become a major phenomenon in the west until the Famine.[6]

By 1820 Ireland's demographic disequilibrium seems to have begun a slow drift toward modification, if not correction, as the country's growth rate approached Western European norms. Between 1831 and 1841 Ireland's population increased by 5.6 percent,

---

2. For population growth see Ó Gráda, *Great Irish Famine*, 5–6; Smyth, "'Mapping the People,' The Growth and Distribution of the People," 13.
3. See Ó Gráda, *Black '47 and Beyond*, 29.
4. Ó Gráda, "Poverty, Population and Agriculture, 1801–1845," 120–21. Ó Gráda suggests that the Irish marriage rate, while within European norms, remained high.
5. The figures do not include Irish people who settled in Britain. See Freeman, "Land and People, c. 1841," 261.
6. Aalen, *Man and Landscape in Ireland*, 184. For emigration from north Leinster and from south and west Ulster, see Ó Gráda, *Great Irish Famine*, 8.

compared to a rise of 13.4 percent during the same period in England and Wales. Overall, the rate of Irish population growth fell from 1.6 percent, during the period from 1780 to 1821, to 0.9 percent by the 1820s and down to a relatively modest 0.5 to 0.6 percent during the 1830s and early 1840s. Nevertheless, demographic *momentum* continued to drive an increasing population already pressing hard on available resources. For example, Donegal's Fanad Peninsula, which numbered around 4,000 people in 1766, held 6,000 by 1800, 8,846 people in 1821 and 9,956 in 1831. The region's population was still expanding when the potato blight appeared in 1845. Nationally, Ireland's population grew from roughly 7.9 million in 1831 to between 8.1 and 8.4 million in 1841. On the eve of the Famine, the population had reached its historic peak, probably numbering between 8.5 and 8.7 million.[7]

Thus, even if there was a Malthusian correction, it lagged behind the relentless momentum of increasing population pressure. At 700 people per square mile of *arable* land, Ireland's agricultural population was among the highest in Europe. Some of the greatest densities were to be found in two areas: in Ireland's remote western peninsulas stretching into the Atlantic and along the drumlin belt in southern Ulster. These rural areas had demographic concentrations equal to Dublin, Cork, Limerick and Belfast.[8] The concentration of population was highest in Ulster's County Armagh, characterized by small holdings sustained by linen, oats and potatoes. Densities of 400 or more per square mile occurred in counties Donegal, Cavan, Down, Monaghan and Tyrone in Ulster and in counties Leitrim, Roscommon and Sligo in the drumlin regions of Connaught. Counties Clare in Munster and Longford in Leinster were little better off, while Mayo and Kerry also had high concentrations of small farms occupying poor land.[9] In the most fertile lands of Leinster, especially in counties Kildare and Meath, however, the densities measured only 201 and 187 per square arable mile, respectively. Throughout Ireland, higher populations tended to correlate with smaller farms on poorer land. For example, 64 percent of Connaught farms were between one and five acres. The corresponding proportion of such farms in the fertile lands of Leinster was only 37 percent.[10]

On the Atlantic seaboard the population crowded along the coasts, where seaweed provided the necessary manure for potatoes. Touring the coastal area of County Clare in

---

7. For Fanad Peninsula see Donald and Mac Suibhne's introduction to Hugh Dorian's *The Outer Edge of Ulster*, 11. For the slowdown in the rate of population growth see Grada, *Black '47 and Beyond*, 25–26; see also his *The Great Irish Famine*, 6. For population in the 1840s see Smyth, "'Mapping the People,' The Growth and Distribution of the People," 13. Historians continue to debate the size and trends of the population in pre-Famine Ireland. Joel Mokyr suggests that census reports suffered from serious undercounting. See *Why Ireland Starved*, 31–33. A contrarian argument for lowering population estimates for the 1841 census (based on higher emigration to Great Britain) may be found in Nusteling, "How Many Irish Potato Famine Deaths?"
8. For density per square mile see Ó Gráda, *Great Irish Famine*, 5. For a map of population density based on Poor Law valuations see Smyth, "'Mapping the People,' The Growth and Distribution of the People," Figure 1, 14.
9. See Freeman, "Land and People, c. 1841," 249.
10. Green, "Agriculture," 89; Smyth, "'Mapping the People,'" 13. For Connaught see figure 6 in Smyth, "The Province of Connacht and the Great Famine," 284.

1841, M. F. Dickson described the six miles between Kilkee and Carrigaholt as looking like one big village. Later, during the Famine, a relief official described the coast road between Sligo town and Ballyshannon as "a regular street of cabins." Even offshore islands seemed to swarm with people. Visiting Cape Clear Island off the southwest coast of Cork, Rev. Caesar Otway wondered at the number of people in a place so barren; he imagined the inhabitants feeding on stones.[11] Thus, while a hypothetical, industrializing Ireland might easily have absorbed its growing population, the actual, largely agrarian Ireland took on a Malthusian cast in the eyes of many observers. One-quarter to one-third of Ireland's population was poverty stricken, often living in one-room mud cabins and subsisting primarily on one crop, the potato. Many farmed five acres or less and were often tenants-at-will. Others were agricultural workers, some of whom had only a patch of potato ground, while others had no access to land at all. With no hope of improvement and at the mercy of whatever malignancies the weather or landlords might throw at them, Ireland's poor lived perpetually on the margin. When conditions deteriorated, they had no place to which they could retreat, except off the island—if they could afford the journey.

Yet amidst continuing subsistence crises, two startling facts emerge. First, despite everything, Ireland's poor were comparatively well fed and generally healthy. The average adult male might eat up to twelve to fourteen pounds of tubers a day, when they were available.[12] If his daily potato diet was monotonous, however, it was also usually plentiful and nutritious. British visitors often described Ireland's ragged peasantry as looking surprisingly healthy. And, indeed, Irish life expectancy, while slightly lower than that of the Dutch and Scandinavians, surpassed that of the Germans and French. This level of health was not maintained equally throughout Ireland, however. The census of 1841 showed that life expectancy was lowest in the west. As T. W. Freeman notes, Ireland could be divided into two regions: "one of poverty west of a line roughly from Derry to Cork and one in happier, if hardly fortunate, circumstances, east of this line."[13] The interesting second fact is that by the eve of the Famine, in addition to more or less feeding its own people, Ireland was exporting enough grain and livestock to support an additional two million people in Britain. This "surplus" has led some historians to argue that the country was not overpopulated. However, with one-third of its population dependent on the potato, the country was not really exporting a "surplus." It was rather selling off food, which, had it been consumed at home, would have led to a less risky, more balanced socioeconomic situation.

So, was Ireland a Malthusian case: too many poor people with too many children competing for limited land, pushing up rents, pulling down wages and barely surviving in the perpetual shadow of starvation? This was indeed the general assumption

---

11. Otway, *Sketches in Ireland*, 240. Dickson, "Letters from the Coast of Clare," 162. For Sligo quote see Anbinder, "Lord Palmerston and the Famine Emigration," 449.
12. Clarkson and Crawford, *Feast and Famine: A History of Food and Nutrition in Ireland 1500–1920*, 73.
13. Freeman, 248. For life expectancy see Ó Gráda, "Poverty, Population and Agriculture, 1801–1845," 111.

of many contemporary observers. Looking back on the period, economic historian Joel Mokyr blames what he calls a governmental "policy of drift" on the British consensus that Ireland was hopelessly overpopulated. Nevertheless, at the time many Irish commentators argued instead that the problem was one of underproduction and underemployment. Their solution lay in creating more farms through government-sponsored land reclamation.[14] And indeed, some historians have also rejected the Malthusian approach to Ireland's problems. Mokyr, for example, sees no evidence that Ireland was in fact overpopulated. His economic analysis does not reveal any convincing relationship between Irish poverty and population pressure.[15] However, other economic historians have not been prepared to completely consign Malthus to the dust bin of discarded theories. By taking into consideration a series of variables concerning the *quality* of the land, especially in the west, Patrick P. L. McGregor has found a Malthusian correlation between poverty and population pressure. "Pre-Famine development may be considered as a westward and southward movement of population to areas where the ratio of wages to rents was highest." In that part of Ireland, the demographics exerted an upward pressure on rents and a downward pressure on wages, causing a lag in the improvement of living conditions. Consequently, the growing population continued to press hard upon the land. In the south and west, McGregor argues, the "hovels stretching up mountain sides were concrete examples of the land constraint upon the economy."[16] Nonetheless, if a country can feed most of its people most of the time, export food and maintain a basic, if minimal, standard of health, is it overpopulated? Addressing that question requires a deeper investigation into the intricate connections between people, land use and food production.

Land Use and the Structure of Rural Irish Society

Ireland's increasing population pressure acted upon tenancy and land use to produce a complex social pyramid, which superficially resembled similar structures in other parts of Western Europe. As noted earlier, in many countries a small, landed aristocracy owned most of the land, which was worked by a large population of peasants. In many instances, the peasants had limited rights of tenancy, if not in law then at least in well-established custom. In many cases the aristocratic proprietors were of the same ethnicity as the peasantry. In Ireland, however, the owners of the land at the top of the pyramid were members of the Anglo-Irish aristocracy, a caste separated from most Irish people by privilege, religion and a history of colonial domination. Moreover, unless they had leases, their tenantry had no rights regarding the land and, outside of Ulster, could claim few customary privileges.

---

14. See Green, "Agriculture," 117. See also Mokyr, *Why Ireland Starved*, 39.
15. See Mokyr, *Why Ireland Starved*, 40–41, 48, 51. For Mokyr's econometric analysis of the Malthusian question see 38–80.
16. McGregor, "Demographic Pressure and the Irish Famine," 236. See also Fitzpatrick, *Irish Emigration, 1801–1921*, 28.

Many of the roughly 10,000 proprietors at the top of Ireland's pyramid did not even live on their estates. By 1800 around one-third of proprietors may have been absentees, many of whom hired agents to manage their land.[17] However, unlike their counterparts in Great Britain, who often had varied commercial interests, many Irish proprietors relied upon rents for the bulk of their income.[18] Unwilling to take financial risks, many, especially absentees, were not inclined to improve their estates or to limit the number of tenants seeking land. Indeed, many found the combination of subdivision and "rack renting" very profitable.

Below the proprietors were the "middlemen," who rented large tracts of land on long-term leases. As land values rose, however, this proved highly detrimental to the owners locked into low rents. Many of these middlemen were "half-mounted gentlemen," often younger sons of Anglo-Irish families. Unable to inherit estates of their own, these "squireens" still desired the lifestyle of the landed gentry, or as much of it as they could afford. Often in debt and living far from the skilled artisans needed to keep up their boxy Georgian houses, they shared with their subtenants a degree of shabbiness that often shocked British visitors.[19] Some middlemen, like Daniel O'Connell, were Catholics, often renting back lands that had once belonged to their families. As part of the Catholic "underground gentry," they often received the deference and respect their co-religionists withheld from Protestant landlords.[20]

Visiting Ireland in the 1770s, agronomist Arthur Young condemned the middlemen for renting vast tracks of land cheaply and subletting small portions at high rents. As a result, "that beautiful gradation of the pyramid, which connects the broad base of the poor people with the great nobleman they support is broken."[21] Nevertheless, in a country with many absentee proprietors, the middlemen often played a role in advancing the commercialization of the agrarian economy, although not always in the most efficient manner. These *tiarnai begs* (or "little lords," as they were called in Irish) were often quite willing to sublet portions of their land to small farmers, leaving the owners with minimal control over their estates.[22] By the second half of the eighteenth century, however, proprietors, residents as well as absentees, began to realize that they could achieve more by employing manager/agents than by depending on middlemen, whose numbers, therefore, began a slow, long-term decline. By the time of the Famine, for example, the Fitzwilliam estate in County Wicklow had managed to reduce the number of holdings

---

17. Dooley, *The Big House and Landed Estates of Ireland*, 18. For numbers see Donnelly, *The Land and the People of Nineteenth-Century Cork*, 12. For land agents see Reilly, *The Irish Land Agent, 1830–60*, 36.
18. Trant, *The Blessington Estate: 1667–1908*, 107.
19. See Scally, *The End of Hidden Ireland*, 56. For effect of long-term leases see Donnelly *The Land and the People of Nineteenth-Century Cork,*, 12.
20. Kevin Whelan, *The Tree of Liberty*, 3–4, 6; For middlemen see 13, 16–18. See also Grace, *The Middle Class of Callan, Co. Kilkenny, 1825–45*, 10.
21. For quote see MacCurtain, "Pre-Famine Peasantry in Ireland," 192.
22. Dooley, *The Big House and Landed Estates of Ireland*, 30, 64–65.

over 300 acres from 40 percent of the estate to 13 percent.²³ There was one problem, however. The middlemen had often acted as a kind of buffer between the landowners and their tenantry. Once removed, tensions between tenants and the landowners or their agents became more intense. In fact, the more proprietors tried to manage the land for commercial purposes, the faster the old paternalistic ties to the small holders— those at the bottom of Arthur Young's socioeconomic pyramid—dissolved, thus contributing to the spread of Whiteboy-type agrarian unrest.²⁴

Below the proprietors and middlemen were their roughly 50,000 major tenants and some 100,000 "snug" farmers renting on the mean 80 and 50 acres, respectively. Outside of Ulster their ranks included some Old Catholic families who formed part of the "underground gentry." By the nineteenth century, strong farmers, especially the Catholics among them, were often rural entrepreneurs who adopted what Kevin Whelan calls "a coherent family strategy." They hoped to keep their holdings intact so that the eldest son would be able to assume the tenancy. Beyond that, they had to save money to educate their children, to place some in religious life and to build up dowries (£50 to £100) for the arranged marriages of their daughters. As noted earlier, to accomplish all this while meeting high rents, many of these farmers shunned the usual trappings of the middle class, thus often rendering their status invisible to most outside observers.²⁵

It would be a mistake to classify all those below the ranks of the solid farmers as part of an undifferentiated mass of "peasants." The complexity of Ireland's agrarian structure extended down into the ranks of the country's poor. As David Ryder and Charles E. Orser, Jr. point out:

> great distinctions occurred within the non-landowning masses, partly because various degrees of prestige could attach to kin-groups irrespective of their access to land, labor and livestock. [...] Rather than construct a rigid system wherein a tenant farmer could sequentially climb the rungs of the "agricultural ladder," extending from labourer to owner, Irish tenure classes tended to overlap and to blend into one another.²⁶

Guided by this caution, it is, nevertheless, possible to distinguish various broad groupings among the poorer classes.

For example, directly beneath the ranks of the big and middling farmers came the small subtenants. By 1841 these numbered around 250,000 families, working on the mean of around 20 acres. They made up most of Ireland's tenantry. Below them were

---

23. Byrne, "The Mechanics of Assisted Emigration: From the Fitzwilliam Estate in Wicklow to Canada," 43. For middlemen see Cullen, *The Emergence of Modern Ireland, 1600–1900*. 99–103. For their decline see Kevin Whelan, *The Tree of Liberty*, 49–52.
24. Dooley, *The Big House and Landed Estates of Ireland*, 21, 52–53. For divisions among landlords, tenants and farmers see Cullen, *The Emergence of Modern Ireland*, 103–104, 131.
25. Kevin Whelan, *The Tree of Liberty*, 29. For dowries see Grace, 26, 28. For numbers see Donnelly, 11.
26. Ryder and Orser, "From Farmers to Defendants: Ballykilcline and Its Historical Context," 23; see also 22.

some 300,000 cottier households subsisting on around five acres or less.[27] Had they been in rural England, these cottiers would have been landless agricultural workers living on cash wages paid by the farmers who employed them. In Ireland, however, they were often "bound" cottiers," farmer/laborers who bartered their family's labor for a cabin, a kitchen garden, some turf and dung gathering rights. In a separate arrangement, they might contract for the use of a plot of plowed and manured potato ground that would supply their families' food.[28] In return for their cottages and plots, bound cottiers might owe their landlords 130 days or more of work at planting and at harvest times; this in addition to cultivating their own potato plots. Living essentially on a "potato wage," cottiers spent many days working off what in monetary terms was often an exorbitant rent. Just the annual "rent" of a cabin might require over 100 days' labor. In County Clare, an acre of land valued at only 15s might rent for £3, a considerable mark up. This link between potato ground and the "potato wage" was, of course, a boon for the employer. By setting his rents at the highest level, the landlord/employer effectively suppressed the cottier's "wages," reducing them to the equivalent of from 4d to 10d a day, except at harvest time.[29] In most cases, steady employment was the exception rather than the rule. Combining his "wages" (potatoes, access to land, occasional cash) with whatever he could earn from the sale of a pig, eggs and/or poultry, a cottier might earn £8 to £16 a year. With perhaps half going to rent, it was a meager amount on which to raise a family. It is not surprising that "loan funds," unofficial banks (often backed by landlords or their agents), sprang up to service and to prey upon the poor.[30]

Although the bound cottiers faced a high work/rent burden, the plight of the 1,000,000 "unbound" cottiers was worse. While they might have had access to a small "pratie patch," generally an acre or less, they had to hire themselves out as best they could in an overcrowded labor market. Some of these laborers were the victims of downward mobility. They might have been sons of small farmers who had been unable to afford rising rents or who had gamboled and lost on the conacre.[31] As their numbers increased, opportunities for work shrank. As farms became divided into smaller and smaller plots at ever-increasing rents, the farmers involved hired fewer laborers, relying on their own families to do the work. Having no leases, most cottiers, whatever their status, were

---

27. For numbers see Murchadha, *The Great Famine: Ireland's Agony, 1845–52*, 5, 6. As with most terms used to describe Ireland's land pyramid, the term "cottier" is somewhat fuzzy. Throughout much of Ireland the term was applied loosely to landless laborers. In certain areas, however, it might refer to a small tenant farmer working up to 10 acres. See Ryder and Orser, "From Farmers to Defendants," 22, 24; Reilly, "'Nearly Starved to Death:' The Female Petition during the Great Hunger," 47.
28. Donnelly, *The Land and the People of Nineteenth-Century Cork*, 17.
29. Vandermeer, *The Ecology of Agroecosystems*, 5. For rents in Clare see Murphy, *A People Starved: Life and Death in West Clare, 1845–51*, 53.
30. For loan funds see Rees, *Surplus People: The Fitzwilliam Clearances, 1847–56*, 18; Reilly, *The Irish Land Agent*, 29. For cottiers wages see also Green, "Agriculture," 95–96.
31. Dooley, *The Big House and Landed Estates of Ireland*, 23. For bound and unbound cottiers see Trant, *The Blessington Estate*, 96. For number see Donnelly, *The Land and the People of Nineteenth Century Cork,*, 12.

essentially tenants-at-will; they could be sent upon the road at any time. Although the unbound cottiers were generally occasional laborers, the entire cottier class represented the principal source of Ireland's agricultural labor force, the chief beneficiaries being Irish landlords and English consumers.[32] Bad as the lot of many cottiers may have been, the situation for those farming the conacre was generally worse.

Conacre, an important feature of Irish agriculture, should not be confused with sharecropping. Rather, it involved a family's gamble that it could contract for an acre or so of land for a single season, grow a crop and end up with enough potatoes to feed itself, while still earning rent money for the following year whereupon the whole process began again. As the Dublin Friend's Central Relief Committee noted during the Famine, these families became "commercial speculators in potatoes." Eventually, since landlords had problems collecting their rent in the wake of bad harvests, many conacre families had to pay their rent in advance.[33] The rents could run between 20s and 40s an acre, although some could be as high as £13, depending on land quality and location. The farmer who held the land would plow and manure the field in return for the rent and a portion of the harvest, while the conacre family would provide the seed and the labor.[34] The system was especially popular with undertenants who could, with minimal risk, earn back some of their own rent by taking on conacre families. Those letting out conacre land were often part of what David Ryder and Charles E. Orser, Jr. call "a vast web of 'middlemen' tenant farmers."[35] For their part, those renting the conacre leveraged the only resource they had: their families' labor. They might grow grain and/or market-quality potatoes to sell, reserving low-quality but more prolific tubers for their own consumption. If the harvest was good, the family would have food plus enough cash for another year's venture. If not, it faced ruin. Either way, the family was often homeless by year's end, since conacre arrangements seldom ran more than eleven months. This gave maximum flexibility to the landlord and none at all to the conacre farmer. The rents were, of course, constantly being pushed up by competition. Indeed, as Henry Blake, proprietor of the Renvyle estate in Connemara put it in 1824, those working the conacre seemed "rapidly advancing to a state of ruin." Oliver MacDonagh notes that by the early 1830s the numbers involved in conacre were growing faster than any other class, "a sure indication that national disaster was possible."[36] Because of its inherent insecurity, the conacre was the last resort for the poorest farmers. Journalist Alexander Somerville estimated that as

---

32. Kevin Whelan, "Pre-and Post-Famine Landscape Change," 20. For narrowing demand for labor see Donnelly, *The Land and the People of Nineteenth Century Cork*, 19.
33. Bourke, *"A Visitation of God?"*, 75. For quote see Society of Friends, *Transactions of the Central Relief Committee of the Society of Friends*, 9.
34. Huggins, *Social Conflict in Pre-Famine Ireland*, 55. For definitions of "conacre" see Byrne, *Byrne's Dictionary of Irish Local History from Earliest Times to c. 1900*, 75–76; Green, "Agriculture," 93; Cullen, *The Emergence of Modern Ireland*, 104–5.
35. Ryder and Orser, "From Farmers to Defendants," 25.
36. MacDonagh, "The Economy and Society, 1830–45," 219. See also the Blake Family, *Letters from the Highlands of Connemara*, 28. Austin Bourke puts the amount of conacre land in 1841 at around 350,000 acres, producing around 2,100,000 tons of potatoes; *A Visitation of God? The Potato and the Great Irish Famine*, 100.

much as four-fifths of the population of Roscommon depended on conacre for survival. For such people, "the refusal [of a conacre contract] is the equivalent to the sentence of death upon the population." It is little wonder, then, that there was also a high level of agrarian unrest in places like County Roscommon.[37]

Below the cottiers and conacre farmers were the *spailpíní*, landless, itinerant agricultural workers who might seek seasonal work as far away as England or Scotland. (Facing hard times, even small farmers sometimes joined the migration, hoping to somehow keep the indignity of their situation a secret.)[38] The numbers involved in such migrations were large. In 1841, 57,651 "spalpeens" went over to Great Britain for the harvest; almost half were from the province of Connacht. In Mayo one-third of the population sometimes joined the migratory movement, seeking work elsewhere in Ireland or abroad.[39] In addition to itinerant laborers there were thousands of squatters. Although they paid no rent, they were still part of the agricultural system in that they, along with many unbound cottiers, were instrumental in reclaiming the bog lands on which they settled.[40] They built what huts they could in roadside ditches, on scrubby wasteland and even in the bogs themselves. Some of these settlements were village size. Where the ground was not too wet, a dwelling might be fashioned out of a "scalp" (from *scailp* meaning "den"), essentially a hole dug into the earth. Crudely thatched and blending into the environment, scalps might be almost invisible to the visitor. Rev. John East noted that, "So little like human habitations did multitudes of these cabins appear, that I was strongly impressed by the aspect of the country as altogether a land without homes." Thomas Cromwell noted that only the smoke drifting up through the roughly thatched roofs might betray the existence of such dug-in dwellings.[41]

These groups, crowding the bottom of the economic ladder, evade hard-and-fast classifications. As Paul E. W. Roberts has pointed out, most were farmers of one sort or another and most were also part of the agricultural workforce. Families often found themselves shifting from one category to another. A tenant-at-will working a few acres could be put on the road at any time, as could the conacre farmer who failed to make rent. Once their potatoes ran out, many families, regardless of their status, had to spend the summer months begging until their own potato crop came in. They were all part of the vast army of Ireland's poor, which, according to Roberts, is how they often defined themselves.[42]

---

37. See Ryder and Orser, "From Farmers to Defendants," 28–29. For Somerville, see his *Letters from Ireland during the Famine of 1847*, 78, 83.
38. Reilly, *The Irish Land Agent*, 33.
39. Green, "Agriculture," 116.
40. Landlords might offer negligible rents to those who would reclaim boggy land. See Donnelly, *The Land and the People of Nineteenth-Century Cork*, 26–27.
41. Cromwell, *Excursions through Ireland*, 2:157; East, *Notes and Glimpses of Ireland in 1847*, 68. For squatters see Austin Bourke, *"The Visitation of God?"* 61.
42. Roberts, "Caravats and Shanavests: Whiteboyism and Faction Fighting, 1802–11," 64.

Subdivision, Subletting and Partible Inheritance

In England, the size of the rural population gradually stabilized while the numbers living in the urban areas grew rapidly. In Ireland, however, an ever-expanding rural population continued to put enormous pressures on both land and rents. While prime arable land could be enclosed and farmed for the market, lower quality land could easily be sublet and farmed for rents. Indeed, since even the best land required draining and manuring, many landlords found it easier and cheaper to harvest rent money. As Anthony Doyle suggests, "Landed estates were businesses whose revenues primarily came from rental incomes."[43] Thus, some landlords, according to Terence Dooley, did no farming and simply lived off rents. An example of rent farming may be found in County Cork where a James Scanlan, paying £85 a year for 46 acres, proceeded to sublet almost all the land to five undertenants for £146, in addition to collecting £30 rent from 10 cabin holders.[44]

The circumstances that encouraged subdivision were in place well before the Famine. Until the passage of Catholic Emancipation, those farming 40-shilling freeholds were enfranchised. Without the secret ballot, of course, the landlords usually controlled the voters, and saw, therefore, an advantage in multiplying their tenancies. In 1822, Lord Ross complained that landlords used to let out farms between 500 and 1,500 acres. "Now landlords, finding that they can get higher rents and have more voters," let out farms of 20–40 acres, "and these, as they multiply fast, again sub-divide them among their sons and daughters as they marry."[45] The 40-shilling freehold franchise was abolished in 1829, but by then the tendency to subdivide for rents was firmly entrenched. Thanks to population pressures, there was no scarcity of those prepared to pay ever-higher rents. As a result, trying to parse status within Ireland's land pyramid can be complicated. For example, an individual could be simultaneously a tenant and a landlord, renting from one person and then letting a portion of that land out to subtenants. In R. B. McDowell's words, if "landlord" were defined as one who receives rents, then "Ireland could be described as a nation of landlords." Daniel O'Connell once observed that there might have been as many as six or seven levels of tenantry between the actual owner of piece of land and an occupier.[46]

When a commodity is divided into smaller portions, the per-unit price often rises, although no intrinsic "value" has been added. Thus, in Ireland, when land was subdivided, the price per acre, as reflected in rent, could rise dramatically. A poor farmer who could not afford to rent twenty acres might manage five, even if the per-acre cost were considerably higher. His landlord might be a tenant himself, subletting portions of his holdings to help cover his own rents. As a result, the highest rents in some areas were not charged by ordinary landlords but by tenant-farmer middlemen.[47] For example,

---

43. Doyle, *Charles Powell Leslie II's Estates at Glaslough, County Monaghan, 1800–1841*, 20.
44. Dooley, *The Big House and Landed Estates of Ireland*, 20. For James Scanlan see Donnelly, *The Land and the People of Nineteenth-Century Cork*, 14.
45. Reilly, *The Irish Land Agent*, 62.
46. Quoted in Huggins, *Social Conflict in Pre-Famine Ireland*, 180. See also McDowell, "Ireland on the Eve of the Famine," 7–8; Bourke, *"The Visitation of God?"* 57–58.
47. Sheil, *Falling into Wretchedness*, 56.

records show that a man in Donegal rented land at 25*s* to 27*s* an acre and then recovered most of his costs by subletting at conacre a dozen or so acres at £13 each. In northwest Tipperary a farmer leased 20 acres at 28*s* an acre and within 10 years had 11 subtenants paying 40*s* an acre.[48] Little wonder that many proprietors and their major tenants found subdivision a profitable alternative to investing in and improving the land. Thus, year by year tens of thousands of families struggled for survival on smaller, more expensive plots of land. In mid-eighteenth-century County Monaghan, the Lucas Estate had 170 tenant families. By 1845 the same amount of land had to support 570 families. Thanks to subdivision, Kilglass Parish in County Roscommon grew from 2,105 people in 1749 to 11,300 in 1841. In 50 years the population on one estate on Valentia Island in Kerry grew from 400 to over 3,000 people.[49]

Obviously, the game of subdividing the land involved not just the great landowners and their middlemen. For example, of the 85,000 acres on the Fitzwilliam estate in County Wicklow only 800 were farmed under the direct control of the proprietor and his agent. The rest were divided up among a hodgepodge of middlemen and their subtenants, each level of the pyramid profiting from the one below it. For instance, Thomas Wall rented around 224 acres directly from the Fitzwilliam estate. He farmed around 90 acres and let the remainder out to 18 undertenants, who, in turn, rented bits and pieces to an unknown number of subtenants.[50] Indeed, the lower on the land pyramid a farmer found himself, the greater his temptation to pass part of the cost of his rent down to the next level. The conacre system, as suggested above, was especially useful in enabling many tenants to shift some of the burden of high rents down to the ranks below them. There were, of course, some problems inherent in the process. Desperate farmers might bid too high and end up defaulting on their rent. Moreover, high rents tended to discourage the tenants from investing in improvements on the farm. Better to exhaust the land and move on.[51]

Given that subdivisions pushed up rents, the system depended on matching a landlord's fiscal necessity (or greed) with someone else's desperate desire for land. One factor driving the process was the old Gaelic tradition of partible inheritance, which involved *access* to the land rather than ownership. As Kerby A. Miller points out, traditional Irish rural society was characterized by strong family bonds and by a powerful attraction to place, especially where Gaelic culture was still strong. Thus, as families grew, there was a compelling desire to keep them intact. A father, wishing to have his adult sons around him, might beg his landlord to further subdivide the holding equally among them, even though the sons would eventually end up paying higher rents per acre for smaller plots of land.[52] In such circumstances, however, as Austin Bourke notes, it was not

---

48. Grace, *The Great Famine in Nenagh Poor Law Union*, 9; For Donegal see Huggins, *Social Conflict in Pre-Famine Ireland*, 55.
49. Trant, *The Blessington Estate*, 79–80. For Roscommon see Dunn, "An Agenda for Researching the Famine," 102. For Lucas estate see Duffy, "The Famine in Monaghan," 177.
50. Sheil, *Falling into Wretchedness*, 28. Fedelma Byrne, "The Mechanics of Assisted Emigration," 46.
51. Trant, *The Blessington Estate*, 108; McDowell, "Ireland on the Eve of the Famine," 8–9.
52. Green, "Agriculture," 91–92. For partible "inheritance" see Miller, *Emigrants and Exiles*, 57–60, 217–18.

the landlord willing to sublet land at high prices who angered the small tenant farmers. Rather, their ire was focused on those landlords who, concerned about managing their holdings, *refused* to subdivide their land under any circumstances.[53]

The victims of "rack renting" were, therefore, often those pursuing partible inheritance, even while being pushed ever closer to the edge of survival. Oliver MacDonagh suggests that by 1830 three-quarters of Ireland's 700,000 farms of 20 acres or less were "non-viable in every modern sense."[54] In Britain, this degree of agrarian subdivision was rare; in Ireland, it was out of control. The country became a land of small farms, tiny plots and a vast poor, rent-burdened subtenantry. In Connacht 60.6 percent of the holdings were under 10 acres. A Parliamentary Commission, headed by Lord Devon, reported in 1845 that 135,000 holdings consisted of less than one acre. According to the 1841 census, a staggering 45 percent of the total holdings were between one and five acres. James Donnelly Jr. points out that during the Famine, there was a strong correlation between holdings of less than 20 acres and high mortality rates.[55]

As mentioned in the previous chapter, some landowners recognized the problems connected to subdivision and tried to curb the system. By the 1830s some proprietors employed managers to both eliminate middlemen and to eradicate small holdings, allowing for the creation of larger, better run farms for their best tenants.[56] Some even imagined that, in pursuing evictions, they were doing their small tenants a favor. John Murray, agent for the Marquis of Downshire's Blessington estate in County Wicklow, argued that, "Surely, a man that looks to the future prospects of his family" should not seek to wish upon them tiny plots of land, which, in the end would produce nothing for themselves nor "pay the owner of the soil." There was a certain logic in this argument, even if those families consequently ejected faced, in the language of the day, "extermination."[57] Indeed, thanks to the Ejection Act of 1815, evictions became easier and cheaper to carry out. Of course, "improvement" by ejection inevitably added to the numbers of land-hungry poor desperately seeking a pratie patch on which to survive. While "improving landlords," such as George Hill of Donegal, generally received a good press, it was often a bad reputation they had among small farmers. Even if no tenants were evicted in the process of estate reorganization, such actions signaled that the old system of subdivision was over and that no additional tenants would be taken on.[58]

A series of government studies recommended large-scale land reclamation to provide new land for the poor. However, neither the state nor the landlords wanted to undertake

---

53. Bourke, *"The Visitation of God?"* 60–61.
54. MacDonagh, "The Economy and Society, 1830–45," 218; see also Austin Bourke, *"The Visitation of God?"* 60–61.
55. Donnelly, *The Great Irish Potato Famine*, 8. For census data see Freeman, "Land and People, c. 1841," 252–53. For Connaught see Smyth, "The Province of Connacht and the Great Famine," 281.
56. Donnelly, *The Land and the People of Nineteenth-Century Cork*, 52–53.
57. Trant, *The Blessington Estate*, 120.
58. For "improvement" and ejections in Donegal see Aalen, *Man and Landscape in Ireland*, 187. For Ejection Act see Hickey, *Famine in West Cork*, 116.

the expense, or tackle the legal complexities involved in turning Ireland's bogs into fertile farmland.[59] Therefore, many proprietors simply depended on their tenants to make improvements. Just as the cost of land was passed down through middlemen, tenants and subtenants, so was the idea of improvements. The problem was that, unlike other types of enterprises, capital investments in agriculture—draining, building up the fertility of the soil, enclosing fields, erecting outbuildings—remained embedded in the land. A tenant's improvements remained behind if he chose or was forced to leave the farm. Nor could he usually claim compensation for improvements from his landlord or from incoming tenants. Thus, without long leases, tenants had little incentive to improve their holdings. Indeed, if they did improve either house or land, their landlord might raise their rent. As one farmer said, "What is the use of improving to have it valued on me at the rent-day, and be made to pay a higher rent for it?" Moreover, indications that landlords were no longer regranting leases would have stifled any interest tenants might have had in improving their farms. So, it was not unusual for small farmers to exhaust the land, knowing that they had no long-term stake in it.[60]

A partial exception existed in Ulster where many Protestant tenant farmers enjoyed some fixity of tenure, meaning that they could remain on the land so long as they paid their rent. Moreover, when they left their holdings, they could often sell the value of any improvements they made to the incoming tenant. Although often referred to as the "Ulster rights," these were more like customs to which tenants tenaciously clung.[61] These customs help explain why British visitors often claimed that Ulster farmsteads looked more prosperous than those encountered in the south, where neither rights nor customs protected small holders. Of course, issues regarding leases and compensation for improvements had little to do with the masses of cottiers and laborers who did not fall into the category of tenantry.

The Potato: The Key to the System

Woven throughout Ireland's vast, ramshackle agricultural system, holding it together and allowing it to spread, was the potato, the principal food (and in many cases the primary "wages") of Ireland's huge rural labor force. The most common Gaelic word for the potato is *práta* (*prátí*, plural) from which is derived the Hiberno-English "pratie." The potato was one of the most important items in the vast Columbian Exchange of animals, plants, people and diseases that moved back and forth between the New and Old Worlds in the wake of the voyages of discovery and colonization. It is not clear how or when the tuber first arrived in Ireland. Since the earliest Irish reference to the potato is in a

---

59. See McDowell, "Ireland on the Eve of the Famine," 6–7.
60. For problems with leases see Mokyr, *Why Ireland Starved*, 82–85. For quote see Hull, "To Drain and Cultivate: Agriculture and 'Improvement' at Ballykilcline," 169. See also Donnelly, *The Land and the People of Nineteenth-Century Cork*, 64–65.
61. In many cases the Ulster customs were not free. In granting them, landlords might have charged as much as 40 times the rent. See Freeman, "Land and People, c. 1841," 255; MacDowell, "Ireland on the Eve of the Famine," 8–9.

County Down text dated 1606, the potato had probably arrived in Ireland sometime in the late sixteenth century. Legend praises (or blames) Sir Walter Raleigh, whose house still stands in Youghal, County Cork, for introducing the tuber into Ireland. Most likely, however, it may have been imported from Spain, the site of its first European cultivation. Significantly, the Gaelic for a certain variety of potato is *an Spáinneach Geal*, "The White Spaniard," possibly deriving from the time when there had been a thriving trade between Galway and Spain.[62]

In Britain and throughout much of Europe the potato was first adopted as a fodder crop and then, because it helps to break up or "cleanse" the soil, as an important element in the new methods of crop rotation. Initially treated as a culinary curiosity in seventeenth-century England, it only gradually came to be recognized as people food. On the other hand, English settlers in Ireland were growing it for both table and stable by the middle of that century. They were closely followed by native Irish farmers, who quickly exploited the potato's food potential out of necessity. Not only was the tuber easily adapted to Ireland's soil and climate, but it came to be recognized as a shield against famine and marauding soldiers during the political chaos of the seventeenth century. An ideal crop in a time of war, it could not be burned, was easily hidden in the ground and was too bulky to carry off. For whatever the reasons, within half a century of its arrival, the potato had a place in the Irish diet not equaled in any other country at the time. As early as 1688, it was already so closely identified with Ireland that anti-Irish mobs in England demonstrated their antipathy by carrying potatoes impaled on sticks.[63]

Although the tuber's adoption in Leinster and in Ulster appears to have been slow, by the middle of the eighteenth century the potato was widely grown in the highly populated province of Munster, possibly because spring frosts—to which early varieties of potatoes were susceptible—were unusual in the southwestern province.[64] As Louis M. Cullen explains, the potato was adopted into a seventeenth-century Irish diet that was beginning to evolve away from its the historic balance between cow and plow—dairy products mixed with occasional grains and vegetables—toward greater reliance upon the latter. Initially, the potato allowed farmers to extend their grain dishes, bread and porridge, over the course of a year. Because the tubers could be lifted starting in August, a family could switch to potatoes in the fall and winter, helping to conserve grains for the following spring when the newly sowed potatoes were still in the ground.[65]

The potato was so well adapted to Ireland that, with hard work and a bit of luck, farmers in some parts of the country might manage two crops a year. Moreover, in a

---

62. For initial cultivation of potatoes in the Canary Islands (1567) and then in Savile, Spain (1573), see Reader, *Potato: A History of the Propitious Esculent*, 88. 91, 113. For County Down see Clarkson and Crawford, *Feast and Famine*, 61.
63. For English mobs and potatoes see Foster, *Modern Ireland: 1600–1972*, 132. For the potato's adoption see Salaman, *The History and Social Influence of the Potato*, 189, 214–15, 234–35; Overton, *Agricultural Revolution in England*, 102. For a summary of the introduction and spread of the potato into Ireland see Dowley, "The Potato and Late Blight in Ireland," 51–57.
64. Ó Gráda, *Black 47 and Beyond*, 14–15, 19.
65. Cullen, *The Emergence of Modern Ireland, 1600—1900*, 145–46.

damp yet temperate climate, the tuber was generally a more dependable, as well as a more productive, crop than grain. While an acre of wheat might feed 2.08 people, an acre of potatoes could feed 4.18.[66] Moreover, since the potato, unlike grain, required no processing prior to consumption, its progress from the field to the pot was simple and left the grower in complete control of his food supply. Finally, in addition to its role in crop rotation, the tuber provided excellent fodder. By 1845, 33 percent of the Irish potato crop, over five million tons, was fed to livestock.[67]

Of course, the potato did not flourish in all types of weather. Dryer conditions, hospitable to grain crops, did not generally favor the tuber. Thus, as Austin Bourke observes, potatoes and grains were good hedges against the failure of one or the other.[68] However, after 1750, encouraged by the increased commercialization of Irish agriculture, what John R. Butterly and Jack Shepherd call "a nutritional transition," the Irish poor gradually moved toward a state of potato dependency. First, providing two-and-a-half times the calories of an acre of wheat, the potato freed up more land for grain without diminishing a family's overall food supply.[69] Second, initially a "winter food" that helped to even out a family's supply of grains, the potato gradually became a substitute food. As the market value of grains increased and the rents rose, the more potatoes a family consumed, the more of its wheat, oats and barley, not to mention livestock, it could sell to help meet the rents. This shift from a varied diet to one dominated by the substitution of potatoes occurred at an uneven pace. Up until the 1770s, Irish potato dependency was associated with only the very poor. Even as late as the 1830s, Tyrone farmers in Ulster still enjoyed a mixed diet of oats and potatoes. However, by then wheaten bread had effectively disappeared from the cottages of many of Ireland's small farmers. To the extent that oatmeal, bacon, cabbage and beef remained a part of the peasant's diet, they were, as L. A. Clarkson and E. Margaret Crawford indicate, "squeezed [...] into the crevices of the year and converted [...] into luxuries."[70] By 1800 farming families working around eight or more acres still enjoyed a mixed diet. Below that acreage, however, most poor Irish farmers and laborers lived primarily on the tuber. It sustained the hundreds of thousands of small holders and cottiers whose labor made possible the increased export of grain to Britain.[71]

The potato was, therefore, not only the foundation of the country's demographic expansion but was central to the growth of its export-oriented commercial agricultural economy as well. Ireland's ability to maintain a dramatically rising population while

---

66. Butterly and Shepherd. *Hunger: The Biology and Politics of Starvation*, 112.
67. Bourke, *"The Visitation of God?"* 56, 104. For adoption of potatoes as fodder see 19, 38.
68. Ibid., 14.
69. For calories per acre see Overton, *Agricultural Revolution in England*, 102. For "nutritional transition" see Butterly and Shepherd, *Hunger: The Biology and Politics of Starvation*, 247–48.
70. For quote see Clarkson and Crawford, *Feast and Famine*, 70. For "wheaten bread" see Crawford, "Provincial Town Life in the Early Nineteenth Century," 49. For the adoption of the potato see Cullen, *The Emergence of Modern Ireland, 1600–1900*, 93, 145–46. For the potato as a substitute food see 157–59.
71. Dickson, "The Potato and Irish Diet Before the Great Famine," 18.

expanding its agricultural exports would have been impossible without a per-capita decline in the domestic consumption of market foods. By the mid-1830s in at least 26 counties, the potato provided 90 per cent of the calories for three-eighths of the population.[72] Yet, because of the potato's nutritional value, the Irish peasants' diet, although lacking *variety*, did not decline in either quantity or quality. Travelers in pre-Famine Ireland often commented on the apparent rude health of even the most ragged peasants and their children. They paid no serious nutritional penalty for potato dependency because the tuber supplied sufficient quantities of most necessary vitamins, especially vitamin C. The notable exceptions are vitamins A and D. However, some sour milk, fish and a bit of sunshine can help make up for these deficiencies. The potato also contains important proteins, starches and amino acids. Some vitamin-rich vegetables, such as cabbage and kale, were occasionally added to a poor family's pot. When not sold, oats could be also an important adjunct to the diet for those who could grow them, especially in the northeastern part of the country. Certain kinds of edible seaweeds, such as dillisk or dulse, as well as some salt fish, added "kitchen"—flavor and texture—to a monotonous dish of potatoes. Peasants living along the seaboard also supplemented their diet with shellfish and herring. On the west coast of Ireland, however, fishing, where it occurred, was usually a part-time and irregular pursuit, there being virtually no infrastructure to support a real market-based fishing trade in the west. Moreover, the shoals were fickle, and herring in particular could disappear from Irish waters at frequent intervals.[73]

The plentitude and the nutritional value of the potato supported rapid population growth in a variety of ways. Its abundance not only reduced mortality but also staved off malnutrition, which, according to Clarkson and Crawford, can delay the onset of puberty and dull sexual drive. The earlier a woman begins having children, the greater her potential fertility. Therefore, as the authors suggest, "when potatoes were abundant, they supported a population of fecund young women and sexually vigorous young men." The authors also note that the ready availability of potatoes and buttermilk may have encouraged early weaning (and, unfortunately, high infant mortality). Since nursing generally delays ovulation, early weaning may have contributed to making birth intervals in Ireland a bit shorter than elsewhere.[74] In various ways, then, the tiny, pratie plots of rural Ireland played a role similar to the factory jobs in industrial England. They enabled poor people to marry and begin families at a young age.

Potato cultivation did have some drawbacks, however. In the marginal lands amid the bogs and on the mountainsides of the west of Ireland, the soil is acidic. To offset this, potatoes required large quantities of animal or plant manures, making their gathering

---

72. Ibid., 19.
73. Clarkson and Crawford, *Feast and Famine*, 78, 81. For fisheries off Clare Island see Mac Cárthaigh, "Clare Island Folklife," 54–55. The lack of curing stations and the tendency of the peasantry to pawn their gear during hard times sharply curtailed the growth of west-coast fisheries; Gráda, *Ireland: A New Economic History: 1780–1939*, 147–48. On the role of oats see Bourke, *"The Visitation of God?"* figures 2 and 3 on p. 21.
74. See Clarkson and Crawford, *Feast and Famine*, 231–32. For causes of high infant mortality see McPartlin, "Diet, Politics and Disaster: The Great Irish Famine," 215–16.

and storing essential to a family's survival—literally a matter of life or death. For those living near the coast, seaweed provided excellent fertilizer. Farmers might use as much as 16 tons per acre. In such areas, guaranteed access to seaweed was crucial. According to Kevin Whelan, a farmer who had rights to gather seaweed was known in Irish as *fear talamh is trá*—"a man of land and strand." Seaweed was so important that kelp "farms" were established at various points along the Irish coast where strategically piled rocks promoted growth and collection. During the equinoctial tides, tourists watched and sketched women and girls filling their creels with seaweed to be carried on their backs up to their fields. The visitors seldom realized that such "picturesque" scenes represented an essential part of the Irish peasant's constant struggle for survival.[75]

Inland, animal waste was the primary source of manure. Apart from a family's pig and possibly a cow and some chickens, however, many small tenants and cottiers owned little in the way of livestock. (Grass and hay for a cow could cost £5 a year.[76]) Therefore, small children were charged with watching the road in front of the cottage so that they could scrape up the droppings of passing horses and cattle. In fact, animal manure was so precious that the collected droppings were piled by the cabin door (augmented by "the sweepings of the cottage," a.k.a. "night soil"). There, the manure could be guarded until used in planting. The sight of the ubiquitous manure pile before almost every cottage appalled British tourists, few of whom understood the extreme value of these noxious collections. Without strict attention to manure, the impressive potato yields of pre-Famine Ireland would never have been realized. Even so, many small farmers adopted the unpalatable Lumper variety because it required less manure than other types of potatoes.[77]

Although potato farming was less complicated than grain production, it was not quite as simple as poking the cutting from a potato into a hole in the ground and waiting for the harvest. As noted above, manure had to be collected and stored. In areas where the topsoil was thin, pratie beds had to be painstakingly built up with seaweed, crushed rock and sand. In the west of Ireland, which enjoys from 175 to over 200 rain-days a year, the soil is not only acidic but very wet.[78] Faced with such conditions, many small farmers, especially those on marginal land, resorted to an ancient raised-bed technique for growing both potatoes and grain in wet soil. Toward the end of the twentieth century, archaeologists uncovered the remnants of Neolithic farmsteads at the Céide Fields in northern Mayo. Visitors there may see the remnants of raised beds dug thousands of

---

75. For tourist descriptions of kelp gathering see William H. A. Williams, *Tourism, Landscape, and the Irish Character*, 55–56. For kelp farming see Bourke, *"The Visitation of God?"* 63–64. For quote see Kevin Whelan, "Landscape and Society on Clare Island," 76. For 16 tons see Knight, *Erris in the "Irish Highlands" and "The Atlantic Railway,"* 82.
76. Donnelly, *The Land and the People of Nineteenth-Century Cork*, 25.
77. Bourke, *"The Visitation of God?"* 64. For night soil see 63. For tourist reaction to the cabin-door manure pits see William H. A. Williams, *Tourism, Landscape, and the Irish Character*, 93–94.
78. In his *Shell Guide to Reading the Irish Landscape*, Frank Mitchell explains that, while the amount of rain that falls in Ireland is not particularly excessive, the *number* of days it rains is very high, impeding drying and drainage, 67.

years ago, when humans first tried to pioneer Ireland's Atlantic seaboard.[79] Millennia later, Irish farmers used similar techniques.

While farmers with enough good land might use their plows to create ridge-and-furrow fields, small farmers employed the spade to build up cultivation ridges, the so-called lazy beds, following the slope of the land to promote drainage. To prepare for planting, they dug the ground on either side of the intended bed, turning the sods inward to produce a ridge, leaving drains up to two feet deep running along either side. The turned-under grass provided some green manure, as well as some degree of weed control. At the same time, the digging process broke the "iron pan" beneath the surface of the soil. This mineral-rich dirt was added to the top of the ridge, along with the seed potato and any essential supplemental manure—seaweed, sand, animal droppings and/or peat dust. Planted on the dome of the ridge, the potato plant could grow above the wettest soil, while also receiving maximum exposure to the sun.[80] Depending on the quality of the soil and on drainage requirements, the raised beds might measure anywhere from three to ten feet across. They were used for grain crops, as well as for potatoes. These cultivation ridges have left their marks upon the Irish landscape. Long abandoned potato beds, some dating from the time of the Famine, can still be seen on hillsides and on long-uninhabited islands.[81]

One of the great advantages of the lazy-bed system was that it required no farm implements other than a spade of special construction, designed more for turning the soil than lifting it.[82] Spade cultivation allowed farmers to cultivate hilly and boggy land that could not be plowed. It also facilitated the careful building up of plaggen or man-made soils, which suggests that the small holders of Ireland were more like gardeners than farmers. Perhaps for that reason, the yields were often impressive. Properly managed, an acre could produce 6 tons of potatoes a year. Thus, a family could be fed for much of the year on the harvest of an acre or even less.[83]

Paring and burning was another ancient agricultural technique practiced by Irish farmers. Also known as "slash and burn," it is still used the world over as a quick method for bringing uncultivated land into use. In Ireland the fire heated the soil in the cold, damp

---

79. For ancient Irish raised-bed farming see O'Connor, *Living in a Coded Land*, 20–21.
80. According to Kevin Whelan, the ridges even create their own microclimate: air flowing from the top to the bottom of the ridges reduced the danger of frost, especially on bog land. See his "Landscape and Society on Clare Island," 74. See also Bourke, who points out that the beds were often shifted each year so that what was trench one season would be incorporated into a ridge the next; *"The Visitation of God?"* 66. For ridge-and-furrow type fields, Hull, "To Drain and Cultivate: Agriculture and 'Improvement'" at Ballykilcline," 170; also Evans, *Irish Folk Ways*, 140–44.
81. For cultivation ridges see Evans, *Personality of Ireland*, 40–41; Kevin Whelan, "Landscape and Society on Clare Island," 50. See also Mac Cárthaigh, "Clare Island Folklife," 52–53.
82. Evans, *Irish Folk Ways*, 145–50.
83. Feehan, "The Potato: Root of the Famine," 30. For potato yields see Bourke, *"The Visitation of God?"* 124; Turner, *After the Famine*, 7. Kevin Whelan claims that by the eve of the Famine, much of the cultivated land in the west of Ireland consisted of plaggan soil, built up over years of adding seaweed, sand and manure; "Landscape and Society on Clare Island," 74.

springtime, while the ash added nitrogen and potash (potassium) to the soil. Where this was the only fertilizer employed, however, the benefits of paring and burning were short lived. In the long run, if repeated too often, the technique can lead to soil exhaustion. Landowners condemned it, but tenants who wanted to sublet part of their holdings could command higher rents because of the practice. As F. H. A. Aalen points out, in the small farmer's never-ending search for more land and potatoes, paring and burning, along with raised-bed cultivation, helped extended the ecological range of Irish agriculture.[84]

Those who lived primarily on potatoes organized their whole lives around the crop. For example, since potatoes seldom last for more than nine months, by the beginning of summer a family's previous year's crop would be gone. Caught between spring planting and the late fall potato harvest, July and August were known as the "hungry months," representing an annual threat of malnutrition for many families, especially those with children.[85] They were also known as the "meal months" to those fortunate families who could afford to substitute oats or Indian meal (imported maize) for their still-growing potatoes. In summer, families with no money often had to take to the road. They would close their cabins and separate, with the men traveling as far as England or Scotland in search of work. For their part, the women and children begged from neighbors, who were usually little better off than themselves. One of the reasons why Irish poverty was so striking to pre-Famine tourists is because the "hungry months" coincided with the height of the summer tourist season, as well as seasonal begging. For example, traveling through Ireland in the 1830s, Leitch Ritchie described a typical family of "pauper peasants" in search of food: "A ragged mother, with a baby on her back, and two or three ragged children at her heels, and more rarely, the ragged father bringing up the rear [...] glide into the huts by the roadside."[86] When fall came and the potatoes were ready for lifting, the family would return to their cabin and pratie patch, hopeful that they would have enough food to see them into the next year.

As the poorer part of Irish society became increasingly dependent on potatoes, the more prolific varieties began to replace those of superior quality, leading to a serious loss of diversity. Austin Bourke points out that by the beginning of the nineteenth century the "superb varieties" that had earlier graced Irish tables were largely gone. For their own consumption, Ireland's small farmers and cottiers grew several kinds of potatoes, which, while below market standards for flavor and texture, were highly productive in boggy, acidic soil. And that was the essential thing: the *amount* of food that could be coaxed from a patch of land. This pressure for quantity over quality also derived from the labor that cottiers owed their landlords. Forced to work during spring and early summer, cottiers planted their own beds later with the lower quality but high-yield potatoes. This "people's

---

84. Aalen, *Man and Landscape in Ireland*, 158. See also Evans, *Irish Folk Ways,* 147; Daniel Grace, *The Great Famine in Nenagh Poor Law Union, County Tipperary*, 36–37; Salaman, *The History and Social Influence of the Potato*, 196.
85. For periodic malnutrition see McPartlin, "Diet, Politics and Disaster," 215. For impact on families with children see 215–16.
86. Ritchie, *Ireland: Picturesque and Romantic*, 2:24–25.

crop," not lifted until late October or even early November, extended the length of the "hungry" months.[87]

Among the most popular potato varieties were the Cup and the Irish Apple. However, the poorest people on the poorest land, especially in the west, relied primarily on just one variety for their own consumption, the "Lumper." This big, white, knobby tuber may have originated as cattle feed in England around the 1770s. Its first recorded appearance in Ireland was in 1808 in County Clare. Although very lumpy in appearance, the name may have derived from the term "Lumpers," referring to a category of workers on the British docks, many of whom came from the west of Ireland.[88] The Lumper was inferior in flavor and consistency; some said it tasted like wax or soap. Yet even when superior types of potatoes were grown for the market, it was the Lumper that the peasant family boiled in its pot. Therefore, although British visitors to Irish cabins were often offered one of the better-quality market potatoes as a token of hospitality, sometimes the Lumper was all that was on hand. In such instances, the visitors found themselves closer to the peasants' reality than they might ever have intended. Their meal would be noticeably undercooked. Half-raw at the center (sometimes referred to as "the bone in the potato"), it supposedly took longer to digest and therefore staved off hunger. Unfortunately, undercooking a potato also leaves many of its nutrients unreleased.[89] While unpalatable and somewhat less nutritious than other varieties, the Lumper had several important advantages. Although it did not keep as long as others, it produced a high-yield crop, 20–30 percent more than the somewhat better-quality Apple and Cup. Moreover, the Lumper could be successfully grown in poor soil with minimal manure. As several historians have pointed out, however, the Lumper's ubiquitous presence among the poorest families in the west was a sign of a declining standard of living. Little grown in the east and northeast, the Lumper predominated in the inferior lands of the west and southwest.[90]

Plentiful and nutritious as it was, the potato had some disadvantages. As already noted, unlike grain, potatoes would not keep a full year. Also, they were a bulky crop, difficult to store and costly to transport beyond local markets. In fact, only two percent of the Irish potato crop was exported. This meant that bumper harvests were used primarily as fodder for Irish livestock.[91] Moreover, because it required no milling or refining, the potato added little to the local economic infrastructure. As the British government was to learn in its attempts at famine relief in the 1840s, areas where potatoes predominated

---

87. Sexton, "Diet in pre-Famine Ireland," 42–43; Bourke, *"The Visitation of God?"* 22, 45–46.
88. Bourke, *"The Visitation of God?"* 38–39.
89. For tourist reports on the "bone in the potato" see William H. A. Williams, *Tourism, Landscape, and the Irish Character*, 98–99. For the nutritional problems of undercooking potatoes see Clarkson and Crawford, *Feast and Famine*, 184. For the Lumper's taste and texture see Bourke, *"The Visitation of God?"* 40.
90. Austin Bourke points out that the Lumper flourished west of a line drawn from roughly the town of Sligo southeast to Waterford, figure 1, p. 21. See also Macdonagh, "The Economy and Society, 1830–45," 222; Donnelly, *The Land and the People of Nineteenth-Century Cork*, 25-26.
91. Mokyr, *Why Ireland Starved*, 279.

often lacked the kinds of market networks that might have facilitated the distribution of imported food. Thus, extensive potato cultivation in the western Ireland probably slowed the evolution of a modern, integrated economy that might have made it easier to deal with the crises caused by the potato blight.[92]

The potato economy presented an additional impediment to the development of modern agriculture in Ireland. As noted earlier, "high farming," the most advanced form of land management and crop rotation, encouraged farmers to replace fallow pastureland with fields devoted to "green crops," nitrogen-fixing plants, such as clover. These increased the fertility of the land while providing fodder for livestock. Unlike natural fallow pasture, however, such crops required fertilizer. Unfortunately, as explained above, potatoes also demanded large amounts of manure. Therefore, with potatoes taking up at least 20 percent of tillage land in most Irish counties, there was not enough fertilizer to support both full-scale modern farming and extensive potato cultivation.[93]

In good years, of course, there were more than enough potatoes. Sometimes harvests were so abundant that part of the crop was left to rot in the fields, leading to deep feelings of guilt when the Famine struck. Not every year's harvest yielded a surplus, however. Just as a good potato harvest produced a positive knock-on effect (plenty to eat, adequate supply of seed potatoes, a well-fed pig to sell), a bad one extended its negative results well into the future. If a family's food supply ran out before spring, the seed potatoes required for that year's planting might be consumed. Also, scarcity meant that there was no surplus to feed a pig, often a family's main source of rent money. In Austin Bourke's words, "The repercussions from a poor potato crop bore hardest on, and persisted longest for, the class least able to bare them."[94]

In good years, however, even poor families might have surplus potatoes, which, along with the stalks, were carefully banked—inside a pig. While British tourists regarded the pig as a half-amusing, half-appalling totem of the Irish peasantry, it was, in fact, an integral part of the potato system. Until the eighteenth century, pigs had been primarily fed on grain and were, therefore, expensive to raise. When farmers eventually realized that potatoes could feed swine, as well as people, pigs became cheap and plentiful and an important part of Ireland's export market. It is no surprise, then, that the Irish porcine population increased along with potato-dependent people.[95] Of course, only better-off farmers could afford to raise pigs for their table. For the average peasant, the pig was never dinner but rather a guest—"the gintleman that pays the rint"—to be fed on the family's surplus potatoes, which otherwise would have gone to waste. A kind of magical piggy bank that could convert spare potatoes and their stalks into much-needed coins, the pig also contributed vital manure, essential to growing its own food.

---

92. Ibid.
93. Ibid., 162–64. See also Grace, *The Great Famine in Nenagh Poor Law Union, County Tipperary* 6. For the extent of potato cultivation see Solar, "The Potato Famine in Europe," 114–15.
94. Austin Bourke, *"The Visitation of God?"* 51.
95. Cullen, *The Emergence of Modern Ireland, 1600–1900*, 151–52.

Since its primary function was to be sold for rent, the peasant's pig had to be properly cared for. Pigs are not hardy enough to thrive outdoors in Ireland's cool, wet environment. Fortunately, the Irish had always admired and looked after their animals. Therefore, the peasantry thought nothing of bringing their pigs in at night to sleep with the family, much to the horror of British observers. Anglo-Irish writer T. Crofton Croker once tried to convince a subtenant to build a small byer for his pig to keep it out of the house. "Sure then," was the response, "and who has a better right to be in it? Isn't he the man of the house? And isn't he that will pay the rent?" Only a few observers came to understand and appreciate the role of the pig in peasant life. Henry D. Inglis learned to "bless the sight [of the pig in a cabin] and to pity more, the poor wretches who possessed no pig." However, as Oliver MacDonagh suggests, since the pig's sole function was to be converted into rent money, his almost ubiquitous presence among poor farmers was not a sign of good fortune but rather one of desperation.[96]

The Rundale System

The potato was the central element within the intricate dynamics of people and land use in Ireland. It lay at the heart of the country's dramatic population explosion, which, according to Kevin Whelan, was "accommodated by massive land reclamation, intensive subdivision and expansion into previously unsettled areas." In other words, potatoes made possible—and necessary—the constant creation of new potato ground. One of the principal mechanisms facilitating this accomplishment was the rundale system. Although similar to agricultural communes found in the medieval and early modern periods, many Irish rundale villages, especially in the west, were the products of distinctly modern economic forces. Beginning in the eighteenth century, many families, faced with rising rents, engaged in a form of joint tenancy by pooling their resources. Often interrelated, these families would rent land in common, usually some combination of tillable patches and rough pasturage. The resulting rundale settlements, sometimes called "clachans," were structured around the traditional infield/outfield system.[97] The tillable "infield" was divided among the families, each having its own individual, unfenced strips. These were periodically redistributed, so that every family received an equal share of both the more, as well as the less, productive land. (The redistribution was carried out by the *argid rí* or "money king," a sort of village headman, who also collected and paid the

---

96. MacDonagh, "The Economy and Society, 1830–45," 222. For T. Crofton Croker see his *Researches in the South of Ireland*, 103. For Henry D. Inglis, see *A Journey throughout Ireland, during the Spring, Summer and Autumn of 1834*, 1:79. For tourist reaction to pigs see William H. A. Williams, *Tourism, Landscape, and the Irish Character*, 91–93.
97. For eighteenth-century origins of the modern rundale system see Dickson, *New Foundations Ireland, 1660–1800*, 123–24. For Kevin Whelan quote, see "Landscape and Society on Clare Island," 73. The word "rundale" originated in England as a term applied to certain types of nucleated villages. Both "clachan" and "rundale" were applied to Scotland before being transferred to Ireland; see Kevin Whelan, "Settlement Patterns in the West of Ireland in the Pre-Famine Period," 63.

rent to the landlord.) These tillable sections usually consisted of a patchwork of glacial drift scattered amid boggy land. Access to seaweed, essential for manure, and peat was also evenly distributed among the families. Moreover, a certain amount of the village's work was carried out through the *meitheal* tradition of communal labor. Thus, in Donald E. Jordan's words, the rundale system "fostered a general spirit of co-operation that minimized the risks associated with cultivating fragile crops in poor soil."[98]

It was not a simple system to administer, however. E. Estyn Evans notes that "the word used to describe the confusion of innumerable scattered plots and tortuous access ways among the infield was 'throughother' [from *trína chéile*], a word which has often been applied to other aspects of Irish life." Robert James Scally, writing about the townland of Ballykilcline, County Roscommon, suggests that "throughotherness" extended to the interpenetration of a rundale settlement's culture and economics with the lives of the inhabitants. It turned their attention inward against the outside world. The apparent jumbled chaos of a rundale village hid an intricate system of relationships—mutual obligations and loyalties—that represented the peasants' defense against an indifferent, if not hostile world. What outside observers saw as typical Irish disorder was the *only* thing that made sense to the rundale inhabitants.[99] Nevertheless, the rundale townlands were by no means closed off from the rest of the world. Artifacts and pottery fragments found at the historical archaeological excavations at Ballykilcline, County Roscommon, suggest that residents were, according to Charles E. Orser, Jr, and David Rider, "the active participants in a widespread market network, and they manipulated the agricultural system—as best they could—to their advantage until hunger and eviction made further resistance impossible."[100]

Rundale outfields, usually consisting of rough pasture, were generally used as commons for grazing. The cattle not only produced milk and butter, much of which was sold to make rent, but also the manure that was essential for the infields' potato and oat beds. In fact, the size and productivity of the infield depended very much on the number of cattle the settlement's outfields could support.[101] In areas where the outfield ran up into hills and mountains, the villagers engaged in a modified type of transhumance called "booleying" (from the Gaelic *buaile* or milking place). In summer, young people would take the livestock into the upland pastures, living there in rough huts while watching over the animals, collecting milk and churning butter. Then in fall they returned the stock to the sheltered lowlands. Booleying also had the advantage of getting the cattle away from the crops growing in the village's unfenced infields.[102] With most of the better-quality produce—oats and barley, along with butter and livestock—slated for market to pay the rent, potatoes were the foundation of a community's domestic economy, indeed its very survival. Thus, as village populations grew and individual holdings became smaller, an

---

98. Jordan, *Land and Popular Politics in Ireland*, 57.
99. Scally, *The End of Hidden Ireland*, 235; Evans, *The Personality of Ireland*, 60. For *trína chéile* see Dolan, *A Dictionary of Hiberno-English: The Irish Use of English*, 271.
100. Ryder and Orser, Jr., "From Farmers to Defendants," 20.
101. Kevin Whelan, "The Modern Landscape," 81.
102. For booleying see Ibid., 80; see also Aalen, *Man and Landscape in Ireland*, 183.

ever-greater portion of the land had to be devoted to potatoes and less to cash crops. By the 1830s only middle-sized individual farms were seriously contributing food to the export market.[103] The rundale townlands largely feed themselves.

A townland's cabins were usually situated on the least arable land nearest a road or along the seashore, often in an apparently haphazard, disorganized fashion. This explains the alternate term for a rundale village—"clachan,"—a Gaelic word suggesting a jumbled, disorganized scattering of stones. One English visitor to Dooagh in Achill, Mayo, described its "miserable huts" looking "as if they had been shaken out of a bag, and had lain as they fell. There was scarcely anything that could be called a street, and a stranger set down in the middle of the village would have found it difficult to get out again." The visual disorder of the clachans often shocked British observers, who saw them as the epitome of both Irish poverty and carelessness. If Irish sloth and want had a home, visitors were convinced it was to be found in the clachans. Shambolic in appearance, the rundale settlements had none of the amenities or internal organization associated with English villages. A correspondent for *News of the World* described one clachan as providing "just room, with care, to ride my horse on the crooked pathway between the dunghills and cesspools."[104]

By the end of the eighteenth century, rundale settlements were spreading into the marginal lands west of the Shannon and the Bann and along the drumlin belt that divided Ulster from the rest of Ireland. Far from being archaic relics of an earlier age, Kevin Whelan describes the rundales as "a response to the surging demographic profile of Ireland between 1600 and 1840." They were "a functioning feature of the aggressive spread of settlement into adverse environmental territory," along the fringes of the Atlantic coast and in the less fertile parts of Ulster. Through this type of settlement, people with little means could survive on marginal lands, leading to a phenomenon that few visitors to pre-Famine Ireland failed to notice: the poorer the land, the denser the population. Once established, clachans usually continued to grow as they absorbed their own ever-expanding numbers. Whelan notes that between 1770 and 1840 the population on marginal uplands increased to five times that of the more fertile lowlands.[105] Historian Breandán Mac Suibhne notes that people who were old in the 1830s had seen the populations of the West Donegal townlands triple, even quadruple in their lifetimes. Some rundales added a second cluster of cabins with their own infields and outfields, pushing into what outsiders might have considered wasteland. However, as Mac Suibhne argues, in the crowded townlands of Ireland there was no such thing as "wasteland." Rather there was at least "rough pasture for cattle and a source of turf, and the odd rabbit, or pheasant, and reeds for thatching."[106]

---

103. Jordan, *Land and Popular Politics in Ireland*, 57.
104. *News of the World*, October 5, 1845 (2). "Miserable huts" quote found in Kevin Whelan's, "Born Astride a Grave," 208.
105. Kevin Whelan, "The Modern Landscape," 84. For quote see Kevin Whelan's "Settlement Patterns in the West of Ireland in the Pre-Famine Period," 62, 64.
106. Suibhne, *The End of Outrage*, 86–87, 89.

A rundale settlement offered several advantages to a landlord. It provided rent from subprime lands without requiring the investment a single penny on improvement. Since the rent was paid in common, the landlord did not have to worry about collecting from individual tenants. Moreover, the clachans, serving as social and economic outlets for an overflowing population, were essentially self-governing. On the other hand, the rundale system did encourage the process of subdivision, which might have frustrated a landlord's desire to consolidate his land. Sometimes, as in parts of Donegal, "squaring the land" involved breaking up clachans and redistributing consolidated holdings among the tenants. The goal, however, was less focused on improving the land than on improving the rents, which might increase by 20 percent.[107] This may be why the number of rundale settlements started to decline after 1815. Even County Roscommon saw a marked decrease after 1830. In the west, where their numbers remained strong, Mayo was the only county where clachans represented the predominant form of land tenure at the time of the Famine.[108]

Nevertheless, rundale settlements still remained an important feature of Irish rural life. They most clearly illustrate the systemic interaction among population pressures, land use and potato monoculture. It was as though the potato itself, through the work of the rundale inhabitants, cottiers and squatters, brought new land, reclaimed from the bogs, into existence. Summing up the role of the clachans, Kevin Whelan contends, "Taken together, the potato and the lazy-bed had a striking long-term settlement impact. They facilitated the shift in population density from east to west, from good land to poor land, from port hinterlands and valleys, to bogs, mountains and islands. The potato, not Cromwell, peopled the west of Ireland."[109]

Monoculture and the Cybernetics of the Potato Economy

To fully understand Whelan's statement, it might be helpful to turn to cybernetics and the concept of feedback loops. According to cybernetics, or systems theory as it is more usually called, the term "negative feedback" is defined as a self-correcting process that maintains the status quo. If things move too far in one direction, negative feedback may pull the system back toward equilibrium. "Positive feedback," on the other hand, may drive a system beyond its norms. Rather than correct a drift from the equilibrium, positive feedback tends to reinforce imbalances within a system. By 1845 one-third of the Irish population—the residents of the townlands and their clachans, along with the conacre families, cottiers and many small farmers—were caught in a cybernetic trap created

---

107. For "squaring" for rents, see ibid., 89, 91. See also Dorian, *The Outer Edge of Ulster*, 236–37.
108. For landlords see also Kevin Whelan, "Settlement Patterns in the West of Ireland in the Pre-Famine Period," 69. For Roscommon see Huggins, *Social Conflict in Pre-Famine Ireland*, 53. For Mayo see Green, "Agriculture," 113. For consolidation of rundale lands see Cullen, *The Emergence of Modern Ireland, 1600–1900*, 49, 79–80.
109. Kevin Whelan, "Landscape and Society in Clare," 76. See also his "Pre-and Post-Famine Landscape Change," 20. For importance of land reclamation see Donnelly, *The Land and the People of Nineteenth-Century Cork*, 26–28.

by a series of positive feedback loops. More people required more land to grow more potatoes to feed more people, who then had to find more land to grow more potatoes, and so it went, with each iteration driving the system further out of balance.

Another way to understand this process is to turn to the related field of ecology and to think of the potato as an invasive species. When an alien plant or animal is introduced into an ecosystem, it often disrupts the established norms within the system by interfering with or bypassing the nexus of preexisting negative feedback loops that had maintained its previous equilibrium. This describes the effect the potato had upon Irish agriculture, even though it was a cultivated rather than a wild plant. Its fecundity, high nutritional value and adaptability disrupted the country's tradition of mixed farming with its strong pastoral influence. The resulting potato monoculture reorganized the foundation of Ireland's rural society. Bypassing traditional restraints (negative feedback loops) on population growth, this monoculture supported the growth of a vast, cheap labor pool of several million people who were primarily dependent upon potatoes for their survival. Moreover, by enabling small farmers to substitute potatoes for market produce—grains, livestock—the monoculture made it possible for them to meet increasingly high rents, thus sidestepping previous demographic restraints. The potato monoculture also underwrote the expansion of grain production, as well as the growth of Ireland's porcine population. Destined for sale and export, Paddy's potato-fed pig was raised to pay the rent, not to feed the family. These rents, in turn, encouraged subdivision throughout the socioeconomic pyramid with rent farming at the upper end and subsistence on tiny plots at the bottom. The monoculture, therefore, supported an ever-increasing poverty-stricken population, which, in the absence of non-farm employment opportunities, was locked into agriculture for its support. This, in turn, maintained increasing pressure on both land and rents. As Kevin Whelan points out, this situation resulted from Ireland's loss of balance between pastoralism and cultivation: "The equilibrium of land use prior to the potato emphasized pastoralism at the expense of tillage. In the west of Ireland, the spread of the potato deranged the traditional balance between tillage and pasture."[110]

The potato's invasive role, therefore, should be understood in systemic rather than in linear terms of simple cause and effect. In a linear system, such as a series of falling dominoes, Factor A impacts Factor B, which in turn impacts Factor C. In systemic interactions, however, Factors A, B and C continuously interact in a loop, as it were. As F. H. A. Aalen suggests, "Population growth and farm subdivision once commenced, reinforced each other in a cumulative way, and cause and effect are thus hard to separate." Aalen thus sees the expansion of potato cultivation as something that "facilitated population growth rather than caused it."[111] To put it another way, potato monoculture was the catalyst that disrupted Irish agriculture.

By 1820, Ireland's potato system was, to borrow another term from cybernetics, in a "runaway" state. Negative feedback loops that might have constrained it were overwhelmed by positive feedback that kept driving the system beyond equilibrium.

---

110. Kevin Whelan, "Pre-and Post-Famine Landscape Change," 25,
111. See Aalen, *Man and Landscape in Ireland*, 158.

Thus, Ireland's population exploded. However, as mentioned earlier, after 1820 marriage rates began to decline, the pace of emigration increased and Ireland's rate of population growth slowed. At the same there was a gradual shift in land usage away from tillage and back to pasturage. The restraints of negative feedback upon the system were beginning to reassert themselves. Nevertheless, their strength was limited while the positive feedback within the potato economy remained strong, continuing to expand the country's population of cheap labor.

Ireland's agrarian labor force was cheap not just because it lived on potatoes. It was cheap because the potato sustained more laborers than could be fully employed. There was never enough work. The average agricultural laborer may have worked three to five days a week but only during planting and harvest seasons. He might have earned 6d to 8d a day for an annual wage of £10 to £15.[112] And yet, even at such marginal wages, the population of the Irish peasantry continued to expand, albeit at a slowing rate. Since they grew their own potatoes, built and maintained their own cabins and often raised some livestock or poultry, this very poor, semi-self-employed labor force was not constrained by the limited opportunities for employment that faced them. In this sense, the Irish rural poor enjoyed a degree of independence unknown to the poor people in industrial England. Thus, even in the face of tightening constraints after 1820, the potato economy shielded many poor people, particularly in the west, from the lure of emigration and even from restraints on marriage. While rising expectations might have encouraged better-off farmers to delay marriage, those with slim hopes for betterment had little incentive to remain single.[113] Caught up in the potato monoculture, they appeared to operate beyond the influence of normal, negative feedback loops. As David Lloyd observes, what the British regarded as the "terrifying abundance" of potatoes allowed "the Irish to defy a fundamental law of political economy, which is that over time the pool of labor comes into equilibrium with the capital available." Lloyd sees the Irish rundale societies as "viable" alternatives to Britain's market-driven agriculture, providing the Irish poor with a degree of independence that seemed subversive within the context of England's wage system. And all the while the system, propelled by positive feedback, enabled the poor to produce an abundance of food, a significant part of which was funneled off to Britain.[114] However, this "viability" was very fragile, akin, at best, to that of life on a shrinking ice flow approaching the equator.

As Ireland entered the 1840s, the positive feedback loops within the potato economy continued to limit the effects of the negative feedback that might otherwise have encouraged a more rapid adjustment of Ireland's population to its resources. Yet, while Ireland's potato system may have appeared stable on a year-to-year basis, no system, especially one in runaway, remains sustainable over the long haul. By 1845 Ireland's population seemed on track to reach nine million by the end of the decade. However, without an extensive broadening of its non-agricultural sector, there seems no way the country could have

---

112. Mac Atasney, *"This Dreadful Visitation:" The Famine; in Lurgan/Portadown*, 17.
113. Jordan, "The Famine and its Aftermath in County Mayo," 42.
114. Lloyd, "The Indigent Sublime: Specters of Irish Hunger," 158, 159-60.

continued to maintain the demographic patterns of continual growth that characterized most of Western Europe. Eventually, neither the potato nor cultural inhibitions regarding emigration could have stayed the buildup of negative feedback pressures pushing and pulling people off the island. Timothy W. Guinnane goes so far as to argue that, in the absence of industrialization, Ireland could not have sustained the pre-Famine levels of its rural population. He maintains that, even without the potato blight, the country's population would still have fallen to the levels actually reached in 1911.[115]

In this sense, perhaps the ghost of Malthus did hover over rural Ireland. The potato system retarded the power of some of the "checks" or negative feedback loops that might have reduced population pressure on inferior land. As a result, the Irish peasantry gradually became trapped in the highly specialized ecological niche of a potato monoculture that seemed to guarantee a year-to-year survival. When the Famine came, however, that promise vanished. This is not to suggest, however, that Ireland's rural poor somehow *chose* their potato niche. Far from it. During the Famine, the Quakers' Central Relief Committee in Dublin summed up the situation very succinctly: "The people lived on potatoes because they were poor; and they were poor because they could not obtain regular employment […] [arising] from the state of the law, and the practice respecting the occupation and ownership of the land."[116] In other words, Ireland's poor were *driven* into the cybernetic trap of the potato economy by the combination of land ownership, land use, commercial agriculture and the lack of non-agricultural employment. When the blight struck there was no way out.

---

115. Guinnane, "The Great Irish Famine and Population: The Long View," 305.
116. Society of Friends, *Transactions of the Central Relief Committee of the Society of Friends*, 9.

Chapter Seven

PHYTOPHTHORA INFESTANS AND THE COLLAPSE OF THE POTATO ECONOMY

Vulnerability or Inevitability

The preceding chapter has shown how patterns of land ownership and use, demographic pressures and monoculture, all tied to the export market, combined to create a situation in which around one-third of the Irish population, some 3.3 million people, survived almost exclusively on potatoes.[1] No system can continue to grow without approaching limits, however, and, as early as the 1830s, Ireland's potato economy was already under pressure. Patrick Duffy's comment regarding County Monaghan's imbalanced "population-resource relationship" may be applied to much of Ireland "The resources of the land clearly had become too fragmented, farms had become minuscule, there were too many people with limited or no access to the land, and fewer and fewer of these had access to non-farm incomes." Thanks, moreover, to excessive subdivision, too many small holdings exhibited the results of overcropping and overgrazing.[2] Traveling around Mount Bellew in County Galway in 1839, Rev. Caesar Otway complained that the land was "miserably cut up and proportioned out into small tenures, where the people pursue their miserable tillage of potatoes and oats." Climbing the slopes of Slieve Gullion in South Armagh in 1839 while gathering information for the Poor Law Inquiry, Jonathan Binns discovered just how dramatically demographic expansion had impressed itself upon the landscape: "The mountain is cultivated as near to its summit as food for man will grow; and the potato and corn [grain] fields are in some places so steep, and apparently so perpendicular, as to resemble, when viewed from the road, pictures in square frames hanging against the walls of a room." By that time cultivation had reached the 800-foot contour level on its way to 1,000 feet.[3]

If a poor potato harvest could spell extreme hardship for those living on the edge of survival, a massive, repetitive failure of the crop could only lead to disaster. But was that inevitable? Was the potato blight simply a deadly random act of nature, unprecedented and unpredictable, which brought down a system that, however vulnerable, might have

---

1. Bourke, *"A Visitation of God?"* 52.
2. Duffy, "The Famine in County Monaghan," 171. See also Jordan, *Land and Popular Politics in Ireland: The Potato and the Great Irish Famine*, 57.
3. For contour levels see Kevin Whelan, "Pre-and Post-Famine Landscape Change," 24, 26. For Caesar Otway see *A Tour of Connaught*, 164, 166. For Jonathan Binns see *The Miseries and Beauties of Ireland*, 1:205.

eventually corrected itself over time? Or, had Ireland finally arrived at the end game for which centuries of colonialism and decades of short-sighted and unwise policies and practices had prepared it? Was the blight the unforeseen result of high-risk agricultural practices? Or, was Ireland's potato economy like a house of cards, an inherently unsustainable construction, awaiting the inevitable bump that would bring it down?

It has long been tempting to see the collapse of Ireland's potato economy foreshadowed in the country's long struggle to feed itself. Through the eighteenth century until 1845, Ireland experienced a succession of subsistence crises of varying severity: 1728–29, 1740–41, 1744, 1757, 1783, 1799–1801, 1816–17, 1822 and 1831. Poor harvests continued in the later 1830s and early 1840s. Not all were due exclusively to failures of the potato crop. Some of the shortfalls represented general crop failures caused by unusual climatic conditions. An infamous example was the terrible crisis of 1740–41, when unusually cold weather followed by draught caused severe hardship throughout Europe and a deadly famine in Ireland.[4] After the 1740s, however, most of Ireland's food crises were localized. Serious widespread excess mortality occurred in only a few instances: 1800–01 and 1816–17, resulting in 40,000 and 60,000 famine deaths respectively.[5] The latter famine was due to a series of cold, very wet summers, most likely generated by several massive volcanic eruptions in Southeast Asia in 1809 and 1815. In the latter year one of the largest eruptions of the millennia occurred on the island of Tambora in Indonesia. The combination of these events seems to have produced a brief period of global cooling, making the decade from 1809 to 1819 one of the wettest and coldest on record. Global temperatures, estimated to have declined by 1.5 degrees Fahrenheit, turned 1816 into the "year without a summer," resulting in the last great general subsistence crisis in Western Europe and North America. In Ireland, unseasonably low temperatures and incessant rain ruined most of the crops and prevented the peat from drying. By 1817 the situation had begun to improve, but by then "famine fever," primarily typhus, ravaged the country.[6] Ireland had barely recovered before it was hit by a less serious crop failure in 1822, followed by smaller one a decade later.

This history of subsistence crises has encouraged some to believe that Ireland was building up to a disaster from which there would be no escape. As Cormac Ó Gráda has observed, "Most traditional historiography, whether Malthusian or nationalist, implies that the Great Famine was part of Ireland's destiny."[7] Ó Gráda, however, regards this as an example of "history written backwards" based on an assumption that events that precede a crisis must in all cases have contributed to it. This creates an impression of inevitability based on a faulty understanding of causation. Ó Gráda can find no evidence

---

4. For dates of food crises see Cullen, *The Emergence of Modern Ireland, 1600–1900*, 97; Clarkson and Crawford, *Feast or Famine*, 126–27. For famines in 1720s and 1740s see Dickson, "The Other Great Irish Famine," as well as his *Artic Ireland*. For 1840s see Ó Murchadha, *Sable Wings over the Land*, 26.
5. Ó Gráda, *Ireland Before and After the Famine*, 4–5.
6. Wood, *Tambora, The Eruption that Changed the World*, 187–88. For volcanic eruptions see 37–39, 41; for temperatures and rainfall see 177, 178, 181.
7. Ó Gráda, *The Great Irish Famine*, 68.

suggesting that the succession of pre-Famine shortfalls in food production were linked or that they were even becoming progressively worse. On the contrary, he notes that Dr. William Wilde's analysis of census data of 1841 failed to identify any deaths by starvation attributable to the crisis of 1831. Moreover, virtually no one, not even those knowledgeable and concerned about conditions in Ireland, had predicted imminent disaster. Ó Gráda, therefore, concludes that, on the eve of the Famine, there was little evidence of life becoming increasingly precarious. If anything, improvements in government relief seemed to have reduced the threat of starvation. Nonetheless, he does admit that, given the economic conditions, Ireland's massive "rural proletariat" did experience increased "immiseration." As Catherine Flanagan, summing up conditions around Kinsale, concludes, while the larger farmers were doing well, small farmers and laborers were getting poorer.[8]

Reviewing the history of food crises between 1700 and 1845, L. A. Clarkson and E. Margaret Crawford argue that, except for 1740–41, none of the critical years in which crops failed in Ireland resulted in "wholesale famines." As noted above, in only a few periods, 1800–01 and 1816–19, do records reveal serious excess mortality. Furthermore, the authors claim that Ireland's food supply was no more problematic than elsewhere in Europe during this period.[9] However, Patrick Fitzgerald has compared 26 subsistence crises in Ireland with conditions in England and Scotland between 1600 and 1845. While such events gradually disappeared from Great Britain, Ireland remained more likely to experience privation. Still, it is important to note that the most severe food crises had been caused by bad weather, which affected all crops, not just the potato. So, according to Clarkson and Crawford, that made what happened in 1845 "unique in cause, scale and timing."[10]

Indeed, the issue of timing was crucial. Ó Gráda contends that it was Ireland's ill-luck that the blight appeared in the mid-1840s. An earlier appearance would have impacted a smaller population. Later, and the belated adoption of bluestone—copper sulfate—to suppress the fungus might have limited the blight's devastating results. In addition, later British governments, less dominated by laissez-faire economics and moralistic philosophies, might have rendered more effective relief. Moreover, demographic pressures might have been eased by increased emigration, thanks to the lure of industrial jobs in post–Civil War America and the advent of cheaper transatlantic fares. Marriage rates might have continued to decline as well, and landlords and farming families might have become less enamored with subdivision, forcing many young people to follow the pull of chain migration to North America and the colonies. Under such circumstances, a later appearance of the potato blight might have impacted a smaller at-risk and perhaps more mobile population, thus averting catastrophe.[11]

---

8. Flanagan, *The Great Famine in Kinsale*, 19. For Ó Gráda see *Ireland: A New Economic History, 1780–1939*, 84–85.
9. Clarkson and Crawford, *Feast and Famine*, 131–33.
10. Ibid., 128. See also Fitzgerald, "'The Great Hunger?' Changing Patterns of Crisis," 102. For the author's list of Irish subsistence crises from 1600–1845 see tables on pp. 115–22.
11. See Ó Gráda, *Great Irish Famine*, 68.

So, instead of viewing Ireland as marching inexorably toward the brink of disaster in 1845, it is quite possible to imagine that, without the blight, the country might have muddled through to a gradual correction, which, as previously suggested, was in fact underway. Still, any transition away from potato dependency and subdivision would have been neither smooth nor painless. Even without a massive famine at mid-century, pressures on landlords and peasants alike would have continued to increase. Expanding periods of hunger and high rates of evictions (to make way for cattle) would very likely have been accompanied by increased agrarian violence and political instability. And the process would certainly have involved significant population decline through immigration. Nevertheless, disaster was not inevitable. Clarkson and Crawford argue, "Had it not been for the fungus and the Great Famine, Ireland would not be burdened with the image of a poor and hungry land. Its history and its historiography would have been different."[12]

While the last part of that statement may be valid, the first part is not, however. Even granting a tendency for British observers to exaggerate the nature of Irish poverty, Ireland went into 1845 with "the image of a poor and hungry land" stamped indelibly upon it. As noted earlier, decades of travel accounts, newspaper articles and government reports had bestowed upon Ireland an almost unique image of poverty. Whatever its validity, that image helped shape Britain's response to the potato blight. And for the bottom third of Ireland's population, the image was accurate enough. Despite some real advances in the Irish economy since the seventeenth century, with the living standards of the lowest third of the population at subsistence level Ireland remained a poor country. As Louis Cullen states, when trying to account for the Famine, "poverty counts." Moreover, Ireland's poverty was not cyclical, but, as Patrick Fitzgerald points out, "sustained and related to structural problems." Describing the townlands of west Donegal, Breandán Mac Suibhne claims that, even in the best of times, the people there lived "barely above the waterline of despair." As John R. Butterly and Jack Shepherd note, since it was only the poor who starved during the Famine, it was poverty that underwrote the crisis. This puts the role of the potato in its proper perspective. In Cullen's words, when the blight struck, "it was not the potato but the inability to replace it in a crisis which is the most relevant feature."[13]

A hungry land may not be a starving land, but it is one in which some large portion of its population exists perpetually on the brink of starvation. Take for example, the seasonal migration of Irish agricultural laborers during the "hungry months" of July and August. Leaving their homes to seek work elsewhere, their wives also took to the road with the children to beg for their survival. Such large-scale migrations are one of the typical responses to the *threat* of famine.[14] In Ireland's case, this seasonal movement marked a practical if difficult response to the stark fact that thousands of Irish families knew

---

12. Clarkson and Crawford, *Feast and Famine*, 197.
13. Cullen, *The Emergence of Modern Ireland, 1600–1900*, 250, 251. Fitzgerald, "'The Great Hunger?' Irish Famine: Changing Patterns of Crisis," 102; Mac Suibhne, *The End of Outrage: Post-Famine Adjustment in Rural Ireland*, 8–9. 102. Butterly and Shepherd, *Hunger: The Biology and Politics of Starvation*, 47.
14. Ó Gráda, *Famine: A Short History*, 81–89.

that they would run out of food *every year*. In other words, they annually faced potential famines that were built into the system.

Nevertheless, burdened by poverty and dependent on the potato, Ireland's agricultural patch-worked system seemed to hold together. For the most part people were fed, *and* food was exported. Clackson and Crawford do not see Ireland's peculiar combination of potatoes, land use and population as "working over centuries toward a tragic climax." In their view, there was nothing inexorable about the Great Famine of the 1840s. They argue that Ireland's agricultural system "kept the Malthusian specter at bay." They do admit that in the process "a precarious ecological edifice was constructed." Yet, they regard this as the "price" to be paid for the country's ability to fully exploit the adoption of a nutritious food, to bring marginal lands into cultivation, to feed its people and to export a surplus to Britain, all the while dramatically expanding its population.[15] Thus, historians like Ó Gráda, Clarkson and Crawford correctly reject attempts to interject simplistic concepts of inevitability into explanations of the Famine. Nevertheless, their recourse to words such as "precarious ecological edifice" and "price" and "immiseration," may leave the door to inevitability at least slightly ajar. An edifice may eventually crumble; prices must be paid; immiseration may end in death. Such words seem only slightly less haunted by inevitability than Kevin Whelan's "potato precipice" toward which he sees Ireland relentlessly sliding.[16]

While Clarkson and Crawford criticize Whelan for implying that the potato economy was creating serious ecological damage to land and plants, his real point seems to be that an agricultural system based on potato dependency, pushing the land beyond its carrying capacity, kept the rural poor at the edge of survival. In a similar vein, Austin Bourke, reviewing the pre-Famine decades, suggests: "So, at an accelerating tempo, the condition of the people spiraled down to an ultimate and unavoidable disaster." Under the subheading "The potato as an instrument of disaster," Bourke states that an "unrestricted potato economy contained the seed of its ultimate destruction." He argues that, over a thirty- to fifty-year period, Ireland had moved ever closer to "inevitable disaster." Except for the word "inevitable," Bourke's comments, along with those of Whelan, do not seem all that far from Clarkson and Crawford's "precarious ecological edifice."[17] Admittedly, Ireland's accomplishment in expanding its food production between 1700 and 1845 was impressive. Yet, surely the ultimate measure of a country's success (as well as the extent of its poverty) resides in its ability to shield its population from famines. What can be said of a system that endured a constant string of food shortages bookended by two massive full-scale famines a century apart, disasters which, as Clarkson and Crawford admit, did break the European mold of agricultural experience, placing Ireland "in a league of its own"?[18] The "exceptions" of 1740–41 and 1845–52 were, in fact, so horrendous that one must question the extent to which Ireland ever really fitted the European mold.

---

15. Clarkson and Crawford, *Feast and Famine*, 133; for "price" see 121.
16. Kevin Whelan, "Pre-and Post-Famine Landscape Change," 26.
17. Clarkson and Crawford, *Feast and Famine*, 131. For critique of Kevin Whelan see 121. See also Bourke, *"The Visitation of God?"* 24, 67.
18. Clarkson and Crawford, *Feast and Famine*, 131.

Louis M. Cullen, for example, does not accept the idea that pre-Famine Ireland can be seen as coping just because food shortfalls seldom led to widespread famine conditions. Rather, he argues, after 1729 the benefits derived by the shift from dairying to farming had already been spent. For instance, those living in the lower tiers of Irish society no longer enjoyed a varied diet. Becoming increasingly dependent upon the potato, the poor were vulnerable to whatever diseases and weather occurrences threatened their principal food. Following its initial positive impact upon Ireland, the potato failed in the long run to protect the country from hunger. Cullen sees the supposed "gaps" [in] food crises, the so-called good years between the bad harvests, as "something of an illusion." "By the 1780s," he explains, "the food supply at the base of the rural community was becoming precarious again." The difference was that the specter of hunger and possible starvation no longer threatened the larger society—only the lower, the poorer third.[19]

Looking at the changes in Irish agriculture produced by commercialization, John R. Butterly and Jack Shepherd see a vast "nutritional transition," as food was drawn from the producers and sold in urban, overseas markets to a more prosperous population, a phenomenon that lies behind many modern famines.[20] What made the Irish situation somewhat different was the high nutritional value of the placeholder—the potato—the substitute for the exported food. For those forced to become dependent upon it, the potato shaped the nature of Irish poverty. For example, the commercialization of Irish agriculture, underwritten by the potato, meant that the growing population of poor were increasingly pushed off the better acreage by grain and cattle and relegated to the sub-prime land on the margins. As a result, by the beginning of the nineteenth century, and at an accelerating rate after 1815, the expanding population of the Irish poor existed in a condition of what Butterly and Shepherd call a state of "silent emergency," a sort of pre-famine condition.[21]

The real question, then, concerns the sustainability of the system rather than the inevitability of its sudden collapse. Ireland's potato system was hardly sustainable over the long run. Like Bourke, Cullen and Whelan, Robert James Scally sees the space for survival at the bottom of Irish society shrinking during the generation before the Famine: "Overpopulation, subdivision, falling prices, lean years, debt and rising evictions" were the markers of a system closing in on itself, sundering one part of Irish society from the other.[22] That sundering becomes visible when comparing Ireland's two "great" famines of 1740–41 and 1845–52. The 1740 event ranks as terrible by any standards. With the country's population at around 2 million, the *proportion* of those who died from disease and starvation may have been higher than in the 1840s.[23] More to the point, the effects of the disaster were experienced widely throughout Irish society. By contrast, in the 1840s privation and death were limited largely to the poorest classes, while around

---

19. For "spending" the benefits of the shift to tillage see Cullen, *The Emergence of Modern Ireland, 1600—1900*, 96–97. For quote see 251.
20. Butterly and Shepherd, *Hunger: The Biology and Politics of Starvation*, 202–8, 246–47.
21. Ibid., 51.
22. Scally, *The End of Hidden Ireland*, 35.
23. Ó Gráda, *Great Irish Famine*, 12-13.

two-thirds of the population successfully, in many cases effortlessly, adjusted to the loss of potatoes. This suggests that after 1740 two different Irelands emerged. Both ate potatoes. However, as participants in the cash economy, medium farmers, not to mention the better-off classes, enjoyed a varied diet. When the tubers were scarce, these groups could purchase or grow alternative foods. Below them, however, were around three million or more people—small farmers, rundale villagers, cottiers, those working the conacre, itinerant laborers, squatters—whose dependence upon the potato was absolute. Surviving at the very edge of the cash economy, their poverty foreclosed their ability to switch to other foods in an emergency.[24]

Ireland's two-tiered economy was, therefore, not a simple tale of wealth versus poverty. It is also a story of vulnerability. As Cullen notes, the shadow of famine no longer threatened farmers above the poverty level. By 1845 two-thirds of Ireland's population lived in a modern European society immune to famines. The other third, however, still lived in a pre-modern society, absolutely vulnerable whenever potatoes became scarce. As Joel Mokyr suggests, the two economies were not separated geographically; instead, they interpenetrated each other down to the county, even the barony level.[25] The gap between the two economies continued to grow, especially after 1815. Cormac Ó Gráda admits that, while the Irish economy may have recovered slowly after 1815, the poor only grew poorer. Nevertheless, he points out that they were still adequately fed and enjoyed a life expectancy comparable to other groups in Europe. He maintains that, based on the very low probability of disaster, Ireland's reliance on the potato "was a relatively low-risk strategy."[26] But was it? While the concept of inevitability may not help to explain the collapse of Ireland's potato economy, neither does the perception of the blight as simply some freak accident of nature, a piece of bad luck traveling eastward across the Atlantic from North America. As noted above, various historians have suggested that something *like* inevitability seems to have been at work in Ireland.

Somewhere between the Accidental and the Inevitable

Sometimes certain destructive elements may be inadvertently incorporated into a system. While failure is not inevitable, their presence forever biases the system toward some sort of disaster should those possibilities ever be realized. For example, at the time of its launch, the *RMS Titanic* had some significant design flaws. For example, the great ship's hull contained a series of separate, supposedly watertight bulkheads, designed to contain a breach below the waterline. In the event of a rupture of the hull, incoming water was to be kept within the damaged bulkheads. Calculating worst-case scenarios, the designers believed that, even if four bulkheads were compromised, the ship would remain stable and afloat. Based on these assumptions (and with construction costs in

---

24. See Cullen, *The Emergence of Modern Ireland, 1600–1900*, 171.
25. Mokyr, *Why Ireland Starved*, 20. See also Cullen, *The Emergence of Modern Ireland, 1600–1900*, 251.
26. For "low-risk strategy" see Ó Gráda, *Great Irish Famine*, 15. For the economy see his *Ireland: A New Economic History*, 162.

mind), they thought it unnecessary to extend the height of most bulkheads more than 10 feet above the water line. This meant, however, that some bulkheads, unsealed at the top, were not actually watertight. Therefore, when the ship's helmsman, attempting to avoid a direct collision with the iceberg, turned the *Titanic* to port, the iceberg scraped along the starboard side of the hull, puncturing and compromising five or six bulkheads along the fore section of the hull. As the bulkheads filled and the bow of the ship began to sink, water poured over the unsealed tops into adjoining "watertight" compartments, one after the other, flooding otherwise undamaged sections. The ship sank two hours and forty minutes after the collision. Well before that, the ship's officers and engineers had concluded that, because of the way the bulkheads had been designed and constructed, the *Titanic* was at that point doomed.[27] The situation that led to the disaster was, of course, contingent upon many circumstances—the speed of the ship at night through an area that might contain icebergs; the decision to try to turn the vessel, thus exposing the side of the hull—to cite just a few. However, because of the ship's design, as well as the failure to consider the possibility that more than four bulkheads could be compromised, once the ship scraped its side against the iceberg, its sinking *became* inevitable. Once certain conditions were met, flaws in the ship's design biased a concatenation of events that lead inexorably toward disaster.

Obviously, the idea of a "design flaw" cannot easily be applied to Ireland's situation in 1845. However, all the factors that left one-third of the country dependent upon a monoculture and too poor to buy alternative food biased the system toward disaster in the event of a massive and protracted potato failure. That danger, although it seemed remote, had, in fact, been recognized in many government reports. But, in the words of Austin Bourke, each team of investigators "in turn lifted the lid of the cauldron, looked helplessly into the mess of injustice, prejudice, starvation and despair, and quietly put the lid on again."[28] Even so, some of Ireland's more professional land agents were concerned enough about the situation to try to improve agricultural knowledge and practices on their estates. Some agricultural "schools" were opened, pamphlets were printed, and agricultural societies were established. Such efforts, however, were scattered and uncoordinated.[29] So, while prudence might have suggested planning for disaster, there seemed little reason to think that it was imminent. Prudence, therefore, with all her attendant costs, was quietly shown the door. Still, unlike the designers of the *Titanic* who were sure they had built an unsinkable ship, those who inquired into the Ireland's potato economy knew that, *if*, for some unknown reason, the potato was to fail on a massive scale, then calamity would surely follow.

Nevertheless, just as the *Titanic* might never have sunk had it not encountered the iceberg, without the potato blight Ireland might have eventually achieved some sort of

---

27. For a survey of the ship's problems see Levinson, "A General Semantics Analysis of the RMS Titanic Disaster," 143–56. There are continuing debates regarding the quality of both the steel used in the hull and the rivets; see Eaton and Hass, *Titanic*, 156–57.
28. See Bourke, *"The Visitation of God?"* 69.
29. See Reilly, *The Irish Land Agent, 1830–60*, 84–86, 91, 93.

equilibrium between population and land usage (although not without some trauma). In such cases, therefore, icebergs and fungal infestations may seem examples of unpredictable, naturally occurring, random elements arriving unexpectedly out of the blue. Yet, the iceberg in question was *not* unexpected. Even before the advent of iceberg tracking (prompted by the loss of the *Titanic*), identifiable ice fields were known to represent hazards to shipping during the North Atlantic spring. The appearance of one off the *Titanic*'s starboard bow on the night of April 14, 1912, was, therefore *not* something out of the ordinary. Indeed, there were lookouts posted, and they did in fact spot it—just before the collision. Unlike the iceberg, of course, *Phytophthora infestans* was an unknown phenomenon, an entirely new disease. As Peter Solar has suggested, its repeated reappearances in Ireland after 1845, causing sequential failures of the potato, were "at the limits of actual experience," and the almost total destruction of the potato crop in 1846 was "far out of the range of actual or likely European experience."[30] Experience, or the lack thereof, however, can be a tricky argument against inevitability. Therefore, another analogy may help.

The Cascadian subduction zone that lies off the coast of Washington state is an area where the continental tectonic plates slide over each other. Periodically, pressure building up along the fault may cause the sea floor to suddenly drop and then rebound between 30 and 100 feet. This can produce a massive earthquake, possibly around 9 points on the Richter scale, resulting in a destructive tsunami, such as one that hit the coast of Japan in 2011. Until a few decades ago, no one knew of this pattern of events off America's northwest coast. Relatively recent research, however, has revealed a cycle of quakes and tsunamis along the Cascadian fault occurring on an average of 243 years. Since the last big quake took place around 1700, the next one is "overdue." Recent geological and historical research, therefore, has extended human experience, allowing northwest-coast inhabitants to anticipate and even prepare for the next Cascadian event, whenever it occurs.[31]

There is, of course, a big difference between plant biology and geology. And the state of science in 1845 did not allow either North Americans or Europeans to fill in the blanks regarding their relatively brief experience with the potato. To them the appearance of *P. infestans* seemed an extraordinary phenomenon. There was no reason why anyone in 1845 should have predicted the sudden appearance of such a disease. Today, however, scientists understand why, under certain circumstances, especially those involving monoculture, plants and the societies that depend on them might fall victim to scourges like the potato blight. So, from the vantage point of today's agricultural science, the potato blight of the 1840s takes on some of the characteristics of an iceberg field or a subduction fault: unpredictable in terms of timing but certainly within the realm of possibility and even, given a long enough timeframe, expectations.

Today's agronomists know what their Victorian ancestors did not. Over time, monocultures become inherently unstable. While monocultures existed elsewhere in

---

30. Quoted in Ó Gráda, *Ireland Before and After the Famine*, 13.
31. See Schulz, "Annals of Seismology: The Really Big One," 52–59.

Europe in the 1840s, few areas came close to Ireland's massive dependence on one crop.[32] Every year vast quantities of potatoes were planted all over Ireland. On the smallest farms and in the pratie patches of the cottiers, potatoes were generally the only crop planted year after year. Moreover, of the 200 varieties of potatoes Ireland had developed, by the 1840s, only a relatively small subset was commonly planted. In fact, on the poorest farms in the west only *one variety*, the Lumper, low in quality but prolific in quantity, was annually cultivated.[33] Unfortunately, planting the same crop, especially the same varieties, on the same farms, sometimes even in the same soil, year after year raises susceptibility to both insect infestations and plant diseases. It is suggestive that, during the Famine, the blight seemed to weaken in 1847. That year saw only *10 percent* of the pre-Famine potato crop planted, representing a large-scale, albeit unplanned, retreat from monoculture. When potato cultivation partially recovered the following year, however, the blight roared back to life, especially in the west where the Lumper predominated.[34] The dangers of intense of monoculture are widely recognized today; in 1845 they were unknown.

For many years it has been assumed that the strain of *P. infestans* that hit Europe in the mid-1840s had originated in Mexico and then spread throughout North America. Eventually designated as US-1, this strain subsequently remained dominant until the 1970s, However, recent scholarship suggests that the deadly pandemic of the 1840s was caused by a different but closely related strain, HERB-1, which may have originated in the United States and then died out by the end of the nineteenth century.[35] The reasons why this strain of the blight was so deadly lie partly in the nature of the potato and its cultivation at mid-century. Current research has demonstrated that the potato's genetic structure compounded the risks of monoculture. Most potato varieties planted in the nineteenth century had very low genetic diversity. This is particularly true of the Lumper, the variety upon which tens of thousands of Irish lives depended. Such genetic limitations may pose a particular problem because potatoes generally reproduce asexually, making them essentially clones. In fact, potatoes are often propagated by cuttings taken from the previous year's crop, thus deriving a clone from a clone. In the 1840s this process facilitated the ability of the pathogen not only to spread rapidly but, once established, to survive in the soil for several years.[36]

---

32. Turner, *Ireland After the Famine*, 5–6. See also Bourke, *"The Visitation of God?"* 20.
33. For 200 varieties see Bourke, *"The Visitation of God?"* 30. For quality of the Lumper see 39–40. For dominance of the Lumper see Ó Gráda, *Ireland Before and After the Famine*, 13.
34. For potato acreage see graph in Donnelly, *The Great Irish Potato Famine*, 58. See also Ó Gráda, *Before and After the Famine*, 80. For 1847 potato harvest see Kinealy, *A Death-Dealing Famine*, 118. For 1848 harvest see 137.
35. Ristaino and Hu, "DNA Sequence Analysis of the Late-Blight Pathogen Gives Clues to the World-wide Migration."
36. Because of the way it reproduced, the virus could overwinter in the soil. Then the spores would infect the tuber, stems and/or leaves, after which the spores might become airborne, moving quickly from one field to another. See Dowley, "The Potato and Late Blight in Ireland," 60–61. For the dangers of monoculture, the low-genetic diversity of potatoes and the Irish Famine see Anon., "Understanding Evolution: Monoculture and the Irish Potato Famine: Cases of

Finally, although the potato was an ancient food in its New World home in the Andes, its large-scale cultivation in North America and Europe dated back little more than two centuries before the appearance of the blight. This meant that, outside of its original homeland, it represented a relatively new plant species, still being tried out in foreign soils, tested by pathogens and by North American and European weather patterns. Austin Bourke explains that it is only after a plant goes from limited to extensive cultivation that previously little-known or even new diseases appear. For example, while European potato farmers encountered leaf curl during the eighteenth century, dry rot did not appear until around 1832. In fact, it was in response to that disease that much of the European stock was replaced by potatoes from North America. Unfortunately, the new stocks were shipped to Belgium between 1843 and 1844, around the same time that *P. infestans* first appeared in the United States. In 1845 the blight, starting in Belgium, spread rapidly among European potatoes that had no genetic defenses against it.[37]

Caught between the accidental and the inevitable, Ireland's potato economy failed. Just as the collision with the iceberg activated the deadly potential for destruction imbedded in the design of the *Titanic's* bulkheads and turned it against the ship, the potato blight exploited the deadly bias in Ireland's potato economy and triggered its collapse. The appearance of *P. infestans* was not inevitable. Once it arrived in Ireland where so many people depended upon the potato, however, some degree of disaster was inevitable. This does not mean that the potato blight fulfilled some dreadful rendezvous with disaster that history had mandated for Ireland. Rather the blight was an event for which history had made Ireland fatally vulnerable. Hindsight provides an understanding of that vulnerability, which was not available 175 years ago. Science today can predict that monoculture involving a crop with low genetic diversity and with barely two centuries of large-scale cultivation behind it may run a grave risk of falling victim to some sort of insect infestation or a disease like *P. infestans*. Like the arrival of the next iceberg or the next Pacific coast earthquake, however, science cannot predict when such tragedies may occur. And, as already noted, timing can be everything.

The initial appearance of the late potato blight was recorded in the United States in the summer of 1843 in areas around New York City and Philadelphia. By 1845 the blight was in the Maritime Provinces and in the southern tier of Canada. In the United States, it had spread as far west as Chicago. By June of that year, it had also made its initial European appearance in Belgium. From there it spread rapidly, arriving in southeast England in mid-August and moving through the rest of the country by the end of the month. By late summer and early fall, it had turned up in Ireland and Scotland. Generally, the earlier in the summer the blight appeared, the greater its destructiveness.

Missing Genetic Variation." See also Watts, "The Dangers of Monoculture Farming." Butler, "Avoiding Monoculture."

37. See Reader, *Potato: A History of the Propitious Esculent*, 194–95. For susceptibility of new crops see Bourke, *"The Visitation of God?"* 25. For previous potato diseases see 26–31. Recent research suggests that the strain of *P. infestans* that entered Europe had not previously encountered cultivated tubers. Uninhibited, it devastated the European and especially the Irish crops. See Callaway, "Pathogen Genome Tracks Irish Potato Famine Back to Its Roots."

In Belgium, the epicenter of the infestation, 90 percent of the crop was lost; in north Holland, 75 percent. In France, Germany and England the losses ranged from 25 to 50 percent.[38] Ireland's greatest losses occurred in the east, suggesting that the Lumpers, which predominated in the west and which would turn out to be very susceptible to the blight, had not yet been fully exposed. Nevertheless, the damage proved serious. About 40 percent of the 1845 potato crop may have been lost. However, because the overall yield was exceptionally high that year, the actual loss to the food supply, compared to previous harvests, was probably between 25 and 30 percent.[39] Ireland's grain harvest for 1845 was generally excellent, however, which proved confusing. Casual observers, accustomed to English harvest standards, did not differentiate clearly enough between plentiful grain, much of which was slated for export, and the reduced potato supply upon which millions of Irish depended.

At this point, two important facts should be noted. First, *P. infestans* represented, as already mentioned, a new disease, completely unknown to both plants and people. Second, famines generally result from *successive* crop failures. Even a large-scale loss of a crop rarely leads to immediate widespread famine conditions, provided the next harvest returns to normal.[40] It is important, therefore, to understand that, unlike most other parts of Europe, the devastating impact of the blight upon the Irish food supply was cumulative. The disease appeared with varying degrees of intensity in every year between 1845 and 1852. There was almost no precedence for this even in Ireland, where crop failures were usually confined to a single harvest season. Therefore, in analyzing the effects of reoccurring crop failures, the calendar year is not the best chronological guide. Ireland's poor lived harvest to harvest, and British relief policy was to some extent shaped by the same seasonal calendar. Therefore, in examining the Famine and its scope, this study will follow the harvest cycle rather than the calendar year; thus 1845–46, 1846–47, 1847–48, 1848–49, 1849–52, with a chapter devoted to each period.

---

38. Solar, "The Potato Famine in Europe," 117. See maps in Freehan, "The Potato: Root of the Famine," 30–31.
39. Donnelly, *The Great Irish Potato Famine*, 47; Dowley, "The Potato and Late Blight in Ireland," 58.
40. Ó Gráda, *Famine: A Short History*, 31.

Part Three

THE FAMINE YEARS

Chapter Eight

THE ARRIVAL OF THE POTATO BLIGHT: 1845–46

The Blight as News

There never was, perhaps, a finer growth of potatoes.

(*Morning Chronicle*, August 30, 1845)

"The potato crop [...] is far from satisfactory. [...] In several districts a rot has set in."
(*The Dublin Evening Mail*, reprinted in *The Scotsman*, September 3, 1845)

Christopher Morash defines the Irish Famine as "a retrospective, textural creation."[1] The Famine as text began immediately upon the arrival of the potato blight in 1845. Then, as now, "news" appears on the back of a story. No story, no "news." Scattered facts and rumors take on meaning only when they are connected and woven into some sort of narrative. While *Phytophthora infestans* spread throughout Europe in the summer of 1845, it appeared late in Ireland and its initial occurrences were sporadic. The intensity of the infestation varied from place to place. Disconnected reports about failing potatoes competed in the papers with glowing descriptions of a generally fine harvest. Was there a problem or was there not? As Cormac Ó Gráda has noted, "preemptive action requires agreement on famine's early warning signs,"[2] As summer turned into fall, Ireland could not agree on those signs.

The blight was first recorded in Ireland on August 20 by the curator of the Dublin Botanical Gardens, Dr. David Moore. It took several days for the word to get around scientific circles. Finally, on September 13, Dr. John Lindley, who had been tracking the progress of the blight in England, issued a stop-press for his journal, the *Gardiner's Chronicle and Horticultural Gazette*. In the journal, he announced that "the potato Murrain [disease] has unequivocally declared itself in Ireland. The crops about Dublin are suddenly perishing." Lindley then asked ominously, "Where will Ireland be in the event of a universal potato rot?"[3] Yet, even a week later, there were only a few reports from the west of Ireland about blighted potatoes. On August 30, the Dublin correspondent for the British *Morning Chronicle* rejoiced at a bounteous potato harvest with prices half those of the previous year. A few days later, the *Clare Journal* exalted, "Our harvest, thanks to

---

1. Morash, *Writing the Irish Famine*, 3.
2. Ó Gráda, *Famine: A Short History*, 6. For the classic warning signs of impending famine see 1–7.
3. For quote see Woodham-Smith, *The Great Hunger*, 40.

Divine Providence, promises to be uncommonly abundant." Nevertheless, constabulary reports on the harvest began to suggest that the blight was already spreading in that area.[4] Thus, the "story" of a potential Irish disaster was still a welter of often conflicting details and uncertainties. For example, *The Scotsman* for September 3 reprinted a report from the Dublin *Evening Mail*. After describing a healthy Irish grain harvest, the article warned that the potato blight had appeared in several districts where "two-thirds of the tubers are found to be rotten within, though large and well looking without." A week later, the *Morning Chronicle* stated that in County Louth, "The potato crop, we regret to say, is giving up fast—many fields becoming withered prematurely. The quantity planted, however, exceeds anything of the kind for many years. They will not, however, be near so productive as the crop of last year."[5]

What was the middle-class Dubliner or Londoner, perusing his newspaper by his fireside, to make of such reports, the good mixed with the bad? *The Times*, Britain's leading daily paper, had yet to comment on the condition of Ireland's potatoes. In fact, in early fall no British paper led with reports on the potato blight in Ireland. Finally, on September 12, the *Morning Chronicle* published a roundup on the Irish potato harvest. Galway's crop was "abundant and good." Tralee in Kerry reported no blight, although there were some complaints in Athlone. Londonderry's harvest seemed sound, although on the Inishowen Peninsula in nearby Donegal whole fields had withered and died. During the first two weeks of October, negative reports from Ireland were sporadic, brief and not particularly disturbing.[6]

Obviously, the blight was not universal throughout Ireland in 1845. Its appearance was spotty. Weather may have played a role in this. Winds from the Continent blowing across the Lowlands and into Great Britain and Ireland probably helped spread the disease. Throughout Europe there had been high humidity, night fogs and thunderstorms, all conducive to propagating the blight, providing temperatures were above 10°C. This may be one of the reasons why upland farms in Ireland with their cooler temperatures largely escaped the 1845 blight.[7] Moreover, the disease did not always make its presence known by attacking the stalks. At this stage, the virus tended to slowly infect the potatoes in the ground, its devastation not detected until the tubers were lifted late in the fall. Thus, only in mid-October did British papers begin to pay more attention to the situation in Ireland. Noting the destruction of potato crops on the Continent, the weekly *Observer* warned on October 19 that "*Famine*, with all its attendant horror, glares [...] from Ireland." This was one of the first times that a British newspaper had used that terrifying word regarding the Irish situation. A few days later, on October 24, the editor of the *Kerry Examiner* expressed concern but insisted that "our market abounds with the finest potatoes. [...] It may be that fear magnifies the danger, at least it is so to be hoped."[8]

---

4. See Ó Murchadha, *Sable Wings Over the Land*, 29–30.
5. *Morning Chronicle,* September 12, 1845. *Scotsman*, September 3, 1845 (3).
6. For news reports see, Leslie A. Williams, *Daniel O'Connell, the British Press and the Irish Famine*, 130.
7. Lamb, *Weather, Climate and Human Affairs*, 168.
8. See MacMahon, *The Great Famine in Tralee and North Kerry*, 26.

Fearful that the spread of the potato blight might strengthen the anti-protectionist campaign against the Corn Laws, there was a tendency in certain Tory quarters to play down the possibility of a subsistence crisis in Ireland. In its October 5 issue, *News of the World* carried a cheerful story about the run of herring off the west coast of Ireland. The catch was so abundant that people could not get enough salt to preserve it. The paper blithely went on to assure its readers, "amongst the many sources of food which Providence has so bountifully supplied this season, the people will be provided with a large stock of this delicious fish." How they were to preserve the catch without salt, which the report noted as scarce, the paper did not say. Such use of contradictory words and soothing images to avoid disturbing realities is typical of British reporting throughout much of the Famine period.[9]

On October 29, the *Morning Chronicle* reprinted two widely contradictory claims regarding the potato, both from the *Sligo Champion*. One report stated that, "The damage in this county is grossly exaggerated, as every farmer must know." And they also knew, the paper suggested, that such reports would help raise market prices. The other piece was a letter written by a Reverend John Coghlan of Sligo:

> It is utterly impossible to convey to you a true picture of the alarming state of despondency into which the people of this parish have been thrown by the extensive rot in the potato crop. It is quite common that a potato field [...] today may be good and sound, and in three days after in a state of melancholy putrefaction. [...] [T]hose poor creatures who depend altogether on the con-acre [sic] potatoes for support, now left without any resource [...] have neither oats, nor money, nor potatoes. [...] May God in his mercy relieve them and revert this scourge from our already impoverished, destitute and suffering people.[10]

If just one Irish paper could not agree on the seriousness of the situation, the British press could hardly be expected to do any better.

Part of the problem was that many of Ireland's poor earned at least a portion of their living by working for their landlords. Unable to plant their own pratie patches until summer, they did not lift their crop until well into the fall. Consequently, the full effects of the blight were not completely known until this "people's crop" was dug toward November. Only then did the extent of the damage become clear. A constabulary report from the area round Kinsale, dated October 29, stated that "Potatoes that were apparently sound have become diseased. More than one quarter of the crop in this district may be considered lost at present." Similar reports from North Kerry confirmed such losses. As a *Morning Chronicle* correspondent noted on November 14, 1845, "in almost all instances where the poor man's garden was dug, it was found that the crop was not only moist and flavorless, but absolutely unfit for human food."[11] As the news regarding the

---

9. For quote see Leslie A. Williams, *Daniel O'Connell, the British Press and the Irish Famine*, 130.
10. Ibid., 134–35.
11. For constabulary report see Flanagan, *The Great Famine in Kinsale*, 23. For Kerry see MacMahon, *The Great Famine in Tralee and North Kerry*, 26. For *Morning Chronicle* quote see Leslie A. Williams, *Daniel O'Connell, the British Press and the Irish Famine*, 142.

"people's crop" came in, it became obvious that, while there was no catastrophe, the situation was very serious. On November 9 the *News of the World* remarked on the confused, often contradictory reports coming in from Ireland. Then, a few days later, it ran a leader headed, "Famine in Ireland—Peel Ministry." Claiming that one-third of the Irish potato crop had been lost, the paper blamed the government for having ignored the impending crisis. As it took shape, the story of the potato blight in Ireland inevitably gathered political implications.[12]

The Politics of the Blight

Apart from the fog of uncertainty that initially surrounds most emerging stories, there were other reasons why it took a while for the press, British and Irish, to grasp the situation in Ireland. Often, before events can be formed into new narratives, they become embedded within preexisting contexts and presented as continuations of old, well-established stories. Thus, British perceptions of the potato blight in Ireland were initially shaped by ongoing debates about other things—previous bad harvests, Irish poverty, Daniel O'Connell's Repeal Movement, agrarian unrest, the Corn Laws, parliamentary politics or concerns about the British economy. All too often, events fitted neatly into Britain's well-established narrative about the Irish, reflecting old suspicions and prejudices. For example, there had been considerable hostility within evangelical quarters regarding Prime Minister Robert Peel's decision in June of 1845 to increase the government's grant to Maynooth College in Kildare for the education of Roman Catholic priests. A Protestant minister, Rev. Tresham Gregg, speaking at a meeting in the Rotunda in Dublin, called news of the grant, "the most frightful that had ever reached Irish shores." The Orange Order's Grand Lodge of Ulster called for all Irish Protestants to stand fast against "the horrors of a civil war." Given this atmosphere, it was inevitable that some Protestants saw the potato blight as God's punishment for Peel's alleged support of Popery.[13]

Then there was Daniel O'Connell, who had long loomed large in the British political imagination. *The Times* was not the only journal in Britain to have virtually demonized O'Connell and his followers. By 1845, *Punch*, as mentioned earlier, had produced cartoons ridiculing "The Liberator." In late November, the satirical weekly published a cartoon labeled "The Real Potato Blight," depicting O'Connell as a giant, malevolent Lumper, sitting on bags of money collected from the peasantry (see Figure 2). A few weeks earlier, it had run a drawing of O'Connell as the swindler Jeremy Diddler, begging Repeal "Rint [Rent]" from near-starving Irish peasants.[14] Thus, Britain's Irish narrative automatically

---

12. *News of the World*, November 16, 1845 (1).
13. For the complicated politics around the Maynooth grant see McDowell, "Ireland on the Eve of the Famine," 79–81. For alleged divine anger, see O'Neill, "The Organization and Administration of Relief, 1845–52," 210. For Rev. Gregg see *Times*, February 11, 1845. (5). For Orange Order see *Times*, November 1, 1845.
14. For "Real Potato Blight" see Donnelly, *The Great Irish Potato Famine*, 193. For "'Rint' v. Potatoes—The Irish Jeremy Diddler" see Leslie A. Williams, *Daniel O'Connell, the British Press and the Irish Famine*, 148.

Figure 2 "The Real Potato Blight of Ireland," *Punch*, December 14, 1845

blamed the Irish people for their country's problems. The landlords were greedy, and the peasants were shiftless, lazy, ignorant and improvident. Like their leader Daniel O'Connell, their seemingly endless appeals for aid could not be trusted. For example, Thomas Campbell Foster, writing in the November 4 issue of *The Times*, ridiculed the peasantry's cry for help: "Has the effect of bygone neglect, and mismanagement, and wrong," he asked rhetorically, "generated a self-defensive resort to suspicious obstinacy, and violence, and fraud?"[15] Although he was reporting weekly from Ireland as the potato blight spread, Foster rarely referred to it. He did, however, continuously blame the peasants for relying on a crop, which he, like many Britons, considered nutritionally inferior and morally suspect—a lazy man's crop that, unlike grain, was too easy to grow. One of Foster's few articles that did touched on the blight, published November 7, 1845, concerned the recent observance of All Saints' Day in Ireland:

> With famine before them, it will hardly be conceived in England that Saturday last, a fine bright, sunshiny day, when the potatoes might have been exposed to the wind and sun and the worst grated into flour, was proclaimed a holiday (no doubt for some good purpose), and not a man was to be seen at work in the whole county whilst their potatoes were rotting. Some will not even take the trouble to dig them, because they are diseased, though there is no question about it but much of them, though rotten may be saved.[16]

Foster, a Protestant, did not share the Roman Catholic devotion to Holy Days of Obligation that required church attendance. On the other hand, better informed and less biased observers did not share his assumption that the rotting potatoes could be somehow salvaged. A week later, on November 19, the *Morning Chronicle* complained about Tory papers insinuating that the Irish people

> will not take advice, nor adopt precautions to preserve any portion of their crops. This is not true. On all sides they are to be seen carting their potatoes into houses, which it is not usual to do until an advanced period of the spring; their women and children are employed constantly in turning them over, and separating the bad from the good; but the disease, which has been well compared to a gangrene, is not to be checked by any means at the disposal of the poor Irish peasantry.[17]

There were, in fact, no means available to anyone for salvaging the diseased potatoes.

The Corn Laws, the Blight and Providence

As explained earlier, when agricultural prices declined after 1815, the United Kingdom's landed aristocracy pushed through Parliament a bill placing high tariffs on imported foreign grain or "corn." These Corn Laws favored the landed aristocracy and their

---

15. See Leslie A. Williams, *Daniel O'Connell, the British Press and the Irish Famine*, 140.
16. Ibid., 117. For the author's analysis of Foster's reporting see 102–21.
17. Ibid., 143.

major tenants in both Britain and Ireland. High tariffs meant expensive food, however, burdening the British working class, who then demanded higher wages from the newly enfranchised middleclass factory owners and shopkeepers. By the 1840s, many people had come to regard the Corn Laws as a tax on the growing urban areas of the Kingdom for the benefit of the landed class. In early 1844, the *News of the World* blamed the defeat of a Whig attempt to debate the conditions in Ireland on the same aristocrats who, through their support of protectionism, "are banded together, and have constituted a Government, for the purpose of restricting the food of the English poor."[18] Adopting the O'Connellite tactics that had proved effective in the struggle to pass the Reform Bill, the Anti-Corn Law League had been formed in 1838. The Tories, under Peel, were seriously divided on the issue of protection. The Whigs, on the other hand, despite their aristocratic leadership, enjoyed more middle-class support, and were, therefore, more sympathetic to repeal.[19]

The conjunction of rising Anti-Corn Law agitation with the onset of the potato blight was one of the first signs that any subsistence crisis in Ireland would inevitably play out within the wider context of British politics. For example, in November of 1845 Whig leader Lord John Russell told the Electors of the City of London that because the potato blight threatened the Kingdom's food supply it was time to end protection.[20] Indeed, any threat to the United Kingdom's food supply was grist for the Anti-Corn Law League and its supporters in the liberal press. Protectionists, on the other hand, were eager to discredit reports of a growing crisis in Ireland, citing them as typical examples of Irish hyperbole. As the *Sligo Champion* complained in January 1846, "Some heartless miscreants there are who have endeavored to give the potato failure a political aspect. They pretend that there is no such thing—that there is abundance of food in the country, and no prospect of want, and this is done to stifle what is called 'the famine cry,' and save the government and the landlords from embarrassment."[21]

Some Tory papers were more nuanced in their views. The previous October, the *Standard*, a supporter of protectionism, apparently decided that a temporary suspension of the Corn Laws might take some pressure off the growing demand for their repeal. The paper even suggested that the threat of famine in Ireland had to be taken seriously: "It is the duty of the state to insure that not one of the Queen's subjects shall perish from famine."[22] By November, *The Times*, ever attuned to shifts in popular opinion, had decided to move into the Anti-Corn Law camp. While, expressing some concern for the situation in Ireland, the paper took a wider view of the situation, declaring that "this is an age of low prices. Our prosperity is to be coincident with low prices. [...] The present corn laws are doomed. It is for the Premier [Peel] to decide whether he will sign the warrant for their execution." A few days later the paper insisted: "The emergency is pressing.

---

18. *News of the World*, February 25, 1844 (1).
19. For Corn Laws see Blake, *The Conservative Party from Peel to Churchill*, 13–15.
20. *News of the World*, November 30, 1845 (3).
21. See Leslie A. Williams, *Daniel O'Connell, the British Press and the Irish Famine*, 152.
22. Ibid., 136. The quote had been reprinted in *Scotsman*, October 25, 1845.

Corn is becoming dearer. Famine threatens Ireland; scarcity is already apprehended in Scotland. [...] Yet, the Minister delays."[23]

Protectionist issues reached beyond politics. A popular strain of Christian economics also came into play. Many evangelicals believed that interference with the workings of the free market went against the divine order of things. The Corn Laws, therefore, represented a violation of the Natural Law. This placed the potato blight and an impending crisis in Ireland in a very particular light. In October 1845 Sir James Graham, Peel's home secretary, wrote to the prime minister

> It is awful to observe how the Almighty humbles the pride of nations. The sword, the pestilence, the famine are instruments of his displeasure [...] he gives the word; a single crop is blighted and we see a nation is prostrate, stretching out its hands for bread. These are solemn warnings, and they fill me with reverence; they proclaim. [...] "doubtless there is a God who judgeth [sic] the Earth."[24]

Varying degrees of providential thinking were common enough at the time, although there was little agreement as to whom or what stood in the shadow of divine wrath. Some extreme Protestants assumed that it was Roman Catholics. Others believed that God was chastising Britain for having allowed the situation in Ireland to go unchecked. *The Times* managed to link providentialism to political economy. It was senseless, the paper insisted, for some of the Roman Catholic clergy and their followers to blame the government for the high price of food. "Providence has thought fit to afflict a nation—a whole nation with a terrible calamity. [...] We ask in all reverence, who is it who has raised the price of food? Who but the ALMIGHTY himself." Many Irish Roman Catholics, such as Daniel O'Connell, took a much broader view. In February 1846 he told Parliament that while the looming crisis was, indeed, a "dispensation of Providence," it was everyone's duty to "perform the part of charitable Christians, by endeavoring to mitigate the evils as they arise."[25]

Prime Minister Robert Peel had his own version of providentialism. Unlike some of the evangelicals, he tried to emphasize the possibility of a positive outcome to the crisis. Given the right response, he suggested, the crisis in Ireland could be a "blessing" from a benevolent God. During the Famine, Peel was to argue in a speech before Parliament in 1849, "It has pleased God to afflict us with this great calamity." Without it, he said, the situation in Ireland might have drifted on for years. "Let us now profit by this solemn warning [...] and convert a grievous affliction into a means of future improvement and a source of future security." Although less outspoken than his home secretary concerning God's judgment, Peel did share with Graham a sense that the Corn Laws were an affront to the moral implications of free trade. More important, as Peel's comments suggest,

---

23. *The Times,* November 6, 1845; November 8, 1845.
24. For quote see Gray, *Famine, Land and Politics,* 99.
25. For O'Connell see Bew, *Ireland: the Politics of Enmity,* 182; For *The Times* quote see the issue for October 14, 1846 (4).

ending protection was merely the first step in a broad transformation of Ireland for which the potato blight seemed to offer a propitious opportunity.[26]

Whatever God's intentions regarding the potato blight, many people in Britain naturally wondered about the impact the loss of so much food in Ireland might have upon the British economy. A few British observers were willing to commit to supporting the Irish people. "T. S." from Liverpool argued in a letter to *The Times* on October 29, 1845: "Let the [Irish] people keep their produce this year and let the Government settle the matter of rents with the landlords." Recalling how the government had paid £20,000,000 to plantation owners when the West Indian slaves were freed, the correspondent asked, "shall we not be charged three or four [million pounds] to save from perishing a much greater number of our near neighbors and brethren?" Although far less generous, even *The Times* flirted with the idea that, if the Corn Laws were repealed, the British would rise to the occasion and minister to the Irish.[27] Nevertheless, concerned about the possibility of a massive food shortage, the *Observer* on October 19, 1845 complained that English charity was always called upon to save the Irish poor, while their landlords shirked their responsibilities: "Now [...] the British public [...] will naturally say that those who have grown rich by extractions from these poor creatures, should maintain them in their destitution. [...] From English charity, therefore, there is little to expect in alleviation of the threatened famine." On November 16, 1846 the *News of the World* insisted that, "It is not fitting that Ireland should become a beggar to England—or that the English people should be called upon to contribute to their maintenance, when Ireland has resources enough to meet the emergency—when she grows food enough to feed her own population, and is rich enough for their support." The article included a phrase that was to become the British mantra throughout the Famine period: "*let Irish money feed Irish poverty.*"[28] Harsh as such pronouncements may sound, in the case of *Observer* at least, they were based on another assumption also widely held at that time. The paper went on to suggest, "Ireland has for years proved a fruitful granary to this country [England]. [...] This year the supply of corn to the British markets must be materially diminished, if not entirely cease unless, indeed, the Irish themselves be abandoned to starvation." In other words, the *Observer*, like some other British papers, assumed that Irish foodstuffs would be kept in Ireland to make up for the loss of potatoes, thus enabling the country to take care of its own problems.[29]

Thus, amid all this welter of opinion, it is evident that, even before famine conditions had appeared, a rough consensus was emerging within Britain public opinion regarding

---

26. See Gray, "Ideology and the Famine," 94. For Peel and Graham see Gray's *Famine, Land and Politics*, 96–102. For quotes see 213–14. For a more detailed discussion of Peel's providentialism see Gray's article, "'Potatoes and Providence,' British Government Responses to the Great Famine."
27. Gray, "'Potatoes and Providence,'" 80. For the "T. S." letter see Leslie A. Williams, *Daniel O'Connell, the British Press and the Irish Famine*, 132–33.
28. For the *Observer* see Leslie A. Williams, *Daniel O'Connell, the British Press and the Irish Famine*, 131; for *News of the World* see 137, emphasis added.
29. Leslie A. Williams, *Daniel O'Connell, the British Press and the Irish Famine*, 132.

the situation in Ireland. Rather than being exported as usual to England, Irish food should be kept in Ireland to feed the hungry. If conditions worsened, then Irish landlords should be charged with the care of their indigent tenants and laborers. British taxpayers should not be involved. It is important to recognize how the two parts of this equation theoretically balanced each other. However, while the second part eventually became government policy, the first part, keeping Ireland's food at home, was never attempted or seriously considered.

Peel's Relief Policies

There was no consensus among scientists regarding the nature of the blight. Was the fungus new, or was it simply a variant of previous fungal attacks on the potato? Were all varieties of potatoes at risk? Would the disease return? Peel appointed a three-man commission to answer such questions. Unfortunately, the panel even failed to recognize *P. infestans* as a new disease. Moreover, the members seemed ignorant of the fact that the blight had been ravaging potato fields in the United States since 1843. Otherwise, they might have anticipated its return in 1846. Finally, failing to understand the nature of the disease—how it spread from plant to plant and from leaves into the soil and eventually to the tubers themselves—they could not suggest how to combat it. A few European scientists and wine growers knew that solutions of "bluestone" (copper sulfate) could inhibit fungal attacks on grape vines in France. Some suggested that it might prevent the spread of blight among potatoes. However, despite a few experiments, the lack of knowledge about the disease, coupled with general skepticism regarding the efficacy of bluestone, meant that it would be years before copper sulfate sprays would be widely adopted to combat the recurrence of the blight.[30] The best Peel's commission could come up with was to recommend storing apparently sound potatoes in special pits that would keep them cool and dry. Unfortunately, even where this was tried, the potatoes rotted anyway. Other suggestions, such as grating blighted potatoes to extract the eatable starch, were even less helpful. The Poor Law Union at Kinsale built a "starch machine" and ran some diseased potatoes through it, but eventually abandoned the fruitless enterprise. On November 10, 1845, Ireland's *Freeman's Journal* concluded that Peel's commissioners had proven that "they know nothing whatever about the causes of or remedies for the disease."[31]

By the new year the partial loss of the potato crop began to make itself felt in Ireland. On January 24, 1846, *The Tralee Chronicle* noted a sudden increase in applications to the workhouse from the families of agricultural laborers. "This is one of the first symptoms of the failure of the food of the peasantry [...] a melancholy state of things for which we were quite unprepared."[32] Reports of such "symptoms" could not have been a great

---

30. Bourke, *"The Visitation of God?"* 150–52.
31. Donnelly, *The Great Irish Potato Famine*, 46. For summaries of the scientific opinions regarding the blight see 44–47; also Bourke, *"The Visitation of God?"* 150–58. For Kinsale starch machine see Flanagan, *The Great Famine in Kinsale*, 24.
32. MacMahon, *The Great Famine in Tralee and North Kerry*, 31.

surprise to Prime Minister Peel, however, who was no stranger to Ireland. He had contended with the country's periodic food problems in 1816–17 and again in 1822, first as chief secretary for Ireland and later as home secretary. He knew the formula for responding to Irish subsistence crises: pull together all relevant governmental agencies; organize local relief committees to raise funds and open soup kitchens; and establish public work projects to employ the poor.[33] Although generally against direct intervention in the market, Peel's free-trade principles did not preclude him from attempting some limited attempts at controlling food prices. Therefore, he secretly imported £100,000 worth of maize, enough to feed one million people for a month. Beginning in March 1846, he held the maize as a reserve food to be stored in government depots and to be released when necessary to keep food prices from escalating. There were 13 main depots connected to sub-depots in coast guard stations and constabulary headquarters scattered throughout Ireland. By May, cornmeal was being sold from government depots for as little as 1d a pound. Intended to control prices, however, Peel's plan did not provide food for those without money.[34]

Although in keeping with Britain's previous experience with Irish food crises, Peel also hoped that importing even a limited supply of maize could have long-range implications. Many within his government shared the popular opinion that the potato was inferior food, both nutritionally and morally. Too easy to grow, it led, in the words of Sir Randolph Routh of the Army Commissariat, "the people to indolence and all kinds of vice, which habitual labour and a higher order food would prevent."[35] For his part, Peel hoped that the blight offered an opportunity for the regeneration of Ireland. Even at this early stage, the seeds of a major goal of British famine relief policy are evident: the restructuring of Ireland's agriculture and its rural society. With the onset of the potato blight and the repeal of the Corn Laws, Peel had decided that Ireland's peasantry could be shifted from a potato wage to a cash income that would support a proper grain diet. He also believed that repeal of the Corn Laws would force Ireland's landlords to move further toward an English style of farming, encouraging them to consolidate and improve their lands, thereby hiring the peasantry to work for money instead of potato ground.[36]

Unfortunately, as they watched their potatoes rot, not many of the Irish poor outside the oatmeal-growing regions of eastern Ulster had easy access to alternative foods. Those on the seacoast might gather shellfish, and farmer/fishermen could take to their boats. However, even in the best of times, the west-coast Irish peasantry was severely limited in its ability to exploit the sea. Therefore, Ireland's chief famine food consisted of maize or "Indian meal," a foreign import. The government saw an advantage in this, however. Since maize had never been common in Ireland, it seemed less likely to compete with the native grains handled by Ireland's merchants.[37] Whatever its imagined moral and

---

33. See Daly, "The Operations of Famine Relief, 1845–1847," 123–25, 127.
34. For depots see Flanagan, *The Great Famine in Kinsale*, 26.
35. Gray, *Famine, Land and Politics*, 119.
36. Gray, "Potatoes and Providence," 81–82.
37. Kinealy, *Great Calamity*, 47. For "famine foods" see Ó Gráda, *Famine: A Short History*, 73–78.

economic standing among plants, however, compared to the potato, maize is nutritionally inferior. Also, like rice, which was also imported, cornmeal was a difficult food to prepare in a culture unaccustomed to it. Maize requires finer grinding than other grains, as well as a longer cooking time. If not prepared properly, it can cause intestinal problems, especially if introduced suddenly into someone's everyday diet. Those problems were compounded by the fact that some of the maize in government depots had gone bad. Little wonder that it became known as "Peel's brimstone," even though much of the meal consumed in 1845–46 was purchased from private grain merchants. Concerned that most Irish people did not know how to prepare cornmeal, Charles Trevelyan, chief civil servant in the Treasury, sought instructions from Britain's diplomatic corps in America for grinding and preparing the grain. As maize became more plentiful as a reserve food, the government distributed recipes with instructions on how to cook it. Elizabeth Smith of Baltiboys, County Wicklow, found them "useful," although "the Dutch oven part might have been left out, even a griddle few of the poor possess, and to talk of yeast and butter and eggs and new milk to perfect paupers is a sort of mockery."[38]

To bring focus and organization to the aid effort, Peel appointed a Relief Commission in November 1845. Among its members were Edward Twistleton, the Poor Law Commissioner, and Randolph Routh, head of the Army Commissariat, both of whom worked closely with Charles Trevelyan of the Treasury, who oversaw day-to-day famine relief. These men remained at the center of relief for much of the famine period. The commission's initial task was to encourage the formation of local Irish relief committees made up of landlords, clergy (Protestant and Catholic) and other prominent citizens. Like those formed during previous subsistence crises, such committees were supposed to raise funds for local relief to pay for food and employment. The government would contribute some matching grants, roughly a third of the expenses. Free food was not to be distributed unless the workhouses were full and, even then, given only to those who were unable to work.[39] The effectiveness of the relief committees varied enormously, depending on local conditions and attitudes. For example, although a relief committee was formed in Coleraine, Londonderry, one member cautioned against accepting premature donations. He had, he declared, "too great a respect for his native town to allow it to go abroad that they were in a worse state of distress than the very poorest classes in the south of Ireland." A landlord in Kings County (present day Offaly) declared that he would not permit his tenants to enter the workhouse, as their well-being was his responsibility.[40] Such reticence would fade rapidly once conditions worsened in the fall of 1846.

Following established emergency procedures, Peel also organized public works to employ the indigent and enable them to buy imported maize. Public works were

---

38. James and Ó Maitiú, *The Wicklow World of Elizabeth Smith*, 61. For private merchants see Daly, "The Operations of Famine Relief, 1845—1847," 127–28. For Trevelyan see Haines, *Charles Trevelyan and the Great Irish Famine*, 182–84. For government food depots see 46–48, 77. For problems with undercooked rice, see Reilly, *The Irish Land Agent, 1830–60*, 105.
39. See Hickey, *Famine in West Cork*, 144.
40. Reilly, "Kings County during the Famine, 'Poverty and Plenty,'" 350. For Londonderry quote see Parkhill, "The Famine in County Londonderry," 150.

unpopular in Britain, however. Back in November 6, 1845, *The Times*, anticipating Peel's move, warned:

> It would be an act of munificent charity, if it were not (as it probably would be) perverted into a monstrous job [fraud]. But remember, if you do this, you will be taking away the money of the English people at a time when money will be scarce, and employment much rarer than it is now, to feed the Irish. Will this be just? Do you think it will be tolerable?[41]

Nevertheless, political economy, laced with a strong dose of Victorian moralism, made even more odious the alternative: the distribution of free food outside of the mechanism of the Poor Law. Employment projects at least made the poor labor for wages. Slow to get started, Peel's works opened in the spring of 1846, as the last of the previous year's remaining potatoes were beginning to run out. By June the works were employing 127,000 people.[42]

Peel's relief efforts provided just enough support to enable the Irish economy to cope with the immediate problems caused by the potato blight. One must wonder, however, if even that much effort would have been expended had not the loss of potatoes initially been inadvertently exaggerated.[43] At any rate, it is important to consider what Peel did *not* do. He failed to address the underlying issues involving land, tenants and landlords. He did not try to control food exports from Ireland. Nor did he clearly declare the crisis an imperial one. Some relief funds came from the Treasury, but most of them were raised locally in Ireland. At no time was Ireland's situation seen within the context of the Act of Union. Although an integral part of the United Kingdom, Ireland, like an errant stepchild, would pay for much of its own relief.

Nonetheless, Peel's limited response proved at least minimally effective; no one starved. Yet, the period from the fall of 1845 to the summer of 1846 was not a happy time for Ireland. Many people were fearful and hungry. There were evictions and protests. Mobs formed and constabulary and dragoons charged. Distress grew in some of the Poor Law Unions. Drawing on Irish newspapers and accounts from its own correspondents, *The Scotsman* recorded many signs of the blight's disruptions in the spring of 1846. On April 8 it carried a story of heavy emigration out of Limerick and Waterford. Most of the passengers seemed to be of the better class of small farmers. The April 15 issue reported on several townlands in County Cavan where some 950 people were threatened with starvation. In Killarney many people had only one meal of half-rotten potatoes a day. On April 22 the paper reported that in Carrick-on-Suir mobs broke into provision stores and shops to carry off meal. In Tipperary rioters seized a dray laden with flour. Later a mob of several thousand gathered in Clonmel demanding food. The military was called out but there was no violence. In response to such incidents, Dublin Corporation, under the influence of Daniel O'Connell, formed a committee to urge the government to place restrictions on the use of grain in brewing and distilling. Also, free trader though he

---

41. See Leslie A. Williams, *Daniel O'Connell, the British Press and the Irish Famine*, 138.
42. Ó Catháoir, "Ireland in the First Year of the Famine," 198.
43. Kinealy, *Great Calamity*, 35.

was, O'Connell wanted a temporary ban on food exports from Ireland. The committee's deputation to the home secretary, Sir James Graham, was coldly received, however. O'Connell salvaged what he could from this rejection, turning his group into the permanent Mansion House Committee, hoping to unite the various Irish factions and to keep pressure on the government. In the end, the effort had little effect.[44]

Interestingly, the Young Ireland faction associated with *The Nation* rejected any and all appeals to the imperial government for aid. A "foreign parliament" that was "ignorant, vain, headlong, insolent and selfish" would only treat all Irishmen, regardless of status, "with indiscriminate insolence." In the journal's pages Richard O'Gorman thundered, "But let us have no begging appeals to England." Such degrading behavior, he insisted, threatened to undermine the only possible solution to the crisis: self-government for Ireland. In the face of rising fears of famine, and despite reservations about his leadership, *The Nation* backed the collection of that year's "O'Connell Tribute," an annual fund-raising effort to support the Liberator as spokesmen for the nationalist cause. Even with catastrophe threatening, ideological purity dominated the group. In December of 1845 *The Nation* solemnly intoned: "Had the destruction of the people's food been [...] complete as was apprehended on the commencement of the season, it would have been much better for the poor."[45]

Peel and Repeal

Initially, Peel and Graham had been cautious in linking the Irish food crisis to the repeal of the Corn Laws. They waited until they were convinced that protection might stand in the way of Ireland's recovery, an approach that annoyed those anxious to abolish protection immediately. In October the *News of the World* noted that, in the face of an "impending calamity," the Government should open the ports to foreign grain. Peel, the paper complained, was too slow.[46] By the end of December 1845, however, the prime minister had decided to significantly lower the grain tariffs with an eye to the eventual repeal of the Corn Laws. Since he knew this would split his Tory party, he tried to keep his decision secret. When *The Times* broke the story, Peel resigned. The Whigs, however, were unable to form a government. Returned to office, Peel determined to act regardless of the political fallout. In the face of strong opposition within the Tory ranks, the bill to repeal the Corn Laws passed in the House of Commons in June 1846 with the help of the Whigs and the O'Connellites. Although the loss of protection disturbed Irish landlords and their principal tenants, O'Connell's liberalism had set him against the Corn Laws. Moreover, the possibility that the repeal would split Peel's party and bring down his government was, for the Liberator, an added incentive. The enmity between the two men was long and deep.[47]

---

44. See Nowlan, "The Political Background," 135–36.
45. For quotes see Bew, *Ireland: The Politics of Enmity, 1789–2006*, 177–78, 181.
46. *News of the World*, October 19, 1845 (2). For Peel and Graham see Gray, *Famine, Land and Politics*, 97–98.
47. Gray, *Famine, Land and Politics*, 117–18.

As O'Connell had hoped, the Tory protectionists, angered by Peel's actions, refused to support him any further. The party split, and Peel's administration finally came to an end shortly after the repeal vote, opening the way for a Whig government headed by Lord John Russell. The specific occasion that brought down Peel was his attempt to pass a severe coercion act for Ireland in response to hunger-inspired unrest. Ironically, Peel saw the act as a necessary accompaniment to the repeal of the Corn Laws and the passage of the public works relief bill for Ireland. It would demonstrate his government's concern for the protection of property, as well as the economic stability of Britain and Ireland. O'Connell pounced on the Coercion Act, and Russell saw he would have support of both the Irish and the protectionist Tories in bringing down Peel.[48]

It is a matter of speculation as to how Peel or Ireland would have fared had he remained in office over the following years. There is little reason to be too generous regarding the hypotheticals. Relief under Peel had not been unstinting. His works program had been slow in starting, and many who needed employment never got on the lists. His imported maize had been intended to hold down prices, not to feed the penniless. As Ciarán Ó Murchadha argues, under Peel the Irish poor "became effectively stripped of the ability to resist the slightest further disruption to their lives. The meagerness of the relief afforded and the purposely scheduled delays in its distribution drove the urban and rural poor to liquidate their every last resource to provide for their families."[49]

Because the blight had arrived after several wet years resulting in bad harvests. Ireland's poor were hardly in a strong position to withstand a severe blow. They did their best, but by the summer of 1846 they had gradually worn down their meager buffers against privation. They had eaten their seed potatoes, devouring the future to placate immediate hunger. They sold their livestock at whatever piece it could bring. In the case of pigs, this meant selling on a suddenly glutted market and spending the proceeds on food instead of rent. The poor also sold or pawned whatever bits of furniture, tools and decent clothing they had. As a result, the pawn trade itself became overwhelmed. Within a few years, it was in decline, as the growing mass of paupers had nothing left to sell and no money to redeem anything. According to one observer in Lurgan, County Armagh, "To dream of finding furniture in the houses of the poor in his district would be folly. There is no such thing; all has gone for food." All these coping strategies are part of an all too familiar pattern seen in food crises today. As Butterly and Shepherd suggest, because such actions at some point become irreversible, they are evidence of impending famine.[50]

Even with the loss of only 30–40 percent of the potato crop in 1845, the base of the Irish potato economy began to crumble, the effects spreading throughout the society. In January 1846, a report stated that many families were living on a single meal of diseased potatoes. As the price of sound potatoes rose, the workhouses initially cut their serving of

---

48. Nowlan, "The Political Background," 138–41.
49. Ó Murchadha, *The Great Famine: Ireland's Agony, 1845–52*, 45.
50. Butterly and Shepherd, *Hunger: The Biology and Politics of Starvation*, Chart 6. 125. For the pawn trade and related quote see Mac Atasney, *"This Dreadful Visitation:" The Famine; in Lurgan/Portadown*, 97–98. For pawn brokers in general see Ó Gráda, *Black '47 and Beyond*, 149–56.

potatoes to just once a day, and then began substituting maze, a serious blow to the nutritional well-being of the inmates.[51] All over Ireland thousands of conacre farmers and cottiers failed to make their rents and, therefore, lost access to the land. At the same time, fewer farmers were willing to put acres out to conacre, unsure of collecting their rents. Where potatoes were scarce, farmers could no longer feed their laborers as part of their wages. Consequently, unemployed workers swelled the ranks of the destitute. Added to their number were bound cottiers who, faced with the loss of their potatoes, withheld their labor from their landlords, flocking instead to the public works. Without laborers, the acreage planted with potatoes in 1846 was far below that of the previous year. Thus, even if the blight had not returned in the fall of 1846, rural Ireland would have still faced food shortages, hardship and a seriously damaged economy.[52]

Thus, Peel handed over to his Whig successors an already battered vessel just before it crashed unto the reef and sank. Yet, because he was no longer at the helm, history has given him a largely underserved pass. Interestingly, once out of power and with his party divided, Peel tended to support most of his successor's subsequent famine policies. Indeed, there were important continuities of policy between Peel and Russell's Whigs, especially concerning the need to restructure Irish agriculture.[53] However, there was one very important difference between Peel and his Whig successors. His relief policies had followed well-established precedents, deploying a vague combination of partial reliance on local Irish resources and imperial intervention in the form of food imports and a shared support for public works. Some British newspapers complained that he had left the door open for Irish penury to become a burden on the rest of the Kingdom. Yet, what did the term United Kingdom imply, if not that, in a crisis, the whole would come to the assistance of one of its members? Nevertheless, sections of British public opinion were disturbed. "We cannot, by any process of reasoning," grumbled *The Times* in September of 1846, "be convinced that the general body of the nation ought to be taxed for the support for particular districts of Ireland."[54] Peel had left ajar a door that his Whig successors would be most anxious to shut and bolt.

Enter the Whigs

Given the crisis that Lord John Russell would soon confront, it is ironic that there could not have been an incoming British prime minister better disposed toward Ireland. Inheritor of the reformist tradition within the Whig party, Russell had a record of trying

---

51. Flanagan, *The Great Famine in Kinsale*, 25.
52. See Ó Murchadha, *The Great Famine*, 45–46. For dismissed laborers see McCavery, "The Famine in County Down," 103. For conacre see Flanagan, *The Great Famine in Kinsale*, 29. For bound cottiers see Donnelly, *The Land and the People of Nineteenth-Century Cork*, 74.
53. Behind the scenes, Peel offered advice to Russell and was almost a mentor to the new Chancellor of the Exchequer, Sir Charles Wood. See Haines, *Charles Trevelyan and the Great Irish Famine*, 64–65, 205–9, 210–12. For continuities linking Peel and Russell see Gray, *Famine, Land and Politics*, 128.
54. De Nie, *The Eternal Paddy*, 107.

to deal with some of Ireland's problems. As previously mentioned, O'Connell had worked closely with the Whigs and particularly with Russell. Granted, the results had been modest at best, but both Russell and O'Connell were still interested in cooperation. The Liberator, in fact, had little choice. Politically weakened by his failed campaign to repeal the Act of Union, and confident that the Tories would do little for Ireland, he felt that he had to support the Whigs again and hope for the best, even at the risk of further defections from among his own supporters. Unfortunately, this focused too much Irish political attention on O'Connell's leadership and not enough on the crisis facing the country. Inside the Repeal Association, the Young Ireland faction rejected cooperation with any party that had opposed Repeal. Therefore, at a time when Ireland desperately needed strong, united leadership, O'Connell faced political challenges at home. The situation came to a head in July 1846 when the Liberator insisted that all association members sign on to his nonviolent approach to Repeal. Young Ireland walked out and soon founded its own organization, the Irish Confederation. While this left O'Connell free to deal with the Whigs, it also left Irish politics weakened at the very moment when the country was about to experience a full-fledged famine.[55]

Nevertheless, O'Connell's new alliance with the Whigs got off to a promising start when Russell appointed John William Ponsonby, the Fourth Earl of Bessborough, as Ireland's new lord lieutenant. Bessborough was on generally good terms with O'Connell. Unfortunately, both men were in declining health; neither would survive the following year. To make matters worse, times had changed since the old Whig–O'Connellite agreement at Litchfield House a decade earlier. The reform-minded faction within the Whig leadership had dwindled, leaving Russell in a weak position as far as Irish affairs were concerned. Russell, therefore, found himself forced to form a government dependent upon powerful politicians who shared little interest in ameliorating the plight of the Irish. Within short order the prime minister became more of a moderator of his cabinet than a leader of his government.[56]

While the Whigs' interest in Irish reform had weakened over the years, the party was more dedicated than ever to the principles of laissez-faire. Having just supported the repeal of the Corn Laws and celebrated their triumph over protectionism, most Whigs had little interest in launching new intrusions into the free market. Some had even been annoyed at Peel's modest interventions in the Irish economy in response to the potato blight. As they took power, however, many Whigs assumed that the crisis in Ireland had passed and that normality would return with the fall harvest. The new government thus set about winding down Peel's relief interventions, which some felt represented assaults upon morality, as well as on economic orthodoxy. Many Britons believed that the Irish had flocked to Peel's public works in hopes of "good wages" for little labor and cheap food. There was, therefore, no enthusiasm for continuing such alleged abuses of the public trust. On the contrary, the Whig leadership and its supporters were anxious to teach the Irish people some lessons in self-reliance. Significantly, many

---

55. Nowlan, "The Political Background," 137, 144–45.
56. Gray, *Famine, Land and Politics*, 147–48.

of the new government's policies regarding Ireland were developed by Sir Charles Wood, chancellor of the exchequer, in conjunction with Earl Grey, the colonial secretary, and Sir George Grey, the home secretary. Ideologically committed to the economics of liberalism, this Treasury faction became skilled in imposing most of its ideas on a weak prime minister and a divided cabinet. They also found a more-than-willing alley in the person of Charles Trevelyan, the assistant secretary of the Treasury.

Trevelyan was politically well placed. His brother-in-law, Thomas Babington Macaulay, the paymaster general, was a well-known author. In addition, Trevelyan had close ties to his minister, Charles Wood, and enjoyed a good relationship with most of the cabinet, as well as with various Whig editors, to whom he passed information, occasionally writing anonymous articles supporting government policies. Trevelyan, an intelligent, dedicated administrator, was one of those workhorses who helped to make Victorian Britain tick. Very articulate and highly opinionated, he had a questionable gift for attracting attention to himself. Because he also inserted himself into the most minute details of famine relief, a careless reading of the history of the Irish Famine could lead to the conclusion that he was the dominant figure in determining relief policy.[57] He was not. Decisions were made in the cabinet. However, while he did not make policies, as the Treasury's chief civil servant, Trevelyan did implement them on daily basis. He was, without doubt, a key figure in the government's handling of the Famine. Obedient, but not always comfortable with Peel's policies, Trevelyan found himself in greater sympathy with the more ideological and moralistic outlook of Wood and his associates. Rarely did he write or say anything that did not reflect the policies passed down by his superiors. Nor had he many serious disagreements with them. For their part, the ministers' positions were made easier by the fact that they could rely on a civil servant who shared their dedication to minimizing costs and to restraining interference in the market.[58] This meant that when the cabinet wanted someone to explain and justify its position to the British public, Trevelyan's indefatigable efforts and skillful pen were at its service. In addition to explaining government policies, he could, when necessary, enforce them in the face of occasional resistance from the Crown's deputies in Dublin and from those relief officials on the ground who had to deal with the reality of conditions in Ireland.

In December 1845, when it was becoming apparent that the Whigs would eventually replace Peel's government, Galway landowner Lord Clanricarde warned Russell that Ireland was facing a critical situation and that it would represent "the most serious difficulty" that the leader of the next administration would encounter. By spring, as the shortage of potatoes became acute among the poor, demands for work came from both local relief boards and laborers alike.[59] Nevertheless, on taking office, Russell's government, firm in its ideological commitment and confident that Peel had overreacted, was

---

57. Ibid., 231–33.
58. Nowlan, "The Political Background," 151. For Trevelyan and the Treasury faction see Gray, "Potatoes and Providence," 83–85.
59. See, for example, MacMahon, *The Great Famine in Tralee and North Kerry*, 33, 47,59, 99. For Clanricarde see Cornwell, *A Galway Landlord during the Great Famine*, 22, 30.

anxious to close down the public works. Under pressure from Irish grain merchants, it also quickly abandoned Peel's policy of importing maize to hold down prices, Clanricarde's arguments to the contrary. Doubling down on its gamble that the blight would not return, Russell's government, against Routh's advice, decided to end almost all relief efforts on August 15, just as disturbing reports about the fall harvest were beginning to appear. Until then, the prognosis for a sound potato harvest had seemed good. In the early summer of 1846 the constabulary, charged with keeping track of the potato crop, reported that many farmers had planned to abandon the tubers that year. However, as those potatoes that had been planted began to grow seemingly blight free, initially reticent farmers changed their minds.[60] On June 9, the *Kerry Examiner* confidently observed: "The weather is delightfully hot […] and as things go on at present, we may, through the bounty of a merciful Providence, expect an abundant harvest." With a good potato crop in the offing, everything seemed aligned for an end to the crisis. Then came the fall harvest. On August 29, 1846, the *Tralee Chronicle* carried the grim news: "The [potato] crop is totally ruined."[61]

---

60. Atasney, "The Famine in County Armagh," 39.
61. For *Examiner* quote see MacMahon, *The Great Famine in Tralee and North Kerry*, 60.

Chapter Nine

THE FIRST PHASE OF THE FAMINE: BLACK '46–'47

The Harvest of 1846

Thomas Ward from Mionloch [Galway] went out to the garden for potatoes for a meal. He stuck his spade in the pit, and the spade was swallowed. The potatoes turned to mud inside. He shrieked and shrieked. The whole town [land] came out. All the potatoes were in the same way.[1]

[…] in one night, [the potato plants were] smitten with the blight and changed from the natural green to that of polished black, the real resemblance of death."[2]

An extremely wet July and August facilitated the rapid spread of the disease. Moving at a rate of about 50 miles per week from the west, it destroyed up to 90 percent of Ireland's potato crop, leaving only one month's supply of edible tubers. In a matter of weeks, much of the country's food supply had disappeared.[3] The rampant and unrelenting spread of the blight was, of course, a devastating blow to those most dependent upon potatoes. One observer reported that "a sort of stupor fell upon the people, contrasting remarkably with the fierce energy put forth a year before. It was no uncommon sight to see the cottier and his little family sitting on the garden fence, gazing all day long in moody silence at the blighted plot that had been their last hope."[4] In early September the *Morning Chronicle* reprinted a piece from the *Ballinasloe Star*. "The fact can no longer be concealed—thousands and tens of thousands of people are starving. There is no middle term to describe their condition: starvation is the only applicable word."[5] From Dublin, the lord lieutenant and his staff warned Russell of an impending crisis beyond anything previously experienced. However, still involved in winding down the remnants of Peel's relief efforts, and with Parliament due to rise at the end of August, the government had no new plans to fall back upon. As matters worsened, it scrambled for a response, while the Treasury and Bessborough's administration in Dublin Castle talked past each other virtually the whole fall. Gradually, however, a consensus formed out of a mixture of evangelical moralism and free-market economics, which, with some modifications, would remain in place for the duration of the Famine.

---

1. Quoted in Ó Gráda, *Black '47 and Beyond*, 200.
2. Dorian, *The Outer Edge of Ulster*, 227.
3. For the spread of the blight, see Bourke, *"The Visitation of God?"*, 145–46.
4. Quoted in Bew, *Ireland: The Politics of Enmity*, 188.
5. *Morning Chronicle*, September 9, 1846 (6).

First, Irish property taxes rather than the Imperial treasury would shoulder most of the burden of relief. This was a popular move in Britain. An April 1846 leader in the *Morning Chronicle* had warned that "to spare the Irish landlord by mulcting the English trades man, whose whole life is one series of tax payings, is a kind of [...] absurdity."[6] Second, the government would not encourage idleness by handing out free food: there would be no dole (a position that would eventually have to be modified). Third, believing that Peel's purchase of Indian corn had set a dangerous precedent, Russell's government insisted that there would be no interference with free trade in the grain market. A fourth principle involved the centralization of famine relief administration to avoid the large-scale waste and corruption that had supposedly characterized Peel's efforts. Since much more money would be at stake this time, the British taxpayers had to be assured that every penny of relief would be accounted for. Therefore, virtually the whole relief effort, private charity as well as public monies, would flow through the Treasury. As noted above, this placed the department's permanent civil servant, Charles Trevelyan, in a unique position to administer the day-to-day aspects of relief.

Finally, as much as possible, the government intended to adopt relief policies that would lead to restructuring Irish agriculture. Even Peel's administration had been adamant that there should be no return to the status quo ante of potato dependency. Sir Randolph Routh, head of the Army Commissariat, reasoned that the necessary transition from potatoes to grain would require a three-to-one increase in cultivated acreage, resulting in an increase in employment, along with higher wages. Imagining the bright dawn that would follow the current darkness, Routh maintained that "it is useless to talk of emigration when so much extra labor is becoming indispensable to supply the extra food."[7] Among the more evangelical members of the government, the idea of reforming rural Ireland promised to give some meaning to the disaster. While Chancellor of the Exchequer Charles Wood perceived a retributive hand at work in the crisis—what he called "a calamity sent by Providence"—his assistant, Trevelyan, claimed to discern "a bright light shining in the distance through the dark clouds which at present hang over Ireland."[8]

Drawing upon evangelical interpretations of the moral law, this sort of providential optimism tended to ignore the restraints of laissez-faire philosophy, along with the gloomy judgments of Malthusian economics. Instead, it encouraged a reinterpretation of the prevailing wages fund theory, turning it into a blueprint for growth. According to the original theory, wages depended on the amount of available capital divided by the numbers of people employed. The standard interpretation was that while the number of workers could fluctuate (more workers, lower wages; fewer workers, higher wages) capital was relatively fixed. However, enthusiasts, like *The Times*' "Commissioner" Thomas Campbell Foster, argued that the real source of wealth was productive labor. In order to finance its own recovery all Ireland had to do was to put more people to work, thus

---

6. See Leslie A. Williams, *Daniel O'Connell, the British Press and the Irish Famine*, 156.
7. Quoted in Salaman, *The History and Social Influence of the Potato*, 307.
8. See Gray, *Famine, Land and Politics, British Government and Irish Society,1843–50*. 232.

expanding the amount of available capital. Alternatively, as Peter Gray points out, some within the Treasury placed more emphasis on land, which they believed was an underutilized source of Irish capital. Therefore, hard work on the part of landlords and peasants alike could create wealth by making the land more productive.[9] To that end, the Irish landlords had to be pressured into improving their land and employing the peasantry. With landlords facing the loss of rents, uncertain agricultural prices and increasing debt, it was not clear how this was to be accomplished.[10] This predilection to create rhetorical bridges between the reality of mass starvation and the desperate desire to conjure up simple (and cheap) solutions to the crisis would seem remarkable were it not so common in the speeches and writings of the time. This continual mismatch between imagined ends and proposed means would soon prove fatal.

Although the government claimed to adhere to the principles of political economy, there remained room for interpretation. This infuriated a liberal ideologue like James Wilson, who had launched *The Economist* in 1843. Demanding adherence to a strict laissez-faire policy, he insisted that British taxes should not finance Irish relief and that the government should not intervene in the economy, regardless of the circumstances.[11] Nevertheless, even he recognized that any meaningful restructuring of Ireland's agriculture would be impossible without some tinkering with the system. So, while broadly dedicated to the ideals of a free market, men like Russell, Peel and even Wilson saw no contradiction in occasionally using governmental power to try to create an economy and a society that would ultimately support and benefit from the free market. They imagined a clear difference between intervening in the economy and changing the society.[12]

Unsurprisingly, the government's efforts to relieve Ireland represented a tangle of contradictory goals. For example, in April 1846 Trevelyan proclaimed: "Our measures must proceed with as little disturbance as possible of the ordinary course of private trade, which must ever be the chief resource for the subsistence of the people, but *coûte que coûte* [at all costs] the people must not *under any circumstances*, be allowed to starve."[13] These were noble words, and presumably Trevelyan's use of French was for emphasis and perhaps intended to flatter his highly educated readers. Unfortunately, "at all costs" was not to become the Treasury's watchword in any language, as it steadily sought to protect the markets and shield the imperial coffers from the threat raised by Irish starvation.

---

9. See Gray, "'Potatoes and Providence,' British Government's Responses to the Great Famine," 87. For Foster, as well as for the Irish wages fund theory, see Gray, *Famine, Land and Politics*, 76–77. For the "moralists'" view on the wage fund see 25, 231–32.
10. For landlord reticence to employ the poor see Donnelly, *The Land and the People of Nineteenth-Century Cork*, 109–10.
11. For Wilson on the Irish Famine see Leslie A. Williams, *Daniel O'Connell, the British Press and the Irish Famine*, 200–4.
12. Gray, "'Potatoes and Providence,'" 76.
13. Quoted by Bourke, *"The Visitation of God?"* 173.

Landlords and Peasants

In the meantime, the pyramid structure of Ireland's potato economy continued to crumble, starting with the laborers at the bottom and then spreading back up through the ranks of subtenants, tenants and finally to the landowners themselves. As previously noted, each level of subdivision had helped underwrite the rents of those further up the ladder. With the loss of the potatoes, rents from conacre and from small tenant farms immediately dried up. Eventually, even larger tenants, petty landlords themselves, often had trouble meeting *their* rents. When they defaulted, the landowners at the top of the pyramid suddenly found *their* income flow severely constricted. If they were already in debt, their situation became dire, eventually forcing the government to deal with the problem of bankrupt estates.

The Irish landlords were outraged that the government blamed them for the situation. Those convinced that Ireland suffered from overpopulation rejected the government's demand that they should employ virtually all the country's rural poor. Instead, many landlords felt that they should be allowed to clear the poorest from their properties, sending them abroad by means of government-assisted emigration schemes. Interpreting the concept of the United Kingdom more generously than London, Irish landlords demanded more government support. In December 1846, an Irish landlord, Bernal Osborne, MP, did the math. Some 2,500,000 people were currently destitute. Each pauper would cost the rate payers £4/11 per annum, for a total of £11,375,000, to be paid by a country whose gross rental amounted to £10,000,000 a year. This was not a question of politics, Osborne insisted. It was one of survival. "Not only property but life is at stake. The winter has already commenced; much valuable time has been already lost." It was time, Osborne insisted, for the landlords to organize an assembly to "advise" the government. A similar call came from landlords in Queens County. "It was time," a statement read, "to turn to England, and to ask her—'Is this just? Is this constitutional? Is there a union between us; and do you leave us to our fate—nay, drive us to destruction?'" The appeal noted that England had spent £20,000,000 to reimburse slave owners in the West Indies. Why could she not help the Irish?[14]

In these, as in so many other controversies, Trevelyan found himself in the first line of the government's defense. Once, in October 1846, in an uncharacteristic display of temper, he accused Irish landlords of displaying "a defective part of the national [Irish] character." Instead of taking responsibility by employing the poor, they "confined themselves to memorials & disputations calling on the Govt [*sic*] to do everything, as if they had themselves no part to perform in this great crisis of the country."[15] Yet, while sticking it to the Irish landlords may have been popular in Britain, hardly anyone (except the landlords themselves) raised the question of how they were to employ more laborers while paying ever-increasing rates in the face of ever-diminishing rent collections. As Irish landlord and former member of Parliament H. Lambert recalled: "Placed between a persecuting

---

14. Both quotes carried in *The Times*, December 11, 1846.
15. Quoted in Haines, *Charles Trevelyan and the Great Irish Famine*, 254.

Government and an inflexible creditor, what chance was left to the unhappy landlord but to destroy, or be destroyed?"[16] Choosing the former, some landlords launched evictions. This, of course, forced more hungry people onto the roads and the relief roles and ultimately back into the pockets of the rate payers. Of course, as the pace of evictions increased in the early summer of 1846, Ireland's landlords appeared more blameworthy than ever. On May 4, the *Morning Chronicle* accused them of being the "aggressors" in the many instances of agrarian crime in Ireland. Because landlords had the power to evict tenants without any compensation, "the Irish peasant has no legal right to existence." The law, the paper asserted, "gives the landlord a discretionary power of life and death."[17]

While the peasantry had no voice in these debates, parliamentary committees and private middle-class citizens had been discussing issues of overpopulation, potato dependency and poverty in Ireland for years. Once the potato economy collapsed, there was no lack of ideas, some quite radical for the time. From October 1846 to January 1847, the *Morning Chronicle* ran a series of articles by John Stuart Mill, exploring the importance of tackling the root causes of Ireland's dire situation. To Mill the catastrophe had turned the entire island into a tabula rasa on which a new social order might be inscribed, erasing centuries of British misrule. Among other proposals, he argued that all tenants should be given fixity of tenure and fair rents. He also suggested that the government undertake to settle some 200,000 families on wasteland, which they would then reclaim and control. Several years earlier, George Poulett Scrope, MP, taking his cue from Prussia, had argued for a similar settlement scheme. He also urged the government to embrace tenant ownership of the land as a general policy. Although largely ignored at the time, the idea of the peasant proprietorship in Ireland had at least been broached and would eventually bear fruit, decades after the Famine.[18]

The most radical ideas regarding land reform came from within the ranks of the Irish nationalists. In 1846 and 1847, James Fintan Lalor, an Irish MP and son of a gentleman farmer, contributed a series of articles to *The Nation*, setting forth an original approach to issues of tenants' rights. He proposed nothing less than a radical rethinking of land and its ownership. The Famine, he argued, had dissolved the existing basis for land ownership, in which case the land should revert to its original owners: the people of Ireland. Under those circumstances, the people could regrant ownership, but only to those who acted in the interests of the community. This meant, among other things, to those providing security of tenure for tenants. Some of the Young Irelanders, like Gavin Duffy, were skeptical of Lalor's ideas, while others, like John Mitchel, took them to heart. Although in poor health, Lalor founded a tenants' rights league in Tipperary. He died in December 1849, and his ideas had little effect at the time. However, he did help to inject the issue of tenants' rights into the debates surrounding Irish nationalism, providing a

---

16. Lambert, *A Memoir in Ireland in 1850 by an Ex-MP*, 80.
17. Quoted by Leslie A. Williams, *Daniel O'Connell, the British Press and the Irish Famine*, 157.
18. For Scrope see Gray, *Famine, Land and Politics*, 13–14. For Mill see Kinzer, *England's Disgrace?*, 44, 47–48, 52–53, 55, 61-71.

radical inspiration for later generations.[19] Even at the time, there was some recognition, reinforced by the Devon Report of 1845, that tenants' rights did, in fact, lay at the heart of Ireland's problems. Nevertheless, radical rethinking of the plight of Ireland's tenants found little support in government circles, although Russell tried, unsuccessfully, to push through his cabinet an unimproved land settlement bill. Unfortunately, the prime minister could never get his modest proposals accepted within his divided cabinet. A weak leader, Russell's well-intentioned ideas went nowhere.[20]

As already noted, however, broad agreement did exist for changes in Ireland's agricultural system. The government wanted to encourage, if not impose, an English-style agrarian model upon Ireland. If Irish landlords would meet their responsibilities by employing the poor to improve estate lands, the poor could then live on their wages and not on potatoes. Russell and his colleagues insisted that, in a similar crisis, English landlords would most certainly employ their poor laborers. As *The Times* loftily observed on November 10, 1846, "we in England consider it the first duty of the landlord to provide extraordinary employment to meet extraordinary distress."[21] Of course, England had not seen this kind of distress in a very, very long time.

Witnessing Famine Realities and British Reporting

> I know, Sir, that I run the risk of having my statements disbelieved: but I solemnly swear no words can exaggerate and no one can describe the misery that the people of this neighborhood are enduring. [Dr. David Donovan]

As the crisis worsened, reports of dire conditions began appearing in Irish and then British newspapers. On January 2, 1847, the *Cork Southern Reporter* published the above statement written by Dr. David Donovan, a regular correspondent.[22] Such firsthand observations, along with reports of coroner's inquests, addressed two issues. They confirmed that people were actually starving in Ireland. In addition, such reports frequently provided the names of victims and described the circumstances of their deaths. The abstract "improvident masses," so frequently conjured up by bureaucrats, economists, editors and politicians, momentarily dissolved into individual human beings suffering the worst horrors of famine. Sadly, Dr. Donovan was right about the degree of disbelief his accounts would encounter. In Britain, a constant drumbeat of suspicion rattled through the press. Reports of hunger and starvation reprinted from the Irish newspapers awakened the skepticism engraved in Britain's Irish narrative. For many, the Irish remained a mendacious people, ever given to exaggeration and lies. Fortunately, some British journals decided to investigate for themselves the realities of the situation.

---

19. For Lalor and the Young Irelanders see Nowlan, "The Political Background," 169–77.
20. Kinzer, *England's Disgrace?* 78–79. For the land reclamation bill see Gray, *Famine, Land and Politics*, 159–64.
21. For quotes see Leslie A. Williams, *Daniel O'Connell, the British Press and the Irish Famine*, 183.
22. For Dr. Donovan's quote see Michael Foley, *Death in Every Paragraph*, 27. For his newspaper reports see 26–30.

For example, Frederick Bayley, editor of the *Illustrated London News* (*ILN*; founded in 1842), decided to inquire into the crisis. Providing pictorial as well as textual coverage, the weekly journal, which found its way into many middle-class English homes, published several investigative pieces starting on January 30, 1847. On that date the front page of the *ILN* carried an engraving of an open cart hauling an uncovered corpse, an image that many readers might have found disturbing. The accompanying text sought to drive home a hard message: "England learns with dismay, that millions of men are dependent for life on its Treasury [...] [which] must for a long time to come, send out grants, loans, advances—must pay the wages of half a nation for this year. [...] To all objections made on principle [...] there is but on answer—it must be done!" A month later Bayley dispatched one of his reporter-illustrators, James Mahony, to Skibbereen, County Cork, "with the object of ascertaining the accuracy of the frightful statements" emanating from that area. The resulting two articles, published on February 13 and February 20, 1847, provided some of the period's best reporting on the disaster.[23]

Irish realities challenged whatever skepticism the *ILN*'s readers might have had. As Mahony wrote for the February 13 issue, "neither pen nor pencil could portray the misery and horror" that confronted him in his native West Cork. While some of the magazine's illustrations were stock images of the Irish countryside, a few may have pushed the envelope of what was acceptable in British middle-class parlors. One engraving depicts a woman begging with her dead baby in her arms. And, while Mahony's sketch of a ragged boy and girl hunting for potatoes in Cahera does not quite reproduce the living skeletons the artist described in his written report, their thin, spikey hair (signs of malnutrition) and pinched features might, nonetheless, have disturbed some readers. Most likely Mahony and his editor were aware of the power of illustrations both to engage but also to repulse readers. In almost every case, the text of the articles, while still discreet, got closer to the grim reality than did the accompanying engravings. For example, in one house near Bridgetown, Mahony recalled seeing "the dying, the living, and the dead, lying indiscriminately upon the same floor, without anything between them and the cold earth save a few miserable rags." The accompanying sketch, however, showed a shabby Irish village with clusters to townsfolk who are too distant to suggest sever privation. When Mahony and a clergyman visited the hut of man named Mullins, the artist found the dying man huddled in a corner on a bit of straw. His ragged children crouched over a few embers to keep warm. Mahony's sketch, however, foregrounds the top-hatted minister seated in the only available chair. In the background are indistinct forms of the children, while the dying man is an equally indistinct bundle of rags. And, although the scene is stark, nothing suggests the hut's ankle-deep fifth Mahony describes in the text. The next engraving is a picturesque depiction of a village, fit for any tourist account.[24]

---

23. For quotes see Leslie A. Williams, *Daniel O'Connell, the British Press and the Irish Famine*, 210. For British press coverage of the period from 1846 to 147, see 168–222.
24. For quotes see ibid., 214. For Cahera illustration see 212. For a description and analysis of the *ILN*'s early coverage of the Famine see 208–18. For further analysis of the journal's Famine illustrations see Crawford, "The Great Irish Famine," 75–88. Also O'Sullivan, *The Tombs of the Departed*, 40–44; Boyce, "Representing the 'Hungry Forties' in Image and Verse."

A glance at the published portions of a journal kept by Elihu Burritt, a visiting American abolitionist and humanitarian, suggests something of what British reporters and their editors held back from their readers. Burritt appears to have visited Skibbereen at the same time as Mahony and may have toured some of the area in his company. Although his style is somewhat stilted, Burritt seemed intent on confronting his readers with the horrific suffering he encountered. In one cabin, a mother held up her 12-year-old son. "The cold, watery-faced child was entirely naked," Burritt writes. "His body was swollen to nearly three times its usual size, and had burst the ragged garment that covered him, and now dangled in ragged shreds behind him." Another mother showed him "a thin-faced baby of two years, with clear sharp eyes that did not wink, but stared stark still at vacancy, as if the glimpse of another existence had eclipsed its vision. Its cold, naked arms were not much larger than pipe stems, while its body was swollen to the size of a full-grown person." Elsewhere, he saw children, who "if they had been dead, could not have been such frightful specters." A child, trying to stand by clinging to a door, "disclosed every joint in its frame, while the deepest lines of old age furrowed its face."[25]

In England a few citizens tried to verify for themselves the differences between Irish realities and British doubts. In March 1847 Lord Dufferin, Frederick Temple Blackwood, left Oxford with a fellow student and traveled to Ireland to investigate conditions there. Near Skibbereen Lord Dufferin paused at a cabin from which emerged a group carrying a woman's corpse

> over which a scanty tattered yellow rag had just been thrown, not sufficient however to cover the whole length of the figure, or to prevent one seeing the livid lifeless arms as they hung down swinging and knocking against the ground. They hastily flung it into the shell, the cart drove off, and the remains were hastily consigned to the earth without a coffin, and without the offices of religion![26]

Later the undergraduate related an incident in which a man, weakened by hunger, tried to bury the body of his wife outside the cabin. The next day neighbors returned her head to him, having retrieved it from scavenging dogs. Dufferin, a future viceroy of India, published his grim account of his fortnight in Ireland as soon as he returned to England.[27]

Whether out of curiosity, compassion or journalistic endeavor, others crossed the Irish Sea to engage in what might today be called "disaster tourism."[28] Some were, in current parlance, "aid workers." For example, William Bennett, an English Quaker, traveled

---

25. Burritt, *A Journal of a Visit of Three Days to Skibbereen and Its Neighborhoods*, 10, 14.
26. Dufferin, *Narrative of a Journey from Oxford to Skibbereen*.
27. Dufferin, *Narrative of a Journey from Oxford to Skibbereen*, 18, 21. Proceeds from his publication went to famine relief, along with £1000 of his own money; Christine Kinealy, *Charity and the Great Hunger in Ireland*, 59–60. The Blackwoods were Anglo Irish. The mother, Helen Blackwood, Lady Dufferin, wrote "The Irish Emigrant," a popular Famine-era parlor song. See O'Sullivan and Lucking, "The Famine World Wide," 213.
28. Based on the author's analysis of publication dates in John McVeagh's *Irish Travel Writing: A Bibliography*, 51. Irish travel accounts were published between 1840 and 1845, while 62 appeared during the famine years of 1846–50. Many of the later concerned aspects of famine relief

through the west of Ireland in 1847, distributing seeds and small monetary grants. Like other members of the Society of Friends who published accounts of their famine missions, Bennett was intent on witnessing, on providing an accurate picture of conditions in Ireland. Unlike those Friends who were devoted to the "plain style" of prose, however, Bennett seems to have harbored a literary bent, which occasionally reveals itself. Visiting Mayo, he stayed with an Anglican rector. In a grim distortion of the literary tendency to use windows to frame picturesque descriptions, Bennett recounted how, during breakfast, the destitute and starving "thronged the windows, which presented framed pictures of living groups of want and wretchedness, almost beyond endurance to behold; yet to keep them off the family had long found impossible." Windows, in fact, frequently figure in these famine travel accounts. While they allowed visitors to see the horrors around them, they also acted as barriers, protecting the observers and keeping the destitute at a distance. Early in his trip, Lord Dufferin recorded that "at the end of every stage, the coach was surrounded by crowds of wretched creatures begging for something to eat, wan little faces thrusting themselves in at the window" of his coach. Doorways played similar roles in famine descriptions, framing a cabin's interior horrors or separating a well-off family from the living dead who crowded near their thresholds. Asenath Nicholson recalled that "the door and window of the kind Mrs. Arthur wore a spectacle of distress indescribable; naked, cold, and dying, standing like petrified statues."[29]

Bearing witness to such appalling circumstances could prove an ordeal. Quaker William Edward Foster, who traveled around Ireland gathering information, wrote: "I have not the nerve [...] to look upon the suffering of the afflicted; it takes too much possession of me, and almost disqualifies me from exertion." One evening another Quaker, Spencer T. Hall, investigating the Famine in 1849, found himself unable to speak, "for had I attempted expression at all, it could only have been in convulsive weeping; and from that hour I resolved to return and plead in England, however humbly, the cause of Ireland among my countrymen." Even that redoubtable American aid worker, Asenath Nicholson, eventually reached the limits of what she could witness. Once, when asked to look into a cabin containing the dead and dying, she had to refuse. "*I did not*, and *could not* endure, as the famine progressed, such sights [...] they were too *real*, and these realities became a dread" (emphasis in original). Initially, she had walked confidently around Ireland, even at night. But "now the fear of meeting living walking ghosts, or, stumbling upon the dead in my path at night" kept her indoors whenever possible. Nicholson and Hall seem to have confronted what David Lloyd has called the "indigent sublime," which momentarily dissolved the boundaries between the well-fed, if sympathetic, observers,

---

and/or reports on conditions. See Fegan, "The Traveller's Experience in Famine Ireland," 361–71. See also Woods, *Traveller's Accounts as Source-Material for Irish Historians*, 142–61.

29. See Kelleher, "The Female Gaze: Asenath Nicholson's Famine Narrative," 128; Dufferin, *Narrative of a Journey from Oxford to Skibbereen*, 7; Bennett, *Narrative of a Recent Journey of Six Weeks in Ireland*, 19. For Bennett and the Quaker "plain style" see Hooper, *Travel Writing and Ireland*, 131–33, 135. For the use of windows in Irish travel narratives see William H. A. Williams, *Tourism, Landscape and the Irish Character*, 60–61. For the use of thresholds see Lloyd, "The Indigent Sublime: Specters of Irish Hunger," 164.

and the skeletal, living dead they had encountered.[30] There was a danger, however, that such descriptions, offered to a reading public attuned to the grotesqueries of the gothic style, might dehumanize famine victims or at least "distance" them from the middle-class readers. *The Scotsman* published a letter from Kerry that described famine victims as being "degraded" and the infants, "not like human beings!" Although sympathetic about their plight, the writer wondered what such children would be like if they grew up? "What sort of population will the Irish be then! These children cannot have brains or ideas in their brains, much superior to those of brutes."[31]

Public Works Resurrected

Whatever their merits, most of the ideas put forward to cure Ireland's underlying ills would take time to implement. With the near total failure of the 1846 potato crop, the government realized that it had to come up with an immediate response. Having disbanded the relief committees, ended Peel's maize imports, and abandoned his public works program, Russell's government now found itself empty handed. It had basically three choices, none mutually exclusive of the others, but all politically and ideological unappealing. For reasons to be discussed below, closing the Irish ports to prevent grain exports was a political nonstarter. This should have made a second option imperative: large-scale importation of grain, not to control prices but to feed those too poor to purchase food. The idea of such a dole, however, also cut too deeply into the prevailing free-market ideology. That left only one alternative: a heavy reliance on the previously banished public works. Thus, like several Continental countries at the time, the government reluctantly found itself forced to deviate from strict laissez-faire orthodoxy.[32] At least, within the liberal lexicon of lesser evils, having the poor work for wages to buy food was preferable to simply doling out either money or rations. Employment at least kept relief attached to some semblance of the market while at the same time observing the minimal moral demands of political economy. Although personally opposed to public works, Trevelyan had no choice but to support the government's policy.[33]

Unpalatable as it seemed, some in the government hoped that the threat of renewed public works financed out of the local rates might induce the landlords themselves to take responsibility and employ the peasantry. Thus, the Labour Rate Act of 1846, which reinstituted public works, prohibited the use of public funds that might benefit individual landowners and their major tenants. The act supported general road building

---

30. See Lloyd, "The Indigent Sublime: Specters of Irish Hunger," 167. For Foster quote see Kinealy, *Charity and the Great Hunger in Ireland*, 72. For Hall, *Life and Death in Ireland as Witnessed in 1849*, 74. For Asenath Nicholson, see Kellerher, "The Female Gaze: Asenath Nicholson's Famine Narrative," 129.
31. *The Scotsman*, July 7, 1849 (3).
32. For policies on the Continent see Kinealy, *A Death-Dealing Famine*, 86–88.
33. According to Robin Haines, Trevelyan would have preferred cost-price sales of food from government depots, supported by charitable purchases where local funds were wanting; *Charles Trevelyan and the Great Irish Famine*, 175–76, 241.

and only a few, limited types of general drainage schemes. So, unless they undertook to employ workers to improve their own lands, the landlords would be forced to pay taxes for projects that were often of minimal value to them. Wood rejoiced that the act could become "a sort of test like the workhouse test" but for the proprietors. "If you don't support your people by wages on your own estates, you will have to pay the county cess." Of course, landlords would pay the cess whether or not they employed the poor. As one land agent in Cork complained, no matter how many people landlords might employ, under the Poor Law "they were taxed as heavily as those who did not employ a single man."[34]

Instead of sharing the costs of projects, as it had under Peel, the Treasury would only advance loans at 5 percent interest. (A small grant pool of £50,000 was available for particularly poor districts in the west.) As it turned out, however, the Labour Rate Act's new public works program contained a serious flaw. The loan repayments were to be spread over 10 years. Who knew what might happen by then? Moreover, since the costs of the projects would fall upon *all* rate payers and not just landowners, no particular group felt any need for restraint in proposing projects. Thus, the demand for public works, instead of being minimized, proliferated, while thousands of the poor, many facing starvation, swamped the relief employment roles.[35]

This was not the only reason why, despite the rapidly growing crisis, initiating projects turned out to be slow and cumbersome. Mindful of criticisms of Peel's earlier program, the government's new public works were to be carefully scrutinized to eliminate jobbery and inefficiency. First, local grand juries were required to make "presentments" (identify projects) and forward them to the Board of Works, which then made recommendations to Trevelyan at the Treasury for approval. Once accepted, the Board of Works had to implement the project. Conditions, however, were so dire that grand juries were pressured into formulating and passing project requests on to the Board of Works as rapidly as possible. Having previously been focused on closing out the remaining works instituted by Peel, the board suddenly found itself seriously understaffed as projects flooded in from panicked groups all over Ireland. The board quickly had to hire 10,000 new overseers and 5,000 clerks, as well as additional engineers, office workers and draftsmen to run 5,000 separate operations. This, of course, generated an enormous amount of correspondence, averaging 800 letters a day. Consequently, delay and confusion abounded, while complaints of inefficiencies and corruption dogged the board. Worse, the whole process was expensive. While trying to keep down the cost of worker's wages, the government spent £48,000 just expanding the Board's bureaucracy. Occasionally, as much as 25 percent of the cost of roads and 50 percent of the drainage projects went into administrative overhead.[36] Thus, in its efforts to minimize jobbery, the government encased the entire relief operation within a cumbersome bureaucratic

---

34. See Donnelly, *The Land and the People of Nineteenth-Century Cork*, 111. For Wood's quote see Gray, *Famine, Land and Politics*, 241.
35. Woodham-Smith, *The Great* Hunger, *Ireland, 1845–49*, 113–14.
36. Ó Gráda, *Great Irish Famine*, 46. For expansion of public works see Kinealy, *This Great Calamity*, 90–91.

carapace. Consequently, projects were slow in starting. In Omagh, County Tyrone, for example, it took two months for the Treasury to approve the first series works and a further month to authorize the remaining projects.[37]

Even so, these attempts to combat waste, fraud and abuse with layers of bureaucracy did not impress the government's critics. In December, *The Times*, ever adept at combining economics, moralism and politics with hyperbole, announced: "A moral has supervened on a physical calamity. [...] There is a grand national embezzlement in the course of perpetration." The paper alleged that not only did the government's projects attract thousands demanding wages for little or no work, but the money they earned would go into buying arms. The "crop" being harvested "is not the golden corn, but the steel blade [...] and firelocks for mattocks. [...] The peasantry have turned famine into a gain, and from its proceeds purchase firearms."[38]

Nevertheless, despite the slow start and bureaucratic stumbles, money eventually began to flow to those employed on the works. According to Cormac Ó Gráda, most of the funds allocated to public works did eventually go into wages.[39] When it came to setting the wage rate, however, the government faced a dilemma. The works were supposed to enable people to earn money to buy food. However, if the wages were too high, people would cling to the works instead of returning to cultivate their fields in spring. Therefore, rates were set at around 2d under the already low pre-Famine standard of 10d a day. At the same time, the Board of Works switched from paying a daily wage to offering only task or piece work. Buoyed up by the optimism available to one far removed from a life of hunger and physical toil, Lord John Russell felt confident that those on task work would be motivated to easily earn enough to feed their families. At the same time, task work promised to control wages. For similar reasons, the government intended to employ only heads of households. Other family members were supposed to be kept off the lists.[40]

Unfortunately, the optimism of well-fed officials sprinted far ahead of the realities of the hungry. Traveling through Ireland in early 1847, journalist Alexander Somerville reported on a family of eight "skeletons," as he called them, trying to survive a full week on the 26 pounds of yellow meal (maize) earned by working on the roads. Unfortunately, driven by their gnawing hunger, they ate most of the meal by midweek, leaving them to starve for the remainder. Somerville noted that most such families spent almost all their money on food, meaning that, if they had to buy their fuel, they could afford only enough for cooking, if that. Consequently, their cabins went unheated during the winter. Several poor law guardians in Kinsale visited two hundred homes and found only two in which there was "any appearance of food," and in scarcely any was there "a particle of fire."[41]

---

37. Grant, "The Famine in County Tyrone," 200. For details on bureaucracy, see Kinealy, *A Death-Dealing Famine*, 75.
38. *The Times*, December 10, 1846 (4).
39. Ó Gráda, *Great Irish Famine*, 46.
40. See Haines, *Charles Trevelyan and the Great Irish Famine*, 241. For inadequacy of daily wages see Grace, *The Great Famine in Nenagh Poor Law Union*, 85; Flanagan, *The Great Famine in Kinsale*, 35. For controlling wages and worker reaction see Flanagan, 34, 35.
41. Somerville, *Letters from Ireland during the Famine of 1847*, 96–97. For Kinsale see Flanagan, *The Great Famine in Kinsale*, 37.

Thus, instead of moving the Irish poor from dependence to self-reliance, Russell's public works shifted them from hunger to starvation wages and harsher living and working conditions. In many cases laborers could not feed their families on what they earned. Therefore, despite the rules, women and children crowded onto the lists. Even so, many of the poor fell into a debt trap, borrowing from merchants to feed their families at high prices, then turning over their week's pay to cover the previous week's debt.[42]

The initial public works operations began in September of 1846, employing 26,000 people. As more projects opened, masses flocked to be hired. In some of the western counties, around one-fifth of the labor force found employment on the projects. In the province of Connaught, the works hired on average one individual per family, as compared to one in 16 families in eastern Ulster.[43] Overall, by November 21, 250,000 people were toiling on the projects. By January 1847, an astonishing 615,000 were on the rolls, the numbers peaking at around 714,000 by March. Although Trevelyan later estimated that those on the public works supported some three and a half million family members, one must question the level of that "support," given all the shortcomings and faults within the system.[44]

Yet, although the numbers employed may seem impressive, there were still too few jobs for the vast numbers hoping to feed their families. On one project near Ennis 700 people turned up to fill only 240 available places. The works in County Cavan employed only 10 percent of the workforce for an average wage of around 4s a week.[45] As the shock waves of the collapsing potato economy reverberated throughout the society, even those not directly involved in agriculture found their livelihoods impacted. For example, around Kinsale, boatman who provided sand used to build up potato beds suddenly found themselves without work. Also, fisherman saw the prices of their catches fall since fewer people had money to buy them. Inevitably, the unemployed staged frequent protests. One relief committee near Kinsale was confronted by the members of some 400 families, proclaiming, "give us work or food, we are starving, we are not beasts, we cannot eat grass." The chairman of the relief committee in Kinsale feared that "the time has come when the people must starve or plunder."[46]

Of the two types of public work projects, road building and drainage, the latter was more expensive but potentially more useful. Drainage schemes or "reproductive works" had the potential to open marginal lands to cultivation. As noted earlier, however, this pushed too hard against Whig ideology. Despite the advice of Bessborough and Clanricarde (who had joined Russell's cabinet), the government insisted that no

---

42. See James and Ó Maitiú, *The Wicklow World of Elizabeth Smith*, 54.
43. Ó Gráda, *The Great Irish Famine*, 51. For provincial tallies see Kinealy, *This Great Calamity*, table 7, 99.
44. See Nally, *Human Encumbrances*, 142. For more data see also Ó Murchadha, *The Great Famine*, 61; Trevelyan calculated that a total of 734,000 workers had been employed; see his *The Irish Crisis*, 64–65.
45. For Ennis see Ó Murchadha, *Sable Wings Over the Land*, 89. For Cavan see Gallogly, "The Famine in County Cavan," 65.
46. Flanagan, *The Great Famine in Kinsale*, 31, 32-33.

individual landowners should benefit from public projects, although they were helping to pay for them through local rates. As Trevelyan stated, widespread drainage would be "a task for which the nature and functions of government are totally unsuited." The controversy over drainage illustrates how almost every detail of Famine relief became the subject of intense and time-consuming debate and disagreement.[47]

Most of the projects, therefore, involved road building, even though Ireland already had a good road system. While isolated areas might have benefited from such improvements, given the pressure to develop projects quickly, many of the new roads were poorly planned and often underfunded. Consequently, many projects ran out of money before they were completed, resulting in the infamous "Famine roads" that disappeared into the bogs. Or in some cases perfectly good roads were dug up so that they could be "improved." Recalling the situation decades later, Dr. Lombe Atthill wrote "there was not a county in Ireland in which many roads were not left in a most impassable state—hills half cut down, hollows partially filled, nothing completed. What between want, waste, ignorance, incapacity and mismanagement vast sums of money were uselessly expended, and thousands of lives lost that might have been saved." Nevertheless, work on the "meal roads," as they were often called, did allow some families to survive the winter.[48]

Despite the depth of the Irish crisis, those dedicated to political economy discerned a moral cloud hanging over the government's public works program. Russell blamed Peel for having set a bad precedent, accustoming the Irish poor to what Russell took to be a promise of "good wages, little labor and a low price of food [...] [which] must be resisted and all such expectations should be crushed." Writing in October 1846, he complained: "The common delusions that government can convert a period of scarcity into a period of abundance is one of the most mischievous that can be entertained. But alas! The Irish have been taught many bad lessons and few good ones."[49] Russell's implication that the Irish were like children who had to be "taught" reveals the role of Britain's Irish narrative in shaping attitudes toward Famine relief. It also reflects moralistic fears that the wrong sort of intervention in the Irish economy would encourage what the British assumed to be the worst aspects of the Irish character. Lady Sligo, engaged in charitable efforts during the Famine, feared that too much government relief "would certainly be the ruin of the people," encouraging them to trust in "anything rather than their own exertions."[50] Apparently, the best way to help the Irish was to reform rather than to feed them. Morality could not be dismissed by hunger.

The government's attempt to base famine relief largely on public works was fatally flawed. Although the program no doubt saved lives, it also claimed them. The winter of 1846–47 turned out to be unusually harsh. February snows in the Wicklow mountains blocked roads, forcing one Poor Law inspector, trying to make his rounds, to dig his horse

---

47. For Trevelyan quote see Nowlan, "The Political Background," 151. For Bessborough and Clanricarde see Cornwell, *A Galway Landlord during the Great Famine*, 30.
48. Kinealy, *A Death-Dealing Famine*, 76. Atthill, *Recollections of an Irish Doctor*, 105.
49. Quotes from Kinealy, *This Great Calamity*, 73.
50. Kinealy, *Charity and the Great Hunger in Ireland*, 161.

out of a drift.[51] Because of the terrible weather and inadequate food, people already malnourished and ill died from exposure while toiling on the works. Having long since pawned their better clothing, they often had little more than rags to protect themselves from the elements. A priest in Dingle, County Kerry, protested that people, working for inadequate and often tardy wages, did not have enough food and were "dying by inches." Sitting on the death of one Denis McKennedy in West Cork, a coroner's jury found that he had "died of starvation, owing to the gross negligence of the Board of Works," which had failed to pay his wages. Writing years after the Famine, Donegal schoolmaster Hugh Dorian unequivocally condemned Russell's public works for "the sending of many a poor honest man to the untimely grave through hunger and cold." The wages were inadequate and out on the works in winter it was what Dorian called "slow murder."[52]

Even had wages been pegged at the pre-Famine level of $10d$ to $12d$ a day, they still might have proven insufficient, given the rapidly rising cost of food. The price of the few available potatoes had risen from around $30d$ per cwt in 1845 to almost $120d$ per cwt in 1847. Oats, the primary alternative food for some small farmers, rose from $80d$ per cwt to almost $140d$. Between October 1846 and January 1847 the prices for oatmeal and maize doubled and, in some areas, even trebled. Even a wage of one shilling a day might have bought only two pounds of grain with which to feed a family of six or seven. Therefore, some families had to get as many members as possible onto the work roles. January 1847 saw an enormous jump in the numbers of boys, girls and women toiling on the projects, a common enough sight in English factories where wages were also low. The number of females on the public works in Castlebellingham, County Louth, increased from 397 in January 9 to 7,042 at the end of the month.[53] As bad as wages and conditions were for those on the works, things were infinitely worse for the unemployed. Captain Wynne, a local Poor Law administers, not normally given to displays of sympathy, complained to his superiors when the works in his district temporarily shut down. Describing the sight of women scavenging fields amid snow and ice for raw turnips and the sounds of their children's screams, he wrote: "I am a match for anything else I may meet with here, but this I cannot stand. When may we expect to resume the works?"[54]

The Scramble for Grain

From the beginning, the government had compounded its relief problems by failing to quickly address two closely related problems: the supply and the cost of food. Whereas Peel had tried to use imported grain as a means of price control, Russell's government intended to stick more strictly to its free-market principles. Grain imported by the

---

51. Rees, *The Surplus People: The Fitzwilliam Clearances, 1845–1856*, 36.
52. Dorian, *The Outer Edge of Ulster*, 215–16. For Denis McKennedy see Hickey, *Famine in West Cork*, 155. For Dingle quote see Kieran Foley, "The Famine in the Dingle Peninsula," 400.
53. Kinealy, *The Great Calamity*, table 4, 96. For wages in general see Ó Gráda, *The Great Irish Famine*, 47. For the rise in food prices see Eiríksson, "Food Supply and Food Riots," 80. For prices per cwt see Kennedy et al., *Mapping the Great Irish Famine*, 66.
54. See Salaman, *The History and Social Influence of the Potato*, 308.

government could be sold (not given away) only in instances when local market supplies became, in the parlance of the Treasury, "exhausted." Even then, that price could never undercut what local merchants were charging, which, in the absence of any attempt at price controls, may have been an invitation to price gauging. In Donegal, maize that cost the government £13 a ton was sold to local relief committees for £19 a ton so as not to compete with the local traders.[55] In addition, the government's attempts to protect local markets may have encouraged some merchants to hold back some of their supplies, thereby preventing the markets from becoming "exhausted" and, thus, keeping prices high. In some areas, such as around Killybegs in west Donegal, the local merchants were unable to import large supplies of grain. Nevertheless, the presence of *any* private grain in the market threatened to keep the government depots closed.[56]

The real problem, which the government tried not to acknowledge and certainly did not want to publicize, was that there was not enough food in Ireland in the winter of 1846 and 1847 to offset the collapse of the potato. Therefore, some officials turned to what might be called "magical thinking," a mixture of ideology and willed ignorance. For example, in response to requests to release food from government depots, Routh insisted that the government's stored grain was never intended as the "primary or principal means of substance [...] but merely to provide a last resource when other means derived from the Home Harvest and Importations shall be exhausted." Touring Sligo markets in the autumn of 1846, Routh was impressed by what appeared to be an abundant harvest, although one largely devoid of potatoes. Since the local markets appeared well stocked, he reasoned that, "The Home Produce has been brought into use only partially," and was, therefore, far from exhausted.[57] Phrases like "Home Produce" and "Home Harvest," resplendent in their official capital letters, have a familiar ring to them. When confronted by problems either too difficult or too expensive to solve, such phrases, sufficiently repeated, can conjure up a pseudo-reality. In Routh's case they magically turned an absence into an abundance. Apparently, he and others in the relief administration assumed that what they saw in the local markets represented but the tip of an iceberg of secret Irish plenty. They conveniently forgot that potatoes had allowed small and middling farmers to sell their grain. Now, without them, oats might have been all many families had left. In such cases, "Home Produce" meant home consumption, not hoarding. One poor-law guardian in County Cork remarked that even "respectable farmers" working 30 acres or more were "suffering," as they were "obliged to consume in their families and in their stables the corn which in former years used to procure clothes and others comforts for them."[58]

---

55. Begley and Lally, "The Famine in County Donegal," 87.
56. See Conaghan, *The Great Famine in South-West Donegal 1845–1850*, 64, 137–38, 152. Nevertheless, Cormac Ó Gráda argues that observers might have mistaken local "supply shocks" for manipulation of the market. Since merchants faced known dangers in hoarding, Ó Gráda argues that the Irish markets operated with a minimum of exploitation; see "The Great Famine and Other Famines," 152–53.
57. Conaghan, *The Great Famine in South-West Donegal 1845–1850*, 67–68, 107–8.
58. Donnelly, *The Land and the People of Nineteenth-Century Cork*, 82. See also 81.

Nevertheless, as reports of scarcity and starvation flooded into the Treasury in the late fall of 1846, Trevelyan and his superiors could not believe that Ireland, a country that exported so much grain and livestock, could be seriously short of food. Surely, landlords and farmers were hoarding their produce. In September 1846, Trevelyan claimed that requests to release government grain supplies were not signs of desperation but rather of "a perfectly natural desire to get food where it can be had at the cheapest rate." Writing to a relief committee, he insisted: "I cannot believe there is no store of food in Roscommon from the oat harvest." Such rhetoric obscured an additional problem. Despite all the parliamentary reports and studies, as well as warnings from officials in the field, the government chose to ignore the fact that in good times small farmers sold, rather than consumed, their grain in order to make rent. And, as one Commissariat official asked, "If the people are forced to consume their oats and other grain, where is the rent to come from?"[59]

At the heart of the crisis in the winter of 1846 and 1847 lay the government's failure to capture a supply of grain sufficient for even its limited purposes. To compound the problem, in addition to the return of the potato blight, a drought had hit the Continent in the summer of 1846, causing heavy losses to grain crops, an essential part of the European diet. Although grain losses on the Continent were generally half those of potatoes, the combined failures caused great hardship, as each had been a reserve food for the other in times of crisis.[60] Thus, while the British government assumed that a free, unregulated market would somehow automatically supply its grain requirements, those European countries less dedicated to the gospel of free trade knew that markets gather available food; they do not produce it. Faced with a shortfall in both potatoes and grain, Prussia and France aggressively entered the international grain market in the summer of 1846, buying up supplies. Meanwhile, the Britain government cautiously sniffed out possible sources within the United Kingdom, while keeping its modest purchases secret for fear of disturbing the Irish market. Such caution was to some extent wasted, since the modest number of Irish grain merchants represented mostly exporters, not importers.[61]

Even when the British government finally began to seriously enter the international market, fears of bidding up the price of grain hindered its progress. By November, however, caution gave way to anxiety, as Britain began scouring Europe for grain, sending ships as far east as Odessa on the Black Sea. By then, however, most of the available grain had already been purchased by other countries. In any event, even had the government been more aggressive and entered the market earlier, it would have still found grain to be expensive and scarce. The agent operating on behalf of the government managed to collect only 16,420 tons of a variety of grains by October, a far cry from the 1,438,324 tons the Relief Commission estimated it would need. To make matters worse, available ships were also scarce, the international subsistence crisis having spread confusion within

---

59. For all quotes see Woodham-Smith, *The Great Hunger: Ireland, 1845–49*, 122.
60. Solar, "The Potato Famine in Europe," 118–19.
61. Kinealy, *This Great Calamity*, 80. For Trevelyan's fear of disturbing the domestic grain market, see Haines, *Charles Trevelyan and the Great Irish Famine*, 99.

European shipping, a situation compounded by unusual weather patterns that becalmed many sailing vessels.[62]

With European markets almost emptied of grain, the government turned its hopes toward North America, which would surely funnel its abundant supplies of maize toward the lucrative transatlantic markets. Unfortunately, the American export trade operated on its own schedule, determined by the time it took the maize harvest to mature, by delays in shipping and then by the virtual closing of the North Atlantic with the onset of winter storms. Even when available, the price of maize out of New York rose from £8 7s 6d per ton in August 26, 1846 to £13 5s by September 1. Not until February 1847 would plentiful supplies of America maize begin flowing into Ireland. Blinded by ideology and strangely ignorant of the mechanisms of the American grain trade, the government faced Ireland's winter of starvation without sufficient food reserves.[63]

Attempting to make the best of the situation, the government hit upon the comforting idea that scarcity should be embraced as a mechanism for conservation. In January 1847, responding to a complaint about the price of grain in Ireland, Trevelyan asserted: "It can […] hardly be necessary to remind you that high prices are the natural check upon the over rapid consumption of an insufficient stock of food."[64] Trevelyan thus espoused rationing for people without rations—based on the hollow logic that, since people cannot consume, rapidly or otherwise, what they cannot afford to buy, the existing supply of food would last longer—the sort of advice that only full stomachs can give to empty ones.

The Question of Exports

> Fainting forms, hunger-stricken, what see you in the offing?
> Stately ships to bear our food away, amid the stranger's scoffing.
> (Lady Wilde, Jane Francesca Elgee)[65]

If any country ever feels in need of lessons on how to generate a bad press that will haunt it down through the corridors of time, it should take note of Britain's decision to allow the continued export of food from starving Ireland. Irish nationalist opinion has long echoed the words of Jeremiah O'Donovan Rossa: "We adopt the English expression and call those years 'the famine years,' but there was no famine in the land […] the English took the food away to England and let the people starve." Even a staunch Ulster Unionist paper like the *Northern Standard* could not ignore the sight of Irish food being exported to England. It once reported that the "dead cart" from the local workhouse found its way to

---

62. Haines, *Charles Trevelyan and the Great Irish Famine*, 341; Kinealy, *This Great Calamity*, 76.
63. For problems with grain imports see Woodham-Smith, *The Great Hunger: Ireland, 1845–49*, 118–22; Haines, *Charles Trevelyan and the Great Irish Famine*, 259–62. For the price of maize see Conaghan, *The Great Famine in South-West Donegal 1845–1850*, 54–55.
64. Kinealy, *This Great Calamity*, 81.
65. From "The Famine Year" by Jane Francesca Elgee, Lady Wilde, quoted in Amy Martin's "'The Skeleton at the Feast:' Lady Wilde's Famine Poetry and Irish International Critiques of Food Scarcity," 150.

the graveyard blocked by a drove of bullocks heading to the nearest port. The "dead cart stopped, that the living luxuries walking on their way into the maws of England might pass on."[66]

As this suggests, it was not just Irish nationalists who criticized the export of food from hungry Ireland. Elizabeth Smith, mistress of Baltiboys estate, wrote: "It seems very unwise in the Government to refuse to interfere with the provisions trade, for the capitalists are buying up all the grain to retail really at an exorbitant price." Elsewhere in her journal Smith questioned, "whether the Government has acted right in declining to interfere with the markets. Extraordinary cases require extraordinary treatment." Abstract principals, she wrote, may be fine for the future, but "one shudders at stepping over mounds of graves in the experiment at this time."[67] Lower down on the social scale, exporting food out of Ireland met with physical resistance. Secret societies, such as the Whiteboys and Terry Alts, threatened farmers if they sold food for export or even tried to move their produce out of their region. In County Clare 50 horses were shot to prevent food leaving the area. Mobs formed to blockade roads. Once the public works began hiring, however, large-scale protests faded. Nevertheless, in many places wagons heading for ports or even adjacent counties were routinely escorted by soldiers and police.[68]

As noted earlier, before the Famine, Ireland had exported to Britain enough food to feed two million people. In addition to grain, the export trade also included livestock and dairy products. Theoretically, Ireland exported *surplus* food not consumed at home. Of course, as already discussed, much of that "surplus" reflected the poverty of those who, facing high rents and unable to afford grain or meat, were forced to live on potatoes. Under the circumstances, could anything fully justify the continued food exports out of Ireland, especially during the first year of the crisis when there was a clear shortfall in the food supply?

First, it is important not to exaggerate the extent of Irish grain exports during the Famine period. For example, even before the crisis 80 percent of the Irish oat crop usually remained in the country. After 1845, grain exports from Ireland declined well below their pre-Famine height. In 1847, only a small portion of the 1.6 million tons of harvested oats left Irish shores. According to Austin Bourke's figures, the net grain outflow from Ireland in 1845, the year the blight struck but before the situation had become critical, measured 485,000 tons of grain. The following year, when conditions were desperate, the outflow fell to 87,000 tons. Although exports continued, they remained considerably below pre-Famine levels.[69]

---

66. See Duffy, "Mapping the Famine in Monaghan," 449. For O'Rossa quote see Donnelly, *The Great Irish Potato Famine*, 210. For Donnelly's discussion of the Irish nationalist view on exports during the Famine see 208–21.
67. See James and Ó Maitiú, *The Wicklow World of Elizabeth Smith: 1840–1850*, 65, 69.
68. For protest actions in Clare see Murchadha, *Sable Wings over the Land*, 77–78. For attempts to block movement of food see 79–80.
69. For data see Bourke, *"The Visitation of God?"* table 3, 168.

The argument that there would have been no famine had all of Ireland's grain been kept in the country runs counter to one simple fact: the failure of the potato left an enormous hole not only in Ireland's food supply but also in its nutritional requirements. Tragically, potato dependency had turned out to be a double trap. The tuber did not just fill up stomachs. It met almost all an individual's dietary demands. Austin Bourke has calculated that prior to the Famine potatoes made up to 60 percent of Ireland's food, while wheat and oats contributed only 25 percent, with other foods accounting for the remainder. Therefore, retaining Irish grains might have increased the Irish food supply by only 15 percent. Even had Irish ports been closed during the critical winter of 1846 and 1847, stopping grain exports would have contributed only 430,000 tons of grain to offset the loss of 20 million tons of potatoes. Such an embargo might have met only one-seventh of the nation's needs.[70]

Peel might be given a pass for not stopping exports in 1845 and early 1846. Facing no actual famine conditions, he had no compelling reason to close the ports. By the time the Whigs came into office in June 1846, however, the situation was rapidly deteriorating. Still, Lord John Russell's government placed its faith in the power of the free market, confident that high prices in Ireland would eventually attract plenty of grain, which, in the long run they did. Andrés Eiríksson points out that the volume of grain imported into Ireland rose to six times that of exports in 1847. Imports grew from 28,000 tons in 1845 to 889,000 tons in 1847, while exports fell from 513,000 tons to 146,000, a net inflow of 743,000 tons.[71] This remained the pattern throughout the remainder of the crisis. Despite the claims of Irish nationalists, Ireland *imported* much more grain than it exported during the entire Famine period. In fact, the military and police were more involved in guarding the movement of imported grain *within* Ireland than in convoying Irish grain shipments to the ports.[72]

Nevertheless, food did leave Ireland during the crisis. Cormac Ó Gráda argues that, in theory, there was nothing wrong with a policy of exporting Irish wheat and oats while importing a much greater quantity of the cheaper maize. However, in a critical situation everything depends upon timing, and in the fall and winter of 1846 time was against the Irish. Between the failed harvest in 1846 and the increase in imports toward the end of the year, Ireland literally faced what Austin Bourke has termed a "starvation gap," within which there was simply not enough food in the country. Under those circumstances, a temporary closing of Irish ports might have made some difference.[73] Why, then, did

---

70. Cormac Ó Gráda arrives at this figure even after allowing grain four times the caloric value of potatoes; see *Black '47 and Beyond*, 124. For percentages of potatoes and grains see Bourke, "The Visitation of God?" 52. Bourke states that the 285,000 tons of grain exported from Ireland in 1846 was the food equivalent of around one million potatoes. He calculates that, had Irish grain been retained, it would have made up for only one-tenth of the potato crop lost that year; 164–65. Christine Kinealy questions some of Bourke's calculations. See "'The Famine Killed Everything': Living with the Memory of the Great Hunger," 16.
71. Eiríksson, "Food Supply and Food Riots," 83.
72. For grain imports and exports see Bourke, "The Visitation of God?" 164–65, table 3,168; Donnelly, *The Great Irish Potato Famine*, 215.
73. Bourke, "The Visitation of God?" 165. Donnelly, *The Great Irish Potato Famine*, 24, 69.

Russell's government fail to impose at least a temporary ban on Irish grain exports in 1846?

During the famine of 1740, a limited embargo had been imposed on Irish food exports, and breweries and distilleries were temporarily closed.[74] However, by the late eighteenth century, the concept of a free market untrammeled by government regulations had gained strength, eventually culminating in the repeal of the Corn Laws. While prudence, humanity and hindsight might have recommended closing the ports in 1846, considerable ideological, as well as practical, obstacles militated against doing so. Trevelyan, especially, entertained a nearly hysterical fear that upsetting the Irish grain merchants would result in their withdrawal from the market, forcing the government to intervene even more. Indeed, the merchants warned that they would not import grain unless the government stayed out of the business. Thus, the idea of curtailing exports from Ireland horrified him, as well as his masters in the cabinet.[75] Even today, governments and non-governmental organizations (NGOs) facing famines are wary of interfering with local markets and existing mechanisms of food distribution.

Even accepting that the closing of Irish ports might have been desirable, such action would have produced its own difficulties. The government would have been faced with the problem of distribution—getting the embargoed food to the hungry. Simply giving the food away went against political economy and Victorian moralism. True, banning exports in 1846 could have modestly increased the grain supply in the Irish markets, perhaps lowering prices somewhat. However, unless the price of grain was low enough or wages on the public works were high enough, simply increasing the grain supply by banning exports would have benefited only those able to buy food. Many lacked the money, and even when the supply of imported grain increased substantially in 1847, large numbers of those on the public works could still not afford to purchase enough food.

Suppose, however, that the British government had decided in 1846 to not only close Irish ports, but also to bypass the markets and to distribute food to those unable to buy it? In this case the government would either have had to seize Irish grain (a political impossibility) or buy it. In the latter case, would purchases have been at market rates, resulting in a high cost to taxpayers? Or, if the government imposed a lower price on Ireland's farmers and landlords, what would have motivated them to try to produce a bumper crop the following year? And how would *they* have paid their bills and taxes? Indeed, while it was the British government that allowed food exports to continue, it was not, contrary to popular opinion, the government that did the exporting. Despite the growing crisis at home, it was Irish farmers, Catholics as well as Protestants, who happily sold Irish food to England. As Andrés Eiríksson argues, tensions regarding exports did not just pit Irish against English interests or peasants against landlords. In Ireland, exports represented "a conflict within the agricultural community, between the starving poor on the one hand and the commercially-minded farmers and tradespeople on the other."[76] It

---

74. Dickson, *Artic Ireland*, 42.
75. See Kinealy, *This Great Calamity*, 89; Donnelly, *The Great Irish Potato Famine*, 69.
76. Eiríksson, "Food Supply and Food Riots," 84. See also Ó Gráda, *Black '47 and Beyond*, 125.

is interesting to note that while some British papers had initially assumed that Irish ports might close, few Irish papers actively supported such a move. Instead, many reflected the open-market opinions of the Irish landowners, major tenants and strong farmers. Finally, in the wake of the defeat of the protectionist Corn Laws, there was little support from opinion leaders on either side of the Irish Sea to reinstitute direct intervention in the market through export restrictions.[77]

Christine Kinealy, however, points out that, while grain exports from Ireland may have fallen after 1845, the amounts of livestock, meat and dairy products flowing out of Ireland remained unchanged.[78] In theory, banning those exports would have certainly increased the Irish food supply. However, the government would again have run into the problem of distribution. The people who were without food generally did not eat meat even in the best of times, for the simple reason that they could not afford it. If the Irish peasantry had trouble buying grain, how would they afford meat? And what existing political principles would have justified the government distributing such "luxuries" to the Irish poor when they were scarce enough among the poor in Britain? Only if a ban on livestock exports had encouraged a reduction of stock and, thus, an internal shift of some edible crops form fodder to human consumption might curtailing the export trade in livestock have had some effect.

The grim fact remains that, from the fall of 1846 to the spring of 1847, Ireland experienced an absolute shortfall of food, leaving a gap that not even an export embargo could have closed. E. Margaret Crawford argues that, even adding all Irish grains and remaining potatoes that went to feeding livestock, the caloric loss still would have been 12 percent. Nevertheless, as Austin Bourke and others have pointed out, preventing grain exports out of Ireland could have made *some* difference during the "starvation gap" that lasted from autumn of 1846 to the arrival of imports of maize toward the end of the year.[79] In the long run, of course, the market did function according to theory. Food came into Ireland and grain prices eventually fell. Unfortunately, theory runs on a smoother road than practice. Even as imports started to increase, food prices continued to rise for some time. Between March and the end of May 1847 wheat averaged 80s 1d an imperial quarter. Only after six months of increasing imports did the price hit a peak of 115s in June before falling. Nevertheless, higher prices did eventually attract substantial amounts of food into Ireland. Of course, it helped that the Europe's grain-destroying drought lasted only one year. The Continent enjoyed bumper grain harvests in 1847.[80]

At that point, however, economics dropped a second shoe. Normally, if the supplies of a commodity increase, then at some point prices decrease. So, as grain imports into Ireland continued to grow, prices eventually fell, causing the bottom to drop out of the United Kingdom's grain market. Many British traders were ruined. They had accumulated what

---

77. Bourke, *"The Visitation of God?"* 165.
78. Kinealy, "'The Famine Killed Everything': Living with the Memory of the Great Hunger," 16.
79. Bourke, *"The Visitation of God?"* 165; Donnelly, *The Great Irish Potato Famine*, 69. For 12 percent see Crawford, "Food and Famine," 65.
80. Haines, *Charles Trevelyan and the Great Irish Famine*, 74.

grain they could at high prices and now had to sell their stocks at market lows. Moreover, three decades of debts stemming from the French wars, a postwar recession resulting in lower tax revenues, and recessions in 1840–42 and 1845 had left the British Treasury at a low ebb. All these factors contributed to an economic crisis that caused the Bank of England, its reserves already diminished, to tighten credit to protect the government's loans to Ireland.[81] Though relatively short-lived, Britain's financial crisis turned out to be one of the century's worst. Even Trevelyan, despite all his access to information and contacts in the bank, had failed to second guess the volatility of the grain and financial markets. It was, after all, still an age in which much of the transport of grain and the data that tracked it still moved at the speed of sail, governed by the whims of wind and weather.[82] Unhappily, the mechanisms of free market capitalism and the empty stomachs of the poor operate on rather different time scales, and, as Lord Keynes once observed, people tend to die over the long run. It took too long for the invisible hand, blindly tracking harvest prices and profits, to do its "efficient," unencumbered duty. By the time the situation improved, "Black '47," the worst calendar year of the Famine, was already well advanced.

The Workhouses

> It is a bold thing for me to expect a coffin
> It is a good thing for me if I get a sheet.
> And, King of Glory, relieve me
> That I may dwell in the churchyard beyond.[83]

While the Treasury comforted itself with abstract arguments about economic theory and back-straightening morality, in many Poor Law Unions the struggles regarding the supply and cost of food were terrifyingly immediate and real. The inmates had to be fed with grain purchased in the local markets. High prices threatened some unions with debt and their inmates with insufficient rations. By early 1847 the price for a ton of meal had risen in some areas from £18 to £27. As costs continued to rise, unions cut back on the quality and even quantity of food.[84]

Despite an increase in inmates in 1845, by summer of 1846 workhouses were still only half full. With the failed fall harvest, however, the occupant numbers exploded. Officially, the 130 union workhouses could hold a total of 94,000 inmates. At the end of 1846 one half of the workhouses were at or over capacity. By February 1847, almost

---

81. Ibid, 71–72; Ó Gráda, *Great Irish Famine*, 39.
82. Haines, *Charles Trevelyan and the Great Irish Famine*, 74–75, 341. For the doubling of imports see Bourke, *"The Visitation of God?"* 164.
83. Translated from Gaelic. See Quinn, "Externalizing Famine, Reconstituting Self: Testimonial Narrative from Ireland," 79–80.
84. Begley and Lally, "The Famine in County Donegal," 86–87. See also Hickey, *Famine in West Cork*, 150. For the effects of reduced rations see Donnelly, *The Land and the People of Nineteenth-Century Cork*, 95–96.

all the unions had reached that desperate point.[85] Overcrowding quickly compounded the deteriorating situations in many unions. In Lurgan, County Armagh, one of the less hard-hit areas, the workhouse population jumped from 313 in September of 1846 to its full capacity of 805 by the end of December, with still more people clamoring for admittance. The workhouse in Skibbereen, County Cork, built for 800 people, held 1,169 by January 7, 1847, 332 of whom had "the fever." Meanwhile, the *Cork Examiner* had a thought for those gentlemen charged with interviewing the applicants begging admittance to the workhouses. "Poor human beings wallowing night and day in their habitual filth is a discouraging reflection to those at a distance, but to those who must witness it, who must in fact come in contact with such contagious impurities, is pollution itself." Some union guardians were tempted to bend the rules. Under the Irish Poor Law of 1838, only those admitted to the workhouses could receive food. However, between 1846 and 1847 almost half of the unions attempted to deliver some sort of outdoor relief. The government was quick to crack down. If a union provided outdoor relief, the guardians were forced to repay their organization out of their own pockets.[86]

Overcrowding plagued not only the workhouses but their graveyards as well. Union burial grounds filled up rapidly. At the Lurgan Union a coffin might hold two to three bodies. Large graves intended for up to twenty bodies filled with water causing the coffins to float, until someone stood on them while dirt shoveled in. Twenty-first century excavations of the intermural burial grounds of the Kilkenny Union have uncovered stacked, multiple remains in individual graves. At least these dead had been coffined. Many inmates, approaching their end, had entered the workhouses just to make sure they would be buried in a coffin. Sadly, with the growing numbers of dead, many unions had recourse to reusable coffins with sliding bottoms. Paupers found dead in their cabins or along the country roads were not entitled to even this minimal privilege.[87] In some workhouses the handling of the dead became a matter of routine. According to one oral account, the "Black Room" in the workhouse in Castlerea, County Roscommon, was situated behind the "Black Gable." There, boards slanting from the room's window ran down into a pit at the foot of the gable end. "When death occurred, the corpse was sent down this slide into the pit beneath, and quicklime was shoveled over the corpse, along the boards and along the wall of the gable," turning it black.[88]

As the winter worsened, workhouse mortality rates rose dramatically. Recorded deaths at the workhouse at Lurgan in County Armagh jumped from 58 in the third week of January 1847 to 96 in the first week February. For the first six weeks of 1847 Lurgan had the highest mortality rates in Ulster. Overcrowded and poorly managed,

---

85. Kinealy, *This Great Calamity*, 107. For total capacity see Crossman, *The Poor Law in Ireland 1838–1948*, 11.
86. Crossman, *The Poor Law in Ireland 1838–1948*, 21. For Armagh see Mac Atasney, "The Famine in County Armagh," 39. For Skibbereen see Hickey, *Famine in West Cork*, 170. For *Cork Examiner* see MacMahon, *The Great Famine in Tralee and North Kerry*, 75.
87. For Kilkenny see Geber, "Burying the Famine Dead," 343–46. For Lurgan see Mac Atasney, "*This Dreadful Visitation?*", 60.
88. See Póirtéir, "Folk Memory and the Famine," 227–28.

the guardians had to close the workhouse doors for several months. In the six parishes on the Mizzen Peninsula of West Cork, 1,125 men, women and children died between September 1846 and January 1847. Then in February another 962 died, followed by 1,838 in March, by 1,710 in April and by 1,194 in May.[89] All these numbers were far above pre-Famine levels.

There was a significant gender and age imbalance within the workhouses. In the Cork workhouse women made up 75 percent of the adult population. In three provinces, the female-to-male ratio was generally two to one; it was three to one in Ulster. While many women were widows or had been abandoned by their husbands, such an imbalance also reflects the results of chain migration. If a husband managed to emigrate, his wife, claiming abandonment, might enter the workhouse with her children, where they awaited the fare to join him abroad. Some poor law guardians believed, however, that husbands simply sought to off-load their wives and children on the workhouses. Whatever the circumstances, families, especially women, tried as best they could to use the system to their advantage.[90]

Most of the male inmates were either very old or very young. In the spring of 1849, a Poor Law Commissioner, visiting a union in County Antrim, discovered that, out of 780 inmates in February 1849, 450 were children and 205 were adult females. Of the 125 adult males, only 20 could do physical work. In general, men died at a higher rate than women. In the six West Cork parishes, the ratio of the mortality for men, women and children was 3:2:4.[91] As Cormac Ó Gráda suggests, while male life expectancy traditionally exceeded that of females in normal circumstances, the reverse is true during famines. The reason may be that, although men have greater muscle mass, women have more body fat, providing them with better chances of survival when food is scarce.[92]

In 1841 over 40 percent of the Irish population had been under 15, a fact mirrored in workhouse populations during the Famine. Many children entered with their families (or with unmarried or widowed mothers). Others were orphaned or abandoned. With the passage of the Irish Poor Law the foundling hospitals that would have taken them had been closed. Therefore, the unions were the only institutions where such children could be placed.[93] As the crisis deepened, the numbers of children in the workhouses jumped from 63,000 in 1847 to 90,000 in mid-1849.[94] Such "snapshots," however, do not take

---

89. For the Mizzen Peninsula Hickey, "Mortality and Emigration in Six Parishes in the Union of Skibbereen," 376. For Lurgan see Mac Atasney, *"This Dreadful Visitation?"* 48–51.
90. See Donnelly, *The Land and the People of Nineteenth-Century Cork*, 98–99; Reilly, "'Nearly Starved to Death': The Female Petition during the Great Hunger," 51; for Cork see Moran, "'Shoveling out the Paupers,'" 27.
91. Hickey, "Mortality and Emigration in Six Parishes in the Union of Skibbereen," 376. See also Dallit, "The Famine in Country Antrim," 25.
92. Ó Gráda, *Famine*, 99–101.
93. Moran, "'Suffer Little Children': Life in the Workhouse during the Famine," 30–32.
94. For data see Moran, "'Shoveling out the Paupers': The Irish Poor Law and Assisted Emigration during the Great Famine," 26. For proportion of children in 1841 population see Conlon-McKenna, "Foreword: The Great Silence," xii. For proportion in workhouses see Kinealy, *A Death-Dealing Famine*, 128.

into account the high death rate among the young. Day by day living arrivals would have replaced the departing dead. For example, in 1851 the Kilkenny Union held around 1,909 children under 15. However, since 2,194 children (53 percent of all inmates) had died between 1846 and then, the overall number of children in the workhouse for that period must have been over 4,000. Writing about Kilkenny, Jonny Geber found that the peak of mortality for children occurred at the age of three. As he notes, that was the age when, according to workhouse rules, children would be separated from their mothers, a practice that probably contributed to the high rates of mortality.[95]

Thanks to dedicated masters and matrons, some unions were reasonably well run in the face of often impossible circumstances. However, despite all the bureaucracy and attempted oversight, conditions and levels of effectiveness varied enormously, especially as the poorer unions came under increasing pressure. Rations were sometimes reduced or diluted with cheaper and nutritionally inferior food. This was particularly hard on children, especially if milk (with its crucial vitamin A) was watered down or eliminated.[96] Faced with overcrowding and at times bad or insufficient food, it is little wonder that discipline sometimes broke down. From the very beginning, the Irish poor exerted what agency they could, making it a struggle sometimes for officials to enforce rules and routines.[97] As conditions grew worse and pressures on the unions mounted, some workhouses fell into confusion and a few into complete disorder. In some cases, inmates misbehaved in order to be sent to jail, where they thought conditions would be better. In May 1847, the inmates of Ballinrobe Union in Mayo took over the workhouse. There, as in 38 other unions, the board of guardians was dismissed, replaced by the government-appointed paid vice-guardians. This was not merely a matter of restoring order and decorum. The vice-guardians had the power to set new rates, often dictated by the government, something locally elected guardians were often reluctant to do.[98]

The boards of guardians were, in fact, involved in an intricate balancing act—trying to follow government mandates, while minimizing costs and, therefore, taxes. Although resident proprietors often sat on the boards, members also included big to middling farmers, as well as town merchants. They represented the interests of the upper and middle-class rate payers, Catholics as well as Protestants. Controlling expenses often became their paramount concern, with the costs of feeding the workhouse inmates closely monitored and adjusted accordingly. During the Famine, for instance, the workhouse at Carndonagh in County Donegal managed to reduce their per-person cost from 2*s* per week in 1845 to 1*s* 6*d* in August 1847 and then to 10*d* by the early 1850s. According to Jim MacLaughlin,

---

95. Geber, "'Wretched in the Extreme': Investigating Child Experiences of the Great Hunger through Bioarcheology," 76. For deaths under three years see 82–83.
96. Moran, "'Suffer Little Children,'" 37.
97. See Crossman, *The Irish Poor Law, 1838–1948*, 15–17.
98. For Ballinrobe see Eva Ó Cathaoir, "The Famine and the Workhouse," 228. For jail preference see Crossman, *The Irish Poor Law, 1838–1948*, 20. Within the workhouses, women, especially young women, seemed to be often unruly. See Moran, "'Permanent Deadweight': Female Pauper Emigration from Mountbellow Workhouse to Canada," 111–12.

the boards managed the Famine in their own interests, "ensuring that poor relief would not constitute an excessive drain upon their comparatively meager resources."[99]

The Soup Solution: The Temporary Relief Act, 1847

By January 1847 the failure, or at least the extreme limitations, of the government's emergency relief efforts had become obvious. Over £5,600,000 had been spent on famine relief since 1845 to limited effect. Hunger, sickness and death continued to increase.[100] The cumbersome public works scheme reinstituted by Russell's government had proven the worst of all possible solutions. The program was expensive, and the wages were too low to allow many people to buy enough food, especially as prices continued to rise. Nor did the projects contribute much to the Irish economy. Very little land was drained and too many new roads went nowhere. At the same time, Ireland's Poor Law system, based on the workhouse, was becoming fearfully overwhelmed. Therefore, Russell's administration set out to fashion a series of new policies that might prove both more efficient and less of a burden to the Exchequer.

In the process of introducing his new bills to Parliament, however, Russell had to walk a fine line. As he told the House of Commons: "And, Sir, while I feel that there is a disposition in this country to do everything that is liberal towards Ireland in this respect, we must also consider the difficulties and privations to which the people of England will be subjected." Russell then had a grim warning for Ireland. "I wish to declare […] that we cannot expect, and that we do not expect […] by any measures of the Government […] to ward off or prevent the effects the awful visitation of which we are suffering (hear, hear, hear). It is not in the power of men to do away with the effects of such a calamity." Concerning the call from certain leading men in Ireland to immediately supply the country with cheap food, the prime minister insisted: "Why, sir, this is a task which it is impossible for us to accomplish."[101]

In revamping its approach to famine relief, the Whig government made two decisions. It would phase out most of the public works and would, instead, move to "outdoor relief"—feeding people outside of the workhouse—something prohibited under the original Irish Poor Law. In certain areas recipients would not have to surrender their liberty and enter the workhouse just to get food, although those who had lost their homes would still have to apply for admission. Organizing these changes would take time, however. In the meanwhile, the government needed a short-term, stopgap measure. Embracing the previously unthinkable, it decided to serve free soup on a massive, national scale.

For years, the provision of free soup had been used by municipalities, as well as charitable and religious groups, to feed the poor in times of extremity. At the onset of the crisis in 1846, small, local soup kitchens, funded by charitable donations, were organized

---

99. MacLaughlin, "The Management of Famine in Donegal in the Hungry Forties." 457. See also 454, 455.
100. For cost see Kinealy, *A Death-Dealing Famine*, 66.
101. Reported in *The Observer*, January 31, 1847 (2).

THE CORK SOCIETY OF FRIEND'S SOUP HOUSE.

Figure 3 "The Cork Society of Friends' Soup Kitchen," *Illustrated London News*, January 16, 1847

in various parts of Ireland. Wherever they appeared they were usually swamped by unemployed laborers and their families.[102] In particular, the success of the Quakers' soup kitchens had caught the government's attention. In the fall of 1846, the Society of Friends, having experience in providing food to the indigent, began to set up soup kitchens in several key Irish towns. In general, the Quaker establishments were well organized, providing nutritious, free soup to those in need, regardless of religious affiliation. They also donated large boilers to local relief groups. In Cork, they set up a kitchen that attracted attention in Britain when an engraving of its operation appeared in the January 16, 1847, issue of the *Illustrated London News*[103] (see Figure 3).

---

102. For examples see McCavery, "The Famine in County Down," 105–10.
103. For the *ILN* report see Leslie A. Williams, *Daniel O'Connell, the British Press and the Irish Famine*, 196–97. For illustration see Donnelly, *The Great Irish Potato Famine*, 80. For boilers see Goodbody, *A Suitable Channel*, 29–31. The author reports that Quaker iron mongers in Britain donated 56 boilers for distribution throughout Ireland, 30. For the Society of Friends own account of their soup operations see their *Transactions*, 53–54.

Although ideologically unsavory, handing out free soup would save lives, and, compared to public works, would be cheap. Indeed, as early as October 1846, Sir Charles Wood, Chancellor of Exchequer, fretting over the costs of the inefficient public works program, realized that, if the potato continued to fail, free soup might be the only alternative for dealing with ongoing starvation. So, in February 1847, the government passed the Temporary Relief Act, mandating soup kitchens to be run out of the individual Poor Law Unions. Parliament voted £2,255,000 to support the measure, with half the amount earmarked as loans.[104]

Amid the preparations for this enormous undertaking, another precursor of modern disaster relief appeared on the scene: the "celebrity aid" champion. In this case, a French chef occupied the role that would today go to an international rock star. Alexis Soyer certainly had a rock star's flair for publicity, although, unlike some of his modern-day counterparts, he brought some relevant skills to his charitable task. Unfortunately, knowledge of nutrition does not seem to have been high on his list. Nevertheless, Soyer gloried in his position as the renowned chef of the Reform Club in London, where many Whigs were among the beneficiaries of his culinary skills. Soyer began by publishing some recipes for charitable soup. Soon, however, he hit upon the idea of going to Dublin and setting up a model soup kitchen to produce palatable but cheap meals. The government gladly took up his offer, and for a moment Soyer provided the only good-news story coming out of Ireland (see Figure 4). Celebrated in the English papers, he was, however, attacked in much of the Irish press. Not everyone admired the regimented way he fed the poor: each sitting lasted just six minutes, allowing for 1,000 paupers per hour. And of course, the bowls and spoons were chained to the tables.[105] Moreover, while his organizational skills were unquestioned (Soyer would eventually oversee the feeding of British troops in the Crimea), his recipes looked none too promising, at least on the receiving end. For two gallons of water, the chef recommended a quarter leg of beef, two onions and other vegetables, a half-pound of flour, a half-pound of pearl barley, some salt and sugar. Considering that this concoction was a substitute for the super-nutritious potato, it is little wonder that it quickly earned the derisive name "poor soup" as opposed to "soup for the poor." The British medical journal *The Lancet* claimed that Soyer's soup provided only one-quarter of a proper day's ration. But at 6*d* for two gallons, 3–4*d* a quart, it was cheap, a fact much appreciated by the government.[106]

Projected on a national scale the whole process of running soup kitchens had to be carefully planned. Convinced that the public works programs had been abused despite massive bureaucratic safeguards, Trevelyan's office encumbered the new food distribution system with even more burdensome rules and regulations. Recipients had to apply to the board of guardians of their local Poor Law Union for food tickets. The unions, in turn, had to submit weekly reports to Trevelyan, accounting for every penny spent.

---

104. Kinealy, "The Role of the Poor Law during the Famine," 113–14. For Wood see Haines, *Charles Trevelyan and the Great Irish Famine*, 241.
105. For regimented feeding see O'Sullivan, *The Tombs of the Departed*, 46.
106. For Soyer see Strang and Toomre, "Alexis Soyer and the Irish Famine," 66–84. For *The Lancet* see Kinealy, *Charity and the Great Hunger in Ireland*, 30–31.

Figure 4 "M. Soyer Model Soup Kitchen," *Illustrated London News*, April 17, 1847

In preparation for the massive operation, the Treasury Department, in true Victorian bureaucratic fashion, ordered 10,000 account books, 80,000 balance sheets and 3,000,000 ration tickets.[107]

The Temporary Relief Act, passed in February 1847, should have been implemented in March as the public works began closing. However, soup did not begin to flow until June. There were several reasons for the delay. The Poor Law unions needed some time to gear up for their new responsibilities. Also, although grain imports were growing, food stocks, desperately low during the winter, had to be built up. Finally, the government may have wanted to force small farmers to go back to the land to plant their crops. Unsupported by free seed and rations, however, this turned out to be a false hope.

So, for whatever reasons, a gap opened between the winding down of the public works in March and the provision of government soup in June, during which time many people were without support. The Quakers' Central Relief Committee in Dublin quickly realized that "the period of transition was likely to be one of extreme severity." The committee offered to match whatever additional funds the Relief Commissioners might supply.

---

107. See Donnelly, *The Great Irish Potato Famine*, 82.

When the government rejected the offer, the Friends, nonetheless, did what they could to meet this new crisis, their efforts enhanced by the timely arrival of contributions from America.[108] At the same time, the private charity known as the British Association, led on the ground by its indefatigable chief agent, Count Paul Strzelecki, saved many lives caught in the gap between government works and government soup. The association released around £30,000 a month to its agents in Ireland to help those without any other support.[109]

Considering that the government's soup ration was not a supplement to the recipients' daily diet but in most instances their sole source of nourishment, it is disturbing that officials did not clearly define what constituted proper soup. By comparison, Soyer's much derided product may have been superior to what came out of many Poor Law kitchens. Eventually, the Relief Commission asked the Board of Health if a steady diet of soup would be adequate for those already malnourished. The board made it clear that soup was not a proper substitute for potatoes, and that a continuous liquid diet would lead to diarrhea. Moreover, the board argued that soup kitchens should not try to substitute bulk for nutrition. Plenty of onions and other vegetables, for example, were necessary to combat scurvy. The appearance of that disease, along with diarrhea, among those receiving soup, suggests that the Board of Health's warnings fell on deaf ears. Eventually, the government began to urge the serving of thick porridges and stirabouts bulked up with meal and rice.[110]

Although marginally more expensive to prepare, the government decided, for various reasons, that only cooked food would be distributed. There was fear, shared even by the Quakers, that uncooked rations could be sold for alcohol. Also, when rations consisted of maize, many of the poor had no idea how long Indian meal had to be cooked to prevent serious gastric problem. From the administrative standpoint, prepared food also improved the management of the dole, since entire families would have to queue up for their rations. Understandably, being forced to accept cooked rations was deeply humiliating for the recipients. Moreover, the daily routine of assembling at distribution points exhausted those who lived some distance from the workhouses. It is hardly surprising that riots broke out in various venues.[111]

Charged with providing cooked rations for masses of people, unions found that they had to acquire the necessary boilers and vats, as well as to expand their bread-baking facilities. Nevertheless, at two to two-and-a-half pence per serving (falling to one penny in certain places), government soup was admirably cheap. The total outlay for the summer of 1847 was £1,724,631, more than half of which had been intended as loans to Poor Law Unions. Amazingly, around £530,000 of the funds Parliament voted to support the effort were never spent because the price of grain had fallen so dramatically by the time the distribution of soup commenced. As noted earlier, during the summer of 1847, Ireland's grain imports had begun to outstrip the country's exports.[112]

---

108. Society of Friends, *Transactions*, 60–63; quote on 62.
109. Kinealy, *Charity and the Great Hunger in Ireland*, 29, 173–76, 185.
110. Salaman, *The History and Social Influence of the Potato*, 312; Kinealy, *This Great Calamity*, 148–49.
111. Kinealy, *This Great Calamity*, 145–46.
112. Ibid., 152.

By the end of July 1847, at the height of the soup operation, 3,020,712 men, women and children were being fed every day—*almost one-third of the Irish population*. Of course, the numbers crowding into the soup stations varied across the country. At the parish level in Connaught, they ranged between 70 and 100 percent of the population. In the Skibbereen area of West Cork, where death and emigration had already harrowed the ranks of the poor, the percentage was 58.[113] Yet, even at over three million, the numbers fed by the government did not include all the hungry. For example, soup was not given to the able-bodied unless they entered the workhouse. Nor was it handed out to those who rented more than two acres of land. Moreover, the burden of supplying the soup fell unevenly among the Poor Law unions, due to the regional differences in demand. Thus, overwhelming numbers of rations were dispensed in the seaboard counties of the West, especially in Counties Kerry, Clare, Galway and Mayo. The unions in these areas were soon deeply in debt, and, while the government gave them some grants and loans, they faced constant pressure to raise taxes or reduce their relief rolls.

The soup dole certainly saved lives and alleviated much suffering. Distasteful as the government found it, the scheme did make serious, albeit temporary, inroads in famine-related mortality. The records of workhouse deaths in six parishes on the Mizzen Peninsula in West Cork tell a dramatic story. After the soup kitchens opened, the death rate dropped from a high of 1838 in March to 307 in June, then down to 148 in July and 48 in August and September. However, the program operated during the summer, when the weather was less likely to take its toll on malnourished bodies.[114] And, regardless of its success as an exercise in emergency mass feeding, the Relief Act produced what some British voters might have considered their worst nightmare. From the beginning of the crisis the Whigs had been petrified that direct aid to the Irish poor would only encourage massive dependency on the British Treasury. Thus, even though the act was not set to expire until the end of September, operations began to wind down in early August.

The Permanent Solution: The Poor Law Extension Act of 1847

Haunted by the specter of a dependent Ireland, Sir Charles Wood, the Chancellor of the Exchequer, wrote to Lord John Russell in December 2, 1846, echoing a common theme of the Irish narrative:

> What has brought them [the Irish masses] […] to their present state of helplessness? Their habit of depending on government. What are we trying to do now? To force them upon their own resources. Of course, they mismanage matters very much. […] If we are to select the destitute, pay them, feed them and find money from hence, we shall have the whole population of Ireland upon us soon enough. It is tending very fast to that already and we must beware of taking further responsibility. […] Let us do all we can to improve the local machinery [of the Poor Law], but for God's sake do nothing so fatal as to cast it aside.[115]

---

113. For Skibbereen see Hickey, *Famine in West Cork*, 205–6.
114. Daly, "The Operations of Famine Relief, 1845–47," 133. For Mizzen Peninsula see Hickey, *Famine in West Cork*, table 15, 212. See also 211, 213, 215
115. Kinealy, *This Great Calamity*, 118.

In bestowing large-scale outdoor relief, first through public works and later through the soup kitchens, government officials like Wood feared that they were perverting, if not completely circumventing, the function of the Poor Law system. They were handing out jobs or free food without strictly applying the workhouse "test" for genuine pauperism. Of course, both the public works and the soup kitchens had been temporary measures intended to minister to Ireland's poor until the next harvest. At that point, even if the crisis continued, members of Russell's cabinet felt the need for a new act that would bring relief completely under the Poor Law. Therefore, just as the temporary soup kitchens were gearing up in June 1847, the government passed the Irish Poor Law Extension Act. Intended to supersede the emergency dole of free food, the act, in the eyes of its authors, also put Irish relief on a bureaucratically sound and politically defensible basis. All relief would be channeled through a somewhat revamped Poor Law system with Irish property mandated to pick up almost the entire bill, a popular policy in Britain. As *The Times* intoned in December 1846, "The Irish poor must have food and employment; *and it must not be from Imperial resources.* [...] It follows that *the property of Ireland must be made legally responsible for the employment or feeding of the people.*" Not everyone agreed with such a policy, however. Some newspapers pointed out that, with one half the population of England, Ireland had only one-fifth the property base to support a much larger proportion of poor.[116]

Given the degree of Irish poverty and the uncertain nature of future potato harvests, the government felt forced to relax some of the previous barriers to relief built into the original Irish Poor Law. Recall that, unlike English paupers, the Irish had no right to welfare; Irish workhouses were not obliged to take in all who qualified. Faced with mass starvation, however, the government decided that it would grant Irish paupers in the worst-stricken areas in the west of Ireland the *right* to relief. Moreover, if a particular workhouse was full or too disease-ridden to safely house more inmates, those destitute who qualified could receive outdoor relief in the form of food and clothing without being confined within the workhouse walls. The sick, infirm and widows with two or more *legitimate* children could also receive aid. Even able-bodied paupers might qualify for outdoor relief for a limited time—if they agreed to hard, degrading work in return. The sharp drop in food prices made the venture seem economically feasible even if it remained ideologically unpleasant. For its part, the British public generally accepted the Amended Irish Poor Law as both just (giving Irish paupers the same right to relief as the English) and necessary. It was what one MP called, "a great act of justice due to the Irish people, due to them by England." Besides, many believed that one of the factors propelling Irish paupers to flee to Britain was the lack of outdoor relief at home.[117]

On the other hand, the Irish landlords, mandated to pay for this extended relief, were shocked. In their minds, it was bad enough that they were already paying high taxes to support the Poor Law Unions. Under the old law, at least, a workhouse's limited

---

116. Bew, *Ireland: The Politics of Enmity,* 191; *The Times,* December 14, 1846 (4); italics original.
117. Neal, "Black '47: Liverpool and the Irish Famine," 131. For quote see Donnelly, "'Irish Property Must Pay for Irish Poverty': British Public Opinion and the Great Irish Famine," 76.

capacities would have theoretically contained costs. But once paupers received the right to relief beyond the workhouse walls, there seemed no limit to how high Poor Law rates might rise. Under these circumstances, many Irish landlords could see only bankruptcy ahead. Yet, their complaints were met with almost universal outrage in Britain. The public blamed the landlords' alleged poor management and rack renting for having created potato dependency among their tenants in the first place.

Even competent and caring Irish landowners faced tightening economic pressures, however. As noted earlier, the weather in the late summer of 1846 had ruined much of the Irish grain harvest, as well as the potatoes. In addition, the cascading effects of a sharp recession in 1847 were probably more widely felt in Ireland than in Britain. The linen industry was in a slump, and agricultural prices had fallen. Elizabeth Smith lamented in her journal that the local Wicklow cattle markets failed to attract buyers: "Banks, merchants, agents, all are bankrupt in all places. […] [P]eople are oppressed by this frightful amount of bankruptcies."[118] For her Baltiboys estate it meant another round of belt tightening. Less fortunate or less careful landlords faced ruin. As many small tenants defaulted on their rents, the results reverberated back up the land pyramid to strong farmers and eventually to landowners. Nonetheless, the Irish landlords in Parliament found themselves politically isolated. They tried to pass several amendments that would have shielded them from some of the costs of the new Poor Law Act. They failed—with one exception.

The landlords did succeed in attaching a clause to the new Poor Law legislation stipulating that families renting more than a quarter acre would have to surrender the bulk of their land to be eligible for outdoor relief. This, they assumed, would limit the number of applicants, thus, keeping the rates in check. Or it would, at least, force people to surrender their tiny holdings, allowing the land to be combined into larger, economically viable farms. This addition to the Poor Law Act became known as the "Quarter Acre" or "Gregory Clause," named after its proprietor-author, William Gregory, who assured the House of Commons that its effects upon the poor would be minimal. In the House of Lords, however, the Irish landowners supporting the clause understood its purpose perfectly well. Referring to the changes taking place in Ireland, Clanricarde insisted that, "those who had hitherto lived by holding small pieces of ground would no longer be able to do so. […] The clause," he maintained, would "make less difficult a change which must take place, and the sooner the better."[119] Although not usually sympathetic to initiatives coming from the Irish landlords, Trevelyan, reflecting the views of the cabinet, also embraced the Quarter Acre clause as necessary to facilitate land consolidation and to bring some order to Ireland's fragmented and, therefore, unmanageable land system. However, he argued that the starving should be fed, regardless of how much land they

---

118. James and Ó Maitiú, *The Wicklow World of Elizabeth Smith*, 95. For economic slump see Mac Atasney, *"This Dreadful Visitation,"* 78–79.
119. See Cornwell, *A Galway Landlord during the Great Famine*, 33. Gregory, who had inherited a large estate in Galway in 1847 when he was already in debt, later became the husband of Isabella Augusta Persse. Lady Gregory, who, along with William Butler Yeats, later founded the Abbey Theater.

held. Nor could he see any justification for burning the roofs over their heads if they did not move.[120] Nevertheless, a good deal of mischief and suffering would spring from the Gregory clause. Its inclusion in the Amended Poor Law Act shows the extent to which the legislation was intended to contribute to the socioeconomic restructuring of rural Ireland during the Famine.

As Christine Kinealy has argued, the revised Irish Poor Law successfully completed the shift of the cost of relief from the imperial Exchequer to Irish rate payers. Having committed over £7,000,000 for famine relief from 1846 to 1847, the government only paid out around £300,000 during the 18 months following the passage of the Amended Poor Law Act. Much of that was intended as loans. Sometime later, Nassau Senior, an influential economist close to some members of the government, stated the case plainly: "The English resolved that the Irish should not starve. [...] We resolved that, for one year at least, we would feed them. But we came to a third resolution, inconsistent with the first, that we should not feed them for *more* than a year." After that it would be up to the Irish rate payers to shoulder the entire burden.[121]

Charitable Giving from Home and Abroad

On December 18, 1846, Henry Labouchere, Ireland's chief secretary, wrote to the prime minister: "The workhouses are full and people are turned away to perish. It is impossible to allow this state of things to continue without making some effectual effort to relieve it."[122] While the government had done its best to shift most of the costs of famine relief onto the shoulders of Irish property owners, it had reluctantly begun to realize that Irish taxes alone could not meet all of Ireland's needs. While many British newspapers continued to complain that Ireland was becoming an increasing burden upon British taxpayers, many people did make a clear distinction between taxation and charity. On January 1, 1847, *The Times* published a letter from an anonymous clergyman arguing that English citizens would rather contribute to Irish relief than to be taxed for it. Clearly, the clergyman insisted, private charity had an essential role in Irish relief. The writer warned that "it becomes us to prepare for the judgment of God upon ourselves" should Britons fail to succor their fellow countrymen in Ireland. He concluded that "a channel must and will immediately be opened through which that charity may flow."[123] As if on cue, the next day *The Times* published a letter signed by two Church of Ireland clergymen, Rev. C. Caufield and Rev. R. Townsend, who described the dire conditions around Skibbereen in County Cork.[124] The letter also announced the establishment of a

---

120. Haines, *Charles Trevelyan and the Great Irish Famine*, 390.
121. Senior, "Relief of Irish Distress in 1847 and 1848," 223.
122. Quoted by Kinealy, *This Great Calamity*, 118.
123. See Leslie A. Williams, *Daniel O'Connell, the British Press and the Irish Famine*, 193.
124. In a follow-up letter to *The Times*, Caufield and Townsend described the cold receptions English groups initially gave their plea to succor, "a cause so unpopular." The two men were shocked to realize how little English people knew of the realities of the crisis in Ireland; *The Times* January 7, 1847 (5). See also, Leslie A. Williams, *Daniel O'Connell, the British Press and the Irish Famine*, 194–95.

committee of leading London businessmen that would organize fundraising for famine relief. This became the British Association for the Relief of Extreme Distress in Remote Parishes of Scotland and Ireland, soon to be known simply as the British Association. Given the sequence of events, the association must have been the "channel" referred to in the earlier anonymous letter. It also seems likely that the government itself was involved in helping to organize the initiative. Certainly, Trevelyan actively supported the formation of the new organization.[125]

Even as England was gearing up for a massive charitable campaign, however, *The Times* seemed intent on acting as a drag against benevolent progress. Referring to Ireland, the paper grumbled:

> Mendicancy, in one form or another, pervades all the classes, institutions and customs of that country. A beggar peasantry, a beggar demagogue [O'Connell], and beggar landlords vie with one another in the exercise of national privilege. "Give, give, give, give," "more, more, more, more," is echoed from every quarter of the Irish compass.[126]

Clearly, whatever progress charity was to make in England, it would face strong headwinds. Nevertheless, on January 14, close on the heels of the announcement regarding the founding of the British Association, Queen Victoria issued an appeal to be read out in all Anglican churches. The "Queen's Letter," reprinted in most British newspapers, urged Her Majesty's subjects to contribute generously to aid Ireland. The resulting sums were considerable. The Royal Letter initially brought in £170,571. The monarch herself contributed £2,000. (While not lavish, given the royal family's wealth, the contribution amounts to approximately £120,834 in 2017 valuation, a bit more than one might have expected from the ungenerous "Famine Queen" of Irish nationalist legend.) Within a short time, the British Association itself raised £269,302. Additional funds continued to come in, boosted in March by the royal declaration of a day of national fasting and humiliation. For the whole of the Famine period, British charitable contributions eventually totaled some £603,535, the equivalent of around £36,463,774.10 in 2017 currency.[127]

Anxious to control every aspect of famine relief, the Treasury itself took control of most of these funds, as well as the distribution of the food collected by the British Association and other charitable agencies. The Treasury thus had a pot of private money, which it could quietly dole out without raising the ire of British taxpayers. In other words, the British Association's funds could be spent on things that the government felt it could or should not undertake, such as feeding and clothing over 200,000 school children for a seven-month period.[128] As Robin Haines notes, under Trevelyan's

---

125. See Haines, *Charles Trevelyan and the Great Irish Famine*, 214.
126. *The Times*, January 8, 1847.
127. For contributions see Haines, *Charles Trevelyan and the Great Irish Famine*, 215. The conversions into 2005 equivalent value are derived from the United Kingdom's online National Archives Currency Converter: 1270-2017.
128. For feeding the school children see Kinealy, "'Attenuated Apparitions of Humanity': The Innocent Casualties of the Great Hunger," 13–15.

control, the Association operated as a quiet arm of the government. In fact, it provided such a useful cover for the interjection of money for distressed Poor Law Unions, that when the Association's funds began to dwindle, the government tried for a time to quietly replenish them.[129]

Charitable giving for famine relief went far beyond the Queen's Appeal and the British Association. The Irish Famine provides the first example of a modern phenomenon: international disaster aid. As Cormac Ó Gráda observes, Ireland became "the first beneficiary of 'globalized' famine relief."[130] From the Sultan of the Ottoman Empire to the Choctaw Nation in America, charitable responses came from individuals, religious groups and organizations large and small from all over the world. Overseas colonial communities, such as those in India, sent contributions. Funds came from Europe, and the citizens of the United States made significant contributions of food and clothing, as well as money. Most of the major east-coast American cities launched fundraising efforts. Among the most effective was the General Relief Committee of New York. Although the Irish in the United States were often involved, much of the impetus for charity came from non-Irish sources. And although the US Congress refused to pass a generous grant for Irish relief, it did permit the temporary decommissioning of several warships to transport American donations to Ireland.[131]

On an even broader, international scale, both the Roman Catholic Church and Anglican Church, each representing worldwide networks, helped organize international aid. In Rome Pope Pius IX was active in appealing for support for Ireland. The Vatican published a pamphlet that underscored the suffering of the Irish people. In addition, the Pope organized a subscription and issued an encyclical soliciting prayer for Ireland. Funds raised by Catholics around the world were generally sent to Rome, from where they were funneled to the Irish archbishops who disseminated them.[132]

Unfortunately, some Protestant organizations in Ireland saw the Famine as an opportunity to combine proselytizing with Christian charity. The largely evangelical Irish Relief Agency, established in 1831, insisted that their grants would be influenced by neither religion nor politics. Nevertheless, providentialism and hostility toward Catholicism frequently appeared in the organization's appeals. And when the body wound up its activities in 1848, the bulk of the remaining funds went to Rev. Nangle's Protestant colony on Achill Island (see Figure 5). Nevertheless, the £42,466.5s the agency raised and distributed helped many who were outside of the Poor Law's relief system. Moreover, it is important to note that most Protestants, worldwide, who contributed to Irish relief, did so without seeking sectarian advantage.[133]

---

129. Haines, *Charles Trevelyan and the Great Irish Famine*, 311, 479–80, 482.
130. Ó Gráda, *Famine: A Short History*, 201.
131. Kinealy. *Charity and the Great Hunger in Ireland*, 119–24, 282–83. For New York Central Relief Committee see 85–106. For an American relief ship see Gray, *The Irish Famine*, 55.
132. Kinealy. *Charity and the Great Hunger in Ireland*, 127–30. See also Kerr, "The Catholic Church and the Irish Famine," 120–29. For Anglican, as well as Catholic fund raising, see Delaney, "Ireland's Great Famine: A Transnational History," 110.
133. Kinealy, *Charity and the Great Hunger in Ireland*, 261–65.

Figure 5 "A View in Achill," *Illustrated London News*, March 3, 1844

Although modest in numbers, the Society of Friends became a highly effective engine for Irish relief. In November 1846 several leading Irish Quakers joined with their co-religionists in England to establish the Society's Central Relief Committee in Dublin. The Quakers brought to the crisis more than spiritual dedication and a strong tradition of charitable works. The many businessmen in their ranks contributed effective organizational skills. The Dublin Central Committee acquired its own office and meeting room with someone to staff the operations. The committee met at least three times a week; daily when necessary. Similar committees were set up in several of Ireland's largest towns, and special sub-committees, one for each province, were established, each with its own secretary. To speed up operations the committee developed questionnaires for those seeking grants.[134] The Friends were also intent on insuring that the funds they raised would actually help those most in need. However, the committee knew little about conditions in remote parts of Ireland where Quakers were thin on the ground. The Central Committee, therefore, built up a network of correspondents and local agents

---

134. Society of Friends, *Transactions*, 36–37, 464, 466. See also Goodbody, *A Suitable Channel*, 4–8, 12–15, 17, 32–33.

throughout the country. A number of Quakers, including two Englishmen, William Edward Foster and James Hack Tuke, traveled through the west of Ireland gathering information. Reporting back to the Central Committee, they recounted appalling scenes of distress, all carefully and vividly recorded in their letters, many of which were subsequently published. As Foster noted, too many people in England thought reports about Irish suffering had been exaggerated. It was, however, impossible to "deepen the blackness of the truth."[135]

The Quakers' Central Committee quickly established a soup kitchen in Dublin, hoping to provide a model for other parts of the country. Friends also organized the distribution of clothing and seeds. Businessmen themselves, they were careful in all their operations to avoid interfering with local markets or resources, preferring to import foods, such as rice, which local merchants did not handle. When they became involved in land reclamation in County Mayo, they imported expensive guano so as not to interfere with local sources of fertilizer.[136]

By giving many modest grants to local relief groups, as well by providing direct aid, the Quakers, alongside other organizations, took on the role of what today would be called NGOs—nongovernmental organizations—sustained by international support from overseas donors. In terms of size and importance, the Quakers' Central Relief Committee with its overseas network was second in importance only to the British Association. The Quakers published reports and correspondence were instrumental in gaining attention and attracting donations, especially in America.[137] Unlike some modern NGOs, the Quakers could tell prospective donors how much actual aid their contributions would provide. The Central Committee's *Transactions*, published in 1852, provide an incredibly detailed accounting of their activities.

The Society of Friends tended to focus on areas where government-directed relief did not reach. For example, once it realized that the government was phasing out the public works well before alternative modes of relief would be in place, the Dublin Central Committee did its best to work within the resulting gap.[138] The Friends also took seriously the lack to proper clothing among the hungry poor, who had early on pawned their best garments to buy food. In addition to physical suffering, the poorly clothed victims also experienced social and personal degradation. In gathering clothing from Britain and America, the Quakers seem to have tapped into networks of women who collected and sewed for Famine victims.[139]

---

135. Goodbody, *A Suitable Channel*, 18. See also Society of Friends, *Transactions*, 39–42, 55. Tuke published an account of his trip, *A Visit to Connaught in 1847*. The Quakers preferred giving small grants, frequently renewed, despite the bookkeeping burden. They felt that this approach reduced "imposition" while affording "means for testing the efficiency and trustworthiness of the guarantees"; Society of Friends, *Transactions*, 55. Most of the grants were made to women, "who were found to be our most efficient almoners," 56.
136. Society of Friends, *Transactions*, 57, 87. Goodbody, *A Suitable Channel*, 59.
137. Society of Friends, *Transactions*, 48.
138. Ibid., 60–62.
139. Ibid., 69–73; Mac Atasney, "The Famine in County Armagh," 57–60. For the clothing situation and women see the author's "'Nearly Naked:' Clothing and the Great Hunger in Ireland," 83–93.

By May 1847, Irish Quakers had donated £4,800, while the London Committee raised £45,051.12s.8d. This was on top of thousands of pounds worth of donated food and clothing. Contributions raised by Friends in America, which included donations from many non-Quakers, eventually surpassed the funds collected by Friends within the United Kingdom.[140] Since the British government paid for the overseas shipment of food and clothing, these donations were then channeled through the government's Commissariat. This, however, enabled the government to recoup some of its expenses by insisting that the grain be transferred from the shipping barrels to sacks, which it sold to the charities at 2s./6d per sack. Such costs, of course, came out of an organization's relief funds.[141]

Operating through their transatlantic networks, the Friends' circulars and printed appeals had an impact beyond Quaker communities. By reprinting Quaker accounts of Irish distress, American newspapers played an important role in spreading awareness of the Famine, making it, as Enda Delany suggests, "the world's first modern famine," a tragedy that "unfolded in the full glare of the global press." Some contributions came from unexpected sources. The Choctaw Nation, having experienced its own ordeal on the "Trail of Tears" just 14 years earlier, sent money to the starving Irish, as did a group of enslaved persons in Alabama. Overall, as much as a million pounds designated for Irish relief may have come from the United States, most of it collected in 1847.[142] Delighted as the British government may have been by the influx of foreign donations, there were those who saw this charitable flow as a rebuke to Britain's parsimonious policies. Reporting the arrival of the USS *Jamestown*, loaded with relief supplies, the *Cork Examiner* suggested: "Let the manner in which a Nation acts that owes us nothing [America] [...] be a model to a Nation [Britain] that owes to us her pre-eminent greatness."[143] The more the Americans donated to the cause, however, the more the story in their newspapers became one of Yankee generosity rather than Irish need. As James M. Farrell notes, "The [newspaper] narratives largely confirm the image Americans had of themselves as a providentially blessed Christian nation, quite in contrast to the image of an Ireland abandoned by God and plagued by famine and disease."[144] The question was, how long the combined motives of pity, piety and national pride could sustain American charity, or anyone else's, at such high levels?

---

140. Goodbody, *A Suitable Channel*, 21–23; Kinealy, *Charity and the Great Hunger in Ireland*, 67.
141. Kinealy, *Charity and the Great Hunger in Ireland*, 71.
142. For the Choctaw see ibid., 104–5. For the international response to the Famine see 41–61, 85–106. For the American aid effort see also Curti, *American Philanthropy Abroad*, 41–64. For press coverage of famine-relief funding in America see Hogan, "The Famine Beat: American Newspaper Coverage of the Great Hunger," 155–79. For quote see Delaney, *The Curse of Reason*, 108.
143. See Delaney, *The Curse of Reason*, 112. For the *Jamestown* and reception of American aid see Merle Curti, 41, 63.
144. Farrell, "Reporting the Irish Famine in America: Images of 'Suffering Ireland' in the American Press, 1845–1848," 72–73.

Politics during the Famine: The Death of O'Connell and the Election of 1847

Although Daniel O'Connell had initially supported the Whigs' return to government, as the crisis deepened, he became frustrated with their parsimonious response. Yet, although he finally denounced the Whigs in December 1846, he had shared much of their economic liberalism based on free markets and the sanctity of private property. This left him short of alternatives. Moreover, O'Connell's health was failing, leaving more of the daily operations of the financially depleted Reform Association in the hands of his son, John. Nevertheless, toward the end of 1846, he appeared to have pulled the factions of the Repeal movement together to form a broad-based parliamentary "Irish party." Both the O'Connellites and Young Irelanders believed that the Irish landlords should accept reforms in land tenure and tenants' rights. They also insisted that famine relief be accepted as an imperial rather than Irish problem. Unfortunately, somewhere between January and May 1847 the "Irish party," such as it was, disintegrated. In the end, Ireland's politicians could not get past the old arguments over Repeal tactics and questions of O'Connell's leadership. Thus, Ireland faced a full-blown famine with Irish political opinion completely fragmented. In the subsequent months, although the Whigs faced severe criticism in Ireland, there was no effective, united opposition to their policies.[145]

Weakened at home, O'Connell soon found Irish concerns less popular than ever in Britain. The continuing costs of Irish relief, along with the financial crisis in Britain, strengthened middle-class radicalism and anti-Irish sentiments within the Whig party. The General Election of 1847 resulted in a dramatic increase in middle-class representation in the House of Commons, as Parliament finally began to reflect the changes instituted 15 years earlier by the passage of the Reform Act of 1832. Many of the newly elected MPs were strongly influenced by the so-called Manchester school of laissez-faire economics. Weak on theory but strong on confidence and opinion, the group, angered by high taxes (especially during an economic recession), also opposed any tendencies of the government to involve itself in economic matters. These MPs and their middle-class supporters were, moreover, suspicious of those above and below them. Wary of their aristocratic leaders, they were also distrustful of any policies that might weaken the "moral fiber" of the lower classes, especially the Irish, even if they were starving. These middle-class radicals were especially unhappy with the government's handling of Famine relief, which seemed both ineffective and expensive. Even Elizabeth Smith railed in her journal at the "feudal Barons" in the government, "supercilious ignoramus's [sic]," who overtaxed the public: "There is too much power in the middle-class, the real strength of the state, to endure longer such misgovernment."[146] The new radical bloc in Commons, around 80 strong, felt much the same way. And they now held

---
145. For the "Irish party" see. Nowlan, "The Political Background," 154–63.
146. James and Ó Maitiú, 110. For the General Election and British middle-class political reaction see Kinealy, *A Death-Dealing Famine*, 118, 120; Gray, *Famine, Land and Politics*, 288.

the balance of power in the House. As head of a minority government, Prime Minister Russell needed the support of the radicals, as well as some acquiescence from Peel's faction of the Tories.

This situation strengthened the power of the Treasury faction, since Sir George Grey, Wood and Trevelyan were sympathetic to many of the attitudes of the radicals in Commons.[147] As a result, Russell, having already failed to gain support for a "comprehensive scheme" for Ireland, which included a Land Reclamation Bill, now found Parliament even less generous toward the island. In fact, he believed that his faction of the Whigs had essentially lost the election because it had done too much for Ireland. With Russell's position within the cabinet weaker than ever, Wood's emphasis on trimming the budget found favor among the Tory Peelites and the Whig Radicals alike. This left the prime minister with little support for more enlightened policies toward Ireland.[148] Therefore, the government clung more tightly than ever to its basic approach to famine relief: Irish property would pay for Irish poverty and Irish agriculture would be restructured. Thus, the Amended Poor Law of 1847 reflected the demands of Whig middle-class supporters. As the *Evening Mail* observed, Russell and his cabinet were in the grip of "anti-Irish [...] English middle-class feeling."[149]

For his part, O'Connell did what he could. The great leader pleaded with Parliament to do for Ireland what it had done in abolishing slavery in the West Indies. Just as Parliament had raised a massive loan to purchase the slaves, O'Connell urged it to come up with £40,000,000 to save the Irish people. In his last appearance in the House of Commons, the Liberator was so weak that his once stentorian voice barely carried to those nearest to him. His final appeal for Ireland fell upon the House largely unheard and unheeded. On May 17, 1847. the ailing leader, having embarked on a pilgrimage to Rome, died in Genoa. Although his powers, political as well as physical, had waned, his passing left a void in Irish politics that would require a generation to fill.[150]

O'Connell's body was returned to Ireland, where a great funeral procession wended its way through the streets of Dublin. His pall-draped triumphal car with its now empty throne paused before his old home in Merrion Square. Although O'Connell's passing received broad coverage in the press on both sides of the Irish Sea, in the end it represented but one death among thousands during what became known as "Black '47."[151]

Black '46–'47

Traditionally, "Black '47" is regarded as the worst calendar year of the Irish Famine. However, in terms of the harvest cycle, 1846–47 represents a unique and desperate

---

147. Kinealy, *A Death-Dealing Famine*, 121.
148. For rejection of Russell's policies see Gray, *Famine, Land and Politics*, 269. For Russell's sense of the General Election of 1847 see 288. For tensions between Russell and Wood's Treasury faction see Kinealy, *This Great Calamity*, 276.
149. See Bew, *Ireland: The Politics of Enmity*, 193.
150. For O'Connell's last appeal see Leslie A. Williams, *Daniel O'Connell, the British Press and the Irish Famine*, 224.
151. For press coverage of O'Connell's death and funeral see ibid., 223–40.

period, the first phase of the Famine, characterized by its own set of problems and responses. Inaugurated by an ecological crisis, the destruction of that year's potato crop, this period was characterized by panic, an absolute shortfall in the food supply, an incredible mustering of administrative machinery, a brief outpouring of generosity from Britain, but also a great deal of suffering and high mortality. Completely unprepared for a return of the potato blight, Lord John Russell's government, only a few months into office, had to quickly cobble together a series of responses that represented a mélange of conflicting policies. Feed the starving. Minimize the drain on the imperial treasury. Encourage Irish landlords and other rate payers to shoulder as much responsibility as possible. Minimize fraud on relief projects. Avoid creating mass dependency on the government. Place the cost of relief on the shoulders of Irish property. Restructure the rural Irish economy. And all these goals had to be accomplished within the ideological confines of political economy. Not surprisingly, the government failed to strike a genuine balance among all these objectives. Only toward the end was there a brief moment when feeding the hungry temporarily took almost uncontested precedence.

The closing of the soup kitchens in late August concluded the first phase of Famine; the implementation of the Amended Irish Poor Law inaugurated the second phase, which set the basic pattern for the next five years. The initial success of these changes would, of course, depend on the harvest of 1847. Unless it was bountiful, those same three million people who had flocked to government's soup kitchens in the summer would be demanding relief from their Poor Law Unions, most of which were already stretched far beyond their capacities. The government, therefore, bet heavily on the blight having finally run its course, and, *mirabile dictu*, the gamble initially appeared to have paid off. The 1847 potato harvest was relatively blight free. The question then centered on the size of the harvest. Had enough potatoes been planted?

Chapter Ten

A FALSE DAWN: 1847–48

The Harvest of 1847

If the land is not sown and planted, the famine next year will be immeasurably more disastrous than the famine this year, and if the people are not fed [...] the land cannot be cultivated.
(Alexander Somerville, January 23, 1847)[1]

When the blight hit Ireland's potato economy, it not only destroyed the productivity of the cottiers' potato ground but also stole the "currency" with which many had been paid. With the loss of potatoes, farmers, having no means to pay them, began dismissing their laborers. As early as November 1846, the *Tipperary Vindicator* warned: "The land is lying idle because [...] the poorer description of farmers cannot possibly pay the labourer, nor could the labourer support himself [on] the wages which the farmer was hitherto accustomed to give him." Under these circumstances, many of the 700,000 employed on the public works preferred to stay with the projects as long as possible, instead of returning to the land.[2] In January *The Economist*, generally critical of the government's relief efforts, warned, "Scarcely any of the small farms are ploughed, and in many instances the pursuits preparatory to the approaching spring appear suspended." One immediate problem seemed to be a lack of horses. Many were employed on the works, and those farmers who might have hired them had no oats for feed. James Wilson, *The Economist*'s founding editor, blamed the situation on the government. The public works had attracted small farmers and cottiers away from their fields. As a result, "The cultivation of the land, and every description of useful and independent labour have been utterly abandoned."[3]

In January 1847, only weeks away from the beginning of the Irish spring, Scottish correspondent Alexander Somerville traveled through Ireland for the *Manchester Examiner*. He noted that peasants were still working on the relief projects for inadequate wages instead of preparing the ground for planting. Should this situation continue, he wondered how those people would have enough time and energy to plant that year's crops? He also noted that men and horses were being hired away from their fields to transport imported grain around the country. In many cases, even those who might have intended to plant a potato crop had no cuttings to put into the ground. Around Kilkenny, Somerville also

---

1. Somerville, *Letters from Ireland during the Famine of 1847*, 31–32.
2. See Daly, "Farming and the Famine." For *Tipperary Vindicator* see Smyth, "Classify, Confine, Discipline and Punish," 134.
3. *The Economist*, January 16, 1847, 59.

noted that many "quarter-acre men," those who rented minimal potato ground, were not buying manure in preparation for spring planting. Lacking seed potatoes, they were instead selling what manure they had previously accumulated at discounted prices. Since it took three acres of grain to replace one of potatoes, it seemed impossible to Somerville that enough land could be prepared and planted in time to feed the nation.[4] Similarly, in March a team of Quakers investigating conditions in the west also reported finding too few people cultivating the land because many small farmers were still dependent on the public works. On the 31st of that month, the *Manchester Guardian* warned: "If the ground remains untilled, and the summer sun shines on unsewn fields, the inevitable result will be another famine, not less appalling in itself, and doubly fatal in its effects because it will visit a people already weighed down by destitution and pestilence." The paper recognized the government's long-term goal of shifting the peasantry from the status of self-sufficient potato cultivators to that of wage-earning workers. The process would take time, however, and, as *The Guardian* noted, it could not be accomplished smoothly, *if at all*. Nonetheless, the journal, like the government, used hopeful words to paper over the cracks in reality: "If, on the other hand [...] every effort is made to replace the potato by less hazardous and more nutritious crops the foundations will be laid—albeit amidst severe privation and suffering—of a permanent improvement in the condition of the country." As Leslie A. Williams notes, both *The Guardian* and the government were caught on the horns of a dilemma: "how to keep the Irish from starving while trying to change their agricultural system."[5]

Still, there seemed reason for hope. Although no one apparently knew how much potato ground had been planted, by the beginning of the summer all crops looked promising. The grain harvest, which came in first, was generally good. This took some pressure off the east and portions of Ulster where oats had always been an important part of the small farmer's diet. At the same time, the good weather raised expectations for the potatoes. In late May 1847 *The Scotsman* carried an optimistic report from Ireland: "There is no plant in the field that looks healthier than the potato, and shows—as far as this season has yet gone—a more decided promise of a happy maturity."[6] And, indeed, as they were lifted, many tubers did look relatively healthy. In fact, in some areas the per-acre yields seemed to rival those of the pre-Famine years. Unfortunately, the *number* of acres under potatoes had declined precipitously to just 10 percent of the pre-Famine level: from around 2.5 million acres in 1845 to little more than 0.3 million acres in 1847.[7] The fears Somerville had expressed earlier in the year suddenly became very real. Though less plagued by blight, the 1847 harvest was far too small to meet the needs of several million people. For all practical purposes, the results of the potato harvest of 1847 proved about

---

4. Somerville, *Letters from Ireland during the Famine of 1847*, 31–32, 33, 60–61.
5. For comment and *Manchester Guardian* quote see Leslie A. Williams, *Daniel O'Connell, the British Press and the Irish Famine*, 243. For Quakers see Goodbody, *A Suitable Channel: Quaker Relief in the Great Famine*, 20.
6. *Scotsman*, May 29, 1847.
7. See graphs in Donnelly, *The Great Irish Potato Famine*, 58.

as devastating as that of the previous year. A small healthier crop was no better than a large diseased one. Privation and suffering would continue.

As the reality of the situation sank in, James Wilson, who had expressed some optimism in September, decried disaster a month later. His lead article in *The Economist* for October 16 tied the fatal decline in potato acreage directly to the government's public works which had taken people away their fields. The government "did what [it] could to make them [the peasants] give up their small holdings. They aimed at producing a change in the agriculture of Ireland." Wilson then quoted Trevelyan: "The change […] from an idle, barbarous, isolated potato cultivation, to corn [grain] cultivation, which enforces industry, binds together employer and employed in mutually beneficial relations […] is proceeding as fast as can reasonably be expected under the circumstances." However, such change, Wilson insisted, could never be accomplished by outside interference, but only by the Irish themselves, presumably under the threat of starvation. Government intervention, he argued, had been a disaster.[8]

While Wilson had the logic of ideology on his side, there may have been another type of logic at work that no one at the time understood: the logic of ecology. As suggested earlier, the apparent weakening of the potato blight in 1847 might have been due to the vastly reduced scale of potato cultivation. In effect, this represented an unintended retreat from monoculture. As far as the future was concerned, would planting more potatoes result in a significant resurgence of the blight? The answer to that question would have to wait for another year. In the meantime, Ireland continued to face disaster, marked by suffering, controversies over outdoor relief, massive movements of population, a drying up of British charity and an attempted revolution.

The Second Phase: The Amended Poor Law and Outdoor Relief

The sharp decline in potato cultivation meant that those who survived the first year of the Famine now faced ongoing malnutrition, making them prey to a variety of diseases, many of which would prove fatal. Adding to the misery, another hard winter followed on the heels of the small potato harvest. With the government soup kitchens closed along with most public works, the continuing crisis pushed hard on remaining relief efforts as they moved into their second phase. Everything was now centered on the Poor Law system, newly augmented with the possibilities for outdoor relief. Threatening higher Irish taxes, the new policy was contentious from the start. To the government's anger, many Poor Law boards of guardians, representing big farmers and landowners, refused to strike—impose—higher rates, which in some areas had increased between 500 and 900 percent in a matter of a few years.[9] As a result, collecting taxes in many areas became ever more difficult. In October 1847, Carrick-On-Shannon's Union collected only 5 percent of its rates. In Clifden, County Galway, attempts at tax collection, which often involved distraining livestock or crops, were met with violent resistance, leaving

---

8. Quoted in Leslie A. Williams, *Daniel O'Connell, the British Press and the Irish Famine*, 245–46.
9. Mac Atasney, *"This Dreadful Visitation,"* 71.

the Poor Law Union there facing financial collapse. In November 1848 the *Galway Vindicator* reported that a military force backing up the tax collectors had taken artillery to use against barricades that had previously blocked the roads. This time, instead of a blockade the contingent encountered a wide and deep trench dug across the road. Planks were searched for but not found, and the force had to about face and march home, its mission unaccomplished.[10]

With the closing of public projects laborers were desperate for work. Even when landlords and farmers did hire the wages were inadequate. Captain Arthur Kennedy of the Kilrush Union complained: "Six days' wages at 5d. would be but 2s/6, not an equivalent to two and a half stones of meal, which a small family on outdoor relief would be entitled to."[11] Meanwhile, the government denounced the rate resistance of those farmers who neither employed the poor nor paid their Poor Law rates. By November, Edward Twistleton, chief of the Poor Law Commission, reversed his previous position and agreed that recalcitrant boards of guardians be replaced with government appointees. Although aware of the burden of higher taxes, he believed that increases were necessary to prevent a drain on the Treasury, which "might be seriously injurious to the Empire." For the greater imperial good, it was essential "to throw the Irish on their own resources, as far as possible."[12]

For all the controversy over outdoor relief, only half of the Poor Law Unions were permitted to offer it and then only to those who passed strict rules of eligibility. However, attempts to distinguish between the able-bodied and the "impotent" poor began to break down as malnutrition and disease eroded the health of most applicants.[13] In the meantime the numbers of those on relief continued to grow. In January 1848, the Mohill Union, County Leitrim, had over 1,000 individuals on outdoor relief, in addition to its workhouse inmates. A month later, it was feeding 7,000, pushing up its costs from £30 to £218 per week. By February 1848, throughout Ireland 445,456 Irish people were on outdoor relief. By September, from a total of 1,433,042 receiving Poor Law assistance, only 525,263 were inmates of the workhouses. The rest were on outdoor relief.[14] Consequently, many unions were in debt to local food merchants, as well as to the Treasury. Therefore, by the summer of 1848, in the wake of the low potato yield the previous fall, many unions were in serious financial difficulties. Trevelyan, therefore, felt that he had no choice but to continue to pare the available cheese, sparingly distributing loans and grants to unions only when justified by serious need. Being too generous would, as he wrote to Twistleton, "revive the mendicant spirit" among the Irish. Besides, any hint at government generosity would have stirred up a wave of protest in Britain.[15]

---

10. *Galway Vindicator* report carried by *Times*, November 10, 1848. For Clifden see Villers-Tuthill, "Clifden Union, Connemara, County Galway," 296–97.
11. See Donnelly, *The Great Irish Potato Famine*, 105.
12. Haines, *Charles Trevelyan and the Great Irish Famine*, 444.
13. Ó Murchadha, *Sable Wings over the Land*, 147.
14. Kinealy, *This Great Calamity*, 198–99. For Mohill see MacAtasney, "The Mohill Union," 307.
15. Haines, *Charles Trevelyan and the Great Irish Famine*, 495.

In charge of overseeing day-to-day relief, Trevelyan had become more powerful than ever. Many private donations, as well as all public relief funds, were channeled through the Poor Law system over which he had ultimate control. In addition, he saw to it that the boards of all Poor Law Unions reported directly to him, rather than to the Irish executive at Dublin Castle. Thus, he could account for almost every penny spent (or loaned) on Irish relief. A dedicated bureaucrat, the concerns that drove Trevelyan in his almost obsessive management of Irish relief were complex. He wanted to prevent starvation, but, as the Exchequer's chief civil servant, he believed it was his duty to minimize the financial strain on the Imperial Treasury and, thereby, the burden on British middle-class taxpayers, of which he was one. Also, like most of the members of Russell's government, he wanted to force Irish landlords, particularly absentees, to shoulder the burden of the disaster, believing that their own careless policies had contributed to the calamity. In addition, Trevelyan was convinced, along with most of the cabinet, that the newly amended Poor Law with its imbedded Quarter Acre or Gregory Clause would force structural changes in Irish agriculture. Finally, as a devout evangelical, Trevelyan believed that the state should inculcate, and certainly not undermine, the moral values of society. Relief had to be given in a way that would not "demoralize" the poor, making them dependent upon the public purse.

Unfortunately, with the Gregory Clause's quarter-acre stipulation in place, the pace of evictions quickened. In July 1848 a correspondent to *The Times*, riding through parts of the west of Ireland, found both sides of the road lined with unroofed cabins. Whole villages had been evicted. The situation was "a natural, inevitable result, of the war now carrying on in the west of Ireland between fast fading property, fast increasing pauperism." The landlords, the correspondent wrote, had no choice but to clear their estates.[16] Indeed, facing the shortfall in rents, the rise in Poor Law rates and the threat of outdoor relief, many landlords now saw their tenants as liabilities. At the same time, Whiteboy activity, which had previously acted as a partial check on evictions, became more difficult for hungry people to sustain. In this atmosphere, the Gregory Clause seemed a godsend to the landlords. It promised to ease the way for clearances, thus preventing their ultimate nightmare: "pauper warrens" in which no one paid rent and where everyone lived off outdoor relief at ratepayer expense.[17]

A Nation on the Move

> There were towns in which the entire population seemed to be in motion, either to administer or to obtain relief.[18]

Visitors to Ireland during the Famine must have felt as if the whole Irish nation was on the move. In a pattern often seen in famines elsewhere, the collapse of the potato

---

16. *The Times*, July 5, 1848.
17. See Ó Murchadha, *The Great Famine*, 116.
18. East, *Notes and Glimpses of Ireland in 1847*, 17.

economy had produced a series of shock waves that sent a large portion of Ireland's population onto the roads.[19] Watching the migration, Quaker William Bennett wrote that "the tide of emigration [...] is truly affecting." He passed lines of emigrants, whole families with their worldly goods packed up in donkey carts, heading for towns and seaports. At each stage, the journey ended for some, regardless of their intended destinations. Sickness, poverty or mere exhaustion prevented some from continuing. Death overtook others. Along the verges of the roads, the migrants passed the dying and the dead, some exposed, others buried in rough, barely covered graves.[20]

As Ireland's overall population declined, many towns grew during the Famine years, as the catastrophe in the countryside poured thousands into their streets. Entering a village in Clare, Rev. Spencer T. Hall, who usually avoided dehumanizing language when writing about the poor, saw "objects" that "I should certainly have believed to be dead already but for their feeble efforts to solicit charity as I approached them." Visiting a soup kitchen in Cork, Rev. John East described "women with infants which could not touch the food. Many of them were mere breathing skeletons, far gone; and their mothers held them up in our faces, with a kind of maniac grin, intimating that the help came too late for these little ones." He found Cork, a "city of destruction." Less careful in his language than Hall, East went on to compare these starving refugees "to nothing but the condition of the *insect tribes* at the fall of the year, when they just move to struggle and to die. Children, wan and livid, were dying or actually dead, in the arms of fathers and mothers, who had scarcely strength to carry them."[21] William Bennett, conscious of the Quaker mission to give witness to what he encountered, described the scene in Kenmare, County Kerry: "The sounds of woe and wailing resounded in the streets throughout the night. I felt extremely ill, and was almost overcome." "I might see several families lying about in the open streets, actually dying of starvation and fever, within a stone's throw of the inn." Never before in Ireland had he seen people "falling on their knees to beg. It was difficult to sit over breakfast after this." Bennett tried to find help within the town, but there was none to be had.[22]

In some towns, the accumulated misery announced its presence, not only to the eye but to the ear as well. Bennett was not the only one to discover that starvation could have a voice. Others recorded the "demonic yells" and "agonizing shrieks" heard in the streets. Sometimes the groans of the hungry crowding around private homes provided a grim accompaniment to a household's meals. A visitor to Cork in April 1847 was haunted by the "low unbroken wail of children. [...] It never ceased, but filled the air, following even long after one had left those quarters."[23] At other times, however, it was the unexpected stillness of the starving that shocked the observer. In Cork, Rev. John East found

---

19. For migrations during famines see Ó Gráda, *Famine: A Short History*, 81–89.
20. See Scally, *The End of Hidden Ireland*, 172. For quote see Bennett, *Narrative of a Recent Journey of Six Weeks in Ireland*, 53.
21. East, *Notes and Glimpses of Ireland in 1847*, 20; Hall, *Life and Death in Ireland as Witnessed in 1849*, 20.
22. Bennett, *Narrative of a Recent Journey of Six Weeks in Ireland*, 127, 128–29.
23. For all quotes see Geary, "'The Living Were Out of Their Feeling': A Socio-Cultural Analysis of the Great Famine in Ireland," 311–12.

that, although the poor where in a "state of helpless, hopeless misery," they beseeched relief "rather by the eye and general aspect than by the tongue" of the practiced beggar. William Bennett recalled that "the silent beseeching look, *without a word spoken*, of some of the women and girls, is what enters into the heart deepest, and is the most difficult to bear."[24] Silent or not, whether in the crowded workhouses, in the lines at soup kitchens or in the streets of the towns and cities, the Famine also had a smell, although generally it was only medical personnel who mentioned that in their journals.

Sometimes begging in the streets could be aggressive, especially as want eroded the traditional social customs so characteristic of pre-Famine Ireland. Bennett noted that, as coaches pulled into a town, the begging that suddenly formed around them could be "very violent." The Scottish philosopher Thomas Carlyle described an ugly scene in Millstreet, County Kerry, when some visitors threw a few halfpence among the beggars, who scramble for them "like rabid dogs." Carlyle recalled: "one oldish fellow […] beating a boy, to keep at least him out of the competition."[25]

The Transatlantic Emigration

> Clinging to and kissing and embracing each other with the utmost ardour, calling out aloud, in broken tones, endeared names of brother, sister, mother, sobbing and crying as if the very heart would burst […] and when the final orders were given to clear the ship and withdraw the gangway, the howl of agony there arose at once from the parting deck and the abandoned pier, was perfectly overpowering.[26]

People were fleeing not just the countryside but Ireland itself. In 1845, before famine conditions had taken hold, about 75,000 people left the country. With the destruction of the potato crop in the fall of 1846, the exodus accelerated. Around 106,000 people emigrated, most during the winter half of the year. Until then, emigrants had usually embarked in the spring and early summer when the Atlantic crossing was relatively calm. However, in 1846, as fall gave way to winter, panic set in as people fled on whatever ships were available, regardless of the season. It seemed, moreover, as if all the old cultural inhibitions that had traditionally limited emigration had been suddenly washed away. In 1847, 214,000 Irish embarked for North America alone, 117,000 to the United States and 97,000 to Canada.[27] By this time Liverpool had already become the major center for the transatlantic passenger trade. Irish emigrants flocked to the English port because most of its the ships were generally larger, the crossings faster and the sailings more frequent than embarkations out of Ireland. From 1846 until 1851 an average of 250,000

---

24. Bennett, *Narrative of a Recent Journey of Six Weeks in Ireland*, 132. East, *Notes and Glimpses of Ireland in 1847*, 17–18.
25. Carlyle, *Reminiscences of My Irish Journey in 1849*, 113. See also Bennett, *Narrative of a Recent Journey of Six Weeks in Ireland*, 52.
26. Forbes, *Memorandums Made in the Autumn of 1852*, 1:202.
27. For emigration data see Kenny, *The American Irish*, 97–98.

Irish arrived in Liverpool annually, between one-half and two-thirds continuing on to North America.[28]

Between 1828 and 1837, Irish annual transatlantic emigration had numbered around 40,000 per annum. This increased to 50,000 a year between 1838 and 1844. If times had been normal, some 437,500 would probably have crossed the Atlantic between 1845 and 1855.[29] Instead, around 1.5 million fled to the United States, while 340,000 sailed to Canada (of whom two-thirds may have crossed the border into the United States). At the same time between 200,000 and 300,000 Irish settled in Great Britain, while some 50,000 traveled to Australia and New Zealand. In all, some 2.1 million Irish people left the island between 1845 and 1855, accounting for roughly one-quarter of the pre-Famine population. Even as the crisis wound down, the exodus continued. Between 1856 and 1860 an additional 900,000 emigrated. Kerby A. Miller states that, "more people left Ireland in just eleven years than during the preceding two and one-half centuries. An entire generation virtually disappeared from the land; only one out of three Irishmen born about 1831 died at home of old age."[30]

For a laborer, the minimum cost of a ticket and sea stores was equal to a year's income.[31] In 1846 and 1847 the cheapest passages were on the timber ships that plied the route back and forth between Canada and Britain or Ireland. Often empty on the westward return journey, their captains were willing enough to be paid for taking on what was, in effect, human ballast.[32] Even before the Famine, conditions for passengers sailing on those ships were terrible and dangerous. With minimal adjustments, no amenities and no effective regulations, emigrants were crammed into dark holds for up to 40 days or more. As they rode out the storms, their sea stores (their primary source of provisions) often spoiled. Disease was an ever-present danger. If someone brought typhoid fever on board, many others would contract it during the crossing. The mortality rate on the Ireland–Canada passage in 1847 stood at around 20 percent.[33]

Sadly, for those traveling to British North America in 1846 and 1847, illness and death, their constant onboard companions, did not abandon them when their ships reached port. Many landed only to die in one of several quarantine stations where officials tried to isolate fever patients from the general population. In Canada the main station was at Quebec's Grosse-Île, established during the cholera pandemic of 1832. At first, most of the 33,000 Irish emigrants arriving there in 1846 were relatively healthy. By the spring of 1847, however, the situation began to deteriorate rapidly. Of the 243 passengers aboard the *Syria*, the first ship to arrive after the breakup of the winter ice on the St. Lawrence, 81 had the fever, nine having already died. Within a matter of days almost all the arrivals were sick. As more ships docked, the numbers of stricken arrivals quickly exceeded the capacity of the island's 150-bed quarantine hospital. Consequently, passengers were

---

28. Tunney and Nugent, "Liverpool and the Great Irish Famine," 509.
29. Donnelly, *The Great Irish Potato Famine*, 178.
30. Data and quote from Miller, *Emigrants and Exiles*, 291.
31. Ó Gráda, *The Great Irish Famine*, 8.
32. For timber trade see Hickey, *Famine in West Cork*, 132.
33. Ó Gráda, *Black '47 and Beyond*, 106.

prevented from disembarking to escape the unspeakable conditions aboard ship. So confined, the sick sometimes shared their bunks with the dead. By the end of May, 40 ships comprised a two-mile cue outside the station, awaiting to unload their human cargo.[34]

Over the following months, matters grew worse. During the ice-free period between May and November of 1848, Quebec received 441 ships from British and Irish ports carrying between 80,000 and 90,000 people. Of these, some 15,000 died. All told, 5,424 Irish men, women and children are buried at Grosse-Île. Taking in consideration those who succumbed at sea or shortly after disembarking, the Canadian crossing may have claimed as many as 17,000 lives in 1847. As for the survivors, it was difficult to keep people who presented no symptoms of fever cooped up at Grosse-Île. Eventually traveling inland, some unknowingly carried the latent diseases with them. The Roman Catholic Archbishop of Quebec wrote to his fellow prelates in Ireland, warning them that many of their countrymen who arrived healthy later succumbed to diseases after traveling on to Montreal and Quebec.[35]

Fortunately, after 1847, the role of these "coffin ships" out of Ireland diminished. As emigrant destinations shifted from British North America to the United States, the Atlantic journey out of Liverpool offered a less arduous and dangerous passage. In 1847, around 45 percent of transatlantic emigrants went to Canada, many then later crossing the border into the United States. After 1848, the proportion dropped to between 10 and 15 percent. Since the Canadian route was the cheapest, its decline suggests that, by 1848, the numbers of the most destitute emigrants had peaked. Most of the poor who could leave had already done so. Also, since most transatlantic passengers were by then sailing from Liverpool on bigger, safer and slightly faster ships, mortality on the United States route fell to around 2 percent. As Cormac Ó Gráda asserts, "given the tragic and chaotic contexts of the journey, it is the low overall mortality of the journey that is significant."[36]

Famine Migration to Great Britain

> The sudden apparition of 20 French war steamers […] may be less evil, less fatal, less destructive, less confounding than the daily importation of thousands who cannot be driven from the shore or resisted at their landing. (*The Times*, April 1847)[37]

In 1849 Rev. Spencer T. Hall encountered Clare emigrants traveling through the night to reach embarkation points along the Shannon Their carts were piled high with boxes, on which perched "women and children, with swollen eyes and wet cheeks; while with grave and downcast looks, men, both young and old, were slowly marching by their sides." Hundreds of thousands crossed the Irish Sea from Ireland's ports to British cities such as

---

34. Quigley, "Grosse Île: Canada's Famine Memorial," 134–36.
35. For Archbishop of Quebec see Hickey, *Famine in West Cork*, 226. For 17,000 lives see Ó Murchadha, *The Great Irish Famine*, 153. For other data see also McGowan, "Grosse Île Quebec," 533 and "Black '47 and Toronto, Canada," 526.
36. Ó Gráda, *Black '47 and Beyond*, 106. See also Miller, *Emigrants and Exiles*, 292.
37. See Fitzgerald, "'The Great Hunger?' The Irish Famine: Changing Patterns of Crisis," 109.

Liverpool, Glasgow, Manchester and London. Liverpool received most of the arrivals, partly because the fares out of Dublin were cheaper, especially for the poorest who traveled as deck passengers. A February 1847 issue of *The Scotsman* reported that observers had seen wretched women and children on the decks trying to sustain themselves with raw turnips, half-eaten by the cattle on board.[38]

As noted above, one-half to two-thirds of those arriving in Liverpool continued on to North America. The rest, having run out of resources, either moved on to other industrial cities in Britain or simply remained where they landed. Even before the Famine, Liverpool already had a sizable Irish population of 49,639, many living in terrible conditions. The Famine produced 296,213 more refugees in 1847 alone. Between then and 1853 the *lowest* number of annual arrivals to the city from Ireland numbered 232,331. This massive influx of mostly Roman Catholics raised sectarian feelings in a city burdened by the poverty, disease and death that accompanied the refugees. By 1847, the Irish had quickly overwhelmed all available relief sources in the city. That year 47,194 individuals were recorded as receiving relief in Liverpool through the English Poor Law system. As Frank Neal points out, however, this number is very likely too low, since the city's record keeping had broken down.[39]

Because they were not established residents, the new arrivals could not claim relief as a right. Nevertheless, those operating the city's Poor Law system still had a legal obligation not to let them die. Even if the newcomers could not be admitted to the workhouses, some sort of outdoor relief consisting of food (bread and soup) and clothing was often available.[40] In England, as in Ireland, the Poor Law was supposed to shield the Imperial Treasury from welfare costs; local rates had to pay for local poverty, regardless from where the paupers came. As early as 1845, therefore, the annual cost of poor relief in the Liverpool jumped from £2,916 to £25,926. In 1847 the Poor Law rates in the city rose four times in that year alone. The rate payers protested, but they fared no better than their counterparts in Ireland.[41] Eventually, new legislation allowed for the repatriation of Irish paupers back to Ireland, returning 62,881 people (many of them children) between 1845 and 1854. Given conditions there, few wanted to return. Even Irish lawbreakers, provided with the choice of a Liverpool jail or deportation, often chose the former.[42] The threat of deportation made many Irish refugees afraid to apply for relief. So, they stayed in the shadows and survived as best they could on private charity. In December 1847, the

---

38. *The Scotsman*, February 20, 1847; for quote see Hall, *Life and Death in Ireland as Witnessed in 1849*, 19.
39. See Neal, "Black '47: Britain and the Irish Famine," 340, 341. For arrivals see Neal, "Black '47: Liverpool and the Irish Famine," 124.
40. Neal, "Black '47: Liverpool and the Irish Famine," 126.
41. For 1845 rates see Tunney and Nugent, "Liverpool and the Great Irish Famine," 505.
42. For deportations see Neal, "The Famine Irish in England and Wales," 66–69, as well as the author's, "Black '47: Britain and the Irish Famine," 341, 352. See also Ó Murchadha, *The Great Irish Famine*, 148.

London Mendicity Society assisted 736 English paupers and 14,945 Irish. In the same month a year later, the society aided 718 English and 21,578 Irish poor.[43]

The wave of Famine refugees to Britain hit industrial cities where previous growth had already outstripped their infrastructure. As the new arrivals brought fevers and dysentery, public health quickly deteriorated. The numbers of Irish fever victims were so great in Liverpool that several ships were commandeered to act as quarantine stations. Fever sheds were built around the onshore workhouse. The city's records show that over 60,000 cases of famine fever and 40,000 of dysentery were treated in 1847. Around 8,434 of the victims died. As Irish immigrants spread around England and Wales between 1846 and 1848, mortality rates climbed 100,000 above normal.[44] In June 1847 *The Times* complained that "the Irish epidemic is rapidly increasing in the metropolis." The London fever hospital was forced to close its doors against new patients. Of the Irish who thronged the streets, the paper insisted: "It is their nature to herd together, and to avoid any opportunity of airy and cleanly lodging that may be afforded them. They prefer to lie in heaps of their own." As a result, there was throughout the city "festering accumulations of misery, dirt and disease, breeding a pestilence that taints the air [...] This is only the beginning, the whole summer and autumn are before us [...] when the heat [...] has penetrated to the depth of the drains, and the temperature of the earth gives fresh activity to the decomposition of their contents."[45]

Unfortunately, the refugees of 1847–48 arrived just as Britain experienced a sharp recession that left large numbers of unemployed English, Welsh and Scottish workers struggling to survive. Minimal as British relief for Irish refugees might have been, it was also minimal for *all* the poor in the United Kingdom. Yet, while the largely Roman Catholic Irish paupers were not particularly welcomed into Protestant Britain, neither were most of them rejected and turned away. "Despite the ideological blindness of the government," Frank Neal writes, "ordinary people in Britain responded to pleas for help."[46] Indeed, many of the Famine refugees in Britain might have fared worse had they stayed in Ireland. According to records, only 50 immigrants to Britain died of starvation in 1847. British charity, public and private, somehow sustained many who, if they had remained neglected at home, might have perished. It is sadly ironic that the refugees from the Famine had to go to Great Britain to find some approximation of the implied promise theoretically embedded in the concept of the United Kingdom.

---

43. Neal, "The Famine Irish in England and Wales," 68. Gallman, *Receiving Erin's Children*, 30; Fitzgerald, "'The Great Hunger?'" 110.
44. Ó Gráda, *Famine: A Short History*, 87. For Liverpool see Neal, "Black '47: Britain and the Irish Famine," 342, 344, 351; Tunney and Nugent, "Liverpool and the Great Irish Famine," 504–5.
45. *The Times*, June 21, 1847 (5).
46. Neal, "Black '47: Britain and the Irish Famine," 356; "Black '47: Liverpool and the Irish Famine," 134.

Assisted Emigration

Largely absent from the vast numbers of refugees fleeing Ireland were those too poor to afford passage abroad; the workhouses remained their only hope. Significantly, George Nicholls, designer of the Irish Poor Law system, had urged the government to share expenses with the Poor Law Unions and landowners to ship off paupers to the colonies, simultaneously reducing the financial strain at home and boosting the development of the empire. The government, however, balked at the expense. Although the unions could tax themselves to support the overseas shipment of inmates, the actual funds raised were minimal and their use restrictive. Yet, after 1845, as pressure on the workhouses grew, there was an uptick in interest in publicly supported emigration. In December 1846, Lord Clanricarde of Galway, a member of Russell's cabinet, argued that some sort of subsidized emigration scheme was necessary. "You cannot effectively and promptly deal with the dense population of rural villages without recourse to it." In 1847 the government decided to allow the unions some matching funds. Yet, on the whole, there was little enthusiasm on anyone's part to pay for assisted emigration.[47]

An interesting exception came in 1847 when the colonial administration of New South Wales offered to pay the ocean passage for female orphans who, upon disembarking, would become domestic servants. An Irish workhouse had to merely select, groom, outfit the girls and get them to the ports. With family connections in Australia, Trevelyan enthusiastically supported a project that promised to cost the Treasury very little. Eventually, 4,114 orphaned girls made the journey. Some unions gladly cooperated, fearing that female orphans, unmarriageable and unemployable, might remain permanent workhouse inmates. Some might even get pregnant, multiplying their upkeep. As one Poor Law inspector in Nenagh bluntly put it: "You will get shut of them for about £5 each, and perhaps a future generation in the bargain." The Australian scheme eventually faded, however. The girls sent out seemed unsuited to the demands of a strange, pioneer country, and there were too many Roman Catholics among them to please Protestant colonists.[48] Nevertheless, the Australian orphan scheme did inspire a few unions to institute their own measures. Having sent out 84 girls to Australia, the Nenagh Union assisted an additional 753 inmates to emigrate between 1849 and 1860. The Clare Unions of Scarriff, Kilrush and Ennis each sent out around 400 in 1851. The Cork workhouse paid passage for 800 individuals between 1852 and 1854. After 1849 unions could send inmates to the United States. The cheaper passage to Canada remained the preferred route, however.[49]

---

47. Moran, "'Shoveling out the Paupers': The Irish Poor Law and Assisted Emigration during the Great Famine." 23. For quote see Cornwell, *A Galway Landlord during the Great Famine*, 48.
48. For quote see Grace, *The Great Famine in Nenagh Poor Law Union, County Tipperary*, 192. For the operation see Abbott, "The Earl Grey Orphan Scheme, 1848–1850, and the Irish Diaspora to Australia," 201–10; Ó Cathaoir, "The Workhouse During the Great Famine," 233; Haines, *Charles Trevelyan and the Great Irish Famine*, 427–30.
49. Moran, "'Shoveling out the Paupers,'" 32, 34. See also Crossman, *The Poor Law in Ireland*, 31. For assisted emigration for female orphans see Moran, "'Permanent Deadweight:' Female Pauper Emigration from Mountbellow Workhouse to Canada," 109–12.

Although Russell overcame some initial reluctance and accepted the concept of assisted emigration, in this, as in so many other instances, he could not muster enough support in his cabinet to create a more liberal policy. The Treasury faction, especially Earl Grey and Sir Charles Wood, steadfastly opposed the idea. There were already complaints from the colonies, as well as from the United States, about Ireland dumping its paupers abroad. Besides, vast numbers were leaving at their own expense, reducing pressure on the Poor Law system without any cost to the British taxpayers.[50] Still, with Poor Law rates rising, some landlords were anxious to clear and reorganize their estates at their own expense, if necessary.

Landlord-assisted emigration may have been most prevalent in Ulster. In County Londonderry, estates owned by the London companies (Drapers, Grocers, Fishmongers, and others) engaged in what Trevor Parkhill has labeled as "clearance by stealth." By 1848 the Drapers Company had quietly rid its lands of over 400 tenants by spending £950 to send them abroad. In County Monaghan, the Shirley estate assisted some 1,500 individuals to emigrate between 1843 and the end of the Famine period. By then the population of the estate had fallen by 8,000, with assisted emigration accounting for approximately 18 percent of this decline.[51] Probably the most successful case of large-scale proprietor-assisted emigration occurred on the vast Fitzwilliam estate in Wicklow, which comprised some 20 percent of the county. Even before the Famine, Lord Fitzwilliam, anxious to reduce the number of small holdings on his lands, had begun paying the fares and sea stores for those who volunteered to leave. Once the crisis hit in the fall of 1846, the proprietor switched to a stick-*and*-carrot approach. (You're being evicted, but we'll pay your way to Canada.) Consequently, the estate sent some 6,000 people across the Atlantic between 1847 and 1856 at a cost of £16,342 11*s* 1*d*. While it is doubtful that any of them enjoyed the voyage, by the standards of the day they fared better than many other Famine emigrants.[52]

Most of those proprietors who engaged in assisted emigration were less generous than Lord Fitzwilliam. In County Sligo the agents for Lord Palmerston, Russell's foreign secretary, had been busy "squaring the land" on his vast estate by getting rid of his middlemen and breaking up the rundale villages. Even before the Famine, Palmerston had been paying the Canadian passage for some of his poorer tenants. Then, already deeply in debt, he faced the sudden increase in Poor Law rates after the crop failure of 1846. This convinced him that it would be less costly to ship several thousand of his hungry paupers overseas. The ships chosen were not the worst, and his tenants were reasonably well supplied with sea stores. However, his agents in Sligo had failed to pay attention to matters of clothing and support once the emigrants landed. Also, the last two ships out of Sligo embarked late in the season and spent more time at sea than had been anticipated.

---

50. Gray, *Famine, Land and Politics*, 299–300.
51. Duffy, "The Famine in County Monaghan," 193, 194; Parkhill, "The Famine in County Londonderry," 164–65.
52. Fedelma Byrne, "The Mechanics of Assisted Emigration: From the Fitzwilliam Estate in Wicklow to Canada," 36, 44. For numbers involved see 52–53. See also Rees, *The Surplus People*, 34–46 125.

When their passengers finally disembarked in Canada in the late fall of 1847, the sight of the penniless and ragged refugees caused their hosts to accuse Palmerston of shipping out his paupers on what were little better than "slave ships." His Lordship had to appear before a parliamentary select committee of his peers to answer the accusation. Nevertheless, Palmerston did succeed in "shoveling out" his estate. While some 3,626 of his tenants had sought relief in 1847, there were only 53 who did so two years later.[53]

Palmerston appears positively generous compared to other landlords who simply sought the cheapest ships and offered only minimal sums for sea stores to their evacuees. In the early days of the Famine, landlords favored the cheap timber ships out of Irish ports making their return journeys to Canada, despite the discomforts and dangers they presented. For example, Major Denis Mahon of Strokestown, County Roscommon decided to rid his lands of "those of the poorest and worst description, who would be a charge on us for the Poor House or for Outdoor Relief." Mahon wanted to consolidate his lands so that Protestant tenants would have larger, more efficient farms on which to grow grain. He therefore chose cheap passage and minimal provisions for 982 of his poorest tenants, whom he sent out to Canada on five ships in 1847. Conditions were so bad on one of the ships, the *Virginius*, that 158 died before they reached Canada, and only a few were able to walk ashore unassisted at Grosse-Île. In fact, only half of the group lived to reach Quebec City. Mahon was assassinated later that year.[54] Irish nationalists condemned landlords like Mahon as "exterminators." Not all of those who sent their tenants abroad deserved the accusation, however. The records of the Shirley estate in Monaghan and the Lansdowne estate in Kerry, both managed by William Stuart Trench, suggest that oversight and support followed the departing tenants to Liverpool and sustained them in the city until they embarked. Under the circumstances, it would be hard to argue that they would have been better off remaining in Ireland.[55]

Regardless of how generously or how meagerly assisted emigration was carried out, those receiving such support accounted for only 5 percent of the vast human tide pouring out of Ireland. The overwhelming majority of emigrants had to finance their own escape—a possibility denied most of the Ireland's poorest. With the emigrant's path closed to them, this group faced either death or the workhouse, which in too many cases amounted to the same thing. This helps account for the surprisingly low levels of emigration from some of the poorest areas where mortality rates were, however, high.[56]

---

53. See Anbinder, "Lord Palmerston and the Famine Emigration," 441–69. See also Norton, "Communication: Lord Palmerston and the Famine Emigration," 155–65. See also Moran, "'Shoveling out the Paupers,'" 37.
54. For the *Virginius* see Campbell, *The Great Irish Famine*, 41–42. For quote see Quigley, "Grosse Île: Canada's Famine Memorial," 141.
55. Duffy, "Emigrants and the Estate Office in the Mid-Nineteenth Century: A Compassionate Relationship?" 77–86.
56. See Hickey, "Mortality and Emigration in Six Parishes in the Union of Skibbereen, West Cork, 1846–47," figure 13, 378.

Who Left? The Social Status of the Emigrants

Although it is difficult to find solid data regarding the economic status of the emigrants, better-off farmers may have accounted for as much as 25 percent of the initial emigrant flow from 1846 into 1847. Newspapers in Tipperary reported in 1847 that that those leaving were mostly the "better class" of comfortable or "snug" farmers, men of "small capital" who had something to sell to finance their trips.[57] By 1847 these farmers were faced with declining grain prices, rising rates and landlords demanding rent. By quietly selling their crops and livestock, while withholding rent and rates, this slightly better-off class managed to raise the money for the passage, disappearing before either the landlord or bailiff descended on them. Some landlords complained that the more industrious, rather than the worst, tenants were leaving. In some cases, those planning to emigrate would swap their holdings for cash paid by their more secure neighbors who would then take over the farm.[58] This is one of the reasons why the number of holdings above 15 acres rose by 16 percent between 1845 and 1847. As conditions worsened, however, even some of those who initially benefited from the hardship of their neighbors may eventually have found themselves on the emigrant trail. By 1851, the growth of holdings over 15 acres had reversed itself and declined by 10 percent.[59] While some landlords may have regretted the loss of their more dependable tenants, many others generally applauded "these thinnings," as did one estate agent in Country Antrim. He argued that emigration allowed for the creation of larger farms for the best remaining tenants and a financial outlook, which was "better for the Estate, for without the potato crop it is quite impossible for small farmers to live and pay rent especially on poor soil."[60]

Of the Irish immigrants landing in New York, the percentage who declared themselves farmers rose from 6.1 in 1846 to 11.2 in the years from 1847 to 1851. Nevertheless, servants and laborers dominated immigration lists both before and after the Famine. After the blight struck, their ranks grew, accounting, for example, for 75 percent of those entering New York City in 1846.[61] How could this group have afforded the passage? Many of those in the servant class, although poorly paid, were generally not liable for rents nor rates, nor did they have to invest in seed or livestock. Thus, some were able to save money for the passage. Once established abroad, they could then send home remittances to bring out the rest of the family. Ignatius Murphy states that remittances were "the key" to the growth of emigration in the Kilrush Union in Clare. One landlord reported that women and children filled the workhouse, waiting there until money orders arrived that would carry them over to America. The results of this chain migration were

---

57. For Tipperary see Grace, *The Great Famine in Nenagh Poor Law Union, County Tipperary*, 189; for 25 percent see MacDonagh, "Irish Overseas Emigration during the Famine," 321–22.
58. Ó Gráda, *Black '47 and Beyond*, 107; Ó Murchadha, *The Great Irish Famine*, 138–39. Kevin Kenny reports that the presence of middling-to-strong farmers among emigrants was highest in 1847, 1849 and 1850; *The American Irish: A History*, 99.
59. See also Smyth, "Exodus from Ireland," 500–1.
60. Quoted in Dallit, "The Famine in Country Antrim," 28.
61. Miller, *Emigrants and Exiles*, 295; Ó Gráda, *Black '47 and Beyond*, 108.

not lost on *The Times*, which rejoiced: "This mighty emigration pays for itself. It seeks no aid from the public purse."[62]

During the early years of the Famine, the geographical pattern of emigration remained much as it had been in earlier decades. The high emigration areas ran through the crowded drumlin belt of south Ulster and north Leinster, extending west to northern Mayo and into Sligo, areas hit hard by the decline in cottage industries. However, as the famine crisis continued, the pattern of emigration began to shift. After 1851, an exodus poured from the north midlands, Munster and southern Connaught, extending east into parts of Leinster. Some of these areas also experienced large-scale evictions.[63]

Throughout much of the Famine period, overall emigration rates tended to track mortality, both rising in tandem. For example, in 1846 the mortality rate was 9.1 percent, with an emigration rate of 9 percent. In 1847 the rates rose to 18.5 and 18.4 percent, respectively. In 1849 the comparison was 17.9 and 18.3 percent. Only after 1850 did the mortality and emigration tracks separate.[64] By then a rough inverse ratio appeared between death rates and the numbers of emigrants. In areas with high mortality, such as Clare, Galway and west Cork, emigration seems to have been relatively low. In many other parts of Ireland where death rates were lower, emigration was higher. This may be explained in part by the higher rates of poverty in the west, coupled with massive clearances. Few among the evicted could afford to emigrate.[65]

It was in cultural terms that the Famine emigration clearly departed from previous patterns. Religion stands out as one major difference. Prior to 1845, Protestants, who made up about a quarter of Ireland's population, had constituted half of those leaving the island. During the Famine, however, Protestants made up only one-tenth of the emigrants. As a result, the high proportion of Roman Catholics emigrating after 1845 had a profound effect on the largely Protestant British and North American cities in which they settled.[66] At the same time, a linguistic shift occurred within the ranks of the emigrants. Before the Famine, emigrants had come from predominantly English-speaking areas. As the tide of emigration moved toward Munster and Connaught, it included more Gaelic speakers. Half of the emigrants from those provinces may have spoken Gaelic. Kerby A. Miller estimates that one-quarter to one-third of those leaving Ireland between 1845 and 1855 spoke Irish.[67] Miller concludes that the overall character of emigration changed during the Famine. Up to that point people had left largely by choice, seeking economic opportunity and social independence. During the Famine, however, many emigrated out of a sense of desperation. They sought escape, as much

---

62. For *The Time*'s quote see Ó Murchadha, *The Great Irish Famine*, 144. For Kilrush Union see Murphy, *A People Starved*, 83.
63. Smyth, "Exodus from Ireland," 496–97, 501–2. Pre-Famine emigration had also extended into the south-central plains involving the counties of Queens, Tipperary and Kilkenny; see Kenny, *The American Irish: A History*, 98.
64. Smyth, "Exodus from Ireland," 494.
65. Ó Murchadha, *The Great Irish Famine*, 137; Ó Gráda, *Black '47 and Beyond*, 106–7.
66. See Miller, "Emigration to North America in the Era of the Great Famine," 220.
67. Ibid., 218.

or more than opportunity. The potato had failed them; the land had failed them; their landlords had failed them; Ireland had failed them. Thus, some carried with them what Miller has identified as an age-old characteristic of Irish emigrants—a sense of exile.[68]

From Generosity to Donor Fatigue

As noted earlier, despite long-held British suspicions about the Irish, the Queen's Appeal for Ireland in February 1847 had resulted in generous public support, which was quickly matched by worldwide contributions. By autumn, however, British public opinion seemed to have soured on Ireland, turning early generosity into something bordering on hostility. There were several reasons for this, not the least involving disappointed expectations. There had been widespread assumptions that the crisis in Ireland would abate with the harvest of 1847. Press coverage of the Famine dwindled, even in Ireland. All hopes were dashed, however, by the relatively sound but disastrously small potato crop, resulting in continued hardship and privation. Moreover, as previously noted, Britain experienced a short but sharp economic downturn that summer and fall. The year of 1847 saw failing banks and runs on deposits, just when the government faced a balance of payments crisis and a poor wheat harvest in England. At the same time, refugees fleeing Ireland were pushing up tax rates in British cities. Finally, as noted in the previous chapter, the General Election of 1847 returned a strong radical-liberal bloc of middle-class MPs who were deeply suspicious about the cost of Famine relief. Many Britons, in fact, felt they could no longer afford to be generous toward Ireland. Few understood that loans—which the government expected the Irish to repay—accounted for most of British tax money expended on the Famine.[69]

To further complicate matters, Charles Trevelyan, despite his best efforts to economize, realized that the funds raised by the British Association were rapidly being depleted. He had been quietly using this money to provide small grants to bankrupt Poor Law Unions. So, with the situation in Ireland as serious as ever, he convinced the government to have the Queen issue a new appeal. In October 1847 a second Queen's letter was read out in Britain's Anglican churches. Trevelyan wrote to the editor of *The Times*, calling for a generous response to the Her Majesty's appeal. He urged the paper and its readers to pity "the unhappy people in the western districts of Ireland, who will again perish by the thousands this year if they are not relieved." At the same time he tried to reassure the public that, as reported in *The Economist*, "the Poor Law will be enforced in Ireland to the utmost extent" and that the "collection of rates will be enforced, as far as it can be."[70] The Queen's appeal was poorly received by the public, however, and in the October 16, 1847 issue of *The Economist*, James Wilson rejoiced: "Never within our

---

68. Miller, *Emigrants and Exiles*, 298–99. For the exile theme see 3–8, 103–7, 304–5.
69. For the British economy see Haines, *Charles Trevelyan and the Great Irish Famine*, 71–72. For decline of Famine news see MacMahon, *The Great Famine in Tralee and North Kerry*, 152.
70. See Leslie A. Williams, *Daniel O'Connell, the British Press and the Irish Famine*, 246. For Trevelyan's letter to *Times*, see Bew, *Ireland: The Politics of Enmity*, 198,

recollection has such a demand met with so cold, so repulsive a response. [...] [T]he daily journals have teemed with letters from rectors, incumbents and curates, declaring that they cannot conscientiously comply with her Majesty's recommendation; that their own poor are suffering and starving; that the Irish do not deserve further relief."[71] A few months later, in his journal's Christmas Day issue, Wilson insisted that neither charity nor government intervention had helped Ireland. They had only perpetuated misery and destroyed what little self-reliance the Irish had left. "Till you make the people of Ireland rely upon themselves and their own resources, you do nothing." Like many other observers, Wilson never tired of giving bootstrap advice to the bootless. Earlier, in January 1847 he had even indulged in an element of fantasy. Alleging that the poor of County Clare were better fed during the Famine than they had been before, he insisted: "To convert a period of distress, arising from natural causes, into one of unusual comfort and ease, by the interference of government money, or of private charity, is to paralyze the efforts of the people themselves."[72] Obviously, segments of British public opinion had hardened. Many newspapers, reflecting the concerns of the middle-class taxpayers, argued that government intervention had gone too far. *The Times* published a letter from Thomas Campbell Foster, who bragged that his book, *Letters on the Condition of the People of Ireland*, based on his series of articles commissioned by the newspaper, accounted for the failure of the Queen's second appeal. The whole endeavor, he contended, had been a gross impiety threatening to "thwart the providence of God" by degrading the Irish into "contentment" to live on charity.[73]

There were factors other than moralism at play. Great Britain was an advanced capitalist, solution-oriented society that prided itself on its ability to get things done. For the Victorians, problems existed to be solved. Early in 1847 the British had responded generously to Ireland's difficulty, hoping that the money would end the crisis. When, by the fall of 1847, it appeared that Ireland was going to go on starving, whether its potatoes were blighted or not, British sympathy, already under siege from all the factors listed above, began to flag. Such a reaction is by no means unique. Today's television audiences may quickly tire of seeing what appear to be the same starving people in refugee camps night after night and conclude that the problem is not amenable to any solution. Likewise, many British citizens in 1847, daily reading what appeared to be the same stories of hunger and starvation, lost patience with, or at least interest in, Ireland's crisis. Moreover, the British disliked being placed in the position of presiding over an annual replay of Irish want and starvation. This generated a sense of frustration and anger at the ongoing nature of a crisis that never seemed to end and that called into question Britain's values and competence. Thus, whereas the first Queen's letter had initially raised £172,000 back in January, just eight months later the second appeal brought in only £20,000.[74]

---

71. See Leslie A. Williams, *Daniel O'Connell, the British Press and the Irish Famine*, 247.
72. *The Economist*, January 16, 1847, p. 58. For previous quote see *Economist*, December 25, 1847, 1475.
73. For quote see Gray, *Famine, Land and Politics*, 290.
74. For £20,000, see ibid. For the Queen's second letter see Leslie A. Williams, *Daniel O'Connell, the British Press and the Irish Famine*, 246–49.

The tide of charity toward Ireland ebbed abroad as well, suggesting that the Irish Famine had inaugurated another precursor of modern disaster relief, what James S. Donnelly, Jr. identifies as "donor fatigue."[75] Unfortunate as the phenomenon may be, it should be remembered that donor fatigue is the reverse side of exuberant charity's coin; it is the inevitable winding down of unsustainable high levels of donor enthusiasm and commitment. During the first half of 1847, the Irish Famine became an unprecedented philanthropic cause. Writing about American involvement, historian Merle Curti compares it to the "Greek fever" engendered by the enthusiastic support for democratic revolutions in the Balkans in the 1820s. Some of the fund-raising techniques pioneered during that event were carried to new heights and dedication under the banner of Irish famine relief.[76] Unfortunately, neither individuals nor societies can sustain such intensity indefinitely. This was especially true in large British and American cities where the sudden influx of thousands of Irish refugees resulted in rising taxes and abrupt demands placed on of local charities, draining away money that might have gone to Ireland. As time went on, Yankee newspapers, some of which had initially heralded the Famine as a punishment from God, began to turn their attention away from the needs of Ireland to the hoard of needy refugees arriving in American ports.[77]

As Donnelly points out, however, there may have been something deeper at work than donor fatigue. In Britain, at least, increasing negativity toward the Irish suggested that the British public was trying to shield itself from guilt for Irish suffering by blaming the victims. Indeed, the Anglican Archbishop of Dublin, Richard Whatley, an Englishman himself, summed up the welter of confusing emotions and resentments in the minds of his fellow countrymen: "The feeling of the English was a mixture of revenge, compassion and self-love. They pitied the suffering poor of Ireland; they had a fierce resentment against the landlords, whom they hastily judged to be the sole authors of those sufferings; and they dreaded calls upon their own purse."[78] As Leslie A. Williams notes in her study of the British press and the Famine, when a society faces a crisis that involves only some of its members, it does so within the limits of what it deems proper and possible.

> When those limits are reached without an end to the crisis, further responses might threaten actions that were previously considered unthinkable, or at least difficult and costly. [...] The alternative is to unconsciously seek out the formula of words that will absolve the society of further responsibility. Reasons are piled up to explain why nothing further can be done. Among the most convenient arguments are those that depict the victims as in some sense responsible for their fate. [...] One blames the victim in order to deflect blame from oneself.[79]

---

75. For donor fatigue see Donnelly, *The Great Irish Potato Famine*, 126–27.
76. Merle Curti, *American Philanthropy Abroad*, 64. The tide of American support ran from November 1846 to the late summer 1847, peaking in February of that year.
77. See Farrell, "Reporting the Irish Famine in America: Images of 'Suffering Ireland' in the American Press, 1845-1848," 81–83. For other examples, see Kinealy, *Charity and the Great Hunger in Ireland*, 9, 231, 254.
78. Quoted in Hickey, *Famine in West Cork*, 271. For victim blaming see Donnelly, *The Great Irish Potato Famine*, 126–27.
79. Leslie A. Williams, *Daniel O'Connell, the British Press and the Irish Famine*, 248.

Such attitudes, already well rooted in Britain's Irish narrative, were assiduously applied to the Famine situation by journals such as *The Times*. On November 5, 1846, the paper had insisted, without any evidence, that there were still usable potatoes in the ground and plenty of fish in the sea, if only the peasants would dig and fish. However,

> the same barbaric thoughtlessness which congregates hundreds together in the hope of getting food without money, or wages without work, makes them [the Irish] treat with contempt all recommendations of patient industry and painstaking precaution. [...] We are pointing out a malady in the national character which has preceded and induced a more fearful malady in the physical condition of the people. The want of food this year results in some degree from the want of enterprise in past years.[80]

The continuous reiteration of such blame-the-victim rhetoric appears to have had an effect. As Edward G. Lengel contends, somewhere between 1847 and 1848 the British public's response to the Famine seemed to have crossed a kind of watershed. At the beginning of the century, with the passage of the Act of Union, British attitudes had reflected a certain optimism and liberality: Irish shortcomings might have been the result of history and poor governance on Britain's part. Therefore, perhaps within the context of the Union, the Irish could be brought into the modern age. Even during the first year of the potato blight, there had been a sense of optimism that a new Ireland would emerge from the crisis. After 1847, what Lengel calls the previous "liberal consensus" began to break down, resulting in diminishing expressions of sympathy for the Irish. In their place grew what Ciara Boylan has called "a mythology of British sacrifice and Irish intransience."[81] Whatever suffering the Irish endured they had brought upon themselves. Only a strict, unremitting pursuit of restructuring agricultural Ireland would produce the needed changes, regardless of the costs—providing they did not fall upon the British taxpayer.

Famine Protests, Revolution and the Irish Narrative

The British public's rather exaggerated perceptions of a rising tide of violence in Ireland made it easier to blame the Irish victim. Admittedly, unrest and crime often accompany famines. As food became scarce in the wake of the potato blight, the Irish crime rate did increase; from just under 20,000 reported incidents during the years 1842–46 to 41,989 in 1849 alone. Interestingly, the number of crimes against persons did not rise. Most of the reported incidents represented attacks on property.[82] Throughout Ireland mobs attempted to break into government grain depots, as well as shops, mills, boats and even fields of turnips and cabbages. One land agent in County Cork complained

---

80. *The Times*, November 5, 1846, 4.
81. Boylan, "Famine," 13; Lengel, *The Irish through British Eyes*, 121. For the Lengel's extended argument see 97–121.
82. Ó Gráda, *The Great Irish Famine*, 36–37. For crime and famines see his *Famine: A Short History*, 52–56.

that sheep and hay were stolen every night, rendering it "useless" for farmers to try to protect their fields or livestock.[83] Food, even when moved around the island, had to be transported under armed guard. "Offenses against the public peace," such as illegal meetings, riots, sabotage and acts of intimidation, represented a separate category of crime. Andrés Eiríksson considers these, along with "plundering provisions," as forms of "popular protest," indicative of a high level of social unrest. Very often they were meant to force strong farmers to sell their food locally and at "fair"—that is, low—prices. In other words, actions the police interpreted as crimes were often intended to force a negotiation over food prices.[84] Unfortunately, such disturbances, frequently reported in British papers, fitted all to easily into the British narrative about the Irish.

For a time, protests also occurred on public works, as people demanded employment and better wages, or, later, protested the closure of the works. As one inspector put it, the projects brought together "large bodies of men, who mutually inflame each other," and "together in masses are taught to understand their own strength." Eiríksson argues that during a 10-month period, starting in the fall of 1846, the Famine produced a "huge wave of often effective and increasingly collective popular protest" before being broken by hunger and despair a year later. When the soup kitchens opened, laborers, diminished in their own eyes to pauper status, became demoralized. This, as much as hunger and weakness, may have curtailed organized protests.[85]

Food riots and labor protests were one thing; murders, widely publicized in the British press, were quite another. On November 2, 1847, Major Denis Mahon of the Strokestown estate, County Roscommon (now the home of Ireland's National Famine Museum), was assassinated. By that time, violence, including attacks on landlords, had actually begun to decline in Ireland. Nevertheless, this much-publicized case caught public attention throughout the United Kingdom. The British press depicted Mahon, related by marriage to the Duke of Wellington, as a "good landlord," cut down by vicious, ungrateful tenants. The killing occurred during his return from a meeting called to try to save the local Poor Law Union from bankruptcy. Much less publicized was the fact that Mahon had a record of evicting his poorest tenants even before the Famine. As noted above, in 1847 he had sent hundreds of his former tenants to Canada on ships so poorly provisioned that many died.[86] Therefore, while they did not condone the killing, Irish nationalists, knowing Mahon's record, depicted him as a heartless monster, thus outraging British public opinion even more. On November 6, 1847, *The Times* warned of a widespread tenant conspiracy to kill landlords. It also predicted that the Mahon murder would completely sour any remaining British sympathy for the Irish. It would, moreover, make it difficult to push Irish landlords to act responsibly toward their tenants: "While we urge men of patriotism and honour to reside on their properties […]

---

83. Donnelly, *The Land and the People of Nineteenth-Century Cork*, 88.
84. Eiríksson, "Food Supply and Food Riots," 71–73. For "protest crimes" see 68–69, 80–84.
85. For first quote see ibid., 89; for second quote see 91. See also Ó Gráda, *Famine: A Short History*, 55.
86. See Scally, *The End of Hidden Ireland*, 39, 40; Stephen J. Campbell, *The Great Irish Famine*, 40–41.

hideous catastrophes drive them back to security and indifference. Who will take British capital and enterprise to Ireland with such expectations?"[87]

James S. Donnelly, Jr. notes that, in reality, there had been surprising little violence in Ireland, due to both forbearance on the part of authorities and the ceaseless efforts of the Catholic clergy to restrain their people.[88] Nonetheless, thanks in part to *The Times*, the Mahon murder roiled the sectarian political waters in both Britain and Ireland. Some nationalist-minded Roman Catholic clerics were outspoken critics of the government's famine relief policies. This annoyed many Protestants in Britain. Papers like *The Times*, always suspicious of Irish Catholics, could not resist spreading the unfounded rumor that a local priest had blessed Mahon's assassination. In a leading article published December 1, 1847, the paper thundered: "The priest sends out his Thug upon a sacred mission. He hallows his cause, he blesses his weapon, he gives absolution for the seeming crime." The word "Thug" refers to the Indian sect of assassins devoted to the goddess Kali. This comparison rhetorically placed Ireland's Catholics beyond the pale of decent Christians. For their part, Irish nationalists and defenders of the Catholic Church returned such bitterness in kind within the pages of their own newspapers.[89]

In the wake of the Mahon killing some Britons wondered when Irish crime would rise to the level of revolution. Since the beginning of the Famine, newspapers like *The Times* had warned that a distressed Ireland might turn once again to rebellion. For its part Irish nationalist rhetoric certainly kept the pot boiling, at least in the disturbed imaginations of British newspaper readers. *The Times* reported every rumor of Irish peasants buying guns and forging pikes. *Punch* published a cartoon of simian-faced Paddies arming themselves.[90] After the Mahon assassination *The Times*' leader for December 2, 1847, warned that Ireland teetered on the brink of revolution: "Armed ruffians are now let loose upon society without check or control. The present tyranny of the Irish assassins is equal to that exercised by the Jacobins in the worst days of the French Revolution; and yet men are found to talk against even the mildest measures for their repression."[91] That the dominant daily paper in Britain would give voice to such hysteria is evidence of the degree to which opinions regarding famine-stricken Ireland were colored by preexisting political and religious passions. It is, therefore, interesting to note Prime Minister Russell's reaction to calls for repression in Ireland. Irish landowner Clanricarde demanded that the government pass a coercion act, arguing that English landlords would not like to be shot. Russell agreed. "But," he argued, "neither does any landlord in England turn out fifty persons at once, and burn their houses over their heads. [...] The murders are atrocious; so are the evictions." In November 1847, responding to Clarendon's plea for a bill prohibiting the sale of firearms in Ireland, Russell complained: "The truth is that a civil war between landlords and tenants has been raging for 80 years, marked by barbarity on

---

87. For quote see Leslie A. Williams, *Daniel O'Connell, the British Press and the Irish Famine*, 251.
88. Donnelly, *The Land and the People of Nineteenth-Century Cork*, 91.
89. For press coverage of the Mahon murder see Leslie A. Williams, *Daniel O'Connell, the British Press and the Irish Famine*, 249–55. For quote see 252.
90. See Donnelly, *The Great Irish Potato Famine*, 129.
91. See Leslie A. Williams, *Daniel O'Connell, the British Press and the Irish Famine*, 254.

both sides." Russell therefore insisted that any arms bill would have to be accompanied by some relief for the tenants. He then pointed out that Irish constabulary records reported only three agrarian murders in 1847.[92]

Nevertheless, many Britons assumed that an Irish insurrection was in the air. Indeed, by 1848 much of Europe seemed engulfed by a revolutionary wave. To young Irish nationalists, the exciting events in Paris may have been as much an inspiration for revolution as the starvation taking place in their midst.[93] With Daniel O'Connell gone and his Repeal Association moribund, the more radical and restless members of Young Ireland wanted to act. Various nationalist clubs, some affiliated with the Irish Confederation, began arming and drilling. And, following the pattern of the Rising of 1798, they sent a delegation to France hoping for support from a revolutionary regime. However, the government there had no interest in adding hostile relations with Great Britain to its problems. The Young Irelanders were on their own.

In the meantime, the combination of a rising tide of revolutionary rhetoric, along with reports of gun sales and drilling, forced itself upon the attention of the British government. In Dublin Castle, Lord Clarendon, the viceroy, imagined the country about to collapse into violence. He pestered London to enact a strict coercion law, suspending habeas corpus. Although concerned, Russell feared that such draconian laws might make the situation worse. Sedition, after all, was a capital offense. Then, in April 1848 the government passed a law reclassifying certain kinds of treasonous acts and expressions as ordinary felonies punishable by imprisonment or transportation rather than by death. William Smith O'Brien, a Protestant landlord, an MP for Clare and head of the Irish Confederation, was quickly arrested and charged along several of his associates, Thomas Meagher and John Mitchel. The evidence against O'Brien and Meagher being meager, they were acquitted. Mitchel, however, who had openly espoused revolutionary republicanism, was found guilty and sentenced to 14 years of penal servitude in Van Diemen's Land, from where he eventually escaped to America. Finally, in July Russell suspended habeas corpus in Ireland and proscribed membership in nationalist clubs. Since the government could now pick up anyone it suspected of seditious sentiments, Young Ireland's more radical and outspoken members realized that they were marked men. A handful led by William Smith O'Brien decided to act while they still had a chance. O'Brien had been traveling around Ireland seeking support for a rising. Nevertheless, by July Young Ireland was a head without a body. Having managed to telegraph their attentions, on July 29 O'Brien and a handful of men staged a miniscule, easily suppressed "rising" in a cabbage patch in Boulagh, County Tipperary. The leaders were tried and sent to Australia. They were eventually rescued, and some went on to have important careers in the United States and even in the United Kingdom.[94]

---

92. See Haines, *Charles Trevelyan and the Great Irish Famine*, 378. For Russell's response to Clanricarde see Cornwell, *A Galway Landlord during the Great Famine*, 49.
93. Connolly, "The Great Famine and Irish Politics," 44.
94. For press coverage before and after the Rising see Leslie A. Williams, *Daniel O'Connell, the British Press and the Irish Famine*, 287–99.

The Times, having fed the public on a steady diet of Irish unrest and impending revolution, was ecstatic. Referring to the few words it took to cover the story of Boulagh, it scoffed: "The *Iliad* in a nutshell is not a greater curiosity than an Irish rebellion in a column and a half [...] never did rebellion make itself so ridiculous. [...] The perpetual puffing and blowing and trumpeting we have had so long has deceived nobody so much as the traitors themselves."[95] The paper had obviously forgotten its own puffing, blowing and trumpeting. Unfortunately, Young Ireland's abortive rising simply added to the negative narrative driving British perceptions of the Irish as a feckless, improvident, violent people who cried for relief and then ungratefully bit the hands that fed them. Those opposed to public expenditure on famine relief found a convenient excuse in the depiction of Irish anarchy. *The Times* insisted that "Guerilla parties" were roaming the country, and that, "but for the unceasing vigilance of the military and police, where a rebel party consists of hundreds today, it would number thousands tomorrow."[96] Such hyperbole demonstrates that, while Ireland was hardly tranquil during the Famine, the Irish rebel existed more as a stock figure in Britain's Irish narrative than as a manifestation of political reality.

The abject failure of Irish politics during the Famine and the almost comic-opera nature of Young Ireland's attempt at a rising did not mean that Irish nationalism was dead. Less than a decade after the end of the Famine physical force returned with the Fenians. Later, constitutional nationalism, kept alive by Isaac Butt, emerged again in the Home Rule campaign under a new charismatic leader, Charles Stewart Parnell. By then the issues surrounding tenants' rights, pioneered by Young Irelander James Fintan Lalor, had come to dominate Irish politics and to eventually culminate in tenant ownership of the land.

The Beginning of the End? Trevelyan's "Great Opportunity" and "The Irish Famine of 1847"

In the dark winter of 1847, with much of the British public losing patience with the situation in Ireland, the government wanted to reassure its citizens that, despite a string of erratic policies, Ireland was finally set on the path to recovery. To make its case, however, the government would have to walk what Robin Haines calls "a tight line" between demonstrating the lengths it had gone to save lives while, at the same time, defending the costs, which, modest as they seem today, nevertheless struck many Britons as exorbitant.[97] No one in the cabinet wanted the task of writing this apologia nor the obligation of putting his names to it. Therefore, Charles Trevelyan, the man at the very center of famine relief, seemed the obvious candidate for the job. Hardworking, obliging, articulate and a compulsive keeper of records, he had all the facts at his fingertips.

---

95. For quote see ibid., 296.
96. For quote see ibid., 298.
97. Haines, *Charles Trevelyan and the Great Irish Famine*, 319–20.

Trevelyan's acceptance of the assignment, which set him on the path to a knighthood, meant that his would become the first published narrative of the Famine. His 90-page article, initially titled "The Irish Crisis," appeared anonymously in the January 1848 issue of the *Edinburgh Review*, a leading Whig journal. It was, of course, widely known that he was the principal author, and when, a few months later, it appeared in book form; his name was on the cover. Yet, although Trevelyan put much effort into the piece, the work was essentially a government document. Principal cabinet ministers vetted it, and Lord John Russell appears to have written at least part of the ending. No one in government seems to have challenged or repudiated any aspect of the report.[98] At the same time, almost every page bares the trademarks of Trevelyan's vigorous and often opinionated style.

Trevelyan's task was fourfold. He had to show that the government had done its best to save Irish lives. In addition, he had to justify the startling shifts in policy between the 1846 and 1847, defending the government in what it had and had not done. He also wanted to show that significant threat to the Imperial Treasury had been avoided. Finally, he argued that Ireland's potato economy had been a social, as well as an economic, disaster. The Irish peasant had to be saved, not just from the blight, but from the potato system itself. "The Irish small holder lives in a state of isolation, the type of which is to be sought for in the islands of the South Sea, rather than in the great civilized communities of the ancient world." What with "poverty, discontent and idleness," the Irish peasant had followed "an agrarian code that is at perpetual war with the laws of God and man."[99] To save the Irish from themselves, Ireland's agriculture would have to be restructured, but only along certain lines. Any idea of peasant ownership of the land was, as far as Trevelyan was concerned, out of the question. Drawing heavily on Britain's Irish narrative, he wrote: "A peasant proprietary may succeed to a certain extent, where there is a foundation of steadiness of character, and a habit of prudence, and a spring of pride, and a value for independence and comfort; but we fear that all these words merely show the vain nature of schemes of tenant ownership for Ireland." Trevelyan also rejected fixity of tenure for the same reasons: "Mere security of tenure is of no avail, without the capital, and skill, and *habits of life*, and above all, the *wholesome moral qualities* required to turn this advantage to good account."[100] Lacking such habits and qualities, the Irish peasants would have

> to live by the wages of their labour. They must still depend for their subsistence upon agriculture, but upon an agriculture conducted according to *new and very improved conditions*. Both the kind of food and the means of procuring it have changed. The people will henceforth principally live upon grain [...] which they will purchase out of their wages.[101]

---

98. Ibid., 400, 402, 405.
99. Trevelyan, *The Irish Crisis*, 5, 6.
100. Ibid., 175, 176–77. For Trevelyan's views about peasant ownership see Robin Haines, *Charles Trevelyan and the Great Irish Famine*, 405.
101. Trevelyan, *The Irish Crisis*, 163–64, italics added.

In many respects Trevelyan's insistence that Ireland could fully adopt the English agrarian model—large farms served by a landless wage-earning workforce—seems like a bit of magical thinking. Questions of climate, land use and cooperation from the Irish landlords aside, the English example should have made clear that modern farming could only employ a limited number of workers. Rural England flourished because its surplus population, pushed off of the land by enclosure, could migrate to its industrial cities and towns. Without its own industrial revolution, the large numbers of Ireland's landless peasantry would find no more work on idealized farms than in imagined factories. Trevelyan's Hibernian utopia would remain pure fantasy.

Even at this distance in time, it is rather breathtaking to recognize that the British government intended nothing less than the restructuring of the Irish agriculture in the midst of a catastrophe. The Whig leadership seemed unable or unwilling to make a connection between the massive changes they intended, the limited means available to attain then and the suffering their policies would add to people already malnourished and sick. Far removed from the sight and smell of death and disease, Trevelyan and his masters could only see the wonderful opportunity offered by what Trevelyan dubbed "the Great Irish Famine of 1847."[102] They believed that they had to seize the moment, thus ensuring that such a crisis would never occur again.

Trevelyan's article ended by declaring the Famine to be the "direct stroke of an all-wise Providence" laid to the "deep and inveterate root of a social evil" "God grant," he intoned, "that the generation to which this *great opportunity* has been offered may rightly perform its part, and that we may not relax our efforts until Ireland fully participates in the social health and physical prosperity of Great Britain, which will be the true consummation of their union."[103] And so, having striven to show how the government had shifted the burden of Famine relief away from the Kingdom as whole and unto the shoulders of the Irish, Trevelyan finished by invoking the glories of the Union.

The fervor with which Russell's government invoked agricultural reconstruction was at least partially the result of a particular kind of providentialism, frequently voiced by Trevelyan, which has been often misunderstood. He did not, as some have alleged, argue that God was punishing the Irish people. He, along with many in the government, believed that divine wrath had been aimed at what he called the "root of social evil"—the potato-based agricultural system that had brought Ireland to the brink of ruin.[104] Unfortunately, in the rhetoric of the day it was difficult to separate the peasantry from the potato, the people from the failed system that seemed to define them.

---

102. Ibid., 1.
103. Ibid., 201, italics added. Part of this section may have been written by Lord John Russell. See Haines, *Charles Trevelyan and the Great Irish Famine*, 401. For an analysis of Trevelyan's *Irish Crisis*, see. Leslie A. Williams, *Daniel O'Connell, the British Press and the Irish Famine*, 257–81.
104. See Bew, *Ireland: The Politics of Enmity*, 202, 211. For the misreading of Trevelyan, *The Irish Crisis*, see 197; also Haines, *Charles Trevelyan and the Great Irish Famine*, 3–26.

A month after his article appeared, Trevelyan sought to reassure a pessimistic Lord Clarendon: "I think we have come to *the beginning of the* end in Ireland."[105] Having rhetorically confined the Famine to 1847, he appears to have harbored little concern about how events might treat this hostage to fortune. As the fall harvest of 1848 approach, he would soon find out.

---

105. Haines, *Charles Trevelyan and the Great Irish Famine*, 515; italics original.

Chapter Eleven

THE RETURN OF THE BLIGHT: 1848–49

The Harvest of 1848

Although Trevelyan's stage-managed sun may have set on the "Famine of 1847," the real sun rose in 1848 on an ongoing crisis. With the approach of fall the Irish situation remained dire, thanks to the disastrously small harvest the previous year. Because the government, in implementing the second phase of its relief efforts, had closed the soup kitchens and most of the public works, many of the surviving small farmers had little choice but to return to the land the following spring. In hopes that the blight had finally disappeared, they increased potato cultivation from 0.3 million acres to 0.8 million, still far below pre-Famine levels.[1] With increased cultivation and fairly good weather early in the summer, hopes arose once again for a good potato crop. For tens of thousands of small tenants, the harvest represented their last chance to retain their holdings. Many of the cottier class and conacre people had already been wiped out, forced upon the road or into the workhouses. Many others had died.

As late summer approached, the potato plants looked generally healthy. A correspondent for the *Illustrated London News* (*ILN*) confidently reported in August 12: "Ireland only requires a few weeks of sunny weather to possess one of the best harvests in many years." Although there were rumors of some blighted plants, the writer asserted: "I have never seen a better growth, or a healthier bloom upon potato fields."[2] And, indeed, the potatoes lifted early in the season did not seem seriously infected by the blight, though the yield per acre fell from 7 tons in 1847 to around 4 tons. However, a few weeks after the *ILN* had issued its rosy forecast, the *Gardiner's Chronicle* carried the grim news that blight had reappeared in the south and west, as well as in parts of Ulster. "Within the last ten days [...] the potato fields are all now laid prostrate; the leaves withered or withering fast; the stalks which, should be still green and healthy, deprived of foliage and withered black."[3] During the first week in September, the Poor Law Commission in Dublin notified Trevelyan that every electoral division confirmed the blight's presence. In a matter of weeks, the disease had claimed about half of an already modest crop. The result was, in Christine Kinealy's words, a "massive destruction."[4]

---

1. Donnelly, *The Great Irish Potato Famine*, 59.
2. Quoted in Leslie A. Williams, *Daniel O'Connell, the British Press and the Irish Famine*, 295.
3. The journal's report was carried in *Manchester Guardian*, August 23, 1848 (8). For previous quote see *London Illustrated News*, August 12, 1848, 92–93.
4. Kinealy, *A Death-Dealing Famine: The Great Hunger in Ireland*, 132. For Trevelyan see Haines, *Charles Trevelyan and the Great Irish Famine*, 488–90. For potato yields see graphs printed by Donnelly, *The Great Irish Potato Famine*, 58.

When compared to the apparent retreat of the blight in in 1847, the renewed virulence of *Phytophthora infestans* in the fall of 1848 may again reflect the ecological nature of the situation. Even a partial return to monoculture appears to have had serious consequences, at least in the Lumper-dominated western counties where the crisis continued unabated. People there were now entering their fourth year of deprivation. Even with falling food prices many of Ireland's poor remained as desperate as ever. The Poor Law Unions in the western counties, already staggering under heavy debt burdens, faced another year of increasing demand for relief. Workhouse death rates rose. By summer, newspapers carried stories of dogs digging up shallow graves and tearing apart bodies, incidents that recalled Skibbereen in Black '47. A correspondent for *The Scotsman* lamented, "It is our belief that the destitution is now as widespread and mortality as great as any period of the terrible and wasting famine."[5] Certainly, conditions in many workhouses remained as bad as ever, as the guardians struggled to deal with overflowing numbers and insufficient funds. Evictions rose, along with proprietor indebtedness. And while the Queen's visit during the summer provided a feel-good moment, mortality rates rivaled those of Black '47.

Malnutrition, Disease and Mortality

> They dug graves twelve foot deep and put seven or eight bodies in each grave. They never put coffins on them at all. Some of the bodies used to swell up and when they were dropped into the grave they would burst and the grave diggers would have to run until the smell would cease. Often they would get the disease.[6]

As noted earlier, with the onset of the Famine the workhouses rapidly became overcrowded. For example, in a matter of months, the Cork workhouse, built to contain 2,000 persons, grew from a population of 1,137 inmates in September 1, 1846, to 2,040 by the beginning of December with more people, most of them women, clamoring for admission. One month later it was hopelessly overcrowded with 2,714 inmates, and the numbers kept on growing. Between January and June of 1847, 7,814 people applied for admission. Under such pressure, the workhouses began expanding, adding capacity for an extra 800 people in 1847. By acquiring additional buildings, the Cork Union was able to house 6,300 by 1849. Even so, in just one month, June of 1849, it had to accommodate an additional 3,331 individuals. A few months later it again expanded. In most cases conditions in the auxiliary units, often containing large numbers of children, were worse than in the original workhouse.[7] Many of the resource-starved unions of the west, often the most overcrowded, could seldom afford such expansions. So, as overcrowding continued, instead of preserving life, workhouses often hastened its end.

---

5. *The Scotsman*, May 5, 1849. For dogs see *The Times*, July 10, 1849 (8).
6. From the County Wicklow oral tradition. See Póirtéir, "Folk Memory and the Famine." 228.
7. Mahoney, *Grim Bastilles of Despair,* 51. For Cork see O'Mahony, "The Cork Workhouse," 153–54. For children see Moran, "'Suffer Little Children': Life in the Workhouse during the Famine," 38.

The arc of workhouse death rates followed overcrowding. Where 486 deaths occurred in the Cork workhouse in 1845, 2,622 inmates died during the first six months of 1847.[8] The death rate was so high in County Clare's Kilrush Union that it became known as "the slaughter house." The union at Ennistymon recorded 3,843 deaths between 1841 and 1851, about a quarter of the total for all of Clare during that period. Partly because of cholera, mortality rates, which had fallen by 1848, rose again in 1849. Nationwide the weekly death toll grew from 7.7 per thousand inmates in January 1849 to 12.4 in May before beginning a decline. Overall, one in four Famine deaths occurred in workhouses, and at least half of those were due to infectious diseases.[9]

The loss of the potato's amazing nutritional bounty left a gaping hole in the diet of Ireland's poor, one that could not be cheaply filled. Substitute foods, even when provided in adequate quantity, proved nutritionally inferior. Only a carefully varied diet could have made up for the loss of the potato's vitamins and calories. For example, there was nothing to compensate for the potato's generous supply of vitamin C to which the Irish population had become conditioned. And since the vitamin cannot be stored in the body, "land scurvy" appeared early in the crisis. Directives were sent to the workhouses to serve well-cooked vegetables. Unfortunately, overcooking tends to deplete their vitamin content.[10]

Since so much relief food had to be purchased abroad, the pressure to economize favored cheaper grains, especially maize or Indian meal, the "yeller Indian" of famine folklore. Properly cooked it might have filled stomachs, but without a significant accompaniment of vegetables and milk it could not stave off malnutrition. Indeed, it created health problems such as pellagra, a condition often encountered among the famine victims. The problem was not only nutritional, however. As previously discussed, maize is a hard grain that is most easily digested when ground in mills made of steel rather than in the conventional stone mills used for other grains. Ireland had no steel grinders at the outset of the Famine, and the customary single pass through a stone mill proved inadequate. Moreover, although it had been imported on a limited scale during previous subsistence crises, the lack of widespread experience in how best to store and prepare maize created difficulties.[11]

Thus, as workhouse conditions worsened from 1846 through 1848 and 1849, inmates in the overcrowded facilities were assaulted by a variety of diseases. Dropsy and protein-energy malnutrition (marasmus or kwashiorkor) threatened more lives than actual starvation. Vitamin deficiency often led to xerophthalmia, a blindness caused by the lack of vitamin A, one of the few important vitamins *not* found in potatoes. Milk could have provided sufficient vitamin A, but the emergence of xeropthalmia suggests its absence from many workhouse tables. Other diseases, such as Scarlatina (scarlet fever) and consumption,

---

8. Michelle O'Mahony, "The Cork Workhouse," table 3, 154.
9. Paschal Mahoney, *Grim Bastilles of Despair*, 46. For County Clare see Murphy, *A People Starved, 1845–51*, 63–64. For national figures see Donnelly, *The Great Irish Potato Famine*, 104.
10. See Crawford, "Food and Famine," 71.
11. See Haines, *Charles Trevelyan and the Great Irish Famine*, 182–85.

were also common, as were dysentery, diarrhea and outbreaks of smallpox. Given the conditions, even measles could be deadly, especially for malnourished children.[12]

Cormac Ó Gráda points out that certain infectious diseases, normally endemic in a population, will become virulent during times of famine. Typhus and recurring fever had been prevalent among Ireland's poor for decades. When the Famine struck, they proved to be the deadliest scourges. According to medical diagnoses, 97 percent of disease and dysentery was attributed to fevers. Dr. William Wilde estimated that around half-a-million people died of fever, a figure that probably falls short of the actual mark. Only cholera, which swept through the west and some ports in 1849, came close to matching the death rate from fevers.[13]

Typhus and recurring fever are often referred to as reticular diseases because they can be carried by body lice. Although relapsing or recurring fever was usually contracted as the result of a louse bite, the typhus microorganisms, clinging to dust in the air, could also be inhaled. Normally, healthy peasants, having built up some resistance to them, could often fight off these infections. Malnourished bodies, however, often succumbed, especially when poor, sick people were crowded together in the workhouses. For their part, healthy middle-class people who had frequent contact with the workhouses and their inmates—doctors, priests, ministers and Poor Law officials—were less likely to have any immunity. They were, therefore, in special danger of typhus and more likely to die if they contracted it. In Innishshannon the better-off classes were 16 times more likely to contract typhus than the poorer people. Middle- and upper-class townspeople naturally feared that the large numbers of poor moving along the roads and into built-up areas carried diseases.[14] In April 1847 the city of Cork, faced with the influx of some 20,000 starving and disease-ridden refugees from the countryside, passed a resolution calling for the expulsion of infected paupers, as well as for the posting of guards to prevent further incursions of rural poor. In his brief visit to Ireland, Lord Dufferin noted that clergymen, Protestant and Catholic alike, often employed men at their gates to protect their households and guests by fending off the fever ridden. Nevertheless, fever had a way of reaching even into the big house. In May 1847 Lord Lurgan, one of Ulster's important landowners, died of typhus.[15]

Many of those eligible for Poor Law relief, but fearful of diseases, delayed applying for admission to the workhouse as long as possible. Consequently, many sick individuals

---

12. See Crawford, "Food and Famine," 71–72. The author suggests that at the time doctors often mistook xerophthalmia for ophthalmalgia. For Scarlatina, etc., see Clarkson and Crawford, *Feast and Famine*, 158.
13. See Clarkson and Crawford, 158, 160. See also Ó Gráda, *Famine: A Short History*, 117. For 97 percent see Flanagan, *The Great Famine in Kinsale*, 46.
14. Flanagan, 41–43. For Innishshannon see 42. See also Geary, "Medical Relief and the Great Famine," 199.
15. Mac Atasney, *"This Dreadful Visitation*, 59. See also Dufferin, *Narrative of a Journey from Oxford to Skibbereen*, 20–22. For Cork see Geary, "'The living were out of their feeling': A Socio-Cultural Analysis of the Great Famine in Ireland," 319–20; Donnelly, *The Land and the People of Nineteenth-Century Cork*, 87.

arrived at their doors too late to be helped. In the poorly managed Lurgan Union infirmary patients averaged two to a bed, although three or four were not uncommon. To make matters worse, the workhouse dead had been buried in graves situated too close to the union's wells, which eventually had to be closed for fear of contamination.[16] For a time, the expansion of workhouses, the building of fever hospitals and the extension of outdoor relief under the Amended Poor Law gradually reduced mortality rates, although at 11 to 12 per thousand in early 1848, they remained high. Then the numbers shot up again when cholera broke out in 1849. Although the fever hospitals received around 580,000 patients between 1847 and 1850, the costs of providing for them fell on the individual, often underfunded unions. Of course, most fever victims probably never saw the inside of a "hospital," however inadequate. It was not until 1851 that the government finally agreed to pay for some of the unions' medical costs.[17]

Outdoor Relief and the Workhouse "Test"

Once again, the government found itself unprepared for the resurgence of the potato blight. Having allowed Trevelyan to proclaim the end of the Famine, the government had started to cut back on outdoor relief as early as March 1848. It was anxious to force those who still had access to land to plant potatoes (although this went against the general policy of agrarian restructuring). Thus, Trevelyan got the British Relief Association to agree to limit their aid for school children to only those whose parents were working their holdings. Once the grim nature of the 1848 potato harvest became clear, however, Trevelyan fell back on his standard operating procedure. He urged Prime Minister Russell to reaffirm a policy of noninterference in the markets to reassure merchants, encouraging them to import as much grain as possible.[18]

The Amended Poor Law Extension Act of 1847 had pushed all the costs of relief onto the individual unions, while allowing those in the west to give outdoor relief to paupers who could not be accommodated inside the overcrowded workhouses. By February 1848, 445,000 people were being fed through outdoor relief. That number reached 834,000 in June of that year, and after a brief drop it climbed back to 784,000 in July of 1849, declining steadily thereafter. By then, the financial damage to certain unions had been severe. In June, only 45 out of 130 Poor Law Unions had favorable balances on their books. Thirty were in serious financial trouble.[19]

Amidst all of this, the government tried to hide an awkward fact. Despite the continued high numbers dependent upon public assistance, the cost of relief per person continued to drop. In July 1848, it cost 6*d* a week to feed an individual on outdoor relief, less than a penny a day. This fact so embarrassed officials that neither the Poor

---

16. Mac Atasney, "Lurgan Workhouse," 165–66.
17. Geary, "Medical Relief and the Great Famine," 205. For the public health structure in Ireland at the start of the Famine see 199–201. For data on workhouse mortality see Donnelly, *The Great Irish Potato Famine*, 104, 105.
18. Haines, *Charles Trevelyan and the Great Irish Famine*, 489.
19. For data see Donnelly, *The Great Irish Potato Famine*, 106–7.

Law Commission nor the Treasury wanted to make it public for fear of being accused of having scrimped at the expense of the hungry.[20] The costs did not decline enough, however, to help underfunded and overburdened Poor Law Unions, which now found themselves caught on the horns of a dilemma. Given spatial limitations, the numbers that could be admitted to the workhouses were finite. However, in the eyes of the Poor Law guardians, the numbers who might be entitled to outdoor relief seemed infinite. Consequently, some unions, such as Loughrea in Galway, refused to appoint the relieving officers required to process applications for outdoor aid.[21] According to a report carried in the *Cork Examiner* in April 1849, the city's bankrupt union cut its outdoor lists and refused workhouse admission to new applicants. As a result, "Our streets swarm with crowds of sickly and disabled unsuccessful applicants. […] Extermination is going on extensively and systematically in the Union; poverty increasing, relief diminishing."[22]

In addition to the cost, many officials believed that outdoor relief undermined the logic of the whole Poor Law system. Based on the rationale of pauper relief (as opposed to famine relief), supplying rations outside of the workhouse made a mockery of the "test," which had been designed to separate paupers from the merely poor. Yet, once a workhouse was full, there might be no alternative. Fortunately for the guardians of hard-pressed unions, the peculiar logic of the Poor Law could be made to work for instead of against them, providing they applied "the test" creatively. The only way to restrain the demand for outdoor relief was to make sure that there were always some available spaces in the workhouse to "test" those applying for outdoor rations. In Skibbereen, for example, "impotent poor" (for whom the Poor Law originally had been intended) were actually removed from the union's workhouse to provide space so that able-bodied individuals, clamoring for outdoor relief, might be tested. If they qualified for admission, but then refused to enter the workhouse, they were no longer entitled to aid of any sort. Therefore, through careful management there might always be places available, allowing for testing of new applicants for aid.[23] As *The Scotsman* noted approvingly in May 1849: "The efficacy of 'the test' in thinning the ranks of applicants for relief is marvelous." It cited Captain Kennedy, a Poor Law inspector, who noted that the Kilrush Union in Clare had been faced with a flood of applicants for outdoor relief, "many of them removed from want." However, "*An offer of the workhouse dispersed them*" (emphasis original). The "test," the paper maintained, "preserves that broad and deep line of separation between paupers and the self-supporting members of society, which is so important to self-dependence and frugality," thus checking "the moral disease of pauperism." Echoing the words of George Nicholls, the designer of Ireland's Poor Law, Kennedy maintained that, while relief should be sufficient to sustain life and health, it "should be made odious" to all those who accepted it.[24] It was this desire to maintain spaces to support of the "test" that

---

20. Kinealy, *This Great Calamity: The Irish Famine*, 239–40.
21. Cornwell, *A Galway Landlord during the Great Famine*, 43.
22. *Cork Examiner*, April 19, 1849.
23. For Skibbereen see Hickey, *Famine in West Cork*, 280. See also Thomas, "Ulster Workhouses—Ideological Geometry and Conflict," 162; Crossman, *The Poor Law in Ireland 1838–1948*, 26.
24. *The Scotsman*, May 5, 1849; italics original.

helped drive the tripling of workhouse accommodations, which rose from 114,000 beds nationally in March 1847 to 309,000 in March 1851. As James S. Donnelly, Jr. suggests, this expansion was for "reasons of economy and not of humanity," as Poor Law Unions sought to defend themselves against the specter of unlimited outdoor relief.[25] The real function of the Poor Law was to ration relief rather than to prevent hunger.

Rate-in-Aid: All-Ireland Relief

Although responsibility for Famine relief rested almost entirely upon the Irish rate payers within each individual union, some unions faced greater demands than others. With the gradual decline of the potato blight in the north and a partial recovery of the linen industry, most Poor Law Unions in Ulster were more or less solvent by 1848 and 1849. Elsewhere, however, workhouses carried varying amounts of debt. In the west where demand was heaviest, 22 unions were effectively bankrupt, dependent upon insufficient government loans that trickled slowly out of the Treasury. The Poor Law system was particularly ill-designed for the west. Not only was the land generally poor, but the unions encompassed too much densely populated territory. The Ballina Union, for example, covered over a half-million acres with a population of 120,000. The Westport Union stretched along 70 miles of coastline. Presented with such distances, many malnourished people faced difficult journeys to the workhouses to receive aid.[26]

Although the system desperately needed more money, the government was convinced that the British public would not tolerate increased Treasury funds going to Irish relief. Russell's administration did manage to squeeze a grant of £50,000 out of a begrudging parliament, a sum which Wood and Trevelyan knew to be inadequate. Granted in February 1849, the fund was exhausted by April. Paltry as the grant was, its passage was greeted with near hysteria in some quarters. *Punch* ran a cartoon, "The English Labourer's Burden," depicting a beleaguered British workingman carrying a wild-looking, aged Paddy on his back. The Irishman grips a shillala in one hand and a bag emblazoned with "£50,000" in the other. *The Times* complained that the grant "has almost broken the back of British benevolence."[27] In the face of such opposition the government insisted that any additional relief funds would have to come entirely from Ireland.

By this time, it was obvious that the bankrupt unions could not be forced to raise any more money. Therefore, in May the government decided to prorate the costs of additional aid for the heavily indebted western districts among all other Irish unions. As originally envisioned by Russell, the money raised by this Rate-in-Aid proposal, augmented by a £1,000,000 loan, would be used to assist emigration out of the distressed unions. However, this proposal found no traction within the cabinet, especially from the Treasury faction, which insisted on using the money solely for indebted Poor Law Unions.[28] Even

---

25. For quote and national figures see Donnelly, *The Great Irish Potato Famine*, 106.
26. See Smyth, "The Province of Connacht and the Great Famine," 287–88.
27. For *The Times*' quote see Gray, *Irish Famine*, 87. The *Punch* cartoon appeared in volume xvi (1849), 79. For reproduction see Donnelly, *The Great Irish Potato Famine*, 120.
28. Gray, *Famine, Land and Politics*, 309–10.

this met with strong opposition. The Rate-in-Aid levy infuriated Irish ratepayers in the solvent unions. It constituted an additional tax on them for the benefit of others, and, as some critics noted, it was imposed only in Ireland rather than throughout the United Kingdom.[29] Nevertheless, the Rate-in-Aid did mark a slight shift in government relief policy. Up to this point, it had insisted that relief was a local matter based on the individual Poor Law Unions. Now it was in effect saying that relief was ultimately a *national*, an "All-Ireland," responsibility, as it were. It was certainly not an imperial one. Russell did offer, as an alternative, to extend the British income tax to Ireland, but the Irish landlords accepted the Rate-in-Aid as the lesser of two evils. This probably had been Russell's intention, as paying for Irish aid out of an imperial income tax would have threatened the firewall that the government was trying to maintain between the imperial treasury and Irish need.[30] Some observers managed to see Rate-in-Aid as furthering the restructuring of Irish agriculture. George Nicholls, for example, argued that the bill was necessary if the Irish were to be weaned from "a crop so uncertain and treacherous as the potato," which they would cling to "so long as they could turn to England to help whenever it failed them." The Rate-in-Aid would cast "the consequences of the failure upon Ireland itself."[31]

Rate-in-Aid roused intense anger in Ulster where the threat from the Famine was retreating. The guardians of the Lisnakea Union remonstrated against such an imposition on "the peaceable, loyal and industrious citizens of the North of Ireland for the support of the lazy, vicious and indolent population of the south and west of the Kingdom who neither fear God, nor respect the law of the land." A gentleman in Lurgan, County Armagh, asked why, given that the potato blight had hit all parts of Ireland, it was the south and west that suffered while the north was "spared"? It was, he insisted, "because we are a painstaking, industrious, laborious people, who desire to work and to pay our just debts, and the blessing of the Almighty is upon our labour." While the words "Catholic" and "Protestant" do not appear, the sectarian implications in these statements are quite clear.[32] As for being spared, during the early years of the Famine, conditions in Ulster had been as bad as in any other parts of Ireland. In 1846 Ulster workhouses filled up about as quickly as elsewhere. As the situation worsened, suffering respected no sectarian divisions. For example, a clergyman in Donagh, County Donegal, reported to the Poor Law Commission in May 1846 that, unless his area received more relief, those likely to be severely affected included 165–181 Anglicans, 120 Presbyterians and 140 Roman Catholics. Had conditions not improved in Ulster (less dependent upon the Lumper than other areas) after 1848, the myth that prosperity, hard work and God had spared the province would have been harder to maintain; likewise the pride and tribal-like identity so essential to the region's Protestants. Occasionally, however, even a stout Orange paper,

---

29. Mac Atasney, *"This Dreadful Visitation*, 85.
30. See Kinealy, *This Great Calamity*, 255–56.
31. Quoted in Nally, *Human Encumbrances*, 153.
32. Quoted in Mac Atasney, "Famine in County Armagh," 35. For Lisnakea quote see Thomas, "Ulster Workhouses—Ideological Geometry and Conflict," 162. See also Kinealy, *A Death-Dealing Famine*, 142-43.

such as the *Ballyshannon Herald*, had to acknowledge reality. "Social disorganization is nearly complete," it lamented in September 1847. "The masses of people are steeped into the lips of poverty. [...] Class is divided against class." For the most part, however, northern newspapers tended to underreport local poverty and workhouse overcrowding. As a result, the reality of conditions in the north must often be gleaned from the reports of religious societies and from occasional letters.[33]

With some 30 Poor Law Unions essentially bankrupt while others staggered further into debt, the government tried to put the best possible face on the situation. Entertaining high hopes as usual for the fall harvest, the government tried to build on Trevelyan's contention that the "Irish Crisis," if not actually over, was winding down. In truth, only the government's financial contributions to Famine relief were winding down. Early in 1849 it began to close the warehouses where emergency stories of grain had been held in reserve. In addition, Trevelyan announced to the Relief Commission in Dublin that very little money would be available for grants to distressed unions. As noted earlier, in lieu of spending Treasury money to help keep unions afloat, he had been tapping into the dwindling funds gathered by the charitable British Association. By 1849, however, the association's reserves were virtually depleted, bringing an end to its daily feeding of over 200,000 needy school children.[34] Convinced they could squeeze no more money out of the parliamentary stone, Wood and Trevelyan urged the government to initiate a voluntary subscription. Members of parliament (including, of course, cabinet ministers) were asked to donate £100 each, while the Queen gave £500. In this way, the government scraped up an additional £10,000, sparing the Imperial Treasury any further damage.[35]

In 1849, Edward Twistleton, chief of the Poor Law Commission in Dublin, looked at the situation and despaired. He had been involved with the commission for years and had been a staunch supporter of the Poor Law system. In constant contact with the unions, he analyzed their financial data, their populations and their needs, passing the information on to Trevelyan in London. Although they agreed on many things, each eventually came to see a different world from their respective positions. Unlike most of his colleagues in London, Twistleton allowed himself to be acutely aware of the contradictions inherent between the relief of paupers, the original intent of the Poor Law, and famine aid, the role foisted upon the system by the government. For a while he tried to cling to a narrow interpretation of the role of the Poor Law. "I confess it does not appear to me," he wrote to Sir George Grey in 1847, "that the responsibility of deaths from starvation outside the workhouse rests either with the Board of Guardians or the Commissioners." Twistleton was not suggesting that people should be left to starve, but rather that those beyond the workhouse system should be relieved by the government, not the rate payers. As London

---

33. For Ulster workhouses see Grant, "The Famine in County Tyrone," 219. For Donagh see Begley and Lally, "Famine in County Donegal," 85. For Lurgan see Mac Atasney, "The Famine in County Armagh," 44. For the *Ballyshannon Herald* see Mac Suibhne, *The End of Outrage*, 63.
34. This project had been initiated by the association's agent Count Strezelecki. When he left the association, the government assured him that, where needed, the children's project would be continued. It was not. See Kinealy, *A Death-Dealing Famine*, 137.
35. See Kinealy, *This Great Calamity*, 256.

shifted most of the burden of famine relief onto the account books of the unions, Twistleton became increasingly frustrated, especially with the Treasury's constant complaints that the commissioners were far too liberal in providing aid. Writing to the home secretary in February 1849, Twistleton complained: "The extent of the calamity which affects the Distressed Unions and the intensity of the distress in them, do not seem to be fully understood in England."[36] By that time, Twistleton's principal concern was feeding and keeping alive as many people as possible within the Poor Law system. Trevelyan, with whom he was in daily contact, however, clung to what he considered his principal task of minimizing the payouts from the Imperial Treasury. Inevitably, tensions built up between the two men. Where their communications had once been genial and then at least professional, a certain testiness began to characterize their relationship. Although policy was clearly set in London and enforced through the Treasury, Twistleton was not shy at expressing his opinions and even occasionally asserting the rights of the commission. In January 1849 when Trevelyan wanted all children removed from the workhouses to make room for able-bodied men, Twistleton simply refused to comply.[37]

After the Rate-in-Aid Bill and the pitifully inadequate £50,000 grant, Twistleton finally felt he could no longer carry out what he took to be his duty—saving lives. In March 1849, he submitted his resignation to Clarendon, the lord lieutenant. Trying to explain Twistleton's position to the prime minister, Clarendon wrote: "the destitution here is so horrible, and the indifference of the House of Commons to it so manifest that he [Twistleton] is an unfit agent of a policy that must be one of *extermination*." Clarendon explained that Twistleton found himself in a position "that no man of honour or humanity can endure." Later, testifying before a parliamentary select committee, Twistleton made it clear that he wanted it on the record that people were still dying for want of food, although "it is quite possible for this country to prevent the occurrence there of any death from starvation, by the advance of a few hundred pounds."[38]

By this time Twistleton had come to reject completely the government's policy that Irish property must pay for Irish poverty, as well as the doctrine that governments should not interfere with the "natural laws" of economics. Apparently clinging to the idea of the United Kingdom, he argued that Famine relief was an imperial, not simply an Irish, responsibility. And the "laws of nature," as interpreted by the government, would, in effect, condemn the destitute to die. "I believe," Twistleton asserted, "it is part of the system of nature that we should feel compassion for them and assist them."[39] In so saying, he rejected the very basis of the policies maintained by Wood

---

36. Quotes from Kinealy, "The Role of the Poor Law during the Famine," 111, 119.
37. Kinealy, *This Great Calamity*, 246.
38. For quotes see Nally, *Human Encumbrances*, 217.
39. See Gray, *Famine, Land and Politics*, 315.

The Landlord's Solution: Ejecting Peasants

In December 1848, landlords from several western unions met in Dublin to petition for tax relief. They argued that the "Poor Law is wholly unsuited to the state and condition of Ireland, and has proved amongst the most lamentable failures of the annals of legislation." Instead of stimulating proprietors to support the poor, they argued, the Poor Law had rendered them powerless.[40] High tax rates were not their only problem, however. Back in 1843 an amendment to the Irish Poor Law had made landlords responsible for the rates assessed to tenants farming land valued at £4 or less. The idea was to encourage landlords to clear out their small holders and consolidate the lands. While some did, others had simply included these taxes in their calculation of rents. Now, however, with rents going unpaid, the landlords were left with ever-increasing tax bills.[41] Under these circumstances, many western landlords realized that it would be easier and more lucrative to replace their tenants with cattle. Thus, the Famine sped up the long-term trend away from cultivation toward pasturage, often resulting in evictions. Conveniently enough, the Quarter Acre or Gregory Clause, inserted into the Poor Law Act of 1847, became an important engine for such clearances. As noted earlier, the clause stated that no tenant renting more than a quarter acre of land could receive any relief, indoor or outdoor, unless he surrendered the bulk of his holding. Taking the broadest interpretation of the law, landlords insisted that those unable to pay their rents could not receive Poor Law assistance unless they give up *all* their land, including their cabin. Even dependents were denied assistance until a tenant surrendered everything. Thegovernment eventually tried to curtail this abuse, but landlords persisted in acting with impunity, since few tenants could afford to go to the courts for relief.[42]

Eviction meant disaster for most cottiers and poor farmers . Too poor to emigrate, the workhouses offered them terrible conditions and high death rates. Their only alternative was to take to the roads to beg and, too often, to die. Some tried to survive in the ruins of their unroofed, tumbled cabins until pushed out by the landlord. From there they might literally disappear into the landscape, seeking shelter in "scalps," improvised huts thrown up in ditches or even dug into holes in the ground. In December 1849, the *ILN* noted that observers had always described the Irish mud cabins as the worst dwellings in the

---

40. *The Times,* December 19, 1848.
41. See Donnelly, *The Land and the People of Nineteenth-Century Cork,* 112.
42. Donnelly, *The Great Irish Potato Famine,* 100, 102, 110–12.

Figure 6 "Scalpeen," *Illustrated London News*, December 15, 1849

world. However, the writer noted that the Irish have proved that even "in their lowest deep there is still a lower deep—that a Scalpeen is worse than a mud-hut, and a Scalp worse than a Scalpeen. [...] There must be more hope of the savages of New South Wales or the Brazils." The article carried an engraving of a recently evicted ragged man standing in front what looks like a hut most likely fashioned from the thatch and bits of wood from his tumbled cabin (see Figure 6). Considering the case of another individual, the article observed:

> Yet the instinctive love of life is so great, so strong is the sentiment by which Nature ensures the continuance of the race, that Brian Connor (see Figure 7) dreads nothing so much as that he shall not be allowed, now that his hut has been discovered, to burrow longer in security; and like a fox, or some other *vermin*, he expects to be unearthed, and left even without the shelter of what may be called a preparatory grave.

SCALP OF BRIAN CONNOR, NEAR KILRUSH UNION-HOUSE.

Figure 7 "The Scalp of Brian O'Conner, Near Kilrush Union-House," *Illustrated London News*, December 22, 1849

An example of the Victorians' difficulty in describing abject poverty without demeaning and objectifying the victims, the comparison of the evicted pauper to "vermin" could have elicited little sympathy for him among the *ILN*'s readers. Nevertheless, the journal did not turn away from the reality of Brian Connor's plight. The article went on to note that with the onset of winter, eviction under such circumstances was tantamount to a death sentence.[43]

To prevent evicted families from returning, many landlords assiduously demolished their cabins. The third Earl of Lucan, declaring that he "would not breed paupers to pay priests," evicted some 2,000 people, methodically destroying each cabin in the process. His efficient wrecking crews managed to demolish up to 20 homes a day.[44] In areas where the traditional Gaelic sense of community remained intact, evicted families were sometimes taken in by their neighbors. In such cases, however, landlords, intent on clearing their holdings, might threaten those tenants harboring evicted neighbors with the "hanging gale," a demand for immediate payment of the half-year's rent. Since few could comply even in the best of times, the sheltered families would usually find themselves back on the road. Even when taken in by their neighbors, an evicted family's prospects remained grim. The *ILN* quoted Captain Kennedy, a poor-law inspector: "None of the homeless class can now find admittance save into some over-crowded cabin, *whose inmates seldom survive a month*" (emphasis in original). The journal commented, "A month's agonies—the result of hunger, dirt and fever—after being expelled from a home suffices to destroy life."[45]

There are no solid numbers on evictions prior to 1849, when the constabulary began to keep records. In that year 13,384 families comprising 72,065 individuals lost homes and land. This figure does not include those who "voluntarily" surrendered their holdings or the thousands of people pushed out in illegal evictions that bypassed the courts and police.[46] While the national eviction rate averaged 20 percent of tenants, the west ranked highest with 30 percent in Tipperary and a staggering 40 percent in Clare. There, 1,200 people were evicted over a single fortnight in May 1849. In the whole of Connaught, evictions of all types might have forced out around 58,000 families. Overall, between 1849 and 1854, James S. Donnelly, Jr. estimates around half a million people were made homeless.[47] This eviction movement, as one might call it, produced profound changes in rural Irish society. For example, the cottier class, which, prior to the Famine, had worked between one and five acres, fell by a quarter between 1845 and 1847. By 1851, one half of the cottiers were gone. Many small farmers fared little better. The loss of farms

---

43. *Illustrated London News*, December 15, 1849, 349. For quotes and illustration see Leslie A. Williams, *Daniel O'Connell, the British Press and the Irish Famine*, 329–30, italics added. The writer of the *ILN*'s article may have been confused in his terms. A "scalpeen" (*scailpín*) with its diminutive ending would be a small "scalp." Therefore, it is hard to see how a "scalp" would be worse than a "scalpeen."
44. Curtis, *Notice to Quit: The Great Irish Famine Evictions*, 25.
45. For Kennedy quote in the *ILN* see Leslie A. Williams, *Daniel O'Connell, the British Press and the Irish Famine*, 330. For "hanging gale" see Donnelly, *The Great Irish Potato Famine*, 154–55.
46. Donnelly, *The Great Irish Potato Famine*, see the table 4, 140.
47. For overall numbers see Donnelly, "Mass Evictions and the Great Famine," 155–56. See also O'Neill, "Famine Evictions," 30–31, 48; Smyth, "The Province of Connacht and the Great Famine." 288–89. For Clare see Kinealy, *A Death-Dealing Famine*, 141.

between 5 and 15 acres doubled between 1847 and 1851, by which time their overall numbers had been reduced by 38 percent.[48]

The press occasionally carried disturbing accounts of starving people being put out on the road with nothing except what they could carry. The *ILN* published some very effective pieces on "ejectment" in 1848 and 1849. Somewhat embarrassed, the government would only insist over and over that it could not interfere in matters involving private property. Nevertheless, segments of public opinion in England and Ireland, especially among the Catholic clergy, expressed outrage at the evictions. Even Russell was forced to agree with the angry remonstrations sent to him by Archbishop MacHale of Tuam. Consequently, the prime minister sought to restrict evictions. As he told his cabinet, "the murders of poor cottier tenants are too horrible to bear, and if we put down assassins, we ought to put down the lynch law of the landlords." Unfortunately, the cabinet contained several Irish landlords actively engaged in clearing their lands. As so often happened, Russell's attempts to ameliorate conditions in Ireland were easily nudged aside. The bill that eventually passed Parliament was so watered down that it provided little real protection to those facing ejection.[49]

The evictions provide an insight into how a government dedicated to laissez-faire principles could still pursue policies intended to radically reshape Irish society. By placing the burden for famine relief on Irish property and by constantly increasing the tax rate, landlords were in effect encouraged, if not actually forced, to eject masses of tenants. The government, in fact, wanted marginal, subsistence farmers cleared, allowing the land to be consolidated and put to efficient, more profitable use. Writing to Russell in March 1848, his foreign minister, Lord Palmerston (who, as already noted, was engaged in "squaring" his vast Irish estates), admitted that, "It is useless to disguise the truth that any great improvement in the social system of Ireland must be founded upon an extensive change in the present state of agrarian occupation, and that this change necessarily implies a long, continued and systematic ejectment of small holders and squatting cottiers." In fact, one of the few areas of agreement within Russell's divided cabinet centered on the idea that the removal of the cottier and small farmer class would advance the commercialization of Irish agriculture.[50]

The Government's Solution: Ejecting Landlords—The Encumbered Estates Act

It was not just the non-rent-paying peasantry who were to be evicted. Non-rate-paying, indebted proprietors were to be ejected as well—or at least forced to sell their lands. Cormac Ó Gráda argues that the bankrupt condition of many Irish estates cannot be

---

48. Smyth, "Exodus from Ireland—Patterns of Emigration," 501.
49. See Donnelly, "Mass Evictions and the Great Famine," 162-63. For quote see 163.
50. Cornwell, *A Galway Landlord during the Great Famine*, 32, 46–47. For Palmerston see Christine Kinealy, "The Role of the Poor Law during the Famine," 117.

blamed entirely on the Famine. Even before the blight, many estates were seriously indebted due to poor management. In addition, James S. Donnelly, Jr. notes that the middleman system had kept proprietors from realizing the full value of their estates. Also, there was a tendency among some owners to anticipate the termination of leases (when they could raise their rents), and thus, to borrow against the future.[51] For years, landowners had used their estates as collateral for loans to sustain an upper-class lifestyle or to make a mark in politics. To take just one example, when he inherited his estate in West Cork in 1818, Lord Audely found that it was £3,400 in debt. By the time he died 18 years later in 1837 his debts had ballooned to £89,400, plus £61,700 in interest and £16,200 in court costs. That estate, worth only £20,000, owed a total of £167,300. Little wonder that, on the eve of the Famine, some 900 Irish estates were in the Courts of Chancery.[52]

The government's great hope of restructuring rural Ireland depended upon liquidating mismanaged estates. The Kingdom's laws of inheritance, however, were extremely complex. Since the Middle Ages, power had been invested in families whose wealth was based on land. The preservation of that essential confluence of power, family and land meant that estates could not be broken up. Most were, therefore, entailed; that is, the entire estate had to be passed on intact to the most eligible male heir. This made it difficult, if not impossible, to sell large, indebted estates and to pay off their creditors. Such issues had to be processed through the Courts of Chancery, a slow-moving, Dickensian bureaucratic sink even in the best of times. In its 1845 report to Parliament, the Devon Commission had recommended bypassing Chancery to speed up processing the backlog of indebted Irish estates. The economic destabilization caused by the Famine only made matters worse.[53] Pressures to deal with the situation came from a variety of quarters. In Britain, radical representatives of the urban middle class denounced the ancient aristocratic monopoly on land, demanding instead "free trade in land." Jonathan Pim of the Society of Friends was confident that resident, middle-class entrepreneurs investing in land would bring much needed capital and better business sense to Irish agriculture. However, that could only happen "by the free sale of land, by the sub-division of estates, and the consequently increased numbers of resident proprietors." Free trade in land was strongly supported by the Dublin Statistical Society, founded by Archbishop Whately of Trinity College. In 1847, one of its members, William Neilson Hancock, argued that Ireland's problems were not due to a failure of the "Celtic" character. All the country's economic ills could be traced to the feudal impediments to agrarian free enterprise embodied in the custom of entail and the failure to reward tenants for improvements made on their

---

51. Donnelly, *The Land and the People of Nineteenth-Century Cork*, 70. For indebted estates see Ó Gráda, *Black '47 and Beyond: The Great Irish Famine in History, Economy and Memory*, 26–27, 133–34.
52. For data and Lord Audley see Hickey, *Famine in West Cork*, 119, table 7. For 900 estates see Dooley, *The Big House and Landed Estates of Ireland*, 24, 146.
53. Donnelly, *The Great Irish Potato Famine*, 162.

holdings.⁵⁴ And who should invest in freely traded Irish land? British public opinion generally supported replacing Irish landowners with English and Scottish landlords and tenants. As Michael de Nie suggests, this marked a retreat from the optimism that had accompanied the Act of Union. No longer confident that the Irish could become anglicized, many now favored a more direct, colonial approach: a new wave of British settlers would take over the task of anglicization.⁵⁵

In 1849 Robert Peel, although in opposition, proposed a new, bold measure. He recommended creating a land commission to handle the buying and selling of debt-ridden Irish estates, thus bypassing the equity courts and speeding up land transfers. Further, he urged that the commission should improve and manage foreclosed estates until new agricultural managers and investors took them over. He called this proposal for Ireland a "new plantation." Unlike the seventeenth-century plantations under James I, however, Peel proposed using capital rather than religion to reinvent Ireland. Violating Whiggish laissez-faire principles, Peel's "plantation" scheme went too far for most of Russell's cabinet. Nevertheless, Peel's ideas caught the imagination of the public. *Punch* ran a cartoon of Peel as the "New St. Patrick," striding confidently through Ireland armed with his bill labeled "New Plantation." Before him slither terrified snakes and other vermin labeled "Destitution" and "Mortgage."⁵⁶

There was too much demand for action to allow Russell to ignore Peel's proposal. So, in place of Peel's "plantation" scheme, Russell brought in a bill that bypassed Chancery but did not involve government purchase or management of land. Peel accepted the loss of his more daring ideas, and with his support the Encumbered Estates Act easily passed Parliament in July 1849. The act allowed anyone with a valid claim against an Irish estate to appeal to a three-judge commission to order the sale of that estate. In most cases, all creditors holding the estate's debt could bid on its lands. Setting aside the old rules of entail, it allowed large estates to be broken up. Moreover, since an estate may have had many claims upon it, the act conferred parliamentary or indefeasible titles upon purchasers.⁵⁷

Although stripped of its more imaginative aspects, the aura of a "new plantation" nevertheless clung to the act. Certainly, many perceived in it a glow of promise, the first real providential fruits of the government's hoped-for opportunity to reconstruct agrarian Ireland. As Peel said in presenting his original bill, "It has pleased God to afflict us with this great calamity—which may, perhaps, be improved into a blessing."⁵⁸ For a

---

54. See Boylan and Foley. "'A Nation Perishing of Political Economy'?" 146–48. For Jonathan Pim see his *The Conditions and Prospects of Ireland*, 237–38. For the politics of free trade in land see Gray, *Famine, Land and Politics*, 199–200, 204–9, 217–19.
55. See de Nie, *The Eternal Paddy: Irish Identity and the British Press, 1798–1882*, 274–75.
56. For a discussion of Peel's bill and the related cartoons see Leslie A. Williams, *Daniel O'Connell, the British Press and the Irish Famine*, 309–12. See also Gray, *Famine, Land and Politics*, 210–16.
57. Dooley, *The Big House and Landed Estates of Ireland*, 31. For Encumbered Estates courts see Donnelly, *The Great Irish Potato Famine*, 164–68.
58. Gray, *Famine, Land and Politics*, 213.

brief time the city of London was abuzz with talk of investments in Irish land. According to *The Times*, the London Council was negotiating with the government to purchase land freed up by the Encumbered Estates Act. Referring to the report, a *Punch* cartoon showed Gog and Magog, mythical figures associated with London, helping a ragged Paddy out of the mire.[59]

All's Well that Ends Well—With a Royal Visit

Hopeful that the potato blight was finally receding, that civil unrest had been contained and that a restructured Ireland was set firmly on the road recovery, the government was eager to announce that Ireland was open for business. To promote this idea, Ireland, cast in a rare rosy glow of optimism, prepared to receive a visit from Queen Victoria. If the country was safe enough for Her Majesty, then it was surely safe enough for English investors in search of economic opportunity. In preparation for the visit, the *ILN* ran several articles aimed at promoting Irish tourism.[60] Nevertheless, the spirit of optimism remained a bit restrained. Because of the continuing distress, the Queen did not visit in state, nor did she venture inland. The Royal visit was limited to the port cities of Belfast, Cork, Waterford and Dublin. Nevertheless, balls, street decorations, bonfires and other displays put both the monarch and many of her Irish subjects in a happy mood. In its August 11 edition, the *ILN* festooned its masthead with harps and shamrocks and, inside, printed an original song, part of which ran:

> Exalt, then, O Erin, VICTORIA shall bring,
> For the winter now passing the glories of spring—
> For the dark beating tempest, clear vistas of blue;—
> And the myriads now weeping shall smile as they sing,—
> *Cead mile failte* [sic], Erin aboo.[61]

It was not all a hundred thousand welcomes, however. Criticism came from various quarters. The Irish Roman Catholic hierarchy was sharply divided over the Queen's visit. When Archbishop Murray drew up a welcoming address, most bishops refused to sign it. Archbishop MacHale bitterly complained that its gushing statements ignored the "the hideous cruelty inflicted [by the Government] [...] on our flocks, whom we see daily [...] perishing unpitied before our eyes." The Limerick clergy wrote their own address, arguing that nowhere else in the world would a government be permitted "to unroof and demolish the homes of fifteen thousand human beings, and turn them out [...] to die

---

59. See Leslie A. Williams, *Daniel O'Connell, the British Press and the Irish Famine*, 311–13. For the failure of these negotiations see Gray, *Famine, Land and Politics*, 220–21.
60. For the *ILN*'s coverage of the Queen's visit see Leslie A. Williams, *Daniel O'Connell, the British Press and the Irish Famine*, 316–18. For other press comments, 319–25; See also Cappock, "Pageantry and Propaganda;" Spurgeon Thompson. "Famine Travel: Irish Tourism from the Great Famine to Decolonialization," 164–80.
61. Quoted in Leslie A. Williams, *Daniel O'Connell, the British Press and the Irish Famine*, 318.

by the slow wasting of famine and disease." As Donald Kerr points out, after 1846 the mood of the Irish Catholic clergy had changed from trust in the government to anger at its refusal to acknowledge the damage caused by its policies. At the Synod of Thurles in 1850, the Irish clergy expressed outrage at the government for following the "False Teaching of the age," which generated "a spirit of contempt, hard heartedness, and hostility to the Poor."[62]

The British press, however, preferred to focus on the pageantry of the Royal visit and the enthusiastic reception offered by Her Majesty's "loyal" Irish subjects. Even *The Times* declared the Queen's visit the "concluding chapter of the history of Irish rebellion." *Punch* went so far as to present a vision of Ireland's future. In a page-length engraving, the Queen, with a ragged Irish family in the background, peers into the waters of Lough Neagh, County Antrim, long fabled for providing glimpses of people leading alternative lives beneath its surface. In *Punch*'s "Ireland—A Dream of the Future," the Queen sees prosperous farms, busy plowmen (English style-farming, not Irish spade work), flocks, dancing country folk, a distant city and a steam train. The latter was presumably necessary to cart off the new Ireland's bounteous produce to overseas markets.[63] Apart from the train, however, the illustration offered no hint of industrial development, which was at least taking place in Belfast. It was the government's vision of an agrarian utopia, a restructured Ireland arising out of the ruins of the old potato economy. It was an Ireland that would be Britain's breadbasket and butcher shop and never an industrial competitor. It was a neat imperial solution. The Queen's visit in the summer of 1849 offered a suitable pageant with which to at last bring down what was surely the final curtain on the disaster.

In April 1849, *The Times* confidently haled what Joseph Schumpeter a century later called capitalism's gift of "creative destruction."

> The rigorous administration of the poor law is destroying small holdings, reducing needy proprietors to utter insolvency, compelling them to surrender their estates into better hands, instigating an emigration far beyond any which a government could undertake, and so leaving the soil of Ireland open to industrial enterprise and the introduction of new capital.[64]

There were still difficulties in the west, but it was finally time to get on with other things. Surely the harvest of 1849 would verify that the Famine was at an end.

---

62. For all quotes see Kerr, "The Catholic Church and the Irish Famine," 135–36.
63. See Leslie A. Williams, *Daniel O'Connell, the British Press and the Irish Famine*, 320–22. For quote from *The Times* see 322.
64. For quote see Donnelly, "'Irish Property Must Pay for Irish Poverty:' British Public Opinion and the Great Irish Famine," 76.

Chapter Twelve

YEARS OF EVICTIONS: 1849–52

The Harvest of "Black '49"

> My host says they [the peasants] are dying in far greater numbers than most people have any idea of […] [I]f this state of things shall continue much longer, the country wil [sic] be cured in the only effectual manner by an immense depopulation. […] Our family are all forbid from going into the village, or near the fever hospital or the graveyard. Yet, even at the distance of several fields, we sometimes smell the latter. There are so many corpses that half of them are exposed above the ground without any coffins, others in open coffins. […] This whole country could make one doubt the goodness of God more than you can believe, unless you had seen it.
>
> (A letter to
> *The Scotsman*, June 29, 1849)[1]

Despite the government's repeated insistence that the Queen's visit marked the end of the Famine, those closely involved with the situation still had reason to worry. By the summer of 1849 around a million people still depended on relief; 227,329 occupied the workhouses with 784,370 on outdoor assistance.[2] In June, Trevelyan received samples of blighted potato leaves from the early harvest in Ireland. He could only hope that the disease's diminishing presence in the east would prove a trend. However, as the government awaited the outcome of the fall's harvest, official correspondence reveals the confused state of policy and leadership. The letters between Lord John Russell and Lord Clarendon indicate a simultaneous fear of both a good and a bad potato harvest. Clarendon worried about a good potato yield "and all the false hopes and bad habits it will entail." Yet, he had to agree with Russell, who maintained: "A good crop of all kinds this year is the only thing which can save Ireland from dreadful scenes in the next two or three."[3] As it turned, out nature and circumstance split the difference, producing a curate's egg of results: good in some parts, terrible in others.

Overall, the harvest of 1849 reaffirmed the drift toward increasingly favorable potato yields per acre, although the number of acres under cultivation remained far below pre-Famine levels.[4] Even previously hard-hit areas such as Mayo showed some improvement. Yet, while some regions, especially in the east and north, emerged largely blight

---

1. A letter from Ireland published in *The Scotsman*, June 27, 1849, quoted in Leslie A. Williams, *Daniel O'Connell, the British Press and the Irish Famine*, 314.
2. Kinealy, *This Great Calamity*, 263.
3. Gray, *Famine, Land and Politics*, 322–23.
4. See chart in Donnelly, *The Great Potato Famine*, 58.

free, the harvest brought little good news for most of the Lumper-growing areas of the southwestern seaboard counties and the Shannon basin.[5] There the blight, now entering its fifth year, remained as virulent as ever. County Clare, where significant agricultural employment had been scarce for several years, was particularly hard hit. The numbers in the Ennis workhouse continued to climb, not reaching their peak of 5,219 until June 1850. In spring of that year, the county still counted 12,000 people in its workhouses with another 30,000 receiving outdoor relief. Kerry, Limerick and Tipperary lagged just behind Clare in the levels of distress. In June 1850, the *Tralee Chronicle* noted that the workhouses around Listowel contained 4,000 inmates with 5,000 on outdoor relief. "As fast as hundreds die away, hundreds of homeless, hungry, sickly skeletons fill up their ranks [...] many are received, many are rejected." In the workhouse of the Nenagh Union, Tipperary, admissions, which had hit 2,939 in 1846 grew to 10,048 in 1850.[6] In fact, despite the partial retreat of the potato blight, the national mortality rate in 1849 reached 240,797, only slightly below Black '47's 249,355 victims. In three of the four provinces, mortality rates were greater in 1849 than they had been in 1847. Ulster, hard hit in the early years of the Famine but quick to recover, presented the dramatic exception. Otherwise, "Black '49" would have edged out Black '47 in the grim tallies of death.[7]

Even where the blight had receded, potato yields failed to fully recover for several reasons. First, the years of blight had weakened the enthusiasm of some farmers for the potato. In addition, as landlords cleared away small plots, those farming larger holdings found the old, highly productive spade cultivation too labor intensive and expensive. In some areas, the recurring blight had also reduced the fertility of the soil. Finally, by this time the Famine had wiped out many clachans, leaving them abandoned or converted into rough pasturage. The old, large-scale, intensive potato monoculture was becoming a thing of the past.[8]

Kilrush and the High Tide of Evictions

With at least the eastern counties of Ireland largely liberated from the depredations of *Phytophthora infestans*, the task of feeding people and saving lives should have become easier. That it did not may be blamed, in part, on the government's enormous error of trying to base famine relief entirely on the Irish Poor Law system. This perpetuated in a more concentrated form the vice-grip that the blight had inflicted on the old potato economy: the loss of food at the bottom and the loss of rents and the increase in taxes at the top. Consequently, both peasants and landlords were squeezed, although only the

---

5. Ibid., 268–68.
6. For Clare workhouses see Ó Murchadha, *Sable Wings over the Land*, 227; Kinealy, *This Great Calamity*, 267. For Tralee see MacMahon, *The Great Famine in Tralee and North Kerry*, 265. For other unions, see Grace, *The Great Famine in Nenagh Poor Law Union, County Tipperary*, 129, 163.
7. Comparing mortality rates for 1847 and 1849: Leinster, 59,208 and 60,360; Munster, 82,496 and 92,737; Ulster, 64,586 and 42,742; Connaught, 43,045 and 44,956. For all data see Christine Kinealy, *This Great Calamity*, 251.
8. For decline in potato yields see Kinealy, *This Great Calamity*, 285.

landlords had some recourse—eviction. By 1849 increasing numbers of the remaining small farmers, no longer able to pay their rents, faced eviction. Since ejections, often enforced by the constabulary and the military, frequently involved the unroofing or even tumbling of cabins, many newspaper readers on both sides of the Irish Sea were outraged, adding to public condemnation of Irish landlords. However, as George Poulett Scrope pointed out, landlords turned to evictions principally because the government had placed the full burden of famine relief on their shoulders. Either they foreclosed on their tenants themselves, or those holding the landlords' debts would foreclose on them. Either way the tenants would be forced out. The Gregory Clause, as previously noted, gave the landlords a weapon, while the increasing rates and the Encumbered Estates Act gave them reasons for using it. Scrope insisted that blame for the disaster that had overtaken Ireland's poor fell upon the government. He predicted that it would be "held responsible [...] by history, by posterity—aye, and perhaps before long, by the retributive justice of God and the vengeance of a people infuriated by a barbarous oppression, and brought at last to bay by their destroyers."[9] However, any British taxpayer tempted to question the government's policies knew quite well where the burden of relief would fall if it was shifted from the shoulders of Irish property. On consideration, therefore, he might have concluded that the Irish landlords could do little else but evict. As for the Irish peasantry? Well, there was always *The Times* to argue once again that Ireland's poor had been the principal authors of their own misfortune. They represented, as the paper assured its readers, "a vast population steeped in the congenial mire of voluntary indigence and speculating on the gains of a perpetual famine."[10]

James S. Donnelly, Jr. has pointed out the "ambivalence" reflected in British public opinion. Initial middle-class concern for the victims of the Famine and hostility toward the Irish landlords gradually gave way to a certain sympathetic understanding of those caught between dwindling rents and rising taxes.[11] The confusion and frustration that characterized British attitudes toward the Irish tenantry and landlords are reflected in the pages of the *Illustrated London News* (*ILN*). When the potato blight struck in 1845, then editor Frederick Bayley had displayed a certain amount of sympathy for the Irish poor. As described earlier, he printed some groundbreaking pictorial reports during the early years of the crisis. In 1848, Charles Mackay, a Scot and a Whig supporter, took over the editor's chair. Generally, MacKay showed little compassion for and much impatience with the Irish. On the front page of the May 29, 1848, issue, he published a leader denouncing the Irish peasant for taking on rents he could not possibly afford in order to sustain a hand-to-mouth existence: "He lives in a wigwam and shares it with a pig. He speaks a barbarous language, and is in arrears with the intelligence of the world. [...] The masses of the [Irish] people cannot be called civilized by any stretch of flattery."[12] Nevertheless, MacKay, contemplating the results of the unceasing evictions, was not

---

9. Quoted in Donnelly, *The Great Potato Famine*, 125.
10. Ibid., 130.
11. Donnelly, "'Irish Property Must Pay for Irish Poverty'," 69.
12. See Leslie A. Williams, *Daniel O'Connell, the British Press and the Irish Famine*, 283.

blind to the sufferings of those Irish still trapped in Famine conditions. In the October 30, 1849 issue, the *ILN* commented:

> Nothing like the misery of the Irish people exists under the sun. Even the gleam of hope that appeared to brighten their prospects a few weeks ago, when a harvest more than usually abundant was ripe for the sickle, has disappeared. [...] The landlords evict [and] [...] the miserable tenants go to the Union, or receive outdoor relief at the rate of seven-eighths of a penny a day, til the munificent allowance lapses in the grave.

It was, however, the Irish landlord who received the bulk of the Mackay's sympathy and understanding:

> If a landlord's property swarms with a tenantry too *ignorant and dispirited* to cultivate the land, and too poor or *dishonest* to pay the rent agreed upon, he must evict them, or become a pauper himself. [...] The truth is, that these evictions [...] are not merely a legal but a natural process; and, however much we may deplore the misery from which they spring [...] we cannot compel the Irish proprietors to continue in their miserable holdings the *wretched swarms* of people who pay no rent, and who prevent the improvement of property as long as they remain upon it.[13]

Nevertheless, Mackay did not shelter his readers from the harsh reality surrounding evictions. On December 16, 1848, under the heading "Ejectment of the Irish Tenantry," the *ILN* carried a page with two powerful illustrations. One engraving showed a family being put out of a cabin as the roof is being demolished to prevent their return. The woman of the house pleads with a man on horseback, either the landlord or a bailiff, while armed soldiers stand by to enforce the eviction order. In the background, the tenant's livestock is being driven off to pay for the arrears in rent. The second picture shows an evicted family before a hut they have thrown up for shelter. The woman nurses a baby while the man stands by, his face buried in his arm. At his feet lies a pitcher, one of the family's few remaining possessions.[14]

A year later, in December of 1849, the *ILN* published "Conditions in Ireland," the first of a two-part series of articles about the evictions around Kilrush, County Clare (see Figures 8 and 9). In the second of the two issues, December 22, the journal ran two adjoining pages containing some of its most powerful depictions of the Famine. On the upper portion of each page engravings extend three columns wide. One shows a group of barely clothed peasants being given clothing (see Figure 10). The top of the facing page depicts the remains of the village of Moveen, the unroofed gable ends of the cottages standing stark against a barren landscape. (see Figure 11). Smaller illustrations throughout both pages suggest the poverty and despair of those evicted, while the text carries hints of some of the horrors the *ILN*'s reporter encountered around Kilrush

---

13. Ibid., 327–28, italics added.
14. See ibid., 303. The same style jug appears in the both illustrations. For the significance of earthenware pottery in the lives of poor tenants see Orser, "The People's Pottery: Irish Course Earthenwares and their Cultural Significance." For jugs see 80.

404   THE ILLUSTRATED LONDON NEWS.   [DEC. 22, 1849.

MISS KENNEDY DISTRIBUTING CLOTHING AT KILRUSH.

CONDITION OF IRELAND.
ILLUSTRATIONS OF THE NEW POOR-LAW.
(Continued from page 404.)

BRIDGET O'DONNEL AND CHILDREN.

SCALPEEN OF TIM DOWNS, AT DUNMORE.

Figure 8 "Conditions in Ireland," *Illustrated London News*

VILLAGE OF MOVEEN.

SEARCHING FOR POTATOES IN A STUBBLE FIELD.

SCALP OF BRIAN CONNOR, NEAR KILRUSH UNION-HOUSE.

Figure 9 "Conditions in Ireland," continued, *Illustrated London News*

Figure 10 "Miss Kennedy Distribution Clothing at Kilrush," *Illustrated London News*, December 22, 1849

(see Figure 12). "The once frolicsome people—even the saucy beggars—have disappeared, and given place to wan and haggard objects. [...] One beholds only shrunken frames scarcely covered with flesh—crawling skeletons, who appear to have risen from their graves, and are ready to return frightened to that abode." The reporter's language is unfortunately more reflective of the manufactured horrors of popular Gothic novels than of objective, journalistic descriptions of death and disease.[15]

One illustration remains particularly riveting, however. A thin mother, barely covered by her rags, stands trying to shelter her two little girls. None of the family have shoes. Although wood engravings did not allow for fine detail, the illustrator had, nevertheless, caught something of the distress and ravage on the face of the mother, Bridget O'Donnell (see Figure 13). Her name, as well as at least part of her story, are remembered today only because the *ILN* reporter did something rather extraordinary for the times: he interviewed a peasant woman, purporting to quote her actual words. This occurred several decades before interviews became one of the principal techniques of modern journalism. The interview stands as but one example of how the Irish Famine forced

---

15. Leslie A. Williams, *Daniel O'Connell, the British Press and the Irish Famine*, 335. For the use of Gothic tropes and language in famine commentary see Ryder, "Reading Lessons: Famine and the *Nation*," 158–61.

Figure 11 "Village of Moyeen," *Illustrated London News,* December 22, 1849

journalists to see the poor as more than faceless abstractions paraded through sermons and the theories of the political economists. Moreover, by deploying the new technique of combining wood engravings and letterpress on a single page, thus enhancing both the visual and the literary impact, the *ILN* had done for Kilrush what it had earlier done for Skibbereen. Through the new media of pictorial journalism, it had created symbolic geographies representing the horrors of the Irish Famine.[16]

The evictions around Kilrush gained notoriety for several additional reasons. West Clare, a popular tourist destination, was one of the more densely populated parts of Ireland. With much of the interior of Clare occupied by the Burren, a large, almost barren area of exposed limestone, the peasants' clachans crowded the coast, where seaweed provided essential fertilizer for their potatoes. The concentration of people around Kilkee rose to 367 persons per square mile. Around 75 percent of the holdings in Clare were valued at under £4, meaning that, if a tenant defaulted on his rent, his landlords had to pay the rates. As noted earlier, this made the small holders prime targets for eviction. In the words of Lord Clanricarde: "The landlords are prevented from aiding or tolerating poor tenants. They are compelled to hunt out all such, to save their property from the £4 clause."[17]

---

16. For reproductions of these pages and an analysis of their contents and layout see Leslie A. Williams, *Daniel O'Connell, the British Press and the Irish Famine*, 331–40. For an analysis of the interview with Bridget O'Donnell, see Michael Foley, *Death in Every Paragraph*, 10–15.
17. Reilly, *The Irish Land Agent*, 129. For Clare see Ó Murchadha, *The Great Famine: Ireland's Agony*, 120. For population density see Murphy, *Before the Famine Struck*, 19.

Figure 12 "Searching for Potatoes in a Stubble Field," *Illustrated London News*, December 22, 1849

BRIDGET O'DONNELL AND CHILDREN.

Figure 13 O'Donnell. "Bridget O'Donnell and Children" *Illustrated London News*, December 22, 1849

A parliamentary committee, formed to consider the evictions in the Kilrush Union, determined that 2,359 families, consisting of 12,000 people, about 17 percent of the area's 1841 population, had lost their homes between 1847 and July 1850. The relentless pressure for eviction took on the character of what Ciarán Ó Murchadha calls a "panic-haste" among the landlords, induced by the specter of ever-rising rates and by the fear that outrage over evictions might force the government to introduce some tenant-rights legislation.[18]

---

18. Ó Murchadha, *The Great Famine*, 125. For data see Donnelly, *The Great Potato Famine*, 147; Murphy, *A People Starved*, 58.

Land sales under the Encumbered Estates Act account for another reason why evictions continued into the 1850s. Purchasers expected their lands to be cleared of small holders, a point which sellers often found advantageous to address. For example, an advertisement for sections of the recently divided Martin estate in Connemara reassured purchasers that "the same Tenants by name, and in number, will not now be found on the Lands." If, however, as often happened, the new owners discovered otherwise, they themselves would engage in wholesale evictions.[19]

As noted earlier, to prevent evicted families from reoccupying their cabins, landlords usually insisted that the dwellings be unroofed, if not actually tumbled. The latter was a simple matter, however, as the bailiffs knew where a few deft thrusts of a crowbar would bring down the roof. Sometimes families were offered money, usually around 10*s*, and forgiveness of rents in arrears, if they helped destroy their own cabins. However, as George Poulett Scrope asserted in Parliament, 10*s* constituted a paltry recompense for losing one's house and access to land. Although evictions in Clare peaked by 1850, they continued at a high rate until 1854 in Mayo, Clare and Tipperary. These massive clearances amounted to what William J. Smyth has labeled a de facto "economic and social revolution."[20] Within a few short years, pre-Famine patterns of land use that had characterized the potato economy were swiftly reversed.

Water from a Stone: Funding the Poor Law Unions in the Late Famine Years

Following the 1849 harvest, the government still faced pressures for intervention, even though critical conditions were limited to large sections of the west. Trevelyan, the sometimes all-too-audible public voice of the Treasury, sought to throw a rhetorical cloak over the situation: "What the patient now requires is *rest and quiet and time for the remedies which have been given to operate.* Continued dosing and dependence upon physicians is not good either for the body politic or corporate." The actual human, Irish body—homeless, diseased and malnourished—did not figure into this convoluted metaphor. Ridiculously inappropriate analogies such as this caused even Russell to complain bitterly about the "harsh Trevelyanisms" that characterized the moralists in the Treasury.[21] Privately, the prime minister occasionally kicked back against the Treasury's easy acceptance of the Irish peasant's suffering as the inevitable price for economic prudence and improved land management. Nevertheless, in his more reflective moments, he decided that the problem lay not with Trevelyan and Wood but "deep in the breasts of the British people," who felt that, for all the money and effort spent on Ireland, they had been repaid only in "calumny and rebellion." Russell felt that there could be "no great plans for Ireland—and

---

19. Quote in Patricia Kelly, *Story of Connemara*, 112.
20. Smyth, "Exodus from Ireland: Patterns of Emigration," figure 5, 498. For Mayo, Clare and Tipperary see Donnelly, *The Great Potato Famine*, 156. For Scrope see Ó Murchadha, *The Great Famine*, 115. For demolition process see Dorian, *The Outer Edge of Ulster*, 238.
21. See Gray, *Famine, Land and Politics*, 323, italics original. For "Trevelyanisms" see 325.

much as I wished it, I have got to see that it is impracticable." The prime minister did favor a bill that would have reformed land tenure in Ireland, but the Irish landowners in his cabinet vehemently opposed it. In the end Russell lacked the power and eventually the will to do much of anything.[22] As always, however, he and his colleagues sought absolution in the doctrine of laissez faire, the glory of which raised doing little to the high level of grand policy.

This did not silence government's critics, however. At the behest of George Poulett Scrope, a select parliamentary committee inquired into conditions in the Kilrush Union. The committee found that, with the government still insisting that local relief had to be paid out of local rates, distressed Poor Law Unions could not meet the demands placed upon them. Consequently, although food in Ireland was generally plentiful and cheap, people still suffered. The select committee concluded that "a neglect of public duty has occurred, and has occasioned a state of things disgraceful to a civilized age and country, to which some authority ought to be held responsible, and would have long since been held responsible had these things occurred in any union in England."[23]

Still, the government did not completely lack initiative. By 1849, it had decided that it was time to expand the number of Poor Law Unions and their facilities. Since the Irish Poor Law had not been designed to provide relief in the event of famine, the oversized western unions had become problematic during the crisis. Therefore, a Boundary Commission recommended the creation of 50 new unions. More than a matter of tidying up after the fact, this was largely a response to the continuing fear of outdoor relief still haunting the most distressed unions. By splitting up some of the large unions and by building more workhouses, enough space might be created to "test" all those applying for relief.[24] Even more important, the creation of smaller, more uniform unions in the wake of the Famine shows the extent to which the Irish Poor Law system, contrary to its original purpose, had become accepted as the official mechanism for crisis relief.

With much of the continuing demand for famine relief limited to some of the western unions, it should have been possible to focus additional resources on those areas. The government did come up with some new loans, and it managed to pass a new Rate-in-Aid Act in 1850. By June 1850, however, when those funds had run out, the government found itself obliged to dispense even more loans to the distressed unions, adding to their burden of debt.[25] With that in mind, Russell's administration decided that it was time for the Poor Law Unions to begin repaying their loans to the Treasury. Government critics, such as James Wilson of *The Economist*, had frequently complained "that a loan to Ireland one year is converted to a gift the next."[26] Although demands for relief were still running well above pre-Famine levels, the Consolidated Annuities Act of 1850 pulled together the debts of each union and established a repayment schedule ranging from

---

22. For quote see Haines, *Charles Trevelyan and the Great Irish Famine*, 517. For rejection of tenure reform see Cornwell, *A Galway Landlord during the Great Famine*, 38.
23. See Kinealy, *This Great Calamity*, 290. For Scrope's committee see 288–90.
24. Ibid., 282–85. See also Donnelly, *The Great Potato Famine*, 107.
25. Kinealy, *This Great Calamity*, 278.
26. *The Economist*, January 30, 1847, 115.

5 to 40 years, depending on a union's circumstances. Still intent on restructuring Irish agriculture, the government hoped that, by putting yet more pressure on rate payers, the debt-repayment legislation would force more small tenants to abandon their holdings and more struggling owners to sell out to investors. So determined was the Treasury to make a show of debt repayment that it allowed some unions to take out *new* loans to pay off the old ones.[27] Thus, in the Dickensian world of the Treasury, relief administration seems to have become less a means to an end than an end in itself; wheels within wheels turned for the sake of turning.

Yet, beneath the surface all this was merely show. By 1849 the government had quietly recognized that the bulk of the loans would never be repaid. Concerned about the political repercussions, however, correspondence to this effect had been carefully edited out of the Blue Books Trevelyan routinely prepared for Parliament. In dealing with this topic, the government had to negotiate a tight rope strung between two threats. If it showed any signs of relenting on debt repayment, Parliament would be in an uproar. Yet, if it pressed too hard for immediate repayments, Ireland (at least its ratepayers) would be furious. So, the Treasury pushed for whatever money it could force from its debtors, and they, individuals and unions alike, resisted as much as they could. Nevertheless, Trevelyan saw potential value in the game. In September 1851, he advised Wood that, by appearing to stand firm on debt repayment, the government might be able to get Parliament to grant the remaining funds from the Rate-in-Aid Bill to the distressed unions. And so it went, wink following nudge, until 1853, when a new government decided to cancel the Famine-loan debts outright. Simultaneously, it extended the British income tax to Ireland, an act that pleased no one on the island. By remitting many of its Irish loans, the government roughly doubled its Famine-relief costs to around £7,000,000 ($755,335,000 in 2020 valuation). Even so, Irish rate payers (along with charitable donors) had contributed an even greater amount for the support of Ireland's poor.[28]

Entering the 1850s: An Altered Landscape

In the subsequent harvests of 1850 and 1851, the trend established in 1849 continued with blight-infected areas largely confined to parts of the west. By 1852, for the first time in seven years, Ireland enjoyed a harvest largely free of the potato blight. Many people felt that the Famine had finally ended. In 1851, Lord Ross of Birr Castle, home of one of Europe's largest telescopes, celebrated the "end" of the crisis with a firework display that cost some £400.[29] Nevertheless, the Famine had left its mark. In its wake, a new social landscape had begun to emerge. According to the 1851 Census, 355,689 fourth-class

---

27. For debt repayment scheme see Kinealy, *This Great Calamity*, 270–77.
28. For the Treasury's private acquiescence on non-repayment see Haines, *Charles Trevelyan and the Great Irish Famine*, 356–57, 528–29. For Trevelyan's suggestion to Wood see 541. For costs of the Famine see Donnelly, *The Great Potato Famine*, 119. For 2020 equivalence in currency see Nye, "Pounds Sterling to Dollars.".
29. Reilly, *The Irish Land Agent*, 352.

mud cabins, 75 percent of the country's housing stock, went "missing." On the Mizzen Peninsula, for instance, most of the cabins that had once housed 83 percent of the area's population were gone.[30] Once unroofed, these sod structures began to dissolve back into the earth. Sometimes only ghostly potato ridges or middens marked the places where families had once lived. Elsewhere, the ruins of sturdier rough, stone dwellings remained, littering the landscape. Throughout the west and southwest, the gable ends of empty houses, denuded of their rafters and thatch, stood naked against the sky. Many of the ruins depicted in the *ILN* show these tall silhouettes, suggesting houses that may have been of stone construction. In 1852, Sir Digby Neave described a ruined village with "the yawning-stone gables of well-constructed homes [...] stone-chimneys [...] and the slate lying around."[31] Neave may have been indulging in poetic license, of course. The fourth-class cabins rarely had any chimneys and the roofs were always thatched, not slated. Yet, his observations, along with other descriptions and illustrations, suggest that, as the Famine progressed, some of the better-off small farmers either abandoned their relative sturdy homes or were evicted.

While workhouse populations gradually declined after 1850, the uprooting and dispersion of the Irish people continued unabated. As stated earlier, around 1.2 million people fled the island between 1845 and 1851. An additional 900,000 emigrated over the next five years.[32] However imperfect the data, the 1851 decennial census provides some idea of the extent of the "scattering." Of special interest were the figures for mortality and depopulation. Since death and emigration rates did not begin to rise significantly until the winter of 1846, the depopulation recorded by the census had occurred in just five years. The data shows that the west and southwest were most affected. The province with the highest mortality from all causes was Connaught where 408,828, three out of every 10 people, died. Of deaths by starvation Connaught's share was a disproportionate 47.2 percent of the total. Munster reported 27.2 percent, while figures for Ulster and Leinster were 5.2 and 4.2 percent, respectively. With less than half the country's population in 1841, Munster and Connaught accounted for two-thirds of Ireland's famine mortality.[33]

The sharp demographic decline had dramatically remade the social and economic structure of Ireland, as illustrated in the following table.

---

30. Hickey, *Famine in West Cork*, 330.
31. Neave, *Four Days in Connemara*, 13, 14.
32. Donnelly, *The Great Potato Famine*, 178.
33. Ó Gráda, *The Great Irish Famine*, 51; Smyth, "The Province of Connacht and the Great Famine," 281. For deaths by starvation see Smyth, "The Province of Munster and the Great Famine," 363.

Agricultural Holdings in Ireland (1845–51)				
Size of Holdings	1845	1847	1851	% change 1845–51
Less than an acre	135,134	73,016	37,728	–71.2
1 to 5 acres	181,950	139,041	88,083	–51.6
5 to 15 acres	311,133	269,534	191,854	–38.3
Above 15 acres	276,618	321,434	290,404	+5.0

This table is based on data in Bourke, "*A Visitation of God?*" 79, 194n23, and in Donnelly, *The Great Potato Famine*, table 5, 161. Most of the data is based on the census reports for 1841 and 1851. However, Bourke explains that, for a variety of reasons, the figures from the 1841 census are unreliable. He developed his data for 1845 primarily from the Poor Law returns for that year; see 77–79.

As can be seen, the numbers of those working holdings under five acres—largely cottiers—were reduced by half, while holdings under one acre fell by 71 percent. Since each holding had supported a family, these figures represent hundreds of thousands of people. The bulk of the losses for families working 15 acres or less occurred during the first years of the Famine, from 1845 to 1847. The one-third reduction in the number of holdings between 5 and 15 acres is especially significant. It represents small farmers who, in normal times, lived a cut above the cottiers and conacre people. The loss of approximately 40,000 of these holdings in the first year of the Famine suggests the precarious position of even this group. However, their biggest losses occurred after 1849. Since these farmers were expected to pay their share of the Poor Law rates, many were forced out as these rates increased. As a correspondent to the *Downpatrick Recorder* argued: "We observe, with regret, that much of the wealth and comfort of this hitherto prosperous county is being transported to the shores of America. [...] Lord John Russell's rate-in-aid scheme is driving some of our farmers out of the country."[34] As suggested earlier, the considerable growth in the holdings over 15 acres between 1845 and 1847 suggests consolidation of vacated land early in the Famine, Nevertheless, the reduction in the number of holdings in this group between 1847 and 1851 points to the cumulative effect of the blight and high taxes in driving out some of those who had initially benefited from the difficulties of their neighbors. In the process this freed up even more land for the stronger farmers.

The 1851 Census returns provide a glimpse of just the early stages of the reconstruction of rural Ireland's social and economic landscape. The process would continue through the remainder of the century. It was, of course, inevitable that, once the blight had destroyed the basis for the old potato economy, a new Ireland would emerge. This was certainly what the government had hoped. The process, however, was not driven by any grand schemes, such as assisted emigration, tenant ownership, land reclamation or investment in Irish manufacturing. Instead, change flowed from the government's adherence to its decision to institute the Irish Poor Law system as the primary instrument

---

34. Quoted in McCavery, "The Famine in County Down," 125. For data see also Smyth, "Exodus from Ireland," 500–1.

of famine relief, thus forcing Irish property to shoulder the costs. This encouraged, if not compelled, landlords to clear their estates, thus eradicating the decades' accumulation of small, subdivided holdings once sustained by the potato. Pushed along by the Encumbered Estates Act, insolvent landlords were themselves forced out, leaving the way open for new investment and types of land management. By following its minimalist but ironclad policy, the government allowed grim events to initiate profound changes in agricultural Ireland. As Trevelyan once confided to Twistleton: "We must not complain of what we want to obtain. If small farmers go, and their landlords are reduced to sell portions of their estates to persons who will invest capital, we shall at last arrive at something like a satisfactory settlement of the country."[35] But would that settlement be the one Trevelyan and the government had envisioned?

---

35. Quoted in Kinealy, *A Death-Dealing Famine*, 148.

Part Four
THE POST-FAMINE YEARS

Chapter Thirteen

POST-FAMINE DREAMS AND IRISH REALITIES IN THE 1850S

Divine Opportunities: Bible Wars, the West and the Famine

The west of Ireland, especially Connemara— western Galway along with parts of southern Mayo—became the focal point for British imperial imagination in both its secular and sacred manifestations. As noted earlier, the so-called Second Reformation produced networks of evangelical clergy and sympathetic landlords, who, backed by money from British and Irish Protestant organizations, established missions, schools and even "colonies" in the west. This meant that, with the arrival of the Famine, charitable aid inevitably breathed the atmosphere of proselytism, especially since many evangelicals interpreted the Famine as a sign of divine punishment. It was a call to Protestants for repentance and action and to Catholics for renunciation and conversion, thus preparing the way for the Second Coming by displacing the Roman Antichrist.[1]

Rev. Alexander Dallas, an English rector from Hampshire, carried this powerful vision into Connemara during the Famine. In 1846 he moved to Castlekerke near Lough Corrib in Galway. There was no time to establish a colony. Instead, Dallas and his supporters organized a series of mission stations around Connemara, each headed by a minister and employing teachers, tract distributors and Gaelic-speaking Scripture readers. As famine conditions worsened, the stations often distributed food and clothing to those attending services. Eventually, these efforts were funded by the British-based Society for the Irish Church Missions, founded in 1849. Such backing also enabled the D'Arcys, founders of the Galway town of Clifden, to hold their so-called Silver Mondays, when shillings were handed out to those who had attended service on the previous Sunday. To Dallas and his associates, it must have seemed that, faced with the God's wrath, the peasantry of Connemara was finally ready to abandon Romish superstitions.[2] Not all Protestants supported the "reformationists," however. Although Rev. Sidney Godolphin Osborne granted the usefulness and sincerity of their aid, he also noted "the utmost enmity of the [Catholic] priests" and the inevitable "domestic divisions" stirred up by the missionary efforts. "But I will say nothing further here on the subject; to touch any of these matters in Ireland, is to handle a sort of controversial 'pitch'—you are sure to be blackened."[3]

---

1. Irene Whelan, "The Stigma of Souperism," 144.
2. Ibid., 145–47. For Rev. Hyacinth D'Arcy's involvement in the missionary movement see Kathleen Villers-Tuthill, *History of Clifden, 1810–1860*, 67–72. For Dallas see Kinealy, *Charity and the Great Hunger in Ireland*, 170–75.
3. Osborn, *Gleanings in the West of Ireland*, 73.

On Achill Island, situated at the head of Mayo's Clew Bay, the evangelical colony of Dugort struggled to help the desperate peasantry while continuing to proselytize in the face of hunger. Like some other Evangelicals, Rev. Edward Nangle, head of the mission, regarded the crisis as God's judgment on Roman Catholicism, an important argument in his fund-raising strategy. Most of those employed on the colony's farms appear to have been converts. Children who were fed at the mission every day received Bible lessons along with their meals, although Nangle insisted that the children and their parents had to agree to the lessons. Of course, there would have been no food without the lessons.[4] The term "soupers" already existed as a label for Catholics who "took soup"—who converted to Protestantism in return for food, clothing or employment. In its looser sense, it referred to situations in which recipients of charity agreed to listen to Bible readings or sermons in return for a meal. During a visit to Dugort, an officer of the Board of Works complained that English charitable contributions were being used as a coercive tactic to advance religion. Nangle, of course, indignantly rejected such charges.[5] Souperism, however, was not the only criticism leveled against the master of Dugort. American independent aid worker Asenath Nicholson, visiting the evangelical colonies in the west, accused the missionaries of exploitation:

> I had looked into the cabins of many of the converts of Dingle and Achill, and though their feet were washed cleaner, their stools scoured whiter, and their hearths swept better than many of the mountain cabins, yet their eightpence a day [earned at the colony] will never put shoes on their feet, convert their stools into chairs. [...] It will never give them the palatable, well-spread board around which their masters sit, and which they have earned for them by their scantily paid toil.

And, since the missionaries apparently found reading to the Gaelic-speaking peasants easier than teaching them to read for themselves, Nicholson argued that the converts "can no more be sure that this religion, inculcated by proxy, emanates from the pure scriptures, than did the prayer-book which they held in their hands when standing before a Popish alter."[6]

Despite such criticisms, the evangelical missionaries in the west of Ireland greeted the end of the Famine confident that their work would yield a bounteous harvest of converts. In 1853 Rev. Joseph Denham Smith published *Connemara: Past and Present*, his celebration of the "Reformation" in western Ireland. In the spirit of providentialism, he cheerfully asserted that the Famine had not been "an unmixed evil." Among its "advantages" had been emigration,

---

4. Ní Ghiobúin, *Dugort, Achill Island, 1831–1861*, 47, 53. Patricia Byrne, *The Preacher and the Prelate*, 119. Nangle raised funds through his newspaper, *Achill Herald*. See Byrne, 56–58. Also Irene Whelan, *The Bible War in Ireland*, 260–64.
5. Ní Ghiobúin, *Dugort, Achill Island, 1831–1861*, 49–50.
6. Nicholson, *Ireland's Welcome to the Stranger*, 339. See also her *Annals of the Famine in Ireland*, 105. For Nicholson and the Nangle see Patricia Byrne, *The Preacher and the Prelate*, 91–95, 129–34.

by which, on the western side of the Atlantic, thousands, once the slaves of Romish intolerance, are becoming the sons of freedom. [...] [I]t remained for [...] the famine to prepare [...] the hearts of myriads for the reception of that seed of divine truth, which is already yielding the first fruits of a goodly harvest. Yes, out of the mortal year of 1846, has come to use to a great degree the Reformation which we witness in 1852. How wonderful are the ways of God?"[7]

Smith then proceeded to recount the history of cooperation among Alexander Dallas of Castlekerke, the D'Arcys of Clifden and Nangle of Achill in spreading Connemara's missionary movement. Indeed, in the early 1850s, as land shaken loose by the Encumbered Estates Act came on the market, Dallas swung the considerable resources of the Society of Irish Church Missions behind the Achill colony. There was, in fact, no time to lose. In 1851 the Catholic Archbishop of Tuam, the redoubtable Rev. John MacHale, had established a Franciscan monastery on Achill Island near Dugort. It was among the first of the Catholic preaching orders that suddenly appeared throughout the region. Anxious to keep as much land as possible out of Catholic hands, Nangle had already purchased some acres the same year. Then, with the help of Dallas and the Irish Church Missions, he was able to expand his colony's holdings on Achill.[8]

Nevertheless, just a decade later reality had begun to temper evangelical hopes for the west. In 1863, Rev. Henry MacManus, a Presbyterian minister, published *Sketches of the Irish Highlands*, a reminiscence of his preaching tour through Connemara in the early 1840s. Although still dedicated to the idea of an Irish reformation, MacManus' piece suggests that time had taken a toll on his conversionary confidence. The author conveys little of the victory-is-at-hand enthusiasm found in earlier missionary accounts. Each "success" he recounts had been hard won and yet often eroded in the face of native resistance and what could be called the Catholic Church's counter reformation.[9]

Back on Achill, the Bible wars had proved costly. Eventually, the Irish Church Missions pulled out and Nangle's Colony found its financial support beginning to dwindle. Nangle died in 1883, and by the end of the century only a small number of Protestants converts remained in Dugort. The story was much the same throughout the areas where evangelicals had attempted to exploit the Famine as an opportunity for proselytism.[10] Although the evangelicals had gained strength within the Church of Ireland and the Presbyterian Synod of Ulster, their "Second Reformation" had failed to weaken the Roman Catholic Church. True, between 1834 and 1861 the country's Catholic population declined by 30 percent, while the smaller Protestant population dropped by only 19 percent. Even so, this meant that, for the first time since the institution of the Penal

---

7. Smith, *Connemara: Past and Present*, 83–84.
8. For MacHale see Patricia Byrne, *The Preacher and the Prelate*, 156–59; for Dallas see 165–66.
9. See MacManus, *Sketches of the Irish Highlands*.
10. See Ní Ghiobúin, *Dugort, Achill Island, 1831–1861*. See also Branach, "Edward Nangle and the Achill Island Mission," 35–38. For the battle of faiths on Achill see Patricia Byrne, *The Preacher and the Prelate*, 155–69.

Laws, the ratio of Catholic priests to people had significantly improved, making it easier to respond to the evangelical challenge.[11]

Sadly, such controversies threatened to obscure the many instances of interfaith cooperation during the Famine. Instead, the bitterness and hostility sowed during the Bible Wars left an angry residue in parts of the west, even as conversions, never overwhelmingly large, melted away. A surviving Gaelic poem from the period warned against the temptation of the missionaries' "sour soup," because *"go mbeirtear ar na franncaig fé chréithir, 's mheallfaí's an madra a tseamlas géire"* ("rats are caught under sieve pots, and the nastiest shambles will tempt a dog").[12] The labels, "souper" and "jumper" (a "souper" who rejoined the Catholic Church) would follow families through generations, an unhappy legacy of the Famine. Thus, the Bible Wars only served to increase Ireland's sectarian divisions. Thanks to the "reformationists," Catholic clergy were extremely suspicious of any Protestants seeking to improve the lot of the peasantry. In its post-Famine triumphalism, the Roman Catholic Church adopted a repressive stance toward anything that did not emanate from within the fold. Irene Whelan sees irony in the efforts of the evangelical missionaries, who, "in their attempts to destroy what they saw as Catholic tyranny […] virtually brought it into creation."[13]

Imperial Visions and the Garden of the West

> Disease has done its worst, famine has done its worst, and panic has done its worst. And now the population is in a greater state of health, and the poor houses are less full, and confidence is more prevalent than, for three years past, has been the case.[14]

On October 30, 1852, the *Illustrated London News* published an engraving titled "Harvest in Kilkenny." It depicts a group of agricultural laborers, men and women, relaxing after having brought in the grain, a few sheaves of which appear in the foreground. Behind the figures lie cleared fields dotted with more sheaves formed into stooks. The engraving illustrates a post-Famine rural Ireland as the British wished to imagine it. Not a potato in sight! No cattle either. Nothing but happy, well-fed Irish peasants and good, healthy grain, ready to be threshed and sent to market. A month later the journal ran an illustration of a pretty, barefoot colleen holding a sheaf of grain she had gleaned from a field. In an accompanying poem the journal maintained that Irish labor was now thriving "in the dawn of a brighter day."[15] However, while the Famine had come to an end, its

---

11. Yates, *Religious Condition of Ireland*, 60, 320–21.
12. Quoted in Ó Gráda, *Black '47 and Beyond*, 221.
13. Irene Whelan, "The Stigma of Souperism," 153. In her study, *The Bible War in Ireland*. Whelan concludes that the powerful Catholic response to the evangelical challenge laid the basis for the Church's concept of the "spiritual empire," the worldwide missionary enterprise, spread in large part by the post-Famine Irish diaspora; 272.
14. *Illustrated London News*, October 19, 1850, 318.
15. For "Harvest in Kilkenny" see O'Sullivan, *The Tombs of the Departed*, 46–47. For "The Irish Gleaner," see Meloy, "'Dawn of a Brighter Day,'" 19–20.

terminal stage dragged on. As late as 1857, 269,800 people remained in the workhouses, with 35,432 receiving some form of outdoor relief.[16]

The 1851 Census confirmed the loss of a million-and-a-half Irish people. The report's editors, nonetheless, did manage to detect a silver lining: masses of paupers had disappeared from the land, along with their tiny, fragmented holdings now consolidated into larger, proper farms. The reconstruction of rural Ireland seemed in progress. The editors even quoted from Trevelyan's *The Irish Crisis*: "supreme wisdom has produced permanent good out of transient evil."[17] As British imaginations indulged in imperial dreams, however, one did not need Providence to underscore the bottom line. The Irish, peasants and landlords alike, had failed to realize the full promise of Irish agriculture, especially amid the scenic splendors of the west. Their nightmare of potatoes and poverty had produced disaster. Now, with the land cleared of its nearly pauperized masses, decent-sized farms awaited newcomers who, by draining the bogs, would realize the land's full potential. New farmers would employ the former tenantry as agricultural workers who would earn cash wages instead of potatoes. With the help of the Encumbered Estates Act, the English style of farming would spread throughout the west of Ireland. English and Scottish agricultural entrepreneurs would turn the region into a veritable garden. It was an imperial vision, carrying echoes of Robert Peel's original Encumbered Estates Bill: the "New Plantation of Ireland."

As with the Bible Wars, Connemara was also the center for these more secular imperial dreams, thanks in part to a series of books linking the area's picturesque scenery to the idea of economic development. As early as 1823, members of the Blake family of Renvyle, Galway published letters extolling the supposed potential of this land of mountains, lakes and bogs.[18] A decade later, in 1834, Scottish editor and writer Henry D. Inglis published a two-volume work recounting his tour through Ireland. Part travelogue and part investigative reporting on economic conditions, Inglis was particularly taken with Connemara's picturesque scenery. At the same time, he also conjured up the region's supposed economic potential in fisheries, marble works and especially agriculture. Like many travelers to Ireland, Inglis never saw a bog that his imagination could not drain and cultivate. About Connemara he wrote: "It was impossible to cast the eye over the vast inclined plains of bog-lands, skirted by fine water levels, which seemed to invite draining, without […] seeing, in perspective, these vast tracts bearing abundant produce." No other place in Ireland, he wrote, was "so well adapted for experimenting on waste lands, and reclaimable bogs." Other visitors to the region expanded on the idea of Connemara as a potential garden. A year after Inglis published his tour, John Barrow proclaimed the region "capable of being converted into one of the most fertile and productive districts in Ireland." Given Connemara's supposed advantage in internal communications via lakes

---

16. Kinealy, "The Role of the Poor Law During the Famine," 119.
17. For Census Report see Willie Nolan, "Land Reform in Post-Famine Ireland." 570.
18. See the Blake Family, *Letters from the Irish Highlands of Connemara*. For a discussion of the book see William H. A. Williams, *Tourism, Landscape and the Irish Character*, 165–66.

and canals, Barrow felt sure that, if the bogs were drained, "population would soon flow into this remote district."[19]

One thing that helped encourage such visions was the fact that Connemara's population was concentrated along the coast. Around 1840 an interior road designed by the ubiquitous engineer Alexander Nemo opened western Galway to tourists. Connecting Galway town to Clifton, it left much of the more highly populated costal land bordering Galway Bay hidden behind the Connemara Hills to the south. Thus, visitors to the region thought that they had encountered an empty land of great agricultural potential just awaiting the touch of capable British hands. Traveling Nemo's road in 1842, William Makepeace Thackeray lavished praise on the region's alleged economic potential, as well as its scenic beauties: "The cultivation of the country is only in its infancy as yet, and it is easy to see how vast its resources are and what capital and cultivation may do for it." Undaunted by the blanket bogs around him, Thackeray, the consummate urbanite, confidently proclaimed that "a little draining" would turn them into rich productive agricultural land. Moreover, the constant sound of rushing water, common to a region of lakes, bogs and plentiful rain, apparently put Thackeray in mind of industrial potential. "Streams and falls of water often dash everywhere," he observed; "they have only to utilize this water-power for mills and factories—and hard by are some of the finest bays in the world where ships can receive foreign and home produce." Thackeray went on to proclaim that once the country's "capabilities are yet brought into action [...] Ireland will be poor Ireland no longer." A few years later, in the depth of the Famine, James Wilson, so critical of the Irish people, was bullish about Ireland's future possibilities. "Ireland possess climate, soil, mines, water-power, fisheries, and every element of wealth to an extent unknown in almost any other country."[20]

Like Thackeray, many visitors to the west of Ireland assumed a connection between Nature's beauty and Nature's bounty. A sort of romantic capitalism inspired the idea that picturesque scenery and economic potential could and should walk hand in hand. This assumption appeared in a clutch of travel-cum-promotional books that appeared in the wake of the Encumbered Estates Act. In 1849 George Preston White published *A Tour of Connemara with Remarks on Its Great Physical Capabilities*. Reprinted in 1851, the book combined visions of economic development with the usual tourist descriptions of picturesque scenery. Much of White's book consists of speculation about the region's potential for fisheries and agriculture. His appendix includes an essay written by Alexander Nemo on draining and reclaiming bog land. A civil engineer himself, White also conjured up visions of great harbors serving the transatlantic trade. White quoted a letter from the famous scientist Sir Humphry Davy, who regarded the west of Ireland as representing an "untouched fund of wealth." At the same time, White, like most of those who visited Ireland at that time, was anxious to allay any anxieties potential settlers might have

---

19. Barrow, *A Tour Round Ireland*, 244, 245; Inglis, *A Journey throughout Ireland*, 2:55, 2:64. For Inglis on Connemara, see William H. A. Williams, *Tourist, Landscape and the Irish Character*, 166–68.
20. *Economist*, February 27, 1847, p. 226; Thackeray, *Irish Sketchbook: 1842*, 180.

regarding security. Despite a certain amount of agrarian unrest in the country, individuals, he insisted, were safe and secure in their life and property.[21]

Also in 1849, Scottish farmer and agricultural writer James Caird published *The Plantation Scheme, or the West of Ireland as a Field for Investment*. Caird had already helped to popularize the concept of "high farming," which combined sophisticated practices of crop rotation with the use of fertilizers and deep-tile drainage. Visiting the dismembered Martin estate in West Galway, he had a discerning eye for which lots might return the costs of draining and which would not. Although confident about opportunities for investors and settlers in the west, he argued for large-scale government loans to advance agricultural improvement, advice which naturally went unheeded.[22]

In 1850 William Tighe Hamilton published *The Encumbered Estates of Ireland*, based on his series of newspaper articles about some of the larger Irish estates that had come on the market. About half the book deals with Connemara. Like Caird, Hamilton was more realistic than others concerning the difficulties involved in acquiring good land and realizing profits from it. Nevertheless, he concluded that "Ireland offers, at this moment, a great opportunity for British capital and enterprise." All the resources were there, he claimed—cultivatable land, manufacturing potential, fisheries, plentiful labor and transportation infrastructure. Nothing was needed, he assured his readers, "but that one thing that Ireland has not got herself—CAPITAL." The magnet that would attract this missing element was, he hoped, the Encumbered Estate Act.[23]

At least Caird and Hamilton brought a dash of realism and some caution to the idea of investing in and developing land in the west of Ireland. Two other authors, however, William Bulloch Webster and Rev. John Harvey Ashworth, exuded untrammeled confidence and enthusiasm. In his *Ireland Considered as a Field for Investment and Residence* (1852), Webster began by dismissing old stereotypes of the Irish as a violent and indolent people. The remaining peasantry would, he insisted, provide good, dependable cheap labor. With the "disaffected and unthriving" leaving and the "industrious and well-intentioned" staying, it merely remained for "a most efficiently organized police force" and "numerous English and Scottish settlers" to "strengthen the cause for order in Ireland." Webster claimed that all the pieces for success were in place from cheap land, affordable wages, reasonably priced food and building supplies to bays and streams teeming with fish. And, he insisted, "there is not a bog in Ireland that cannot be drained."[24] Webster's colonial vision made it sound as if Ireland was a newly discovered country, open and ready for settlement. He quoted J. R. McCulloch's *Statistical Account of the British Empire* (1837), which praised the "luxuriance" of Ireland's pastures and the "extraordinary fertility" of its crops. However, Webster did not include McCulloch's warning that, since its climate rendered Ireland better fit for grazing, the country was decidedly inferior when it came

---

21. For Humphry Davy quote see White, *A Tour of Connemara*, 145. For security issue see xii. For White's book see Hooper, *Travel Writing in Ireland*, 148–49; William H. A. Williams, *Tourism, Landscape and the Irish Character*, 178–79.
22. Caird, *The Plantation Scheme*, 50, 179.
23. W. T. H. [William Tighe Hamilton], *The Encumbered Estates of Ireland*, 107, emphasis original.
24. Webster, *Ireland Considered as a Field for Investment and Residence*, 5, 117.

to cultivating grain. And, although Webster was bullish on draining the bogs, McCulloch cautioned about the feasibility of such efforts: "At present, however, it appears to us that there are no good grounds for thinking that their cultivation, if undertaken upon a great scale, would be otherwise than ruinous."[25]

The same colonizing mentality that inspired Webster is evident throughout Rev. John Harvey Ashworth's *The Saxon in Ireland, or the Rambles of an Englishman in Search of a Settlement in the West of Ireland* (1851). Glenn Hooper notes that Ashworth saw settlement opportunities in Ireland through an imperial lens. Might not Ireland, the "Saxon" inquired, be more appealing to English settlers than the Antipodes or the "burning Cape [of Good Hope]?" It was not just convenience yoked to opportunity that drove Ashworth's argument, however. As Hooper points out, Ashworth's enthusiasm for Ireland suggests a kind of "moral imperative," indeed, almost an imperial duty to realize the potential of a land so long misgoverned and neglected.[26] More than any writer at the time, Ashworth's imagination allowed the promise of economic development to revel amid Connemara's romantic landscape. "Beautiful scenery," he wrote, "will have its influence on the mind of an immigrant." His book includes many appealing descriptions of Connemara and Mayo. Fortunately, in his view the picturesque held no risk to the pocketbook. It is often remarked, he wrote, "The more beautiful, sometimes, the more unproductive […] but not here. The mountains often afford the finest pasture, and valleys the richest soil." This potential, however, had to be developed. Gazing over the area around Ballycroy, Mayo, Ashworth proclaimed: "Apart from the occasional beauty of the scenery, it wears at present a wild and dreary aspect; but the agricultural eye wanders over it at the same time with delight and impatience: delight to witness such an accumulation of capability; impatience to see them undeveloped."[27]

Saxons and Celts: Colonialism, Race and Imperial Rhetoric

Ashworth did discern some potential problems, however. Development ultimately depends upon the availability of cheap labor, as well as land, and he wondered if, between eviction and emigration, there would be enough laborers left to complete the transformation he envisioned. This concern also worried other observers. Samuel Reynolds Hole, visiting Ireland in 1859, praised the Encumbered Estates Act: "one of the cleverest, cleanest cuts that surgeon ever made to save his patient from mortification." However, where, he wondered, "are the hands to ply the matchlock pick?" Given the country's depopulation, "there seems to be no staff on the spot for any large undertakings."[28] And what of the quality of the labor that remained? In a sense, the authors of these promotional books

---

25. Ibid., 1:28. For J. R. McCulloch quotes see his *Statistical Account of the British Empire*, 1:517, 359.
26. See Hooper, "'Strangers in Ireland,'" 158–59, 170–71.
27. Ashworth, *The Saxon in Ireland*, 169, 97. For Ashworth's book see Glenn Hooper, "'Strangers in Ireland,'" 157–62, 166–68, 170–72; William H. A. Williams, *Tourism, Landscape and the Irish Character*, 179–81.
28. [Samuel Reynolds Hole], *A Little Tour of Ireland*, 87, 86. See also Ashworth, *The Saxon in Ireland*, 112.

had to write themselves out of a cul de sac formed by Britain's Irish narrative. If Irish laborers were as ignorant, improvident, shiftless, resentful and even violent as the narrative often suggested, then British investments would come to naught. Happily, according to these writers, a winnowing process had been at work in Ireland. While few of these authors ever alluded to famine mortality, they hailed clearances and emigration for ridding the land of a pauper class that had clogged the pathways to progress. Those peasants who remained were "intelligent," "industrious" and even "docile." Once exposed to "Saxon" knowledge and example, the Irish could be depended upon to work. Under Saxon direction, and relieved of their fatal insistence upon occupying some sliver of potato ground, they would happily labor for wages rather than for food, just like English agricultural workers.

This image of the subdued, pliant Irishman was new. As Edward G. Lengel has pointed out, prior to the Famine the more optimistic British observers expressed the hope that, once the Irish were freed from oppressive landlordism, their moral stature would rise. By the end of the Famine, however, such optimism had faded as racism began to merge with the rhetoric of imperialism. As Lengel points out, writers promoting British settlement in Ireland presented the Irish as a distinct race, the "Celts," who—lacking the "Saxons'" moral fiber and self-reliance—were nonetheless fit, under proper guidance, for "work and servitude." Writing in 1857, one visitor to Ireland stated that the Irish peasants were beginning to appreciate "the brain power, the judgment, and, above all, the indomitable perseverance and energy, of the Saxon."[29]

Although it occurred before the 1859 publication of Charles Darwin's *On the Origin of Species by Means of Natural Selection*, the Irish Famine seems to have encouraged a growing tendency to invoke racial terms to explain supposed British superiority over Irish inferiority. In 1850, a year before Ashworth's *The Saxon in Ireland* appeared, Robert Knox published his *The Races of Men*, comparing the superior virtues of the "Anglo-Saxon" to the degradation of "the Celts," an argument that was beginning to seem obvious to many in England. As the Famine progressed, half-starved Irish paupers had poured into British cities, haggard, unwashed, barely clothed and, to many observers, barely human. As Robert James Scally notes, the Irish refugees were often described as "passive," "resigned," "stunned" and "mute" beings who, fearful of deportation or having their families split through quarantine, hid themselves away in cellars, even from those who sought to help them. What might have previously been considered an underclass now appeared to some as a sub-human race. By 1860, Charles Kingsley, an early enthusiast of Darwinism, was describing Irish peasants as "white chimpanzees."[30] By that time, Anglo-Saxon racial superiority had become a virtual obsession on both sides of the Atlantic.

In his book *Rhetoric of Empire*, David Spurr explains how such assumptions of racial superiority were part of what he calls "the colonial discourse," whereby the would-be colonizer rhetorically appropriates a land and its peoples to his benign vision of prosperity

---

29. Weld's *Vacations in Ireland* (1857), quoted in Hooper, "'Strangers in Ireland,'" 155. See also Lengel, *The Irish through British Eyes*, 135–36.
30. For Kingsley see Curtis, *Apes and Angels*, 143. See also Scally, *The End of Hidden Ireland*, 213.

and "civilization." Rather than admit to antagonism between the colonizer and the colonized, the former seeks to dominate the latter "by inclusion and domestication," imagining them co-beneficiaries of the colonial enterprise. In similar fashion, what Spurr calls the "rhetoric of empire" resolved the perceived dichotomy between landscape aesthetics and poverty, which echoed throughout many Irish travel accounts. For example, contemplating Connemara's combination of breathtaking scenery and abject poverty, Ashworth wrote: "Strange it is that, where nature is so lovely, man should be so degraded and so wretched." However, he goes on to assert: "*Ireland has seen her worst days.*" The impending arrival of Saxon capital and Saxon know-how would change everything.[31] It is interesting, therefore, to see how Ashworth's frequent bursts of enthusiasm for Connemara's picturesque scenery fitted easily into the colonial discourse. Marveling at the view from the summit of Corranabinna, 2,500 feet above Clew Bay, Ashworth claimed: "The words of Goldsmith were at my heart though not upon my lips: 'Creation's heir—the world—the world is mine.'"(Glenn Hooper, citing the work of Mary Louise Pratt, calls attention to the importance of the "prospect view" in colonial narratives. In surveying the landscape from a prominence, the observer stands at the "interface of aesthetics and ideology," between the appreciation of beauty and dreams of power and profit.[32]) Then, as if taking possession of them, Ashworth, proceeds to name the landscape features he saw from his vantage point. This naming continues as he and his guide descend into the valley below. As they walk, however, Ashworth's attention gradually shifts from the splendors of the landscape to its potential utility. He notes where springs might be diverted and where catch basins could be established to dry out the ground. "I never saw any tract of land," he confidently asserts, "where extensive and highly remunerative operations could be so easily and economically carried out." Thus, as Ashworth descends the mountain, naming gradually turns into claiming. The whole process illustrates Spurr's contention that the colonial discourse "claims the territory surveyed as the colonizer's own." Yet, Ashworth does not focus on his personal ambition but rather upon the improvement of the land. Thus, the would-be colonizer appears less aggressor or prospector than benefactor who would realize the land's potential supposedly for the benefit of all.[33]

According to Spurr, by drawing attention to the "chaos that calls for the restoration of order, of absence that calls for reaffirming presence, of natural abundance that awaits the creative hand of technology," the colonial discourse "transfers the locus of desire onto the colonized object itself." This process naturalizes the aggressive desire for conquest or appropriation. As Spurr suggests, "The colonizing imagination takes for granted that the land and its resources belong to those who are best able to exploit them according to the values of a Western commercial and industrial system." As a writer in the December 1851 issue of the *Quarterly Review* put it, both Ireland and the British empire would benefit from "colonizing [Ireland] as extensively and systematically as possible with a race differing from the native in origin, in religion, and in character." The enterprise and

---

31. Ashworth, *The Saxon in Ireland*, 40, 43. See also Spurr, *Rhetoric of Empire*, 32.
32. Hooper, "'Strangers in Ireland,'" 17, 167; Ashworth, *The Saxon in Ireland*, 140.
33. Spurr, *Rhetoric of Empire*, 28. For quotes see also Ashworth, *The Saxon in Ireland*, 144.

knowledge of the colonizers would "guide the industry and stimulate the emulation of its inhabitants." This reveals the broad imperial context out of which promotional writing about the west of Ireland emerged in the wake of the Famine. Ashworth's rhapsodies over Irish landscapes, promising to unite aesthetics and utility, were soon to be echoed by British imperialists in Africa. According to Spurr, under the gaze of explorers such as Henry Morton Stanley, the African landscape seemed to have prepared itself for "the marriage with civilization."[34] The same was implied about Ireland.

Irish Realties

In addition to agriculture most of the post-Famine promotional books about Ireland also reveal a keen interest in transportation and communications, internal and external. Significantly, William Dargen's newly completed Midland Great Western Railway linking Dublin and Galway became a part of the effort to promote investment in Ireland. According to the 1854 edition of the *Irish Tourist's Illustrated Handbook*, Mr. Frederick Twining, an Englishman who purchased 900 acres in Connemara, had originated the idea of special railway excursion tickets to accommodate visitors evaluating land for purchase. Twining's scheme was inspired by the 1853 opening of the Irish International Exhibition in Dublin, which was heavily promoted by Dargan. The *Handbook* expressed confidence that prospectors, having visited the exhibition in Dublin, would then travel to the west where they would be impressed by both Connemara's scenery and "its capabilities for agricultural and even commercial progress." Certainly, such promotions provided a boost to tourism in the years immediately following the Famine. One upper-class visitor complained that, where once Irish tourist sites had been visited by "persons of rank and fashion," now it was crowds of English businessmen, "all with one eye for the picturesque, and another for discovering new outlets for the profitable investment of capital." In fact, with so much property seemingly about to fall into English hands, the guidebook suggested that Connemara already had "the stamp of the Saxon in Ireland," a clear reference to Ashworth's work.[35]

Some visitors found at least one blot of the imperial landscape, however. Even Ashworth, traveling around Achill Island, discovered that "visible; roofless buildings were too frequently met with in pleasant nooks and grassy dingles." Contemplating the disappearance of the former occupants, Ashworth wondered, "Why where they compelled to desert their native land?" Then this visitor of unbounded curiosity, whose book is full of detailed information, draws a convenient blank: "It is certainly an enigma, not easily solved by a wandering Saxon."[36] Ashworth seems to have momentarily forgotten that the

---

34. For the Stanley quote see Spurr, *Rhetoric of Empire*, 30. For other quotes see, 28, 31. For *Quarterly Review* quote, see Hooper, "'Strangers in Ireland,'" 159.
35. See *Tourist's Illustrated Handbook for Ireland* (1854), 174, 173. For the *Handbook*, as well as excursion tickets, see Thompson, "Famine Travel: Irish Tourism from the Great Famine to Decolonization," 165–70. See also Dube, "Enabling Instructions and Disabling Illustrations." For the businessmen quote see Lengel, *The Irish through British Eyes*, 141. For Dargan and the Dublin Exhibition see Meloy, "'Dawn of a Brighter Day,'" 34-37.
36. Ashworth, *The Saxon in Ireland*, 161.

unroofing of those houses and the eviction of their occupants lay at the heart of a process that made his dream of Saxon settlement seem possible. Other visitors were occasionally more honest in noting the connection between progress and destruction. Traveling through Connemara in 1852, Sir John Forbes recorded the "melancholy" sight of the stark gables and roofless walls, the reminders of the "horrors of recent evictions," which momentarily pushed from his mind "all the theoretical considerations of agricultural improvement, and all abstract principles of political economy […] [which] might have pleaded in excuse, or even in justification of such a system." Touring at about the same time, Sir Digby Neave was also disturbed by the ruined, abandoned cottages he encountered in Connemara. While he expressed no doubts as to the necessity for the evictions, he found it "humiliating" to think that the former inhabitants had fled to what they considered a "distant and *better* country," meaning America. England, he assured his readers, would do its best to "induce the Irish to alter that verdict."[37]

Eager to grasp the promise of this brave, new world waiting to be created out of a depopulated west of Ireland, these authors were, perhaps, assuaging their consciences by shedding a rhetorical tear for an evicted peasantry. Other observers, however, were made of sterner stuff. Writing in 1852, Sir Francis Bond Head, after admiring some newly consolidated fields in Connemara, "teeming with crops, green and brown," claimed that this new system required "an advocate." "In all the regions of the world, it has been, and is, the stern decree of Providence that civilization, sooner or later, should override and overrun those feeble tribes who are innocently reveling in what is usually called a state of Nature." All around the world "the virtuous and simple aborigines […] have rapidly melted away, as they themselves figuratively express it, 'like snow before the sun.'" Even if the Irish peasants owned their land, "it would be impossible for them as it has for the Red Indians to withstand the torrent of civilization that is steadily and irresistibly rolling over the world." Such decrees of Providence, Head insisted, were "dark, mysterious, and unfathomable."[38]

Journalist Harriet Martineau also toured the island in 1852, intent on producing a series of newspaper articles on Ireland. Having written extensively about the subject of political economy, Martineau may have regarded post-Famine Ireland as a kind of laboratory for its principles. Traveling through Mayo she encountered a dreary landscape: "Those soaked, and perished, and foul moorlands, relapsed from an imperfect cultivation; those hamlets of unroofed houses […] graveyards overgrown with thistles, while cattle go in and out of the crumbling earthen fence; signs of extensive former habitation, amidst which we see two or three human beings moving about like some chance survivors from a plague." These were, she wrote, the "features of a lapsed country." All was not lost, however. "But presently we met a gentleman, riding a fine horse, and looking as if business carried him on so briskly." It turns out that Martineau's gentleman was not Irish but English, "one of seven or eight settlers who have large farms near Westport." She

---

37. Neave, *Four Days in Connemara*, 13–14, italics added. See also Forbes, *Memorandums Made in the Autumn of 1853,* 226–27.
38. Head, *A Fortnight in Ireland*, 148, 149.

devoted one of her chapters to "English Settlers in the 'Wilds of the West'" in which she briefly surveyed the English and Scots she found farming in Connemara.[39]

Indeed, in 1854 a writer in *Ainsworth Magazine* exalted: "A new era has dawned on Ireland. The Englishmen and the Scotsmen have come over to farm." By 1859, when he published *The Agricultural and Social State of Ireland*, land agent Thomas Miller claimed that there were some 800 English and Scottish settlers in western Galway and Mayo. He even printed a map showing their residences. A few years earlier, Rev. Joseph Denham Smith rejoiced that "English, Scottish farmers and yeoman are already taking possession of large portions of the soil, turning it almost at once into great fruitfulness and beauty."[40] The opening of Connemara and adjoining areas had clearly succeeded in attracting British attention. The collapse of so many of the area's Irish landlords had forced extensive land onto the market. With so much available in so short a time, prices fell, inevitably drawing in some land speculators. The most notorious was London's Law Life Insurance Company, which acquired much of the vast Martin estate centered on Ballynahinch in Connemara. Instead of trying to improve the land, the purchaser simply sat on it, waiting for land prices to rise.

One reason why the company decided against any serious attempts at improvement may have been the results of a report it commissioned to evaluate its purchase. The assessor group, which visited Connemara in 1853, was headed by Thomas Colville Scott, a Scottish surveyor.[41] Although his report has not survived, Scot's notes have, and the story they tell is rather different from the usual glowing visions of Connemara as the future garden of the west. The area Scott surveyed, the old Martin estate, had been heavily depopulated. The Law Life Insurance Company, like most of the other new proprietors, had been assiduous in clearing its lands and tumbling cabins. "At present," Scott wrote, "the face of this country & its people look as desolate as if the whole region was about to be abandoned." Searching for large stretches of promising arable land around Roundstone, the assessor found instead patches of rich plaggen soil which the former inhabitants had built up through years of what Scott called "misapplied labour." These plots were too small and scattered to be commercially viable. "There is no room," he noted, "for a single large Farm in this district." The previous occupiers had survived through intensive use of seaweed and by dint of their own labor, whereas "hired labour would ruin a large occupier." In another area, he found three lots, which, if consolidated, might make one good farm. But he wondered who would choose to isolate themselves in such a spot and forgo the annual rents, while building the infrastructure that might attract tenants? Almost every previous writer had touted Connemara's potential for developing an internal transportation network, based on a canal linking Lough Corrib to Galway town and its harbor. Scott, however, remained unimpressed: "I am at a loss to know what

---

39. Martineau, *Letters from Ireland*, 92–93. Martineau was reporting for *Daily News* and later published her articles in book form.
40. Smith, *Connemara: Past and Present*, 81, 83–84. For Miller see Donnelly, *The Great Irish Potato Famine*, 159; Hooper, "'Strangers in Ireland,'" 162–64. For *Ainsworth Magazine* see Hooper, "'Strangers in Ireland,'" 170.
41. See Tim Robinson's introduction to Thomas Colville Scott's *Connemara after the Famine*.

the new traders on the Lough are going to carry, seeing that the surrounding country is hopelessly barren." Although Scott eventually found some decent-sized arable plots, potential stock farms and marble quarries, the overall tone of his notes suggests that his report to the Law Life Insurance Company must have been essentially negative.[42] One must, then, wonder about Harriet Martineau's assertion in 1852 that the agent for the Law Life Insurance Company was actively reclaiming bog land. Subsequent observers found just the opposite. In 1862, journalist Henry Coulter, reported: "The land remains in exactly the same state as when it came into their [the company's] hands, undrained, unfenced, unimproved in any respect." A few years later, Dr. William Wilde observed the old tilth fields on what been the Martin estate going back to bog.[43]

Some new purchasers did attempt to realize Connemara's fabled agricultural potential. Moving beyond what had been the Martin estate, Coulter did find some "exquisite" examples of drained bog land turned into farms. Nevertheless, reviewing the reclamation efforts of the community founded by the Quakers near Letterfrack, Galway, he commented: "The expense incurred in thoroughly reclaiming the bogs has been so great, that, in a pecuniary point of view, a serious loss has been unquestionably sustained." Coulter believed that more modest efforts could prove successful, and for a while some did.[44] Ireland's arable acreage did increase from 1847 into the 1850s, although this was in part a response to continued food deficiency within the country and to an increase in the production of animal fodder. However, wheat production sharply declined after the 1850s. Then, after two decades of continued expansion, Ireland's tillage acreage began to contract. By the end of the century much of the reclaimed land in the west had reverted to bog or had been converted to pasture.[45]

Rev. Henry MacManus, assessing the situation in Connemara in 1863, had to acknowledge that the hopes for agricultural reform, which had often accompanied the evangelical missionary movement, had to be tempered by the realities of geography and climate. He admitted that the bogs of Connemara constituted an "impassable barrier to the farmer."[46] Two long-term factors had weighed against efforts to make the west bloom. First, as feared by some promotional writers, continued evictions and emigration threatened development. Ciarán Ó Murchadha notes that in some places clearances had been so extensive that no farmers remained to take up newly consolidated holdings, thus, leaving the land fallow for years. In fact, the steady outflow of people gradually robbed the west of Ireland of the cheap labor that extensive land reclamation required. As a result, it became easier and less expensive for many landowners to shift from farming to pasturage. This, in turn, encouraged still further depopulation. Michael Turner calls attention to the systemic relationship between grazing and emigration. Increased pasturage

---

42. Ibid., viii–xix. For quotes see 14, 22, 28, 7, 33–34.
43. For Wilde see Patricia Kelly, *The Story of Connemara*, 110. See also Martineau, *Letters from Ireland*, 84; Coulter, *The West of Ireland*, 95.
44. For quote see Coulter, *The West of Ireland*, 122.
45. See Turner, *After the Famine*, 18; see also 35–36.
46. MacManus, *Sketches of the Irish Highlands*, 13.

reduced job opportunities, while the resulting shortage of laborers made cattle more attractive than cultivation.[47]

Ironically, part of the problem was tied to the initial response to the potato blight. In repealing the Corn Laws and ending the protection of domestic grain crops, the United Kingdom had committed itself to a long-term policy of cheap food based on imports. As the old tariffs on foreign grain gradually disappeared, American grain flooded in. Amid falling prices, grain grown on reclaimed Irish bog land often did not return investment. On the other hand, prices for Irish meat and dairy products increased. As Michael Turner asserts, while the decline in grain production occurred even in England after 1870, the Irish had already moved away from farming to dairying and pasturage in response to a growing market for their meat and butter.[48]

For all the enthusiasm of those promoting the garden of the west, only a minority of landowners in the region were prepared to invest their time and money in high farming. Even before the Famine, some observers had been skeptical about the extent to which the bogs could be drained. Samuel Reynolds Hole felt obliged to remind his readers of J. R. McCulloch's warning that in the west of Ireland nature favored grazing over cultivation.[49] After the Famine most of the landlords and their major tenants eventually agreed. As James S. Donnelly, Jr. points out, the massive clearances in West Galway and Mayo were preludes to the accelerating shift into pasture. Even many of the new settlers from Britain became graziers.[50] Pasturage became more appealing in the west for several reasons. First, although much of the western land was mountainous and boggy, it's rough pastures could sustain modest levels of sheep and cattle with none of the expense and effort required to drain bogs for cultivation. Added to that, by clearing away hordes of small holders and by consolidating the land for grazing, landlords rid themselves of an insolvent peasantry and the risk of having to pay their Poor Law rates.[51]

The Times had once looked forward to the day when "a Celtic Irishman will be as rare in Connemara as the Red Indian on the shores of Manhattan."[52] However, even Harriet Martineau, pleased as she was to see English and Scottish farmers in Connemara, had to admit that most of the purchasers of encumbered estates were in fact Irish. For all

---

47. Michael Turner, *After the Famine*, 10–11. See also Donnelly, *The Land and the People of Nineteenth-Century Cork*, 134. Turner also points out that, without cheap labor, the high pre-Famine crop yields, based on intensive spade labor and manuring, could not be maintained. He notes that the potato yields, which had been as high as 14.8 million tons in 1844, declined to 2.6 million tons in the 1850s; 29–30. See also Ó Murchadha, *The Great Famine*, 126.
48. Michael Turner also notes that a declining Irish population reduced the demand for domestically produced crops; *After the Famine*, 22.
49. [Samuel Reynolds Hole], *A Little Tour of Ireland*, 84n1.
50. Donnelly, *The Great Potato Famine*, 159. According to Michael Turner, arable acreage (not including land given over to growing fodder) declined from 4.6 million acres in 1851 to 2.2 million in 1911, while pastureland increased from 9,995 million acres to 12,359 million acres during the same period; *After the Famine*, 32.
51. Jones, "The Transfer of Land and the Emergence of the Graziers during the Famine Period," 95.
52. Quoted in Kinealy, *A Death-Dealing Famine*, 148.

the talk about Ireland needing English capital, there was in fact enough money in the country, as Martineau explained, to allow Irish investors to take advantage of the sudden glut of cheap land on the market. Purchasers included established Irish landowners, especially Irish grazers already involved in cattle fattening.[53] Others who invested in land were Irish businessmen, such as publicans, solicitors and land agents, all seeking profit and status by acquiring land and livestock. In West Cork, most of those who purchased parcels of encumbered estates turned out to be local landlords or members of Ireland's professional classes. Opportunities did present themselves for some English and Scottish investors and settlers who had experience in upland grazing. However, large-scale attempts to attract British farmers to take up vacated tenancies generally came to naught. For all the hullabaloo about the "the Saxon in Ireland," the Encumbered Estates Act wound up returning most of the land to Irish hands. By 1857, despite propaganda for British settlement and investment in Ireland, only 4 percent of those who purchased land were non-Irish. Although it involved the largest transfer of Irish land since the mid-seventeenth century, only £3,000,000 of the £20,000,000 invested in 3000 Irish estates came from outside the country.[54]

The assumption that the west of Ireland represented a veritable garden awaiting Saxon investment had proved a self-induced delusion on the part of its promoters. It paralleled the belief in post–Civil War America that semi-arid conditions on the western high plains could be reversed by farming; rain would somehow follow the plow. It did not.[55] Such dreams rested on the assumption that nature could be somehow transformed by human will and effort. Usually, reality was on the side of nature. On the American high plains, the rains were cyclical; in the west of Ireland they were unrelenting. Thus did post-Famine Irish realities diverge from imperial "Saxon" dreams of making the west bloom. The Famine had contributed to the restructuring of Irish agriculture, but not in the way many in Britain had hoped. Musing on the general failure to turn Connemara into a garden, Rev. Henry MacManus continued to admire the landscape. "While the world lasts, its magnificent scenery will expand the soul of its visitors, and inspire them with thoughts that wander through eternity. It is no waste, then, though it bears no crops. Who finds fault with a picture gallery for not being a dining room?"[56] Perhaps tourism would succeed where agriculture and evangelical missions had failed.

---

53. Martineau, *Letters from Ireland*, 94. For Martineau on Ireland see Glenn Hooper's introduction to her book, as well as his *Travel Writing in Ireland*, 172–89.
54. Reilly, *The Irish Land Agent*, 147. See also Turner, *After the Famine*, 70–71; Hickey, *Famine in West Cork*, 305. For failure to attract British tenants see Donnelly, *The Land and the People of Nineteenth-Century Cork*, 116–17.
55. Smith, *Virgin Land*, 240.
56. MacManus, *Sketches of the Irish Highlands*, 13.

Chapter Fourteen

IN THE FAMINE'S WAKE

Most of the changes long attributed to the Famine were already in progress before 1845. Emigration, the rural to urban demographic shift, the movement away from potato dependency, the change from tillage to grazing, the increasing influence of the Roman Catholic Church—all would have happened to some degree without the Famine. Time, however, defines the flow of history. It makes a difference whether events span decades or are concentrated within a few years. The speed and intensity of the changes wrought by the Famine between 1845 and the early 1850s had consequences. The precipitous collapse of the potato economy, the enormous suffering, the deaths and the disruption of the lives of hundreds of thousands of people, the sudden flight of thousands out of the country—all occurring within five years. This concentrated concatenation of events influenced the nature of change in Ireland for decades to come. It would take a shelf full of books to fully explore the immediate and long-term, wide-ranging consequences of the disaster. This chapter can only suggest some brief observations regarding some of the more obvious effects the crisis had upon the following areas: demographics, agriculture and land use, family structure, living standards, emigration, the Irish diaspora, as well as upon politics, language and religion.

Demographics

As noted earlier, the decennial census reported that Ireland's population had declined from 8,175,124 in 1841 to 6,552,385 in 1851, a loss of around one-fifth. Since excess mortality and the dramatic upsurge in emigration did not begin until the late fall of 1846, this demographic collapse occurred within just five years. And, appalling as the census figures appear, they do not reflect the size of the population as it was in 1846. As noted earlier, the momentum of population growth, although slowing after 1820, could have pushed the Irish population to between 8.5 and 8.7 million by 1846. In fact, as the census report itself suggested, if the Famine had not occurred, the country's population was projected to have been around nine million by the end of the decade.[1] Moreover, the Census of 1851 occurred while mortality and emigration rates remained high. Therefore, assuming a population of around 8.5 million in 1846, instead of a fall of 1.6 million, Ireland's losses might have totaled two million or more—almost a quarter of the population. No other modern European country has experienced such a demographic collapse.

---

1. Kinealy, *This Great Calamity*, 295–96.

Even the terrible famines that hit India and parts of Africa in the late nineteenth and early twentieth centuries failed to match the *proportion* of Ireland's loss.

It is estimated that around a million people died during the Famine. The numbers of actual deaths will never be known, since the official statistics are incomplete. Many died in their cabins where their bodies often remained. Others died in fields, their corpses left to vermin or to be buried unrecorded in common graves. The deaths of many infants and children were seldom registered. And then there were the averted births; children who, under normal circumstances, might have been born had it not been for the Famine. Including these forestalled births, Joel Mokyr's recalculations produced an "upward bound" figure for excess mortality of around 1,498,000 for the period 1846–1851.[2]

Famine mortality was not evenly spread throughout the country. As explained earlier, its impact was regional, with the west being hardest hit. Connaught accounts for 40.4 percent of the total excess deaths, while the figure for Munster is 30.3 percent. Five western counties had the highest death rates (calculated in excess mortality per thousand): Mayo (58.4), Sligo (52.1), Roscommon (49.5), Galway (46.1) and Leitrim (42.9). Three Ulster counties, Cavan (42.7), Fermanagh (29.2) and Monaghan (28.6), also suffered high mortality rates, as did the southwestern counties of Cork (32), Clare (31.5), Tipperary (23.8) and Kerry (22.4). Rates were generally lower for counties in Leinster and eastern Ulster.[3]

Usually, famine-stricken populations make very unmalthusian recoveries; that is, after a few years the survivors repair the losses and population growth resumes. The absence of a demographic rebound in Ireland stands as the most dramatic evidence of the Famine's deadly long-term impact. It turned a slowing growth rate into a sudden dramatic collapse, followed by a population decline that continued for the remainder of the century. In addition to the obvious role of emigration, which will be discussed below, there are several reasons for this. First, Irish birth rates failed to follow the usual pattern of post-famine recovery. Although direct information about birth rates is not available, long-term census data suggests that the number of children 0–4 years old declined from 12.6 percent of population in 1841 to 12.0 percent in 1861 and then to 11.1 percent in 1881. This decline does not reflect a drop in the fertility rate *within* marriage, which remained high, but rather, the results of a fall in the marriage rate itself and an accompanying rise of celibacy in the aftermath of the Famine. The percentage of those aged 45–54 years who never married rose from 10.2 among males and 12.5 among females in 1841 to around 14 percent for both sexes in 1861 and then to 23.8 for males and 21.9 for females by 1900.[4] The increase in celibacy and the subsequent drop in the marriage

---

2. For one million excess deaths see ibid., 168. See also Mokyr, *Why Ireland Starved*, table 9.1, 266. Mokyr's figures include some 45,000 emigrants who probably died in the North American passage. His "lower bound" figure for excess mortality is 1,082,000 people.
3. See Donnelly, *The Great Irish Potato Famine*, table 6, 176 and graph on 177.
4. For birth rates see Ó Gráda and O'Rourke, "Migration as Disaster Relief," 22. For celibacy rates see Ó Gráda, *Ireland: A New Economic History*, table 9.2, 215. F. S. L. Lyons notes that between 1864 (when accurate figures first became available) and 1870, the marriage rate in Ireland was averaging around 5.1 percent in a thousand. Between 1881 and 1890 the rate fell to an average of 4 percent; *Ireland since the Famine*, 33.

rate was the result of the systemic interaction among various factors. These include changes in cultural and religious attitudes, as well as the decline in potato yields coupled with a dramatic abandonment of the subdivision of land—all factors that prior to the Famine had once facilitated early marriages among the poor. The above figures represent national trends. As always, regional patterns differed. Strong variations manifested themselves between east and west. Not until the latter part of the nineteenth century would the initial post-Famine demographic trends characterize virtually all of Ireland.[5]

Agriculture

As noted earlier, the gradual shift from tillage to pasturage had begun prior to 1845. During the Famine, however, acreage dedicated to grain crops declined from 3.8 million in 1845 to 3.1 in 1851. Acres devoted to root crops fell from 2.8 to 1.5 million. After that, however, the decline in tillage slowed considerably—by only a further 4 percent between 1851 and 1859. In fact, shortly after the Famine tillage briefly expanded, probably due to a renewed planting of flax and the use of root crops as fodder. Nevertheless, the long-term trend shows a renewed movement away from cultivation toward grazing. Thus, over the nine years following 1859, total tillage dropped by 14 percent. Between 1847 and 1910, acreage devoted to grain fell from 3.3 million acres to 1.3, while pasturage increased from 8.75 million acres in 1851 to 10.5 in 1900.[6]

To some extent, of course, these changes reflected European-wide shifts in land-holding and land use. Traditional agrarian patterns were breaking down in many areas under the impact of modern, market-driven forces. Thus, the trend away from tillage to pasturage would probably have continued in Ireland regardless of the Famine.[7] For example, it has been argued that agricultural "price shocks," especially the fall of grain prices after 1875, quickened the movement toward grazing. This in turn reduced the demand for labor, thereby maintaining the pressures on emigration. Using econometric analysis, however, Kevin O'Rourke has tested some of the assumptions involved in this argument. He concludes that, without the potato blight, the price shocks would actually have sustained tillage and slowed the shift to pasturage. The reason? The potato played a major role in feeding livestock as well as people. Cows and pigs, in turn, provided a major source of manure, so essential to potato cultivation. Healthy potatoes with their traditionally high yields would have nourished stall-fed livestock, which would have produced abundant manure, thus supporting tillage and, thereby, feeding a cheap labor force. Slowing the movement from tillage to grazing, therefore, would have supported a higher level of employment and reduced some of the impetus for emigration. Instead, thanks to the Famine, labor became more expensive, and potato cultivation, already weakened by the blight, shifted to less labor-intensive methods. The results were lower crop yields along with fewer opportunities for employment. Without the triumvirate of plentiful

---

5. Davis, "The Historiography of the Irish Famine," 21–25.
6. Lyons, *Ireland since the Famine*, 28, 35–36.
7. See O'Rourke, "Did the Great Famine Matter?" 1–4.

potatoes, sufficient manure and cheap labor, many farmers eventually abandoned the tilled fields for pastures with their promise of low labor costs and a good livestock market in Britain. With fewer agricultural jobs at home and industrial work beckoning from Britain and America, emigration rates, therefore, remained high after the Famine.[8]

Concerning the size of land holdings, even where tillage held sway, the post-Famine consolidation of holdings did not result in a continued or significant increase in farm size. True, as previously noted, the proportion of holdings under 15 acres dropped from 80 percent in 1841 to 50 percent by 1851, reflecting the demise of many of the smallest farmers, conacre families and cottiers. At the same time, holdings over 15 acres rose from 20 percent to over 50 percent. Then, however, the process slowed. From 1850 to 1900 farms under 15 acres declined by only a further 17 percent, while holdings over 15 acres grew by only 7 percent. The Famine certainly had an immediate impact upon the patterns of landholding. However, although many small holdings were swept away, the size of the remaining farms remained limited. Ireland continued to be a land of small to medium-sized farms.[9]

Moreover, even though it eliminated much of Ireland's poorest population in a few short years, the Famine did not, according to F. S. L. Lyons, change the fundamental problem of Irish rural society. It failed "to alter the structure of Irish agriculture in response to the changing pattern of British demand." Thus, even as its population continued to shrink, Ireland still produced more people than its largely agrarian economy of modest-sized farms could absorb. Nor, apart from its northeast corner, did Ireland industrialize significantly after the Famine. Even as the steady drumbeat of subsistence crises gradually faded during the second half of the nineteenth century, high levels of emigration continued; the pull of opportunity abroad matched the steady push of under employed people out of Ireland.[10]

Family, Land and Society in Rural Ireland

Ireland's current tourist landscape of sweeping vistas, often unbroken by human habitation or else dotted with picturesque ruins, is largely a post-Famine creation. Over the last century or so, it has been difficult for visitors to imagine that large stretches of almost empty land were once crowded with the cabins of cottiers and poor tenant farmers. By the end of the nineteenth century, thousands of small farms had been swept away; whole clachans had been emptied. While the remains of the abandoned Famine-era cabins disappeared through weathering and the reuse of the stone, other ruins took their place, as each year the outgoing tide of emigration left newly abandoned dwellings in its wake.

The post-Famine demographic decline remained a largely rural phenomenon. Between the Famine and World War I, Ireland's rural and village population declined

---

8. Ibid., 20.
9. Fitzpatrick, *Irish Emigration: 1801–1921*, 37. For data see Schrier, *Ireland and the American Emigration*, 71. See also Lyons, *Ireland since the Famine*, 38–39.
10. For quote see Lyons, *Ireland since the Famine*, 31.

from 7 million to less than 3 million. At the same time, the share of the town/urban population rose from one-seventh to one-third.[11] Nevertheless, for several decades after the Famine, parts of the west of Ireland still contained far more people than the agricultural economy could support. In fact, along the Atlantic seaboard certain areas, especially in Connemara, retained the pre-Famine demographic patterns of subdivision, potato dependency and high population densities. Not until the 1870s and 1880s did crop failures begin once more to force significant emigration upon these areas.[12] Even so, in 1891 the government created the Congested Districts Board to improve opportunities for those living in the Irish-speaking areas of the western seaboard, where subprime land failed to sustain even the remaining population. The board eventually became involved in land transfer from landlord to tenant ownership. As part of that process, small parcels of land in the congested districts were broken up and recombined to make somewhat larger holdings, resulting in so-called ladder or striped farms." Their fields, carefully bounded by stonewalls, can still be seen today climbing from the valleys up the sides of the hills.[13]

These changes on the ground reflected the even greater impact of the Famine upon both the Irish family and rural society in general. As discussed earlier, prior to the crisis, many families, wishing to keep their grown children around them, had pressured their landlords to continually subdivide their holdings. The Famine gradually changed that. Around 1851, Thomas Scott, agent for an Englishman who had purchased an estate near Skibbereen, tried to explain the new order of things to his tenants. "Send your sons and daughters out into the world," he urged them, "and retain your farms unbroken, instead of trying, as you do now, on how small a spot of earth you can contrive to exist." As James S. Donnelly, Jr. demonstrates, the battle against subdivision continued in West Cork well after the Famine. Over time, however, with landlords and their agents often adamant in resisting a return to subdivision, farming families had little choice but to alter their strategies for dealing with the future.[14] As a result, the farm became even more of a family enterprise than it had been before the Famine. With the emptying of the rundale townlands, the old cooperative *meitheal* system declined, and with it the sense of shared risks and rewards. Less able to hire a few laborers, families on small farms now did most of the work themselves.[15]

---

11. Ó Gráda, *Ireland: A New Economic History*, 213.
12. Davis, "The Historiography of the Irish Famine," 23. See also Moran, *Fleeing from Famine in Connemara*.
13. A congested district was defined as an area where the total rate valuation divided by the number of inhabitants equaled less than 30s. In 1891 such districts totaled 3.5 million acres and contained over half a million people. By 1910 the designated area had doubled. See Byrne, *Byrne's Dictionary of Local Irish History*, 76–77. For "ladder farms" see 173. For "striped farms" see Aalen and Whelan, "Fields," figure 12, 138.
14. See Donnelly, *The Land and the People of Nineteenth-Century Cork*, 158–63. For quote see 159. See also Dooley, *The Big House and Landed Estates of Ireland*, 36.
15. Mac Suibhne, *The End of Outrage*, 14, 97–98.

Well before the shift to tenant ownership occurred near the end of the nineteenth century, the decline of subdivision often meant that only one son, usually the eldest, succeeded the father in managing the farm. Of course, the father did not usually relinquish control of until he became too old or infirm to work, often forcing the inheriting son to delay marriage. In the meantime, the family did its best to provide a dowry for at least the eldest daughter and, if possible, educate one of the younger sons for the priesthood. Given enough resources, it might have endowed a younger daughter to become a nun. With neither land nor dowry to support a marriage, the rest of the children, if they chose to stay at home, would have remained unmarried and dependent, helping the eldest brother run the farm and living under his control. Thus, the well-known pattern of fewer and delayed marriages, dependent spinsters and aging bachelors, as well as large numbers of priests and nuns—all characteristic of rural Ireland well into the twentieth century.[16] The burden of these changes fell heaviest upon the younger members of the family, especially the women. Even before the Famine, the cottage industries, which had once involved many women, had already declined throughout much of Ireland. After the Famine, women's role in the rural economy shrank even further, along with their social life. Unmarried women lacked their bachelor brothers' freedom of movement about the townlands. Under the control of the Church and their brother or sister-in-law, they found themselves trapped in the tiny world of the farm—unless they left home, which for most meant leaving Ireland.[17]

Thus, by the end of the nineteenth century, Irish emigration to America had assumed a unique profile. While most other European immigrant groups consisted of some combination of single males and entire families, the post-Famine Irish immigrants coming into America were mostly unmarried young men and women, the latter eventually outnumbering the former. Between 1850 and 1887 around 66 percent of the Irish entering America were single, aged between 15 and 35. Over the rest of the century this group grew to 80 percent with an average age between 20 and 24. In their letters home, immigrants often maintained that America was a country for *only* the young.[18]

Opportunity in the New World did not necessarily mean complete independence from the family back home, however. Emigration became part of a family's, and not just an individual's, strategy for survival. Those who left were expected to send home money or tickets to "bring out" the younger siblings. Between 1850 and 1900, immigrants, many single women, sent $260,000,000 back to Ireland, an average of $5,000,000 a year. Forty percent of remittances consisted of tickets for the American passage. The rest, usually small amounts of money, went to parents or siblings to help pay rents and maintain the farmsteads. In fact, after 1890, when tenants could own their land, these remittances helped maintain Ireland's status as a land of small farms. Thus, immigrant children

---

16. Lyons, *Ireland since the Famine*, 39.
17. Janet Nolan, "The Great Famine and Women's Immigration from Ireland," 64–65.
18. Schrier, *Ireland and the American Emigration*, 4, 25. For female emigration see also Ó Gráda, *Ireland: A New Economic History*, 225–27; Janet Nolan, "The Great Famine and Women's Immigration from Ireland," 62–63.

sustained a large portion of Ireland's post-Famine social landscape. As David Fitzpatrick points out, emigration constituted a form of insurance for many Irish families.[19] However, this phenomenon of remittances tied to emigration reversed the potential dynamics for change in rural Ireland. Instead of modernizing the country, the steady outward flow of young people and the return stream of money underwrote and preserved the archaic, small-farm character of much of Ireland's agricultural economy. In James S. Donnelly, Jr.'s words, "American money" made it possible for many in the west "to maintain an otherwise hopeless position on uneconomic holdings and to persist in an irrational, if understandable, resistance to emigration."[20] Thus, the overseas drain of population had a general stultifying effect on both the society and economy. With the decline in population, Ireland's internal markets steadily shrank, and tax rates increased. At the same time, Britain's far-flung colonies often offered more attractive opportunities for the young than did Ireland. As a result, by removing people, especially the younger part of the population, and increasing the flow of remittances, the institutionalization of emigration eased pressures for dynamic social and economic transformation.[21]

Nevertheless, tensions within Ireland's rural society not only remained but also intensified in some areas. Surviving small farmers resisted landlords continuing efforts to "square" the land and force out small holders. For example, King's County experienced new waves of evictions, with more taking place in the later 1850s than had occurred during the famine years.[22] In later decades the "land wars" pitted tenants against landlords. However, as average people began to accumulate access to land, class divisions within rural society began to shift. Once dominated by landlord–tenant relations they became characterized by tensions between big and small farmers, as well as between the farmers and their laborers. "Strong farmers" controlling large farms wielded considerable power within the community. The "bog farmers" with small holdings on poorer land had little status. By the end of the nineteenth century, the cumulative effects of Catholic emancipation and the gradual extension of the franchise, along with the declining political influence of the landlords, produced new power combinations in Ireland. The post-Famine decades not only saw businessmen investing in land but strong farmers buying (or marrying) into local business. By the twentieth century, the triumvirate of strong farmers, town businessmen (publicans, bankers, merchants) and the parish priests had come to dominate the typical rural community.[23] Poorer farmers and workers lived on the other side of the new class divide. The resulting class tensions attracted the attention of writers such as John B. Keane. In his *The Bodhran Makers*, set in the 1950s, the small bog farmers, seeking freedom from the domination of town, money and Church, decide

---

19. Fitzpatrick, *Irish Emigration*, 30, 38; Janet Nolan, "The Great Famine and Women's Immigration from Ireland," 66; Schrier, *Ireland and the American Emigration*, 107, 151. For small farms see Lyons, *Ireland since the Famine*, 38.
20. Donnelly, *The Land and the People of Nineteenth-Century Cork*, 232.
21. See Fitzpatrick, *Irish Emigration*, 37, 38–39. For emigration and taxes see Schrier, *Ireland and the American Emigration*, 83.
22. Reilly, *The Irish Land Agent*, 149, 155.
23. Dooley, *The Big House and Landed Estates of Ireland*, 35.

to emigrate to England. Writers like Keane were among those who questioned the old emigration-as-exile theme. In doing so, they sought to diminish its power to shield their fellow countrymen from the unpleasant realities of class conflict.

Living Standards and the Post-Famine Economy

There are two ways to raise a country's standard of living. One is to "grow" the economy so that everyone benefits: "A rising tide raises all boats," as it is commonly said. On the other hand, sinking the smallest craft would at least increase the average size of the remaining boats. The Famine accomplished something like that in Ireland. With the almost immediate loss of over two million people, Ireland had fewer mouths to feed and fewer hands to employ. As a result, the country experienced a gradual rise in living standards among the remaining small farmers and laborers.[24] Wages rose, especially in the areas where they had been lowest. Among other things, this opened the emigrant's trail to some of the surviving poor. Consequently, the number of agrarian laborers fell from 1.2 million in 1845 to 0.7 million in 1861. By that time wages may have risen by 57 percent. The resulting tighter labor market also produced a higher land–labor ratio, along with a reduction in pauperism. In the long run, wages appear to have doubled between 1850 and 1894. Initially caused by the loss of many laborers during the famine years, higher wages were sustained by the continued drain of emigration, as well as a falling birth rate due to fewer marriages.[25]

Some improvements in living standards were a grim reflection of the class-based impact of the Famine, which, among other things, swept away most of Ireland's worst dwellings, along with their occupants. By 1851 only in County Kerry did fourth-class cabins account for more than 25 percent of the housing stock. A decade later only one-tenth of the Irish population occupied such houses.[26] In addition to living in better dwellings, many small farmers and laborers managed to shift their diet from total dependency on potatoes to a greater inclusion of cereal foods, such as oatmeal or maize. Further signs of a rising standard of living may be seen in the higher consumption of luxuries such as tobacco, tea and sugar. More significantly, average life expectancy, under 40 years before the Famine, reached 50 by the early 1870s. The literacy rate (surprisingly high to begin with) rose from 47 percent in 1841 to 53 percent in 1851, reaching 90 percent in 1911, partly due to depopulation and partly to the success of the National School system.[27]

---

24. For the rise of living standards and overall quality of life, see Donnelly, *The Land and the People of Nineteenth-Century Cork*, 219–50.
25. For agricultural workers see Ó Gráda, *Ireland: A New Economic History*, 205–6; for wages see 236, 239, 242; Schrier, *Ireland and the American Emigration*, 77. While cottiers and spalpeens outnumbered farmers in 1845, by 1900 they had virtually disappeared. See MacCurtain, "Pre-Famine Peasantry in Ireland: Definition and Theme," 198.
26. For fourth-class housing see Kennedy et al., *Mapping the Great Irish Famine*, Map 32, 83. For housing data see Schrier, *Ireland and the American Emigration*, 82–83.
27. Ó Gráda, *Ireland*, 239–40, 242.

As the return of blight-induced, localized famine conditions in the 1860s and in 1870s demonstrated, primary reliance on the potato had not ended completely for all Ireland's remaining poor. Nevertheless, after the passage of the Land Act of 1870, which granted tenants some security of tenure and compensation for improvements, remaining potato dependency began to fade.[28] The potato's loss of dominance can be explained, in part, by the fact that the crop never regained its pre-Famine level of productivity. Although the occasional return of the blight was a factor, farmers, as noted earlier, employing a smaller, more expensive work force, could no longer afford the kind of highly labor-intensive efforts that had once produced massive potato harvests.[29]

For a time, things also improved for Ireland's landowning class, which included fewer members of the old Ascendancy. Land values, depressed by the Encumbered Estates Act, eventually recovered, and for a while the shift from cultivation to grazing offset higher labor costs. Between 1850 and 1900, the total area under cultivation (excluding hay fields) shrank by 50 percent. At the same time, meadowlands for pasturage increased by 65 percent.[30] As noted in the last chapter, however, this change, along with the gradual decline of unprotected grain prices, ended the dream of extending to the west of Ireland an English-style, high-farming economy. By the 1870s, land agitation, political changes and falling agricultural prices began to reduce the power of Ireland's landowners. Toward the end of the century, the British government began buying them out and selling the land to a new class of farmer/owners. In the 1890s tenant ownership, proposed half a century earlier by George Poulett Scrope and John Stuart Mill, finally came to fruition.[31]

Emigration

As suggested earlier in this chapter, emigration was the main reason for Ireland's continual decline in population. Had the famine-induced exodus stopped after the early 1850s, Ireland's population might have recovered. However, the drain continued. In the decade between the 1845 and 1855, 2.1 million Irish people fled the country. By 1900 around five million people had emigrated, leaving Ireland's population roughly where it had been in 1790—about 4.5 million people.[32] It did not start to grow again until the latter part of the twentieth century.

Cormac Ó Gráda and Kevin O'Rourke have focused attention on several factors that link the effects of this long-term emigration to the Famine. First, in most acute subsistence crises, while the hungry often migrate if they can, they usually remain close to their

---

28. Salaman, *The History and Social Influence of the Potato*, 329. For limitations of the Land Act see Donnelly, *The Land and the People of Nineteenth-Century Cork*, 204.
29. Ó Gráda, *Ireland*, 207. By the 1860s and 1870s potato harvests were averaging half of their pre-Famine yields. See Ó Gráda, *Black '47 and Beyond*, 227–28.
30. Schrier, *Ireland and the American Emigration*, 72.
31. Terrence A. M. Dooley notes that landlordism in Ireland did not really end until the Irish Free State government passed the confiscatory Land Acts of 1923, 1931 and 1933. See the author's "Landlords and the Land Question, 1879–1909," 135–36.
32. Ibid., 147; see also Miller, *Emigrants and Exiles*, 291.

home areas. Today, food donations often help keep them in place. Therefore, when the crisis passes, many survivors return home, resume their lives and contribute to the process of repopulation. However, whereas food is shipped to today's famine victims from the outside, during the Famine "the hungry went to where the food was, and they never returned." In this respect, the Irish Famine had "a permanent impact," establishing a pattern that did not change. Ó Gráda and O'Rourke estimate that, without continued emigration, Ireland's population might have recovered in 15–20 years. As it was, unlike many other European immigrant groups, once they left home, the Irish did not return. There were relative few "birds of passage" in their ranks.[33] Ó Gráda and O'Rourke's second factor is a bit more complicated. Prior to and during the Famine, many, who might have emigrated, lacked the money to do so. They were caught in a "poverty trap," which, in effect, limited the effectiveness of emigration in mitigating the deadly impact of the crisis. As noted above, thanks to the sharp fall in population due to death and initial emigration, wages for laborers rose, breaking the poverty trap that had kept the poor at home. At the same time, declining costs for transatlantic travel, along with remittances from abroad, made emigration affordable, while industrializing America's need for workers made it increasingly feasible. Jolted into existence by the Famine, continued large-scale emigration foreclosed Ireland's potential for long-term demographic renewal.[34]

There were, of course, cultural factors that had inhibited emigration prior to and even during the Famine. Before the crisis, traditional attachments to family and place hindered migration. The Irish landscape, for example, was and remains named to a degree that is hard for most outsiders to appreciate. Within a townland almost every hill, field, lake, stream, even rocks, carry names related to previous inhabitants, to historical events or to Irish mythology. The surrounding hills and mountains often bear testimony to ancient legends, events and graves. For those born into it, this landscape encouraged a special kind of cultural literacy; a native could read the land like a book. It was part of his or her *dúchas* or inheritance. Little wonder than that, according to Kerby A. Miller, many emigrants treated the prospect of leaving home as a sort of exile. Who, they might have wondered, would voluntarily choose to leave such a richly inscribed land to try to live in the unfamiliar, essentially blank, unreadable world of the stranger across the seas? Only dire necessity would force people to abandon loved ones, friends, neighbors and the meaningful landscape in which they had been raised. At a very deep level, the Famine initiated the weakening of these traditional bonds to home and townland, especially among those born into traditional Gaelic communities. The catastrophe began the process of shattering those inhibitions, producing what David Fitzpatrick calls, a "transformation of mentality," more powerful than "any calculation of costs and risks, which insured that the Irish would become an emigrant people." Once initiated, the process

---

33. For quote see Ó Gráda and O'Rourke, "Migration as Disaster Relief," 5; see also 3–4, 17–18. For the weak attraction of "return immigration" to Ireland, see Ó Gráda, *Ireland*, 227–28. Schrier, *Ireland and the American Emigration*, 152.
34. Ó Gráda and O'Rourke, "Migration as Disaster Relief," 5, 16, 19.

was, nevertheless, slow to take hold in certain areas. As James S. Donnelly, Jr. suggests, despite poverty, resistance to abandoning hearth and homeland remained strong in parts of the post-Famine west.[35]

Nonetheless, traditional inhibitions did eventually weaken in the face of other factors that encouraged emigration. One was the systemic link between grazing and employment. As noted above, the movement from cultivation to less labor-intensive ranching resulted in the loss of employment opportunities, increasing the pressures to emigrate. Arnold Schrier found that in 18 Poor Law Unions, a decline of 35 percent of the rural population was matched by a 60 percent loss of tillage land. Between 1851 and 1881, there is a clear correlation between the expansion of pasturage, the reduction of plow land and the continued decline of the population.[36]

Gradually, through a combination of forces, emigration became an established feature of Irish life. Between 1845 and 1890, the annual emigration rate dropped below 55,000 in only two periods: 1857–64 (around the time of the American Civil War) and 1876–80 (a period of widespread economic depression). By 1890 only three-fifths of those born in Ireland still lived there; three million had moved off the island. As stated above, by the end of the century, the Irish population had declined to around 4.5 million, where it stabilized even as an average of 38,000 continued to leave Ireland annually until 1914.[37] The resulting depopulation became an enormous burden to the country. Discovering that eventually one Irish child in three was born to emigrate, one observer wrote: "The moral and psychological effect of that fact is immense. It paralyzes certain areas. It is a dead weight upon the spirit of the whole country, a dead hand upon her economy."[38] No doubt there were many young people who saw emigration as a clear-eyed, although hardly casual, choice in response to the sever lack of economic and social opportunity in Ireland. However, enhanced by the Famine experience, the traditional belief that emigration was something forced upon the Irish, prevented some people from acknowledging responsibility for their choices. The "exile" theme also shielded an emerging nationalistic, bourgeois Catholic Ireland from recognizing the inequalities and contradictions within Irish society. It was easier to blame the continued exodus on the English and the landlords.[39]

The demographic patterns did not change even after Irish independence in the 1920s. Admittedly, worldwide depression and wars presented enormous obstacles to the new country. Nevertheless, the failure of an independent Ireland to support all its reduced population did little for national self-confidence. Although conditions improved after World War II, the Irish economy grew slowly at best, and emigration persisted as a fact

---

35. Donnelly, *The Land and the People of Nineteenth-Century Cork*, 230–31. See also Fitzpatrick, *Irish Emigration*, 26. For exile and *dúchas* see Miller, *Emigrants and Exiles*, 105–6. For traditional Irish attitudes toward emigration see 131–32, 193–279.
36. Schrier, *Ireland and the American Emigration*, 74.
37. The dates for emigration rates are approximate, based on David Fitzpatrick's graph in figure 1, 4; see also 5. For other data see Turner, *After the Famine*, 10.
38. Rev. A. A. Luce, quoted by Mac Éirni, "Famine and the Irish Diaspora," 595.
39. See Miller, *Emigrants and Exiles*, 427–29, 478–82.

of life for many young people even into the 1970s and 1980s. This reversed itself temporarily in the 1990s and early 2000s, as Ireland morphed into the "Celtic Tiger." The subsequent economic collapse, however, reminded many young Irish man and women that the long post-Famine emigrant trail was still open.

The Diaspora

The Famine had a direct impact on almost every aspect of Irish emigration, from transportation to reception overseas and settlement in the receiving countries. As noted in previous chapters, the numbers of Irish immigrants arriving in Britain and in North America jumped dramatically during the Famine. In 1841, only 6.2 percent of those born in Ireland lived abroad; in 1851 the percentage was 22.8, rising to 38.8 percent by 1891. In 1841 there were 291,000 Irish-born living in England and Wales and 126,000 in Scotland. In 1861 the numbers had climbed to 602,000 and 204,000 respectively.[40]

The sudden upsurge in Irish emigration contributed to the restructuring of the transatlantic immigrant traffic out of Ireland through Liverpool. Surveys of Irish-born immigrants in Albany, New York, in 1854 and 1856 revealed that 67 percent had sailed from Liverpool. Only six percent had embarked from Cork, Sligo or Galway.[41] Arriving in the United States by the thousands, the sudden surge in Irish immigrants proved almost overwhelming for the receiving cities. As Kevin Kenny has noted: "Never before or since did the Irish account for so high a proportion of American immigration as during the famine era." The Irish constituted 45.6 percent of all immigrants in the 1840s and 35.2 percent in the 1850s. In that decade two-fifths of the foreign-born in the United States were Irish.[42]

The impact of the Famine migration is best understood by focusing on receiving cities rather than on countries and regions. By 1852, for example, 22.3 percent of Liverpool's population had been born in Ireland, making it Britain's most Irish city. In the United States, the largest East Coast cities received the bulk of the famine immigration. In 1850 the Irish-born made up 26 percent of New York City's residents, accounting for about half of its immigrant population. They also constituted most of the city's charity cases and inmates in its almshouses.[43] In Philadelphia, one half of the 72,000 Irish-born in the city had arrived between 1846 and 1850. Around 9,000 came in the first nine months of 1849. The numbers in Boston were equally dramatic. Prior to the 1840s, immigrant arrivals never topped more than 4,000 in any given year. In 1849 alone, the city received 28,917 newcomers, mostly Irish. Oscar Handlin describes the effect upon the city: "By their immobility the Irish crammed the city, recasting its boundaries and disfiguring its

---

40. Mac Énrie, "Famine and the Irish Diaspora," 592.
41. Byron, *Irish America*, 61*n*. The survey involved those expressing their intention to become citizens.
42. Kenny, *The American Irish*, 104.
43. Mac Éinrie, 592, 593. 595. See also Kenny, *The American Irish*, 106, 107.

physical appearance; by their poverty they introduced new problems of disease, vice and crime, with which neither they nor the community were ready to cope."[44]

Reginald Byron divides the Famine emigration to America into roughly two groups. The first, arriving mostly in the early years of the crisis, resembled pre-Famine emigrants and included somewhat better-off representatives of the middle or lower middle class (some of whom were Protestants), who were literate, fluent in English and had relatives in America. Bringing with them some education, skills and capital, Byron suggests that this group would today be labeled "economic refugees," seeking to improve their lot. By contrast, most of Byron's second group, whom he calls the "true refugees," were mostly poor Catholics, driven more by an instinct for survival than by any plan to climb up the next rung of the economic ladder. Although most spoke English, many were the products of rural, Gaelic culture. They possessed few skills and little experience beyond those of the spade farmer. Moreover, unlike the first group, they were less likely to have relatives to meet and help them. After the initial flood of people fleeing the Famine, however, the status of those leaving Ireland reverted to the pre-Famine profile: they were economic migrants in search of a better life.[45] As noted above, this post-Famine exodus was by no means haphazard. As those belonging to the Famine wave settled in, the survivors began to attract family members or neighbors from Ireland. As a result, subsequent arrivals often had names and addresses to contact when they landed. Those already established in America often sent steamship tickets back to Ireland, along with their remittances, to help "bring out" other family members. The power of this "pull" or "path-dependent" factor helps account for the continued high rate of emigration even after the "push factors" of hunger and fear slackened and Irish living standards rose.[46]

By forcing so many people to emigrate in so short a time, the Famine created conditions in the receiving cities that would affect how new arrivals lived and how they were treated. During the Famine, many people left Ireland in a panic, without having had time to plan and prepare for such dramatic changes in their lives. In Oscar Handlin's words, "This was flight, and precise destination mattered little." Of those disembarking in New York City, around 75 percent were laborers and servants, compared to 60 percent of arrivals in 1836. Kerby A. Miller suggests, therefore, that the Famine immigrants were less able than their predecessors to fend for themselves. Many had spent what money they had on the trip and arrived at their destinations almost penniless. Coming from rural areas, most immigrants had no commercial or industrial skills that would have eased their way into their adopted countries. Yet, lacking the resources (and often the desire) to return to farming, the average Irish immigrant, compared to the native-born American, was more likely to become an urbanite.[47]

---

44. Handlin, *Boston's Immigrants*, 88; for data see 51–52. For Philadelphia see Gallman, *Receiving Erin's Children*, 32.
45. Kennedy, *Unhappy the Land*, 25. See also Byron, *Irish America*, 52–53.
46. See Ó Gráda, *Ireland*, 231; Ó Gráda and O'Rourke, "Migration as Disaster Relief," 21–22. J. Matthew Gallman reports that family members in America often wrote advice and instructions of the reverse sides of the tickets sent back to Ireland; 2.
47. Kenny, *The American Irish*, 105. See also Handlin, *Boston's Immigrants*, 51; Miller, *Emigrants and Exiles*, 296. For 75 percent see 295.

While later generations of Irish immigrants built powerful religious, charitable, cultural and political institutions in America, mere survival became the primary challenge for those who arrived during the Famine. Although they and their children did begin the slow climb up the economic ladder, poverty lay at the heart of the Famine generation's experience. Fleeing hunger and unemployment in Ireland, they found themselves gripped by deep, grinding destitution in their new homes. Industrializing America with its expanding cities needed laborers. However, the hard, backbreaking work open to the Irish afforded them with only the worst sorts of housing in whatever city they settled. Heirs to all that often accompanies poverty—violence, disease, alcoholism, mental illness—the difficult lives of many of the Famine emigrants were often short. Many did not live to see the impressive successes Irish America would eventually achieve. For the most part, the Famine generation of the Irish diaspora in America did not thrive; it endured.[48]

The Famine occupied an uncertain place in the memories of subsequent generations. During the remainder of the nineteenth century, it was hard for emigrants and their descendants to shake off the stigma of association with the ragged, half-starved Irish Catholic paupers who, in the words of Mary C. Kelly, were seen to occupy "a contemptable and odious state in the annals of city and regional history." For those attracted to nationalistic fervor, however, the pain and shame of the Famine became an enduring wrong to be righted. For such people, hating the British precluded forgetting the disaster. Gradually, however, the emergence of an independent Irish nation and the solidifying of an Irish American sense of success pushed awareness of the Famine into the background. Then, it gradually reemerged during the decades after World War II.[49] Primed perhaps by interest in the Holocaust and by the success of Alex Haley's *Roots*, not to mention "the Troubles" back in Ireland, by the sesquicentennial of the Famine in 1995, Irish America was finally prepared to accept the Great Hunger as an integral part of its history and identity. Famine memorials appeared, along with curriculum designs for schools. In 2013 Quinnipiac University opened Ireland's Great Hunger Museum.

Politics in Ireland

Irish politics, which seemed moribund by the end of the Famine, revived during the 1870s and early 1880s as "the land question" became the predominant issue. The Famine had liquidated much of the pauper class, while the landlords continued to clear out many of the poorer farmers. Ironically, this "clarified" the class structure in rural Ireland by helping to create solid, middle-class tenant farmers, who, working larger holdings, could now begin to imagine better lives for themselves and their families. They began to demand the so-called three Fs— fair rents, fixity of tenure and fair sale—lower rents, security of tenure and compensation for improvements they made on the land. Tenants'

---

48. See Miller, *Emigrants and Exiles*, 319; Kenny, *The American Irish*, 107–8.
49. For a detailed account of the memory of the Famine within Irish American culture, see Kelly, *Ireland's Great Famine in Irish-American History*. For quote see 24.

rights eventually became the rallying cry of the Land League, which dominated Irish politics in the late 1870s and the 1880s.

It is important to keep in mind that these tenants' issues reflected the needs and ambitions of a newly emboldened farming class, not those of the remaining small holders and laborers who had been the principal victims of the Famine. Indeed, the better-off farmers were, as S. J. Connolly has pointed out, the beneficiaries of the disaster. The removal of so many of the rural poor through death, eviction and emigration enabled tenant farmers to gradually become the dominant class in rural Ireland, allowing them to claim that *they* represented "the people of Ireland."[50] (At the same time, the reduced agrarian labor force, motivated by the example of the tenant farmers, tried to champion their own economic advancement by demanding better wages.) The movement for tenants' rights became the halfway house for the more profound demand for tenant ownership. Young Islander James Fintan Lalor had helped place the question of land ownership at the heart of Irish nationalism. Once launched, ideas for land reform grew along with Land League agitation. In this, by eradicating most of the bottom rung of rural Irish society, the Famine had once again played its role. As long as the Irish "peasantry" had appeared as an indistinguishable blur, a ragged, seemingly impoverished mass that refused to organize itself into a "proper" class structure, the idea of tenant ownership had seemed absurd to most British observers. However, as solid Irish farmers gradually emerged from the ranks of the old peasantry, perceptions began to change. The combination of political agitation and declining grain prices in the later part of the nineteenth century led to a series of acts in 1881, 1885 and 1891 that facilitated the purchase of land by Irish farmers. By the end of the century, Ireland's "land question," as it had been framed for much of the nineteenth century, had been settled. The "*Irish* question," of course loomed larger than ever.

Although constitutional nationalism had been considerably weakened by the split in the Repeal ranks and by O'Connell's death during the Famine, the cause did not die. Kept alive by Isaac Butt, it received strength at the hands Charles Stewart Parnell. Just as O'Connell had built Repeal on the back of Catholic Emancipation, Parnell moved from the Land League and its battles with the government and the landlords to resuscitate the Liberator's dream of a reestablished Irish Parliament. Home Rule, having finally passed the British Parliament in 1912, was to have gone into effect in 1914, when World War I changed everybody's plans.

Although constitutional nationalism had widespread popular support in Ireland during the second half of the nineteenth century, the appeal of revolution espoused by the Young Irelanders managed to survive. Almost 20 years after their rising in 1848, the Fenians revived the separatist dream of independence. Drawing part of their inspiration and anger from the failure of the British to prevent mass starvation during the Famine, the Fenians staged an abortive rising in 1867. Although initially no more successful than the Young Irelanders attempt at insurrection, the Fenian movement, part of which evolved into the Irish Republican Brotherhood (IRB), established branches

---

50. Connolly, "The Great Famine and Irish Politics," 47–49.

in the United States and in Europe. To F. S. L. Lyons, this internationalization of the "Irish question" marks the principal political consequence of the Famine. Irish resentment against England, intensified by the experience of the disaster, traveled along with the millions who left the island between the 1840s and 1900. Emigrants and their children provided emotional, as well as organizational and financial support, without which active nationalist movements, from Home Rule to Fenian agitation, could not have been sustained.[51] Eventually, it was a cell of the Fenian IRB that laid the plans for Dublin's Easter Rising of 1916, the act that eventually led to the Anglo-Irish War of 1919–21 and the establishment of an independent 26-county Ireland.

Religion and Sectarian Tensions

During the Famine, many Protestant and Catholic clergymen risked their lives to tend the needs of the sick and dying, regardless of their faith. Unfortunately, as explained earlier, the disaster also created situations that exacerbated sectarian tensions. Among Ulster Protestants, the crisis hreatened a sectarian worldview based on the assumption that they were divinely favored to prosper while Catholics were destined to bear God's wrath. The fact that the Famine hit all segments of Ulster society had to be obscured if not denied. As Christine Kinealy argues, the Famine sowed the seeds for one of the key myths of Protestant exceptionalism: that Ulster had escaped the ravages of the Famine, a myth that official history in Northern Ireland has been keen to maintain. Yet the Famine claimed 17 percent of Ulster's population, a higher proportion than that of Leinster. And, of course, the dead included Protestants as well as Catholics. Once the decline in population densities in Ulster is considered, the true impact of the Famine there is revealed.[52]

There was more at stake, however, than simply the idea of Protestant exceptionalism. Acknowledging the depredations wrought by the Famine might have threatened the Protestant power structure within the province. This, in turn, might have endangered allegiance to the Union and exacerbated class tensions among Protestants. Downplaying the sufferings of the Protestant poor also made economic sense for those at the top. It justified the generally parsimonious response from Ulster's landlords. In 1846, when as many as 40 percent of the residents of certain Protestant areas of Belfast were dependent on private soup kitchens, a letter appeared in a local newspaper complaining of the silence of the wealthy, who preferred "the fine philosophy that would starve the poor for the honour of the rich."[53] Overall, the Famine experience encouraged Ulster's Protestant community to turn inward. Having denied the pain inflicted upon their own community,

---

51. Lyons, *Ireland since the Famine*, 4.
52. Bew, *Ireland: The Politics of Enmity*, 206. For percentage of decline in population densities see Kinealy, "'The Famine Killed Everything,'" 22–25.
53. Kinealy, "'The Famine Killed Everything,'" 24. See also Miller et al., "The Great Famine and Religious Demography in Mid-Nineteenth Century Ulster," 431–32.

many Protestants chose to withdraw even further from their Roman Catholic neighbors into an imagined exceptionalism long embodied in Ulster's "moral landscape."

The Roman Catholic Church in Ireland had a rather different experience. Despite its expansion after 1820, at the time of the Famine the Church still lacked both sufficient churches and priests to fully minister to Ireland's continuously growing population. Among the uneducated, folk beliefs, some derived from the ancient pagan past, mingled freely with imperfectly understood religious doctrine. Only about half of the Catholic population could be considered "regular" communicants, then defined as attending confession and mass at least twice a year (Christmas and Easter). Writing about the Catholic tenantry of Donegal, Breandán Mac Suibhne notes that, apart from marriage, baptism, funerals and "making the pattern," for most people "chapel and clerical-directed devotions did not have a central place in their lives."[54] However, as a result of the Famine, the Church lost nearly one-third of its communicants, while the number of priests increased by a quarter. Between 1847 and 1860 the priests-to-people ratio grew from one in 2,800 to one in 1,500. (By the early twentieth century it was one in 1,100, the lowest in the world.) As more churches were built, for the first time in three centuries most of Ireland's Catholic population could be accommodated on any given Sunday.[55] This helped the Church establish greater doctrinal and institutional control over the religious ideas, not to mention the behavior, of its communicants, thereby extending its influence over the culture and society. What Emmet Larkin has called the "devotional revolution," its roots already established in pre-Famine society, consolidated its influence during the latter part of the nineteenth century. It expanded into the "cultural vacuum" caused by the Famine. Kevin Whelan describes Irish Catholicism as "a crucial bearer of order and identity in a nineteenth century world of unprecedented flux," producing what he calls a "modernizing crusade."[56]

A number of factors facilitated the interpenetration of the Church throughout much of Irish society. As the parish priest became a ubiquitous and, by virtue of his clerical status, a commanding figure in most communities, power inevitably moved in his direction. He was often the best educated Catholic in a community. In many cases the son of a farmer, he came from the people he served, and his position gave him natural authority. At the same time, he belonged to a vast hierarchical network headed by bishops and archbishops, ultimately responsible to the Pope, all of which greatly augmented the voice of the Church when it chose to speak out on issues. This was significant, since, during the post-Famine period, increased democracy within the United Kingdom resulted in placing local government in the hands of the Roman Catholic majority throughout much of Ireland. At the same time, the absence of an Irish Parliament created a power vacuum into which the Church could and did step, making religious affiliation, in Kevin Whelan's words, "a surrogate for national identity."[57] Even after Irish independence, Catholics as

---

54. Mac Suibhne, *The End of Outrage*, 3.
55. Larkin, *The Pastoral Role of the Roman Catholic Church*, 214. For lowest priest-people ratio see Kevin Whelan, "The Cultural Effects of the Famine," 274.
56. Kevin Whelan, "The Cultural Effects of the Famine," 275. See also Larkin, "The Devotional Revolution in Ireland, 1850–75."
57. Ibid., 274.

a group seemed willing to hand over many functions, such as education and social services, to the Church, allowing the bishops to wield virtual veto power over certain kinds of social legislation. The Irish Constitution of 1932 recognized the Roman Catholic Church's "special role" in Irish society. This clause was finally dropped by referendum in the 1990s.

Language

By the eve of the Famine, the daily use of the Irish language had all but disappeared in most areas east of the Shannon and the Bann. Nevertheless, population increase, especially in the west where Gaelic remained strong, meant that there were at least as many Irish speakers in 1845 as there had been in 1800. The census of 1851 suggests that, nationwide, a quarter of the population, over a million and a half people, spoke Irish, although only 4.88 percent of them were Gaelic monoglots. The bulk of Irish speakers lived in the provinces of Munster (43.91 percent) and Connaught (50.77 percent). In Ulster only Donegal had a significant number of Irish speakers, half of whom spoke only Gaelic. Thus, according to the census, Gaelic remained the everyday speech of more than one half of the inhabitants along the western seaboard. However, the Census figures probably represent an undercount, since the authorities had placed the question regarding language at the end of the form, almost as a kind of footnote. Recent estimates place the number of Gaelic speakers at the time of the Famine at between three and three and a half million, which would have been a historic high.[58]

Nevertheless, the language had been declining within certain key sectors of Irish society for centuries. Beginning with the Tudor reconquest and extending through the end of the seventeenth century, English became the primary language of power and governance throughout Ireland. By the eighteenth century, it predominated in commerce, trade and employment, taking on an aura of authority and progress. It also become the language of literacy. While Gaelic literature continued to appear in the eighteenth century, by the beginning of the nineteenth few new works in Irish were being written. Thus, the Irish language rapidly became confined to oral communications. Few of those who spoke Irish daily could read or write it. Therefore, outside of the face-to-face communities of the Gaelic-speaking townlands, the language faced stiff competition from English. After 1800, class and geography largely determined who spoke Gaelic. By then the Catholic middle class had largely abandoned the language. As a result, it became the speech of the rural poor living in the west of Ireland. Under such circumstances the question of linguistic survival depended upon the conscious decisions made by its speakers, as they sought to balance their Gaelic-infused culture and traditions against the economic

---

58. Ó Gráda, *Black '47 and Beyond*, 216. For the geography of the Irish language see maps in Ó Cuív, *A View of the Irish Language*, 138–40; Nic Craith, "Legacy and Loss: The Great Silence and its Aftermath," 580–81. For numbers of Irish speakers see 582–83. Gearóid Ó Tuathaigh reports that before 1881 the undercount of Irish speakers might have been as high as 40 percent; *I mBéal an Bháis: The Great Famine and the Language Shift in Nineteenth-Century Ireland*, 10.

and social prestige of English.⁵⁹ Although all these factors had been in play before the potato blight, the Famine dealt Gaelic a double blow. First, Irish speakers tended to live in the areas that suffered the highest mortality and/or significant emigration rates. Kerby A. Miller estimates that between one-quarter to one-third of Famine immigrants in America spoke Gaelic. Adding in the number of immigrants who were only one or two generations removed from using Irish in everyday speech, Miller concludes that mid-century Irish America had a distinctly "Gaelic cast."⁶⁰

The second problem was that back home, Ireland's remaining Gaelic speakers had to contend with a significant loss of confidence in the language. The Famine had further diminished the status of Gaelic, linking it to poverty and helplessness, while conversely increasing the economic and cultural prestige of English. In such circumstances, what did it mean to speak Gaelic? What value could it have, especially when many of one's children would have to emigrate to Britain or to America where Gaelic would be useless? Some leaders, like Archbishop MacHale of Tuam, Galway, urged bilingualism: "Keep the Irish which is your own and learn English," he advised. Nevertheless, as more children went to the National Schools, parents in Irish-speaking areas were usually more anxious for them to learn English than to retain Irish. In many instances, they even coopted the school masters, using the infamous tally stick to punish their children when they used Irish at home.⁶¹ This forced march into the Anglophone world no doubt had devastating effects upon the linguistic abilities of an entire generation of Irish children. Forced to abandon the Gaelic fluency of their families and communities, many of these children had to negotiate the broader society with an imperfect command of English. As Seán de Fréine has argued, the system represented a kind of "linguistic vandalism," resulting in poor levels of education, low levels of self-esteem and self-confidence, and a "stage irishry" patois that made it difficult for English speakers to take "Paddy" seriously.⁶² As emigration became the expected path for much of Ireland's youth, some families stopped speaking Irish even in the home so that their children would not waste time learning a language that would have no currency in "the land of the stranger." By 1911 only 12 percent of Ireland's population spoke Gaelic. The decline continued well into the twentieth century, despite the efforts of the newly independent Irish government to support the language. As David P. Nally has observed, among European countries that gained independence, the Republic of Ireland alone has failed to fully revive its hereditary language.⁶³

---

59. Fulton, "Hegemonic Discourse in Brian Friel's *The Freedom of the City*," 64–65. For middle-class abandonment of Gaelic see Grace, *The Middle Class of Callan, Co. Kilkenny, 1825–45*, 31.
60. Miller, *Emigrants and Exiles*, 297–98. Daniel Cassidy's *How the Irish Invented Slang: The Secret Language of the Crossroads* suggests the extent of the linguistic legacy of Miller's "Gaelic America."
61. The "tally stick," hung around a student's neck, was notched each time a child spoke Irish at home. The next day the school mater would mete out the punishment for each offense. For this and for MacHale's quote see Wall, "The Decline of the Irish Language," 86.
62. De Fréine, "The Cultural Consequences of the Great Famine," 149.
63. Nally, *Human Encumbrances*, 205. See also Tymoczko and Ireland, "Language and Tradition in Ireland: Prolegomena," 12.

Of course, the loss of Gaelic meant the gain of English. As Maureen Wall, an historian fluent in Irish, pointed out, the increasing involvement of the Irish people in politics from the late eighteenth century on gave a special impetus and purpose to their use of English. The campaigns for Catholic emancipation, Repeal, the Land League and Home Rule were all carried out primarily in English. Although Gaelic became a sort of linguistic icon within the republican movement, English was the dominant language of nationalist politics.[64] And, of course, landing in America, Irish immigrants, even most of the Irish speakers among them, had an immediate linguistic advantage over almost anyone coming from the Continent.[65] Ironically, this advantage helped to further undercut the position of Gaelic back home. Since Irish was essentially an oral language for most of those who used it, the highly valued "American letters" (often with dollars enclosed) from a family's overseas children were invariably written in English. In many Gaelic-speaking households it may have fallen to the local school master or a school-going child to read these letters to illiterate parents.[66]

Contrary to the stereotype of the romantic, impractical Celt, it seems that after the Famine many Irish speakers made the hard, pragmatic decision to make sure that their children could speak and read English, leaving Gaelic behind. This, in effect, meant that the Irish themselves seem to have willed the decline of their language. Gearóid Ó Tuathaigh, however, warns against a premature embrace of that word "pragmatic" and all it suggests. Even before the Famine, all the centers of political, economic, administrative and even social power were confined to the Anglophone world. Until 1890, no significant Irish organization supported the preservation of Gaelic. Neither the Roman Catholic Church nor most of the earlier nationalist groups incorporated Gaelic into their visions for the Irish people. Under such circumstances, and aware that so many of their children were fated to emigrate to English-speaking countries, it is hard to say that the Irish "pragmatically" chose to abandon Gaelic.[67] A hungry person is hardly being pragmatic in reaching for a proffered meal.

Yet, Ó Tuathaigh does ask why acquiring English meant abandoning Gaelic for so many families? Bilingualism is common in other countries. Why not in Ireland? Ó Tuathaigh points out that the alternative of bilingualism may have been lost early in Ireland. Many educated Gaelic-speaking leaders were driven out of the country in the seventeenth and eighteenth centuries. With a few exceptions, the Catholic leadership, clerical and lay, could see no benefit in promoting the language. Nor did the Catholic bourgeoisie, from whose ranks so many political, business and religious leaders emerged.[68] Although he held forth in Gaelic at his manorial court at Derrynane, Daniel

---

64. Kennedy, *Unhappy the Land:* 66. Wall, "The Decline of the Irish Language," 88. See also Ó Tuathaigh, *I mBéal an Bháis*, 28.
65. Reginald Byron speculates that, when compared to other immigrant groups, the relatively rapid social and economic rise of the Irish immigrants in Albany, New York, was due to their command of English; *Irish America*, 62.
66. Such a moment is captured in James Brenan's painting "News from America," See Ó Tuathaigh, *I mBéal an Bháis*, 34.
67. Ibid., 25.
68. Ibid., 39–40.

O'Connell led the drives for Emancipation and Repeal in English. Thus, the Famine struck at a time when Gaelic enjoyed little broad social and political support. Given the impact of the communal trauma created by the Famine, it would have taken a good deal of cultural confidence for individuals and families to hold on to the language of their ancestors. Nevertheless, the Irish language has survived. In fact, it seems to have moved beyond the Gaeltach into Ireland's urban areas. It is spoken on radio and television, and, more importantly, perhaps, it is reclaiming its role in Ireland's intellectual and artistic life. Whether or not it thrives in the twenty-first century, it seems destined to at least survive.

Silence, Memory and Selectivity

On the surface, it may appear that, as it slipped into the past, the Great Famine became enveloped in a "Great Silence." Perhaps the searing pain of the event may have been too much to sustain, much less encourage, memories of the experience. However, through the work of the Irish Folklore Commission during the first half of the twentieth century, it turns out that quite a bit had been remembered and passed down from parents to children and then on to grandchildren.[69] Of course, in the process of oral transmission, much information became lost, forgotten, suppressed or misinterpreted. Moreover, the memories that survivors choose to share with posterity were shaped and filtered through the culture, as well as the mores and the needs, of their communities. The oral tradition, therefore, is not a ragbag of memories and myths. It is an active, selective process, a winnowing of what might be remembered from what the community might wish forgotten or repressed. As Cormac Ó Gráda notes, folk memory, often flawed and confused, can be "consciously or subconsciously—selective, evasive and apologetic." For example, there may have been family and community reputations to uphold. According to Piaras Mac Éirni, "The intolerable intimacy of what was done and what was known, must have been one of the reasons why the folklore of the Famine often recounted that the greatest mortality occurred in the next parish, not one's own." Other people's families went into the workhouse, toiled on public roads or queued up for soup—but not those of the informant.[70]

Much of the material that the Folklore Commission collected was transmitted through Irish. The Gaelic-speaking culture of the west of Ireland carried its own mental constructs, its traditional templates, that determined which events might be recalled and how they were to be presented. Moreover, the survivors could only reflect the world as they understood and experienced it. For example, some form of providentialism made as much sense in Ireland's Roman Catholic townlands as it did in English middle-class, evangelical circles, although with different interpretations. So, for example, the oral tradition recalled that, prior to the Famine, the occasional abundance of potatoes had been

---

69. For a brief summary of the work of the Irish Folklore Commission in collecting Famine material see Ó Gráda, *Black '47 and Beyond*, 196, 198–99.
70. For quote see Mac Éirni, "Famine and the Irish Diaspora," 589. See also Ó Gráda *Black '47 and Beyond*, 195.

abused. Cathal Póirtéir cites the story of a farmer who, returning from market with unsold potatoes, "emptied them into the ditch on the roadside, for 'they weren't worth the sacks they were in.'" Afterward, people claimed that the Famine was a just retribution from God for the great waste of food. The account ends with the saying: "A willful waste makes a woeful want."[71]

The oral tradition also reflects a local, face-to-face world, not much inhabited by distant bureaucrats dipping their pens into abstract economic theory. While local landlords, both good and bad, were sometimes remembered, little seems to have been said about the political leaders in Dublin or London. Neither Trevelyan or the "Famine Queen" favorite bogy creatures of Irish nationalists, figure very much in the lore.[72] On the other hand, while abstract concepts of official policy were generally alien to traditional culture, memories often favored the uncanny and dramatic. Irish-speaking areas preserved tales of the miraculous appearances of abundant food, stories that follow age-old models found in international folktales.[73] Traditional culture also shaped memories of the first appearance of the potato blight in a townland. Since few people within the Gaelic culture read newspapers, they might not have been unaware of the advance of the disease across the country. Thus, the shock of the first spade full of rotten tubers or the overnight blackening of potato stalks became seared in memory, often accompanied by thunder or strange mists. The unburied dead left in cabins, or the attempts of a half-starved family (never the informant's own) to dispose of a loved one's body, engraved striking images unto collective memories. Peig Sayers, Irish speaker and famous memorialist from the Blasket Islands, recalled the story of a girl who fastened her mother's corpse to her back with a rope and carried it to the graveyard. Sayers concludes her story: "Don't they say that no matter where in Ventry churchyard, big though it is, you might dig a hole, you might find bones, because they were buried there without coffins or sheets?"[74] Such accounts are reminders that within the oral tradition, the specific often provides a face for the general. Moreover, while such images suggest a grim intimacy with famine conditions, the way Sayers conveyed the story tells much about the how she wanted her Gaelic-speaking community, both its victims and its survivors, to remember and be remembered.

Although the oral tradition tended to be protective of the community, it did not completely ignore the existence of those who took advantage of their less-fortunate neighbors. These stories are complicated, however. They do not just involve evicting landlords and proselytizing missionaries. Local merchants, better-off farmers, land speculators and those employed as functionaries of the relief system might have been beneficiaries of the disaster, regardless of their ethnic or religious background. In each locality it was no secret who were the winners and who were the losers—which families had disappeared, and who had picked up their holdings and survived, even thrived. An

---

71. Póirtéir, "Folk Memory and the Famine," 221.
72. Ó Gráda, *Black '47 and Beyond*, 197–98.
73. For importance of Gaelic language material see ibid., 199. For miraculous food see 213–15.
74. Ibid., 200–1.

old man from Cork recalled: "I used to hear the old people discuss the awful cruelty practiced by farmers who were fairly well off against their poorer and less comfortable neighbors. [...] [They] used to offer the rent of their farms to the landlord and grab their [neighbor's] farms." Little wonder that sometimes in the aftermath of the Famine, a community's survival may have depended upon the suppression of certain memories. As the old man put it: "Several people would be glad if the famine times were altogether forgotten so that the cruel doings of their forbearers would not be again renewed and talked about by their neighbors."[75]

If, on the everyday, community level, private memories of the Famine were surrounded by a certain public silence, on the national level there was a different kind of memory, written rather than spoken, consciously cultivated rather than reluctantly recalled. In his *Jail Journal*, John Mitchel provided an early description of the disaster. Interestingly, in his later account of the Famine in *The Last Conquest of Ireland (Perhaps)*, although published in 1873, he does not carry his account beyond 1851, the stopping point in his *Journal*. Christopher Morash argues that this creates "a suspension of history." In effect, Mitchel erases the "pastness" of the Famine, describing it as though it was contemporaneous with his readers. Subsequent novelists and popular historians did not just repeat Mitchel's sense of outrage. They continuously reused his images of suffering, making them signifiers of the Famine, fixing them "in the domain of public memory."[76] This was, of course, a highly selective memory. Moreover, while folk memory retained the names of at least some of those who died and those who thrived, the Mitchel-inspired nationalist "memory" placed the question of winners and losers on a broad ideological stage. It was England against Ireland, the landlords against the people, and, by implication at least, Protestants against Catholics.

Writing in the *London Review of Books* in 1998, Colm Tóibín addressed this question of nationalist memory. He noted that the social and economic dynamics of the Famine involved not only English officials and the Protestant landlords: "An entire class of Irish Catholics survived the Famine; many, indeed, improved their prospects as a result." It was not just Protestant landlords who engaged in eviction. Catholic middle-class tenant farmers often found it useful to eject their cottiers and dismiss their laborers. As time went on, however,

> there began a great silence about class division in Catholic Ireland. It became increasingly important, as nationalist fervor grew in the years after the Famine, that Catholic Ireland, or simply "Ireland" (the Catholic part went without saying), was presented as a nation, one and indivisible. The Famine, then, had to be blamed on the Great Other, the enemy across the water, and the victims of the Famine had to be this entire Irish nation, rather than a vulnerable section of the population.[77]

---

75. Póirtéir, "Folk Memory and the Famine," 230. Cormac Ó Gráda notes, however, that such accusatory stories are uncommon, and that when incidents were recalled names were seldom mentioned; *Black '47 and Beyond*, 212.
76. Morash, "Making Memories: The Literature of the Irish Famine," 42–43, 48.
77. Tóibín, *The Irish Famine*, 15, 17.

Contrary, therefore, to nationalist memory, it was not the "Irish people" who were starved and driven out. Rather it was a class—the Irish poor—who suffered. The most vulnerable, the least important in Irish society were the ones who disappeared. And in doing so, they made ample room into which the classes above them comfortably expanded. In most cases the winners and losers shared the same religion and ethnicity. As Liam Kennedy has suggested: "the cataclysm can [...] be viewed through the prism of class conflict, in which property holders in Ireland, irrespective of religion or political affiliation, acted like property holders anywhere else in the capitalist world, with the added benefit of the ideology of the free market economy as their rationalization." Kennedy asserts that it was not just the British government or the Irish landowners who must bear responsibility for what happened to the Irish poor. For most members of the Irish upper and middle class, Protestant and Catholic, life during the Famine went on pretty much as usual.[78]

What Was Lost?

Tá scamall éigin os coinn na hÉireann
Nár fhan dúil i gcéiliocht ag fear ná ag mnaoi; [...]
Níl ceol in aon áit ná suim ina dhéanamh
Is ní aithním glao cheart ag bean chun bídh.

[There is some (dark) cloud over Ireland
Men and women desire no courtship [...].
There's no music anywhere nor desire to make it
And I hear no clear call to food from any woman.][79]

The data regarding mortality and emigration hardly conveys the magnitude of the suffering, dislocation and destruction that define the Great Famine. Whole families were wiped out. Entire clachans were emptied, their former inhabitants dead or scattered. Tens of thousands were forced to flee their townlands to seek survival in foreign cities. Statistics can be compiled, but they say nothing of the lives they represent. What did all those people take with them into their graves or across the seas? What did Ireland lose in the demise of so many of its poor? Many in London, Dublin and in the big houses around the country considered Ireland's human loss, sad though it may have been, an economic and social gain. Long regarded as a millstone around the country's neck, the drag of Ireland's poor had been finally cut away.

Of course, this grimly rosy view of things ignored the fact that Ireland's poor had provided an essential pool of cheap laborers, most of whom paid rents which worked their way up the landholding pyramid. Furthermore, the poor cottiers and small tenantry had been a vital part of the culture, especially in the Gaelic-speaking areas. As noted

---

78. Kennedy, *Unhappy the Land*, 96. For quote see 114.
79. From *Amhrám ná Ghorta*, a traditional post-Famine song from the Dingle Peninsula. See Ó hAllmhuráin, "The Great Famine: A Catalyst in Irish Traditional Music Making," 121.

earlier, their passing contributed to the decline of the Irish language, and with it, the worldview embedded within it. It was not just the phrases, the stories, the songs, the tunes and the local lore that faded from many areas. Meaning seeped out of the landscape itself. What Gearóid Ó Allmhuráin calls "the cultural geography" of "the *seanchas* and *dinseanchas*—folklore and place-name lore"—gradually faded from many locales.[80] With the obliteration of many clachans and the depopulation of once crowded and vibrant townlands, the skill sets of musicians and instrument makers, of craftsmen and healing women, of storytellers and dancing masters declined, in some instances disappearing all together. Keening the dead, *caoineadh*, the exclusive art form of women, faded, eventually suppressed by the Church where it had survived at all. The "silence" that survivors often commented on was in large part a cultural silence that settled over rural Ireland in the wake of the Famine. The "merry" wakes and the wild weddings, the Saint's day "patterns" with their unsettling premodern mixture of the sacred and the profane, the *meitheal* gatherings for communal work—all once parts of a vibrant culture—receded into the past or survived within the ever-shrinking areas of the Gaeltacht. Certain aspects of the old rural culture, such as dancing and hurly, were selectively modernized and institutionalized as tokens of respectable national identity.[81] Thus, the collapse of the potato economy and the subsequent shambles called the Irish Famine initiated the fading away of a whole way of life. In the wake of the old traditional culture came the English language, commerce, a censuring and controlling Church, and politics—all powerful elements of the modern world.

It will not do, of course, to romanticize such losses. Rich as the oral culture of clachan and townland may have been, it was at best minimal compensation for a level of poverty that few today would tolerate. Although the Irish peasant's body was better fed than many of Europe's poor, it was ill-clothed and ill-housed, prone to disease and condemned to hunger every summer. Any serious disjuncture between weather and crops, any sudden increase in leaf curl or dry rot in the pratie beds, threatened starvation, which could be relieved only by uncertain charity. And, except for those who could find the economic and psychological wherewithal to emigrate, death provided the only exit from the daily round of work, potatoes and want.

Yet, despite the hardship, there were those during the Famine years and after who yearned for a return of health to their beloved praties and the old way of life. Having recounted her experiences during the disaster, Asenath Nicholson, the independent American evangelical missionary and aid worker, tried to explain why some people might have preferred digging their lazy beds to wielding the sickle for any landlord who might hire them. In her attempt, this very serious, generally unsentimental widow, seldom given to whimsy, sought for something that might illuminate, however dimly, the way of life the Famine destroyed. What she found was that one item of material culture so essential to the life of the Irish peasant: the spade.

---

80. Ibid., 127.
81. For keening, dancing and hurly see Kevin Whelan, "The Cultural Effects of the Famine," 274–85.

The spade has a thousand associations, entwined in and about the hearts of parent and child, which no other instrument of husbandry can claim; it has cut the turf that has lighted up the mud-walled cabin, and boiled the blessed potato [...] it has piled the manure-heap at the corner, mountain high; it has planted the ridge which has furnished their daily bread; it has made the ditch, and repaired the road; it has stood by the hearth or door on many a dark and stormy night, to guard the little stack [of fodder] for the cow against the tithe gatherer; it has been a fireside and field companion; and above all and over all, it has measured and hollowed out many a last sleeping bed for a darling child, a beloved husband or wife, and in the dark days of the Famine it has been the only companion to accompany the father, mother, husband, wife, or child, who has had the corpse of a hunger-stricken relative in a sack, or tied to the back, to convey it to the dread uncoffined pit, where are tumbled, in horrid confusion, the starved dead of all ages.[82]

The Long Shadow of the Famine

Stretching into the future, the Famine casts a shadow, the true length of which will never be known. However, some researchers have begun to make connections between the Famine and the mental and physical health of the descendants of the survivors. There is, for example, the unusually high rate of mental illness that characterized Ireland from the nineteenth into the twentieth century. As Oonagh Walsh has pointed out, Ireland has had a "unique profile" in terms of mental health and treatment. For example, in 1841 the Connacht District Lunatic Asylum in Ballinasloe, County Galway treated around 1,600 patients, with perhaps another 1,500 mentally ill scattered in the region's jails and workhouses. By 1900, a half century after the Famine, *and despite the district's sharply reduced population*, it was treating some 17,000 patients, as well as another 8,000 "lunatics" who could not be accommodated within the institution. Similar patterns were repeated elsewhere. Thus, twentieth-century Ireland's unique, mental health profile: as the population declined, admission rates in mental institutions rose. The problem, moreover, was also found within the diaspora. In overseas immigrant communities the Irish were disproportionately overrepresented among those committed to asylums. In addition to mental illnesses, there was a rise in type 2 diabetes among post-Famine generations. This parallels problems among descendants of those who survived Holland's "hungry winter" of 1944–45.[83] That individuals who experience the ravages of famine and other such traumas might later present physical and mental health problems seems intuitive. But how to account for repeated health problem in subsequent generations? How could something like the Irish Famine affect the health of descendants of the survivors?

According to the emerging science of epigenetics, if an organism encounters extreme stress, the effects may be passed down through several generations. Although an organism's genome, its DNA, may only change slowly through random mutations and natural selection, its epigenome may be altered in response to immediate environmental

---

82. Nicholson, *Annals of the Famine in Ireland*, 164.
83. See Walsh, "'An Invisible but Unescapable Trauma,'" 175–77.

stressors. So, while the DNA may remain unchanged by environmental influences, the altered epigenome may influence gene expression, determining which genes are turned on and which are turned off. Since the epigenome is inherited, the effects it has on the genome may be carried for several generations.[84] While much work remains to be done on linking epigenetics to catastrophic events such as the Irish and Dutch famines, as well as the Twin Towers 9/11 disaster in New York City, it now seems possible that the impacts on traumatized populations may be passed on through succeeding generations.[85]

Looking deeper into Irish society, what connections, if any, might link the Famine to the darker side of twentieth-century Ireland, as revealed by the institutional abuse of some of the country's weakest members? How to explain the mistreatment of poor children and unwed mothers in the industrial schools, the orphanages, the "Magdalene laundries," and the so-called mother and baby homes, accounts of which still appear in Irish newspapers?[86] Does the shadow of the Famine extend that far? While the answers to that question will never be known, it does not appear that the extermination of the poor during the Famine embed within Irish society, as deeply as it might have, an abiding compassion for its marginalized citizens.

There is, however, also evidence that those who look within the shadow of the Famine may find something like a usable past. Over the past several decades "Famine walks" have been staged throughout Ireland. In remembering the Great Hunger, these events also condemn the damage done by colonialism elsewhere, and they call attention to contemporary threats of food insecurity in other countries today, as well as looming ecological dangers around the globe.[87]

---

84. Ibid., 175–76, 178–80. Walsh points out that incidence of cardiovascular disease and hypertension, which had been high among the post-Famine Irish, seem to have peaked by 1980; 177. In "How an 1836 Famine Altered the Genes of Children Born Decades Later," *New York Times*, August 23, 2013. David Epstein discusses evidence of epigenetic research on generational survivors of the 1836 famine in Överkalix, Sweden, as well as Holland's "hungry winter." The author points out that while animal studies have been progressing, the relationship in humans between epigenetic changes and environmental stress is still fragmentary.
85. See Martinez, "How Your Diet Could Affect Generations to Come," *Irish Times*, January 13, 2017.
86. For the scandal regarding the St. Mary's Mothers and Baby Home see "The Lost Children of Tuam," *New York Times*, October 28, 2017.
87. See, for example, https:/www.afri.ie/tag/famine-walk/

CONCLUSION

Parsing the Famine

The Irish Famine was the result of a concatenation of evens set off by an ecological crisis resulting in the repeated impact of blight upon Ireland's potato economy. Created by the systemic interaction of land use and ownership, population pressures and a potato monoculture, this legacy of colonialism had become an ecological trap. The blight took away a principal source of sustenance that was extremely difficult to replace. Even when adequate supplies of alternative food began to arrive in Ireland by the summer of 1847, nothing could supplant the potato's high nutritional content. By then, however, an ecological crisis had quickly become a political one. With around one-third of the Irish population facing immediate hunger in the winter of 1846, the unsettled state of politics in both Ireland and Great Britain meant that the United Kingdom was poorly prepared for such an unprecedented challenge. Although there is no evidence to suggest that the Tories would have been more generous to Ireland's poor than were the Whigs, the fall of Sir Robert Peel in the summer of 1846 removed one of Britain's more effective and imaginative leaders from government. In his place the weaker Lord John Russell presided over a divided cabinet. Russell's position was made worse by the growing assertion of the power of Britain's middle class. Anti-protectionist liberals, having gained the repeal of the Corn Laws on the heels of the appearance of the potato blight, were hardly likely to embrace new, extensive state interventions in the economy, regardless of the circumstances. Then the General Election of 1847 introduced into Commons a large bloc of middle-class radical liberals dedicated to strict laissez-faire principles. This group, already suspicious of the aristocrats in the government, also had deep concerns about the potential price tag of famine relief, even after most of the costs had been pushed unto the shoulders of the Irish themselves. Nothing in this complex situation encouraged the kind of bold leadership and political imagination that might have produced more successful relief policies. Leadership was also lacking in Ireland. Weakened by the death of Daniel O'Connell, the split within the Repeal ranks, and the abortive rising in 1848, Irish politics could not muster an effective voice to counter policies emanating from London.

Complicating matters further, Britain's well-established narrative of the Irish Other acted as a kind of background radiation, contaminating all other factors. True, the negative aspects of the narrative did not completely dominate public opinion, as proven by the generous outpouring of British sympathy and donations in the spring of 1847. Even so, many Britons thought of the Irish as inferior, dependent and seldom trustworthy. Less charitable expressions were blatantly anti-Irish, bordering on outright racism.

Cultural and social attitudes also played their roles in the crisis. Anti-Catholicism, long an important ingredient in the Irish narrative, surfaced in a particularly virulent form during the Famine. Some Evangelicals voiced a brand of providentialism that identified the Famine as God's judgment against Roman Catholicism. However, such views were recognized as extreme at the time, and there is no evidence that they dominated the public discourse or had direct influence on policy making. More broadly, however, evangelicalism supported the moralistic attitudes that pervaded Victorian culture, impeding more generous responses to the Famine's victims. Folding such moralism into political economy, James Wilson, founding editor of *The Economist*, wrote in February 1847: "The peculiar suffering of Ireland at such a moment is a vindication of those great principles which God has established for the moral government of the world."[1]

Of course, this "peculiar suffering" did not fall upon the Irish *people*, as subsequent Irish nationalist propaganda would have it. Rather, the catastrophe fell upon the Irish *poor*, suggesting the degree to which Britain's response to the Famine reflected Victorian attitudes toward class and poverty. As economist M. Rein argues, capitalist societies tend to have a problem with poverty: "It is not so much the misery and plight of the poor but the discomfort and cost to the community which is crucial to this view of poverty. We have a problem of poverty to the extent that low income creates problems for those who are not poor."[2] In other words, the poor can make other people feel bad, even angry. Poverty acts as an accusation that the better off have failed to run things properly. Since the British middle class found their own poor disturbing enough, the Irish victims of the Famine presented an even greater affront to Victorian composure and self-regard, as well as a threat to the public purse.

Almost instinctively, some politicians, bureaucrats and editors deployed language that shielded or distanced comfortable, middle-class Britain from the desperate plight of the Irish poor. Observers objectified them by describing their condition in abstract terms, while allowing the passive voice to mask governmental and societal agency. Commentators deployed euphemisms that blurred reality and irrelevant metaphors that masked unpleasantness. For example, In *The Irish Crisis* Trevelyan attempted to explain why the government had reverted to public works in the autumn of 1846, having shut them down a few months earlier. He argued that, since the Irish peasants were accustomed to growing their own food instead of earning wages to buy it, they had to be given work rather than rations. "It was therefore necessary to adopt some means of giving the people a *command* over the new description of food [maize]." As a result, the government paid hungry people inadequate wages for outdoor work in the depth of winter, supposedly enabling them to buy high-priced grain. The idea that this would give them anything like "command" over their food supply would have been ludicrous had the situation not been so dire. Trevelyan's words sought contentment in the fantasy that the Irish crisis had been met by a clean and simple solution. Such rhetorical strategies, even when

---

1. *The Economist*, February 27, 1847, 227.
2. M. Rein, quoted by Amartya Sen in *Poverty and Famine*, 9.

unconsciously deployed, tended to obscure, even dehumanize famine victims, making, as David Lloyd has observed, "their extirpation thinkable and admissible."[3]

The Famine not only challenged concepts of class and morality. The validity of the doctrine of laissez-faire capitalism embedded within political economy was also at stake. The Irish Famine was one of the greatest challenges faced by nineteenth-century British capitalism, and, by its own internal logic, capitalism did not fail. It functioned more or less as predicted and as intended. Food was in short supply. Prices then rose, attracting necessary imports. Greater imports eventually closed the subsistence gap, and food prices declined accordingly. Of course, by the time theory caught up with practice many people were dead and many more seriously malnourished. So, to the extent that Britain's goal had been to feed starving people, laissez-faire capitalism got in the way. It was the wrong tool for the task. Its mechanisms were irrelevant in the face of immediate mass starvation and privation. Yet, Treasury officials seemed to believe that an enormous problem of poverty and hunger could be addressed by the free play of markets. However, as noted earlier, markets cannot create food; they can only gather it, price it and deliver it within a time frame that may or may not have relevance for the hungry. Moreover, the markets cannot distribute food to those unable to buy it; only private charity and/or government intervention can manage that. Laissez-faire economics, in combination with moralism and class and ethnic prejudice, therefore, seriously limited the British government's effective response. In Liam Kennedy's words, the most doctrinaire economists behind the theories of political economy were "not misanthropic monsters but well-intentioned individuals" who were "drunk" on the idea that they had "uncovered the laws of nature that governed society."[4]

As Amartya Sen argues, famines are more often *economic* disasters rather than simple subsistence crises. Such emergencies are seldom due to an absolute lack of food, but rather to questions involving who is *entitled* to food.[5] Those who have money are entitled to buy whatever food is available. Those without money lack the prerequisite entitlement. Societies may, of course, grant limited entitlements to the underprivileged through various sorts of welfare systems, such as the Irish Poor Law. In Ireland, however, only the "deserving poor" qualified for what was at best minimal support. Under the Amended Poor Act Law of 1847, this group amounted to well over a million people. There were, however, many more who, for whatever reason, were deemed "undeserving" and therefore without entitlement—without food. In effect then, a reliance on political economy

---

3. Lloyd, "The Indigent Sublime: Specters of Irish Hunger," 156. For Trevelyan see Leslie A. Williams, *Daniel O'Connell, the British Press and the Irish Famine*, 265; italics added. For other examples of the manipulation of language see 120–21, 160–62, 264–66, 350–51.
4. Kennedy, *Unhappy the Land*, 103. For the liberal defense of political economy during the Famine see Boylan and Foley. "'A Nation Perishing of Political Economy?'"
5. Sen, *Poverty and Famine*, 161. Cormac Ó Gráda warns against a simplistic application of Sen's entitlement approach to the Irish Famine. He points out that, during the winter of 1846 and 1847, there was an absolute shortfall in the Irish food supply. Questions of entitlements are better applied to later conditions in the south and west of Ireland. See "The Great Famine and Other Famines," 147–48; *Black '47 and Beyond*, 124–25.

based on laissez-faire doctrines set up a concept of justice that competed with, rather than complimented, the needs of the poor. Consider, for example, *The Times* response to Catholic prelates in Ireland when they argued that "Hallowed as are the rights of property, those of life are still more sacred." The paper retorted angrily: "In England, we do not terrify and paralyze the rights of property by proclaiming them subordinate to the 'rights of life,' but we teach and enforce the *duties* of property. We compel property to sustain life. Such is the basis of our Poor Law."[6] However, the Irish Poor Law, as overseen by Charles Trevelyan and his accountants in the Treasury, turned out to be a procrustean bed upon which the hungry poor were made to lie.

According to accounting historian Warwick Funnell, the crucial decision to channel all Famine relief through the Treasury was hardly a trivial administrative detail. It meant that Trevelyan and his clerks were duty bound to track the expenditure of every penny, while also making sure that the government did not undercut private enterprise through a careless release of grain from its depots. This was considered a matter of fundamental principle, not bureaucratic detail. As Funnell argues, accountancy at that time represented more than a technique for keeping track of money. It operated under a concept of justice based on the primacy of property rights, which lay at the heart of laissez-faire capitalism. Individuals had a *moral* right to their lawfully gained property. To take any portion of that property without their consent or that of their political representatives was unjust.[7] Even when Parliament approved the expenditure of funds to help famine victims, the threat of potential "injustice" still hung over the proceedings—unless officials were vigilant in barring waste, fraud and abuse. Even private donations had to be managed by the Treasury accountants, lest a careless distribution of alms threaten the all-important moral distinction between the deserving and undeserving poor. Maintaining this essential difference was one of the reasons why the Poor Law remained the primary mechanism of famine relief.

It was, therefore, through Trevelyan and his Treasury accountants that laissez-faire ideology became institutionalized within famine relief. Funnell argues that, "in a capitalist society the form of justice which accounting can serve is that based on property entitlements. Indeed, accounting is essentially and substantially a technology for enforcing those entitlements." Applied to famine relief, the accounting approach too often denied legitimacy—entitlement— to the those most in need of aid. As Luke Gibbons has observed, the British could grant victims of the Famine pity and charity but not justice for those without property.[8]

---

6. *The Times*, October 28, 1847.
7. Funnell, "Accounting for Justice: Entitlement, Want and the Irish Famine, 1845–7," 192–94. Funnell bases his views of justice and accounting on the writings of R. Nozik, author of *Anarchy, State and Utopia*.
8. Gibbons, *The Limits of the Visible*, 20. See also Funnell, "Accounting for Justice: Entitlement, Want and the Irish Famine, 1845–7," 190–91.

The Failure of Conflicting Priorities

What does it mean to suggest that Great Britain "failed" the Irish? And where does the failure begin? At first glance it might seem that Britain's most obvious failure lay in its long refusal or apparent inability to do anything about the acknowledged dangers of massive dependency on a potato monoculture. Unfortunately, societies have a poor record when it comes to preparing for recognized but "unscheduled" dangers. For example, since 1918, pandemics have been more predictable than were fungal blights in the 1840s. Yet, in 2020, confronted by the novel coronavirus, COVID-19, the United States, having failed to maintain its public health system in a state of readiness, blundered sadly in its response. Beyond that, even the threat of global climate change, which comes with a frighteningly immediate timetable, has yet to galvanize a serious response from most nations.

This is not to excuse British failure to purse some sort of land reform. Still, it is difficult to think of any type of reform that would have significantly relieved the poverty of one-third of Ireland's population. Tenant ownership or at least tenant rights might have helped those who rented viable tracts of land. However, such changes would have done nothing for those working tiny plots without leases nor for the masses of conacre farmers, cottiers and landless laborers. More to the point, to be successful, any type of land reform would have had to rein in, if not reverse, the intense subdivision of land that supported Ireland's population of potato-dependent poor. Any strong reversal of subdivision, however, would have been disastrous for the poor unless accompanied by a massive program of employment and/or assisted emigration. Significantly, the post-Famine land reforms—the implementation of tenant's rights, eventually followed by tenant proprietorship—were accomplished in the wake of a significant depopulation of the countryside and the erasure of the poorest class.

Government-subsidized land reclamation might have temporarily relieved some of the pressure of population upon the land. However, if the results were simply an increased number of small holdings, the cycle of poverty and potato dependency might have remained unbroken. In fact, without a significant increase in emigration, even the breaking up of the estates and a redistribution of the land (the wild stuff of revolutions) might not have freed Ireland from its land–potatoes–people–poverty nexus. Potato dependency could only have been addressed by a significant growth of nonagriculture employment: the extension of industry beyond Belfast. How this could have been accomplished without significant government involvement in the economy is hard to imagine. The relatively new and heady free-market doctrines, not to mention the sanctity of private property, along with English disinclination to encourage Irish manufacturing competition, stood as immense conceptual barriers to any significant industrialization of Ireland. And regardless of how it might have been accomplished, an industrialized Ireland, even if it did manage to break the cycle of potato dependency, would probably have traded clachans for slums—agrarian privation for urban poverty.

When it comes to famine policy, Britain's failures can be more clearly identified. As mentioned earlier, Peel's actions in 1845–46 were minimal, just barely enough to respond to a partial failure of the potato crop. A more generous policy would not have left Ireland in such a weakened position as it faced the crucial harvest of 1846. The failures of Russell's incoming government began almost as soon as it assumed power. A more prudent, less doctrinaire administration might have held off winding down Peel's relief measures until the results of the fall harvest where fully known. Having ignored prudence, Russell's government had to start its reaction to a full-blown disaster from a dead stop.

Responding to disasters is seldom a simple matter. In addition to the inevitable logistical complications, problems involving culture, ideology, economics and politics inevitably arise. Consequently, a variety of factors may influence relief policies, producing a series of competing goals, only a few of which might provide direct relief to the afflicted. Confronted by the destruction of the potato crop in the fall of 1846, the British government did adopt the preservation of Irish lives as a goal. Unfortunately, the government allowed other priorities and concerns to get in the way. For example, the moralism of the day seemed to rule out a dole, especially on a massive scale. Also, laissez-faire ideology blocked the temporary closing of Irish ports. In addition, the crisis seemed to offer an ideal opportunity to teach Irish peasants to work for wages and to buy, rather than grow, their own food. Finally, the government made every effort to protect British taxpayers from the threat of "jobbery." Indeed, it sought to protect the Imperial Treasury itself from the potential drain of Irish relief. Trying to juggle these competing goals, the government settled for a ponderous bureaucratic scheme of public works. Although a well-tested response to the less critical subsistence crises of the past, channeling large-scale famine relief through public works in the fall and winter of 1846–47 turned out to be the worst decision the government could have made. It was slow moving, cumbersome and expensive, often resulting in useless projects. Moreover, because it forced malnourished, ill-clad people to work for low wages in bitter winter weather, it claimed lives as well as saved them. Once the government tacitly acknowledged the failure of its public works program, it rearranged its priorities —temporarily. For three months in the summer of 1847, feeding some three million people became the government's primary goal. And by the standards of the day it was successful, although hardly something that could be justified in terms of political economy.

With the passage of the Amended Poor Law Act, feeding the hungry once more reverted to being but one objective among several. In addition to staying within the confines of moralistic, laissez-faire capitalism, the government felt it had to shield the Imperial Treasury from the costs of the crisis. Nevertheless, while this meant that Irish property would pay for Irish poverty, almost all other aspects of the famine relief were very much an imperial affair. London, the heart of the empire, controlled everything. The Imperial Treasury, under daily supervision by Trevelyan, linked the Army Commissariat, which maintained government food depots, to the Irish Poor Law Commission and the Irish executive in Dublin Castle. And none of these entities represented the Irish people; all were creatures of the imperial government. Although the Irish viceroys, along with the leadership within the Commissariat and Poor Law Commission, occasionally tried to push back against London, the government invariably prevailed. And, without its own parliament, Ireland had no effective voice.

CONCLUSION

Throughout the Famine, the reform of Irish agriculture remained a constant goal. Many in Britain blamed the crisis upon a potato dependency allowed, if not encouraged, by careless and greedy Irish landlords. Since the system of subdivision and rack renting appeared to be collapsing, the government sought to grasp the opportunity to use the crisis to restructure Ireland's agrarian economy. Whatever else happened, that particular goal had to be met, a point reiterated time and again by members of the government. For example, in July 1848 Lord Clarendon appealed to the London Corporation, asking for British investment in Irish agriculture. Referring to Ireland's past and present problems, he asserted: "It is manifest then, that a complete change of system as regards agriculture, the tenure of land, and the social habits of the people, has become indispensable."[9] Yet, this apparently important objective was not embodied in any single piece of legislation. Instead, it was expected to flow from the combination of all the relief efforts, especially the Amended Poor Law Act of 1847 and the Encumbered Estates Act. By placing the burden of Famine relief on local Irish rate payers, the former act threatened to penalize landlords who had fragmented their lands among tenants no longer able to pay their rents. So, without having to mandate evictions, the government's tax policy made them all but a necessity for many landlords. The government assumed that, having cleared away subdivisions, capable landlords would then consolidate their tenancies, embrace "efficient" (meaning English) farming methods and hire the displaced, landless laborers. By simply enforcing a burdensome tax policy on Irish property owners, the government let the landlords do the dirty work of clearing the land. Those landlords too indebted or incapable of proper management would be forced to sell out, a process facilitated by the Encumbered Estates Act. The only support for the evicted came from the locally financed, hopelessly underfunded Poor Law system. Under such circumstances, the aim of restructuring became incompatible with insuring the well-being, much less the survival, of the poor. Through tolerating, if not actually encouraging, evictions, this policy created victims instead of aiding them. Blinded by the arrogance of pride and position, members of the cabinet assumed that they could remake Ireland by conjuring a handful of theories and inviting some like-minded Englishmen and Scots to drain the bogs and make Ireland bloom. In doing so, they invoked the same colonialist mentality that was driving the empire in so many other parts of the world.

The human costs of prioritizing agricultural restructuring did not go unnoticed by some of the government's critics. In December 1849 the *Illustrated London News* complained, "The present condition of the Irish [...] has been mainly brought on by ignorant and vicious legislation." During the worst period of the crisis, the journal continued, the peasantry had been fed by government and private charity. Subsequently, however, the "false theory" of political economy had "led the landlords and the legislature to believe that it was a favorable opportunity for changing the occupation of the land, and its cultivation of the soil from potatoes to corn" or to the raising of livestock. Between evictions and the Poor Law, the parliament managed to make "the terrible but

---

9. Quoted in *The Scotsman*, July 7, 1849 (2).

temporary situation of a potato rot the means of exterminating, through slow process of disease and homeless starvation, nearly the half of the Irish people."[10]

Alternative Solutions

It is one thing to blame the British government for confusing its priorities and making bad decisions. However, given the complexity of the situation and all the factors reviewed above, what alternatives did the government actually have? Could it, in fact, have averted more of the tragedy? This is an important question, because, without better options, then, as some "revisionist" historians have suggested, the British government did its best in the face of unprecedented circumstances.

The challenge of counterfactual history lies in anchoring imagined alternatives to the realities of the past. In this case, Victorian political culture must be taken as a given. A good starting place, then, might be the government's one unmitigated success: the mass feedings carried out over three summer months under the Soup Act of 1847. Mortality rates fell, and pressure on the workhouses eased. Had the program been maintained, many subsequent deaths and much hardship might have been averted. However, at best, this would have been only a partial solution. Nutritional problems aside, it is unlikely that the program could have been continued over several years. The specter of feeding one-third of Ireland, a dole of unimaginable proportions, appalled and frightened the British. It would have been politically untenable for any government to have committed to an open-ended continuation of the program. It was difficult enough for the Russell administration to maintain the drastically limited food dole subsequently conducted under the rubric of outdoor relief.

On the other hand, a more effective program for getting food to the hungry could theoretically have been structured in a way that might have been both politically acceptable and practical. The stigma of the dole could have been reduced by tying direct food aid to a modified public works program coupled with better support of the Poor Law system. Families able to work could have received food and clothing in return for labor, even on their own holdings if no other employment were available. Those individuals and families unable to provide labor would have been supported on outdoor relief through an adequately funded Poor Law without concern for the workhouse "test." To make the public works economically meaningful, the emphasis could have been placed on draining bogs instead of building useless roads into them. Indeed, had the government been willing to invest in "reproductive works," even if they did benefit individual landlords, more useful employment would have been available to the poor. Of course, this would have meant using public funds to improve private lands. Since the landowners were already paying high taxes to support paupers, however, they could have been offered some meaningful relief (or long-term, low-interest loans) if they hired workers. In cases where landowners were too indebted to carry out such efforts, the government could have adopted Peel's original Encumbered Estates Act, which would have allowed a land commission to take over bankrupt estates and run them for a few years, employing labor

---

10. *Illustrated London News*, December 15, 1849, 394.

to bring the lands up to market value. The plan could even have included some movement toward tenant ownership.

Of course, no alternative plan would have worked if it had permitted landlords to constantly manufacture new paupers through mass evictions. Again, it would have been difficult to challenge the taboo against interfering with private property. However, existing laws regarding evictions could have been strictly enforced. Also, alternative tax policies, instead of encouraging evictions, might have been drafted to curb them. In addition, the government could have provided for a significantly greater degree of assisted emigration to Canada or Australia, providing funds to help emigrants settle in their new homes, even if the high costs involved would have limited the scope of such a program. Finally, the government would have had to redefine the crisis as one involving the United Kingdom as a whole, rather than just Ireland, thus shifting the relief burden from Irish property to the Imperial Treasury.

The point is that, even within the framework of mid-Victorian society, given the right leadership, there were alternative policies available that did not completely violate the principles of political economy. Although clearly beyond the imagination and courage of Prime Minister John Russell and his cabinet, most of the ideas suggested above did in fact circulate in one form or another during the crisis. Although some critics would have dismissed them as radical, if applied, they might have altered and reordered government priorities without necessarily abandoning any of them. Certainly, humanitarian needs would have had to come first. Other goals, such as the restructuring of Irish agriculture, would have had to move at a slower pace. The Irish Poor Law would have remained in place, not as a broken engine of famine relief, but as a welfare program for paupers, the purpose for which it was originally created. True, a more generous form of outdoor relief would have been required. However, providing food for work to healthy laborers and their families through a revised public works program would have relieved pressure on the workhouses. Such actions certainly would have stretched the limits of laissez-faire ideology, but not much more than some of the government's own actions. Also, although they would have pushed the envelope of the moralistic attitudes of the day, they would have done so without completely abandoning them. Whenever possible, people would have been given food in return for labor.

There were, of course, no panaceas hidden in any of these alternatives. Nothing suggested above would have completely solved Ireland's problems. A quick, painless "solution" to the crisis did not exist. Given the rapid collapse of the potato economy, extensive hardship and suffering were inevitable. Nothing could have spared Ireland's poor from some degree of disruption, death and panicked emigration. And, of course, none of these plans would have been easy to adopt, especially since they would have necessitated breaching the firewall between Irish relief and the Imperial Treasury. Yet, while more than the £8,332,000 the government did ultimately spend on famine relief, the costs would probably have been considerably less than the £69,000,000 the United Kingdom spent on the Crimean war a few years later.[11]

---

11. See Kinealy, *This Great Calamity: The Irish Famine*, 295.

It should be clear, then, that the British government did not casually turn its back on obvious, easily implemented alternative solutions. Nothing outlined above lay within easy reach. Each alternative would have faced enormous political and economic challenges. Yet, while these might seem like easy excuses for Victorian Britain's failure in Ireland, they, nevertheless, correspond to the justifications given today to explain inaction on any number of serious twenty-first century social and economic problems. Now, as then, the difficulty often lies in a lack of leadership.

Failure or Genocide

In her essay on the Famine, Ciara Boylan observes that "single convulsive historical events can become historiographical behemoths" that challenge academics and excite the popular imagination. "It is difficult at times to avoid a sense that the Famine has been burdened with a weight and a set of meanings that can serve as much to obscure as to illuminate our understanding of it."[12] To some extent this is due to the difference between history as inquiry and understanding and history as accusation and judgment. In the case of the Irish Famine, the accusations began early. During the Famine, some writers involved with *The Nation*, especially Lady Wilde (who wrote under the pen name "Speranza"), were quick to accuse the British government of what is today called genocide.[13] It was, however, the Young Irelander John Mitchel who later stated the accusation most succinctly. In *The Last Conquest of Ireland (Perhaps)*, published in 1861, he famously proclaimed, "The Almighty, indeed, sent the potato blight, but the English created the famine." By that time, living safely in the United States, the clarity of Mitchel's moral vision had been significantly modified by his enthusiastic embrace of American racism and Southern slavery (including a proposed revival of the slave trade). Nevertheless, Michel's accusation became a staple among Irish nationalists, who assume intent by pointing to statements that sound genocidal or to policies that seemed to have been purposely designed to exacerbate the situation.[14] Certainly, it is not hard to find levels of British callousness that go beyond the boundaries of ignorance, innocent misjudgment or ideological blindness. For example, while Russell wrung his hands over the evictions, at least some members of the government were calm in the knowledge that many of those ejected had no resources of their own to fall back upon. They also knew the Poor Law Unions were grossly underfunded and offered scant protection. Yet, they also believed

---

12. Boylan, "Famine," 18–19.
13. See Lee, "The Famine as History," 170. See also Martin, "'The Skeleton at the Feast': Lady Wilde's Famine Poetry and Irish International Critiques of Food Scarcity," 149–60. See also Ryder, "Reading Lessons: Famine and the *Nation*."
14. For quote see Mitchel, *Last Conquest of Ireland (Perhaps)*, 219. A recent contribution to the genocide argument is *The Famine Plot* by Tim Pat Coogan, former editor of the *Irish Press* and author of important biographies of twentieth-century Irish nationalist leaders. Coogan offers up damning anti-Irish statements made by British politicians and publicists, and he calls attention to the admittedly appalling results of some of the government's policies. Yet, he fails to establish intent, an actual genocidal "plot."

that clearing tens of thousands of people from the land was a first, essential step in revitalizing Irish agriculture. They did not necessarily give up on the goal of providing some assistance to the hungry and homeless, but they did not make such relief their overriding priority. It is this cold, detached willingness on the part of some to knowingly pursue policies that put helpless people at risk that has fed the accusations of genocide.

Although seldom accepted by historians in its rawest, most extreme form, many have, over the past several decades, moved closer to Mitchel's bitter position, agreeing that many Famine deaths and much suffering were due to British policies.[15] Some go further. William B. Rogers, for instance, has argued that the main problem with the accusation of genocide rests in the crucial, perquisite component of intent. (There was no British equivalent of the Wannsee Conference at which the Nazi leadership put together the "Final Solution" that led to the Holocaust.) However, he suggests that, if genocide was treated like murder charges—with varying degrees of guilt ranging from manslaughter to first degree—might not Great Britain be justly accused of something like "*unintentional genocide*"?[16]

While an interesting point, it, nevertheless, avoids the question regarding the role that genocide might play in understanding the Famine. The accusation of genocide can become an obstacle, rather than a conduit, to comprehending the crisis. Unless one's intention is blatantly propagandistic, the application of any term or label to an event ought to initiate a process of illumination, of comprehension. It should draw people in, leading them to explore the interconnecting factors that have created the event. In the context of the Irish Famine, however, the term "genocide" may have the opposite effect. It can push the Famine into a grim cul de sac, cutting it off from the broader paths of history that link the past to the present. It can close off rather than facilitate understanding, encouraging denunciation rather than inviting investigation. It can obscure the complexities that make up the reality of a situation. The term may focus too much attention on a handful of "evil" men in the Whig cabinet and in the British press who, allegedly, sought to eradicate as many Irish as possible to further their racist, colonial and capitalistic agendas. Their supposed malevolent intent does not invite analysis of the broader forces at work. Thus isolated, they become monsters who dominate the landscape, obscuring the complexities of the situation.

This is not intended to dismiss the genuine emotions and sense of grievance roused by the Irish Famine. For many people who are Irish or who claim an Irish heritage, the Famine has become a part of their identity. It remains a hunger unappeased, a wound that never healed. However, as Chris Morash suggests, since its earliest accounts, the Famine has been represented by a limited series of images of suffering, death, eviction and exile—"shards of memory"—unconnected to sequential narratives. Unexplained and without context, these oft-repeated examples of massive misery come to represent an "atrocity" that demands remembrance. However, Morash warns, "In keeping these memories alive, we may be doing no more than bearing witness, trying to make whole

---

15. See Davis, "The Historiography of the Irish Famine," 16–21.
16. Rogers, "The Great Hunger: Act of God or Acts of Man?" 253–54.

that which the form of these images tells us can never be made whole. But such a longing for wholeness is not without its dangers."[17] Indeed, pursuing the genocidal charge risks isolating the Famine itself, turning it into a kind of historical horror show, while encouraging the sort of Irish victimhood as suggested by Liam Kennedy's term "MOPES"—"Most Oppressed People Ever." On April 22, 2014, Kennedy Googled the terms "Irish Famine Genocide" and "Irish Famine Holocaust." The former received around one-third of a million hits, while the latter scored 465,000. While these results cannot be taken too literally, they do suggest the popularity of these concepts. An extreme example is the tendency to proclaim the Famine "the Irish Holocaust," which Donald Harmon Akenson regards as a specimen of "famine porn," "a presentation that is historically unbalanced […] distinguished by a covert (and sometimes overt) appeal to misanthropy and almost always an incitement to hatred."[18]

Nevertheless, how injustices are remembered is important. In order to prevent what he calls "the slide of memory into nationalist nostalgia," Kevin Whelan calls for the "redemptive model of *radical memory* [which] must also continue to acknowledge the irredeemable losses that lie at the core of historical injustice, loss so absolute as to be beyond redemption, as has been powerfully argued in the case of the slave trade, the Shoah or the Irish Famine."[19] This is not to suggest that there is some sort of grim quantitative equivalence among these atrocities. Rather they fall into a category of events which change (or should change) the way human beings think about their world. This is why they must never be forgotten. Thus, although today's organizers of Ireland's "Famine Walks" may sometimes incorporate the accusation or the assumption of genocide into their speeches, these events, nevertheless, offer something more than a sad or angry remembrance of victims and victimhood. By linking the commemorations to current injustices threatening poor people in various countries, they provide the Irish Famine with a useable past that speaks to today's global society.

Finally, the term genocide may obscure what should be disturbingly familiar elements in the British government's response to the Famine. The Victorian world of the Russells and the Trevelyans may not be all that far removed from the concerns and rhetoric of the twenty-first century. Once past the historical trappings—the top hats, frock coats, mutton chops and horse-drawn hackneys—one can recognize many familiar elements linking contemporary democratic societies to the Victorian past. For example, although "the media" today extends far beyond the printed word, it still molds, amplifies and manipulates public opinion, as it did in the nineteenth century. Then again, many of today's middleclass taxpayers are just as suspicious of the poor and as deeply

---

17. Morash, "Literature, Memory, Atrocity," 118.
18. For Donald Harmon Akenson see "A Midrash on 'Galut,' 'Exile,' and 'Diaspora' Rhetoric," 13. The author points out that the term "Irish Holocaust" may be deeply offensive to members of the Jewish community. For Liam Kennedy see *Unhappy Land*, 84. For MOPES see 1, 36. The author of this study repeated Kennedy's searches on July 7, 2020 and received 529,000 and 10,200,000 results respectively. However, when quotation marks were applied, the results were 29,100 and 1,820 hits, respectively.
19. Kevin Whelan, "The Cultural Effects of the Famine," 286.

concerned about the cost of welfare as were their Victorian predecessors. Conflicts still occur between public welfare and individual morality. Moreover, the links between evangelical moralism and free-market capitalism remain as strong today as they were in the past. Racial and ethnic tensions still distort today's cultural and political landscape and policy debates. Also, within the current revival of neoliberalism may be heard echoes of the debates over Great Britain's famine policy. Indeed, the British government's insistence on pursuing agriculture restructuring during the Famine could stand as an early example of the economic "shock therapy" neoliberals confidently prescribed to former Communist countries toward the end of the last century. Finally, while famines no longer stalk modern democracies, politics and economics still combine with prejudice and xenophobia to muddle the citizen's will and ability to address today's pressing humanitarian problems. With all this in mind, the Irish Famine may represent something just as disturbing as an accusation of genocide—disturbing because it is more familiar. This is the failure of those who lacked the vision, imagination, courage and empathy to rise to a challenge which, while extremely difficult, was within their capacity to more effectively address. In this respect, Victorian Britain is not unique but an all too representative example of how modern governments and societies may fail their weakest members.

It is not a trivial matter for today's citizens to judge the dead—especially when the verdicts are based on the supposedly advanced humanitarian standards that today's beleaguered and frequently stalemated democracies claim but, nonetheless, struggle to uphold. If valid judgments upon the past are to be made, they should be made in a spirit of inquiry, shaped by humility and understanding, full in the realization that, in the dance of time, those who would sit in judgment today will themselves be judged tomorrow. In that spirit, the past, instead of becoming the repository for anger and blame, might act at times as a revealing, although perhaps an embarrassing, mirror in which the present may glimpse itself.

BIBLIOGRAPHY

Aalen, F. H. A. "The Irish Rural Landscape: Synthesis of Habitat and History." In *Atlas of the Irish Landscape*, 4–30. Edited by F. H. A. Aalen, Kevin Whelan and Mathew Stout. Cork: Cork University Press, 1997.

———. *Man and Landscape in Ireland*. New York: Academic Press, 1978.

———, and Kevin Whelan. "Fields." In *Atlas of the Irish Landscape*, 134–44. Edited by F. H. A. Aalen, Kevin Whelan and Mathew Stout. Cork: Cork University Press, 1997.

Abbott, Rebecca. "The Earl Grey Orphan Scheme, 1848–1850, and the Irish Diaspora to Australia." In *Women and the Great Hunger*, 201–10. Edited by Christine Kinealy, Jason King and Ciarán Reilly. Hamden, CT: Quinnipiac University Press, 2016.

Akenson, Donald Harmon. *Discovering the End of Time: Irish Evangelicals in the Age of Daniel O'Connell*. Montreal: McGill-Queens University Press, 2016.

———. "A Midrash on 'Galut,' 'Exile,' and 'Diaspora' Rhetoric." In *The Hungry Stream: Essays on Immigration and Famine*, 5–15. Edited by E. Margaret Crawford. Belfast: Queen's University Press, 1997.

Altick, Richard D. *Victorian People and Ideas: A Companion for the Modern Reader of Victorian Literature*. New York: Norton, 1973.

Anbinder, Tyler. "Lord Palmerston and the Irish Famine Emigration." *Historical Journal*, 44:2 (2001), 441–69.

Anon. *The Irish Tourist or, the People and Provinces of Ireland*. London: Barton, Harvey, 1827.

Anon. *Journal of a Tour in Ireland during the Months of October and November, 1835*. London: Samuel Bently, 1836.

Anon. *The Sportsman in Ireland, with His Summer Route through the Highlands of Scotland by a Cosmopolite*. 2 vols. London: Henry Colburn, 1840.

Anon. The *Tourist's Illustrated Handbook for Ireland*. London: Crownynill, Jones, Lover, 1854.

Anon. "Understanding Evolution: Monoculture and the Irish Potato Famine: Cases of Missing Genetic Variation." https://evolution.berkeley.edu/evolibrary/article/agriculture_02 (accessed June 22, 2020).

Ashworth, Rev. John Harvey. *The Saxon in Ireland, or the Rambles of an Englishman in Search of a Settlement in the West of Ireland*. London: John Murray, 1851.

Atthill, Lombe. *Recollections of an Irish Doctor*. Whitegate, County Clare: Ballinakella Press, [1911] 2007.

Barrow, John. *A Tour Round Ireland, through the Sea Coast Counties, in the Autumn of 1835*. London: John Murray, 1836.

Barry, Dan. "The Lost Children of Tuam." *New York Times*, October 28, 2017. https://www.nytimes.com/interactive/2017/10/28/world/europe/tuam-ireland-babies-children.html.

Bartlett, Thomas. "'An Union for Empire' The Anglo-Irish Union as Imperial Project." In *The Irish Act of Union, 1800: Bicentennial Essays*, 50–57. Edited by Michael Brown, Patrick M. Geoghegan, James Kelly. Dublin: Irish Academic Press, 2003.

Begley, Anthony, and Soinbhe Lally, "The Famine in County Donegal." In *The Famine in Ulster: The Regional Impact*, 77–98. Edited by Christine Kinealy and Trevor Parkhill. Belfast: Ulster Historical Foundation, 1997.

Bennett, William. *Narrative of a Recent Journey of Six Weeks in Ireland, in Connection with the Subject of Supplying Small Seed to Some of the Remoter Districts with Current Observations on the Depressed Circumstances of the People, and a Means Presented for the Permanent Improvement of Their Condition*. London: Charles Gilpin, 1847.

Bew, Paul. *Ireland: The Politics of Enmity, 1789–2006.* Oxford: Oxford University Press, 2007.
Bighton, Stephen A., and Jessica M. Levon-White. "Teacups, Saucers and Dinner plates: English Ceramic Exports to Ballykilcline." In *Unearthing Hidden Ireland: Historical Archaeology at Ballykilcline, County Roscommon,* 109–39. Edited by Charles E. Orser, Jr. Bray, County Wicklow: Worldwell, 2006.
Binns, Jonathan. *The Miseries and Beauties of Ireland.* Vol. 2. London: Longman, Orme, Brown, 1837.
Blake Family of Renvyle House [Henry Blake, Martha Louise Blake and Anne Attersol]. *Letters from the Highlands of Connemara, 1823–1824.* Edited by Kevin Whelan. Clifden, Galway: Gibbons Publications, 1995.
Blake, Robert. *The Conservative Party from Peel to Churchill.* New York: St. Martins, 1971.
Bourke, Austin. *"The Visitation of God?" The Potato and the Great Irish Famine.* Edited by Jacqueline Hill and Cormac Ó Gráda. Dublin: Lilliput, 1993.
Boyce, Charlotte. "Representing the 'Hungry Forties' in Image and Verse: The Politics of Hunger in Early Victorian Illustrated Periodicals." *Victorian Literature and Culture,* 40 (2012), 421–49.
Boylan, Ciara. "Famine." In *The Princeton History of Modern Ireland,* 404–24. Edited by Richard Bourke and Ian McBride. Princeton, PA: Princeton University Press, 2016.
Boylan, Thomas A., and Timothy P. Foley. "'A Nation Perishing of Political Economy'?" In *Fearful Realities: New Perspectives on the Irish Famine.* 138–50. Edited by Chris Morash and Richard Hayes. Dublin: Irish Academic Press, 1996.
Brady, Ciaran. *Interpreting Irish History: The Debate on Historical Revisionism: 1938–1994.* Dublin: Irish Academic Press, 2008.
Branach, Naill R. "'Edward Nangle and the Achill Island Mission." *History Ireland,* Vol. 8, No. 3, Autumn 2000, pp. 35–38.
Burritt, Elihu. *A Journal of a Visit of Three Days to Skibbereen and Its Neighborhoods.* London, Birmingham, 1847. [A longer extract from his journal was published in *Elihu Burritt, A Memorial Volume: A Sketch of His Life and Labors,* 34–52. Edited by Charles Northend. New York: Appleton, 1879.]
Butler, Nancy I. "Avoiding Monoculture." *Potato Grower,* May 3, 2009, http://www.potatogrower.com/2009/05/avoiding-monoculture (accessed June 22, 2020).
Butterly, John R., and Jack Shepherd. *Hunger: The Biology and Politics of Starvation.* Lebanon, NH: University Press of New England, 2010.
Byrne, Fedelma. "The Mechanics of Assisted Emigration: From the Fitzwilliam Estate in Wicklow to Canada." In *The Famine Irish: Emigration and the Great Hunger,* 41–54. Edited by Ciarán Reilly. Dublin: The History Press Ireland, 2016.
Byrne, Joseph. *Byrne's Dictionary of Irish Local History from Earliest Times to c 1900.* Cork: Mercier, 2004.
Byrne, Patricia. *The Preacher and the Prelate: The Achill Mission Colony and the Battle for Souls in Famine Ireland.* Newbridge, County Kildare: Merrion Press/Irish Academic Press, 2018.
Byron, Reginald. *Irish America.* Oxford Studies in Social and Cultural Anthropology. Oxford: Clarendon, 1999.
Caird, James. *The Plantation Scheme, or the West of Ireland as a Field for Investment.* Edinburgh: Blackwood, 1850.
Callaway, Ewan. "Pathogen Genome Tracks Irish Potato Famine Back to its Roots." *Nature,* May 21, 2013. http://www.nature.com/news/pathogen-genome-tracks-irish-potato-famine-back-to-its-roots-1.13021 (accessed July 5, 2017).
Campbell, Stephen J. *The Great Irish Famine: Words and Images from the Famine Museum Strokestown Park, County Roscommon.* Strokestown, Ireland: Famine Museum, 1994.
Campbell, Thomas. *A Philosophical Survey of the South of Ireland in a Series of Letters to John Watkinson, M.D.* Dublin: Whitestone, 1778.
Cappock, Margarita. "Pageantry and Propaganda: The *Illustrated London News* and the Royal Visit to Ireland." *Irish Arts Review Yearbook,* 16 (2000), 86–93.
Carlyle, Thomas. *Reminiscences of My Irish Journey in 1849.* New York: Harper, 1882.
Cassidy, Daniel. *How the Irish Invented Slang: The Secret Language of the Crossroads.* Petrolia/ Oakland, CA: Counter-Punch/AK Press, 2007.

Chatterton, Lady Henrietta. *Rambles in the South of Ireland in the Year 1838.* 2 vols. London: Saunders, Otley, 1839.
Clark, Samuel, and James S. Donnelly, Jr. "General Introduction" and "Introduction." In *Irish Peasants: Violence & Political Unrest, 1780–1914,* 3–21, 25–35. Edited by Samuel Clark and James S. Donnelly, Jr. Madison: University of Wisconsin Press, 1983.
Clarkson, L. A., and E. Margaret Crawford. *Feast and Famine: Food and Nutrition in Ireland, 1500–1920.* New York: Oxford University Press, 2001.
Colley, Linda. *Britons: Forging of the Nation, 1707–1837.* New Haven, CT: Yale University Press, 2009.
Conaghan, Pat. *The Great Famine in South-West Donegal 1845–1850.* Killybegs, County Donegal: Bygones Enterprises, 1997.
Conlon-McKenna, Marita "Foreword: The Great Silence, Children of the Great Hunger in Ireland, xi-xx. Edited by Christine Kinealy, Jason King, and Gerard Moran. Hamden, CT: Quinnipiac, 2018.
Connell, Peter. "County Meath during the Famine." In *The Atlas of the Great Irish Famine,* 334–40. Edited by John Crowley, William J. Smyth and Mike Murphy. New York: New York University Press, 2012.
Connolly, S. J. "The Great Famine and Irish Politics." In *The Thomas Davis Lecture Series.* 34–59. Edited by Cathal Póirtéir. Dublin: Mercier, 1995.
———. *Priests and People in Pre-Famine Ireland, 1780–1785.* Dublin: Four Courts, 2001.
Coogan, Tim Pat. *The Famine Plot: England's Role in Ireland's Greatest Tragedy.* New York: Palgrave Macmillan, 2012.
Cornwell, John Joseph. *A Galway Landlord during the Great Famine: Ulick John de Burgh, the First Marquis of Clanricard.* Maynooth Studies in Irish Local History Number 47. Edited by Raymond Gillespie. Dublin: Irish Academic Press, 2005.
Coulter, Harry. *The West of Ireland: Its Existing Condition, and Prospects by Harry Coulter, Correspondent for Saunder's News-letter.* Dublin: Hodges, Smith, 1862.
Crawford, E. Margaret. "Food and Famine." In *The Great Irish Famine.* The Thomas Davis Lecture Series, 60–73. Edited by Cathal Póirtéir. Dublin: Mercier, 1995.
———. "The Great Irish Famine, 1845–9: Image Versus Reality." In *Ireland: Art into History,* 75–88. Edited by Raymond Gillespie and Brian P. Kennedy. Dublin: Townhouse, 1994.
Crawford, W. H. "Provincial Town Life in the Early Nineteenth Century: An Artist's Impression." In *Ireland: Art into History,* 43–60. Edited by Raymond Gillespie and Brian P. Kennedy. Dublin: Townhouse, 1994.
Croker, T. Crofton. *Researches in the South of Ireland: Illustrative of the Scenery, Architectural Remains, and the Manners and Superstitions of the Peasantry with an Appendix Containing a Private Narrative of the Rebellion of 1798.* New York: Barnes & Noble [1824] 1969.
Cromwell, Thomas J. *Excursions through Ireland Comprising Topographical and Historical Delineations of Leinster.* 3 vols. London: Longman, Hurst, Rees, Brown, 1820.
Crossman, Virginia. *The Irish Poor Law, 1838–1948.* Studies in Irish Economic and Social History, No. 10. Dundalk: Dundalgan Press, 2006.
Cullen, Louis M. "Economic Development, 1750–1800." In *A New History of Ireland. Vol. IV. Eighteenth Century Ireland, 1691–1800,* 159–95. Edited by T. W. Moody and W. E. Vaughan. Oxford: Clarendon, 1986.
———. *The Emergence of Modern Ireland, 1600–1900.* New York: Holmes, Meier, 1981.
———. "Man, Landscape and Roads: The Changing Eighteenth Century." In *The Shaping of Ireland: The Geographical Perspective.* Thomas Davis Lecture Series, 123–37. Edited by William Nolan. Cork: Mercer, 1986.
Cunningham, John. "The Famine in County Fermanagh." In *The Famine in Ulster: The Regional Impact,* 129–45. Edited by Christine Kinealy and Trevor Parkhill. Belfast: Ulster Historical Foundation, 1997.
Curti, Merle. *American Philanthropy Abroad.* New Brunswick, NJ: Routledge, 2017

Curtis, Jr., L. Perry. *Apes and Angels: The Irishman in Victorian Caricature*, rev. ed. Washington, DC: Smithsonian Institution, 1997.

———. *Notice to Quit: The Great Irish Famine Evictions*. Ireland's Great Hunger Museum. Hamden, CT: Quinnipiac University Press, 2015.

Dallit, Cahal. "The Famine in County Antrim." In *The Famine in Ulster: The Regional Impact*, 15–34. Edited by Christine Kinealy and Trevor Parkhill. Belfast: Ulster Historical Foundation, 1997.

Daly, Mary E. "Farming and the Famine." In *Famine 150: Commemorative Lecture Series*, 29–48. Edited by Cormac Ó Gráda. Dublin: Teagasc, 1997.

———. "The Operations of Famine Relief, 1845–1847." *The Great Irish Famine*, 123–34. Edited by Cathal Póirtiér. Thomas Davis Lecture Series. Cork: Mercier, 1995.

———. "Revisionism and Irish History: The Great Famine." In *The Making of Modern Irish History: Revisionism and the Revisionist*, 71–89. Edited by D. George Boyce and Allen O'Day. New York: Routledge, 1996.

Davis, Graham. "The Historiography of the Irish Famine." In *The Meaning of the Famine*, 15–39. The Irish World Wide: History, Heritage, Identity, v. 6. Edited by Patrick O'Sullivan. London: Leicester University Press, 2000.

De Fréine, Séan. "The Cultural Consequences of the Great Famine." In *The Famine Lectures / Léachtaí an Ghorta*, 144–51. Edited by Breandán Ó Conaire. Boyle, County Roscommon: Comhdáil an Chraoibhín, 1995–97.

De Nie, Michael. *The Eternal Paddy: Irish Identity and the British Press, 1798–1882*. History of Ireland and the Irish Diaspora. Edited by James S. Donnelly, Jr. and Thomas Archdeacon. Madison: Wisconsin University Press, 2004.

Delaney, Enda. *The Curse of Reason: The Great Irish Famine*. Dublin: Gill, Macmillan, 2012.

———. "Ireland's Great Famine: A Transnational History." In *Transnational Perspectives in Modern Irish History*, 106–26. Routledge Series in Modern History, 15. Edited by Nial Whelehan. New York: Routledge, 2015.

Dickson, David. *Artic Ireland*. Belfast: White Row, 1997, 1998.

———. *New Foundations Ireland, 1660–1800*, 2nd rev. ed. Dublin: Irish Academic Press, 2000.

———. "The Other Great Irish Famine." In *The Great Irish Famine*, 50–59. Thomas Davis Lecture Series. Edited by Cathal Póirtiér. Cork: Mercier, 1995.

———. "The Potato and Irish Diet Before the Great Famine." In *Famine 150: Commemorative Lecture Series*, 1–27. Edited by Cormac Ó Gráda. Dublin: Teagasc, 1997.

———. "The State of Ireland before 1798." In *The Great Rebellion of 1798*, 15–25. Thomas Davis Lectures. Edited by Cathal Póirtéir. Cork: Mercier, 1998.

[Dickson, M. F.]. "Letters from the Coast of Clare," *Dublin University Magazine*, 28 (July–December) (1841), 161–79.

Dolan, Terence Patrick. editor. *A Dictionary of Hiberno-English: The Irish Use of English*. Dublin: Gill, Macmillan, 1999.

Donnelly, Jr., James S., *The Great Irish Potato Famine*. Gloucestershire: Sutton Publishers, 2001.

———. "'Irish Property Must Pay for Irish Poverty': British Public Opinion and the Great Irish Famine." In *Fearful Realities: New Perspectives on the Famine*, 60–76. Edited by Chris Morash and Richard Hayes. Dublin: Irish Academic Press, 1996.

———. *The Land and the People of Nineteenth-Century Cork*. London: Routledge Kegan Paul, 1975.

———. "Mass Evictions and the Great Famine: The Clearances Revisited." In *The Great Irish Famine*, 155–73. Thomas Davis Lecture Series. Edited by Cathal Póirtiér. Cork: Mercier, 1995.

———. "Pastorini and Captain Rock: Millennialism and Sectarianism in the Rockite Movement of 1821–4." In *Irish Peasants: Violence & Political Unrest, 1780–1914*, 102–43. Edited by Samuel Clark and James S. Donnelly, Jr. Madison: Wisconsin University Press, 1983.

Dooley, Terence A. M. *The Big House and Landed Estates of Ireland: A Research Guide*. Maynooth Research Guides for Irish Local History No. 11. Dublin: Four Courts, 2007.

———. "Landlords and the Land Question, 1879–1909." In *Famine, Land and Culture in Ireland*, 116–39. Edited by Carla King. Dublin: University College Dublin, 2000.

Dorian, Hugh. *The Outer Edge of Ulster: Memoir of Social Life in Nineteenth Century Donegal*. Edited by Breandán Mac Suibhne and David Dickson. Dublin: Lilliput, 2000.

Dowley, Leslie J. "The Potato and Late Blight in Ireland." In *Famine 150: Commemorative Lecture Series*, 49–65. Edited by Cormac Ó Gráda. Dublin: Teagasc, 1997.

Doyle, Anthony. *Charles Powell Leslie II's Estates at Glaslough, County Monaghan, 1800–1841*. Maynooth Studies in Irish Local History Number 38. Edited by Raymond Gillespie. Dublin: Irish Academic Press, 2001.

Dube, Colleen Margaret. "Enabling Institutions and Disabling Illustrations: Images of Connemara in Tourist Handbooks, 1850–1880." M.Phil Dissertation, University College, Galway, 1994.

Dufferin, Lord [Frederick Templeton Blackwood]. *Narrative of a Journey from Oxford to Skibbereen, during the Year of the Irish Famine*. Oxford: Parker, 1847.

Duffy, Patrick J. "Emigrants and the Estate Office: A Compassionate Relationship." In *The Hungry Stream: Essays on Immigration and Famine*, 71–86. Edited by E. Margret Crawford. Belfast: Institute of Irish Studies, 1997.

———. "The Famine in County Monaghan." In *The Famine in Ulster: The Regional Impact*, 169–95. Edited by Christine Kinealy and Trevor Parkhill. Belfast: Ulster Historical Foundation, 1997.

———. "Mapping the Famine in Monaghan." In *The Atlas of the Great Irish Famine*, 440–49. Edited by John Crowley, William J. Smyth and Mike Murphy. New York: New York University Press, 2012.

Dunn, Mary Lee. "Agenda for Researching the Famine Experience in Kilglass Parish, County Roscommon." In *Ireland's Great Hunger: Silence, Memory and Commemoration*, 88–120. Quinnipiac University Studies in the Great Hunger. Edited by David A. Valone, and Christine Kinealy. New York: University Press of America, 2002.

Dyke, Ian. *William Cobbett and Rural Popular Culture*. Cambridge: Cambridge University Press, 1992.

East, Rev. John. *Notes and Glimpses of Ireland in 1847*. London: Hamilton, Adams, 1847.

Eaton, John P., and Charles A. Hass. *Titanic: Destination Disaster, The Legends and the Reality*. New York: Norton, 1996.

Eiríksson, Andrés. "Food Supply and Food Riots." In *Famine 150: Commemorative Lecture Series*, 67–93. Edited by Cormac Ó Gráda. Dublin: Teagasc, 1997.

Epstein, David. "How an 1836 Famine Altered the Genes of Children Born Decades Later." *New York Times*, August 23, 2013. https://io9.gizmodo.com/how-an-1836-famine-altered-the-genes-of-children-born-d-1200001177.

Evans, E. Estyn. *Irish Folk Ways*. London: Routledge, Kegan Paul, 1957.

———. *Personality of Ireland: Habitat, Heritage and History*. Dublin: Lilliput, 1992.

Farrell, James M. "Reporting the Irish Famine in America: Images of 'Suffering Ireland' in the American Press, 1845–1848." In *The Famine Irish: Emigration and the Great Hunger*, 67–86. Edited Ciarán Reilly. Dublin: The History Press Ireland, 2016.

Feehan, John. "The Potato: Root of the Famine." In *The Atlas of the Great Irish Famine*, 28–37. Edited by John Crowley, William J. Smyth and Mike Murphy. New York: New York University Press, 2012.

Fegan, Melissa. "The Traveller's Experience in Famine Ireland." *Irish Studies Review*, 9 (2001), 361–71.

[Fisher, Lydia Jane]. *Letters from the Kingdom of Kerry in the Year 1845*. Dublin: Webb, Chapman, 1847.

Fitzgerald, Patrick. "'The Great Hunger?' Irish Famine: Changing Patterns of Crisis." In *The Hungry Stream: Essays on Immigration and Famine*, 101–22. Edited by E. Margret Crawford. Belfast: Institute of Irish Studies, 1997.

Fitzpatrick, David. *Irish Emigration: 1801–1921*. Irish Economic and Social History, No. 1. Edited by Peter Roebuck and David Dickson. [Dublin]: Dundalgan: Press, Economic and Social History Society of Ireland, 1984.

Flanagan, Catherine. *The Great Famine in Kinsale*. Maynooth Studies in Irish Local History Number 134. Edited by Raymond Gillespie. Dublin: Irish Academic Press, 2018.
Foley, Kieran. "The Famine in the Dingle Peninsula." In *Atlas of the Great Irish Famine*, 398–405. Edited by John Crowley, William J. Smyth and Mike Murphy. New York: New York University Press, 2012.
Foley, Michael. *Death in Every Paragraph: Journalism and the Great Irish Famine*. Ireland's Great Hunger Museum. Hamden, CT: Quinnipiac University Press, 2015.
Foley, Tadhg. *Death by Discourse: Political Economy and the Great Famine*. Ireland's Great Hunger Museum. Hamden, CT: Quinnipiac University Press, n.d.
Forbes, Sir John. *Memorandums Made in the Autumn of 1852*. 2 vols. London: Smith, Elder, 1853.
Foster, R. F. *Modern Ireland: 1600–1972*. London: Allen Lane/Penguin, 1988.
———. *Paddy and Mr. Punch: Connections in Irish and English History*. London: Allen Lane/Penguin, 1993.
Freeman, T. W. *Ireland: Its Physical, Historical, Social and Economic Geography*. London: Metheun, 1950, 1960.
———. "Land and People, c. 1841." In *A New History of Ireland, v. Ireland Under the Union, I, 1801–1870*, 242–71. Edited by W. E. Vaughan. Oxford: Clarendon, 1989.
Fulton, Hellen. "Hegemonic Discourse in Brian Friel's *The Freedom of the City*." In *Language and Tradition in Ireland: Communities and Displacements*, 62–83. Edited by Maria Tymoczko and Colin A. Ireland. Amherst: University of Massachusetts Press, 2003.
Funnell, Warwick. "Accounting for Justice: Entitlement, Want and the Irish Famine, 1845–7." *Accounting Historians Journal*, 28:2 (December 2001), 187–206.
Gallman, J. Matthew. *Receiving Erin's Children: Philadelphia, Liverpool and the Irish Famine, 1845–1855*. Chapel Hill: University of North Carolina Press, 2000.
Gallogly, Fr. Dan. "The Famine in County Cavan." In *The Famine in Ulster: The Regional Impact*, 59–75. Edited by Christine Kinealy and Trevor Parkhill. Belfast: Ulster Historical Foundation, 1997.
Geary, Laurence M. "Famine, Fever and the Bloody Flux." In *The Great Irish Famine*, 74–85. The Thomas Davis Lecture Series. Edited by Cathal Póirtéir. Dublin: Mercier, 1995.
———. "'The Living Were Out of Their Feeling': A Socio-Cultural Analysis of the Great Famine in Ireland." In *The Famine Lectures/Léachtaí an Ghorta*, 308–28. Edited by Breandán Ó Conaire. Boyle, County Roscommon: Comhdáil an Chraoibhín, 1995–97.
———. "Medical Relief and the Great Famine." In *Atlas of the Great Irish Famine*, 199–208. Edited by John Crowley, William J. Smyth and Mike Murphy. New York: New York University Press, 2012.
———. "What People Died of During the Famine." In *Famine 150: Commemorative Lecture Series*, 95–111. Edited by Cormac Ó Gráda. Dublin: Teagasc, 1997.
Geber, Jonny. "Burying the Famine Dead: The Kilkenny Workhouse." *The Atlas of the Great Irish Famine*, 341–48. Edited by John Crowley, William J. Smyth and Mike Murphy. New York: New York University Press, 2012.
———. "'Wretched in the Extreme': Investigating Child Experiences of the Great Hunger through Bioarcheology." In *Children of the Great Hunger in Ireland*, 75–94. Edited by Christine Kinealy, Jason King and Gerard Moran. Hamden, CT: Quinnipiac, 2018.
Gibbons, Luke. "Did Edmund Burke Cause the Great Famine? The Moral Economy and Colonial Ireland." In *The Famine Lectures/Léachtaí an Ghorta*, 28–51. Edited by Breandán Ó Conaire. Boyle, County Roscommon: Comhdáil an Chraoibhín, 1995–97.
———. *Gaelic Gothic: Race Colonization and Irish Culture*. Galway: Arlen House, 2004.
———. *The Limits of the Visible: Representing the Great Irish Famine*. Ireland's Great Hunger Museum. Hamden, CT: Quinnipiac University Press, 2014.
Goodbody, Rob. *A Suitable Channel: Quaker Relief in the Great Famine*. Bray, Ireland: Pale Publishing, 1995.
Grace, Daniel. *The Great Famine in Nenagh Poor Law Union, County Tipperary*. Nenagh, County Tipperary: Relay Books, 2000.

Grace, Pierce A. *The Middle Class of Callan, Co. Kilkenny, 1825–45*. Maynooth Studies in Irish Local History Number 120. Edited by Raymond Gillespie. Dublin: Irish Academic Press, 2015.

Graham, Robert. *A Scottish Whig in Ireland, 1835–1838. The Irish Journals of Robert Graham of Redgorton*. Edited by Henry Heany. Dublin: Four Courts, 1999.

Grant, Jim. "The Famine in County Tyrone." In *The Famine in Ulster: The Regional Impact*, 197–222. Edited by Christine Kinealy and Trevor Parkhill. Belfast: Ulster Historical Foundation, 1997.

Gray, Peter. *Famine, Land and Politics: British Government and Irish Society, 1843–50*. Dublin: Irish Academic Press, 1999.

———. "Ideology and the Famine." In *The Great Irish Famine*, 86–103. The Thomas Davis Lecture Series. Edited by Cathal Póirtéir. Dublin: Mercier, 1995.

———. *The Irish Famine*. New York: Discoveries/Harry N. Abrams, n.d.

———. "'Potatoes and Providence': British Government Responses to the Great Famine." *Bullán: An Irish Studies Journal*, 1:1 (Spring, 1994), 75–90.

Green, E. R. R. "Agriculture." In *The Great Irish Famine: Studies in Irish History, 1845–52*, 89–128. Edited by R. Dudley Edwards and T. Desmond Williams. Dublin: Browne, Nolan, 1956.

Guinnane, Timothy W. "The Great Irish Famine and Population: The Long View." Papers and Proceedings of the Hundredth and Sixth Annual Meeting of the American Economic Association. *The American Economic Review*, 84:2 (May 1994), 303–8.

Haines, Robin. *Charles Trevelyan and the Great Irish Famine*. Dublin: Four Courts, 2004.

Hall, Samuel Carter, and Anna Maria Hall. *Hall's Ireland. Mr. and Mrs. Hall's Tour of 1840*. 2 vols. Edited by Michael Scott. London: Sphere Books, [1841–1843] 1984.

———. *Ireland: Its Scenery and Character & etc.* 4 vols. London: Jeremiah How, 1843.

Hall, Spencer T. *Life and Death in Ireland as Witnessed in 1849*. Manchester: J. T. Sparkes, 1850.

[Hamilton, William Tighe]. W. T. H. *The Encumbered Estates of Ireland*. London: Bradbury, Evans, 1850.

Handlin, Oscar. *Boston's Immigrants: A Study in Acculturation*. rev. ed. New York: Athenaeum, 1976.

Head, Francis Bond. *A Fortnight in Ireland*. London: John Murray, 1852.

Hickey, Fr. Patrick. "The Famine in the Skibbereen Union (1845–51)." In *The Great Irish Famine*, 185–203. Thomas Davis Lecture Series. Edited by Cathal Póirtiér. Cork: Mercier, 1995.

———. *Famine in West Cork: The Mizen Peninsula Land and People, 1800–1852. A Local Study of Pre-Famine and Famine Ireland*. Cork: Mercier, 2002.

———. "Mortality and Emigration in Six Parishes in the Union of Skibbereen, West Cork, 1846–47." In *Atlas of the Great Irish Famine*, 371–79. Edited by John Crowley, William J. Smyth and Mike Murphy. New York: New York University Press, 2012.

Hilton, Boyd. *The Age of Atonement: The Influence of Evangelicalism on Social and Economic Thought, 1785–1865*. Oxford: Clarendon, 1988, 1991.

Himmelfarb, Gertrude. *The Idea of Poverty: England in the Early Industrial Age*. New York: Knopf, 1983.

Hoare, Richard Colt. *A Tour in Ireland, A. D. 1801*. London: Miller, J. Archer, Mahon, 1807.

Hogan, Neil. "The Famine Beat: American Newspaper Coverage of the Great Hunger." In *The Great Famine and the Irish Diaspora in America*, 155–79. Edited by Arthur Gribben. Amherst: University of Massachusetts Press, 1999.

[Hole, Samuel Reynolds.] *A Little Tour of Ireland. Being a Visit to Dublin, Galway, Connemara, Athlone, Limerick, Killarney, Glengarriff, Cork, etc. by an Oxonian with Illustrations by John Leech* [1859]. 3rd edition. London: Edward Arnold, 1896.

Hooper, Glenn. "'Strangers in Ireland': The Problematics of the Post-Union Travelogue." *Mosaic*, 28.1 (1995), 25–48.

———. *Travel Writing and Ireland, 1760–1860: Culture, History Politics*. New York: Palgrave Macmillan, 2005.

Huggins, Michael. *Social Conflict in Pre-Famine Ireland: The Case of County Roscommon*. Dublin: Four Courts, 2007.

Hull, Kathrine L. "Forget Me Not: the Role of Women in Ballykilcline." In *Unearthing Hidden Ireland: Historical Archaeology at Ballykilcline, County Roscommon*. 140–60. Edited by Charles E. Orser, Jr. Bray, County Wicklow: Worldwell, 2006.

———. "To Drain and Cultivate: Agriculture and 'Improvement" at Ballykilcline." In *Unearthing Hidden Ireland: Historical Archaeology at Ballykilcline, County Roscommon*, 161–75. Edited by Charles E. Orser, Jr. Bray, County Wicklow: Worldwell, 2006.

Hunt, Tom. *Portlaw, County Waterford, 1825–76: Portrait of an Industrial Village and Its Cotton Industry*. Maynooth Studies in Irish Local History Number 33. Edited by Raymond Gillespie. Dublin: Irish Academic Press, 2000.

Inglis, Henry D. *A Journey throughout Ireland, during the Spring, Summer and Autumn of 1834*. 2 vols. London: Whittaker, 1834.

James, Dermot, and Séamus Ó Maitiú. *The Wicklow World of Elizabeth Smith: 1840–1850*. Dublin: Woodfield Press, 1996.

James, Kevin J. *Handloom Weavers in Ulster's Linin Industry, 1815–1914*. Dublin: Four Courts, 2007.

Johnson, James. *A Tour of Ireland with Meditations and Reflections*. London: S. Highley, 1844.

Jones, David S. "The Transfer of Land and the Emergence of the Graziers during the Famine Period." In *The Great Famine and the Irish Diaspora in America*, 85–103. Edited by Arthur Gribben. Amherst: University of Massachusetts Press, 1999.

Jordan, Donald E. *Land and Popular Politics in Ireland: County Mayo from the Plantation to the Land War*. Cambridge: Cambridge University Press, 1994.

Kellerher, Margaret. "The Female Gaze: Asenath Nicholson's Famine Narrative." In *Fearful Realities: New Perspectives on the Famine*, 119-30. Edited by Chris Morash and Richard Hayes. Dublin: Irish Academic Press, 1996.

Kelly, Jennifer, *The Downfall of Hagan: Sligo Ribbonmen in 1842*. Maynooth Studies in Local History Number 77. Edited by Raymond Gillespie. Dublin: Four Courts, 2008.

Kelly, Mary C. "The Famine in Roscommon." *Atlas of the Great Irish Famine*, 308–17. Edited by John Crowley, William J. Smyth and Mike Murphy. New York: New York University Press, 2012.

Kelly, Mary C. *Ireland's Great Famine in Irish-American History: Enshrining a Fateful Memory*. Plymouth, UK: Rowman, Littlefield, 2014.

Kelly, Patricia. *The Story of Connemara*. Dublin: 1989.

Kennedy, Liam. *Unhappy the Land: The Most Oppressed People Ever, the Irish*. County Kildare: Merrion, 2016.

———, Paul S. Ell, E. M. Crawford and L. A Clarkson. *Mapping the Great Irish Famine*. Dublin: Four Courts, 1999.

Kenny, Kevin. *The American Irish: A History*. Harlow, Essex: Pearson Education, 2000.

Kerr, Donald. "The Catholic Church and the Irish Famine." In *The Famine Lectures/Léachtaí an Ghorta*, 115–43. Edited by Breandán Ó Conaire. Boyle, County Roscommon: Comhdáil an Chraoibhín, 1995–97.

Kinealy, Christine. "'Attenuated Apparitions of Humanity': The Innocent Casualties of the Great Hunger." In *Children of the Great Hunger in Ireland*, 3–26. Edited by Christine Kinealy, Jason King and Gerard Moran. Hamden, CT: Quinnipiac, 2018.

———. *Charity and the Great Hunger in Ireland: The Kindness of Strangers*. London: Bloomsbury, 2013.

———. *A Death-Dealing Famine: The Great Hunger in Ireland*. London: Pluto, 1997.

———. "'The Famine Killed Everything': Living with the Memory of the Great Hunger." In *Ireland's Great Hunger: Silence, Memory and Commemoration*, 1–37. Quinnipiac University Studies in the Great Hunger. Edited by David A. Valone and Christine Kinealy. New York: University Press of America, 2002.

———. *This Great Calamity: The Irish Famine, 1845–52*. Boulder, CO: Robert Reinhart, 1995.

———. "The Role of the Poor Law during the Famine." In *The Great Irish Famine*, 104–22. Thomas Davis Lecture Series. Edited by Cathal Póirtiér. Cork: Mercier, 199.

———, and Trevor Parkhill. "Introduction." In *The Famine in Ulster: The Regional Impact*, 1–14. Edited by Christine Kinealy and Trevor Parkhill. Belfast: Ulster Historical Foundation, 1997.

Kinzer, Bruce L. *England's Disgrace? J. S. Mill and the Irish Question*. Toronto: University of Toronto Press, 2001.

Knight, Patrick. *Erris in the "Irish Highlands" and "The Atlantic Railway."* Dublin: M. Keene, 1836.

Lamb, Herbert H. Weather, *Climate and Human Affairs: A Book of Essays and Other Papers*. New York: Routledge, 2012.

Lambe, Miriam. *A Tipperary Landed Estate: Castle Otway, 1750–1853*. Maynooth Studies in Irish Local History Number 17. Edited by Raymond Gillespie. Dublin: Irish Academic Press, 1998.

[Lambert, H.] *A Memoir in Ireland in 1850 by an Ex-MP*. Dublin: McGlashan, 1851.

Larkin, Emmet. "The Devotional Revolution in Ireland, 1850–75." *American Historical Review*, 77 (June 1972), 625–52.

———. *The Pastoral Role of the Roman Catholic Church in Pre-Famine Ireland, 1750–1850*. Washington, DC: Catholic University of America Press, 2006.

Lee, Joe. "The Famine as History." In *Famine 150: Commemorative Lecture Series*, 159–75. Edited by Cormac Ó Gráda. Dublin: Teagasc, 1997.

Lengel, Edward. G. *The Irish through British Eyes: Perceptions of Ireland in the Famine Era*. Westport, CT: Praeger, 2002.

Levinson, Martin H. "A General Semantics Analysis of the RMS Titanic Disaster." *A Review of General Semantics*, 69:2 (April 2012), 143–56.

Lewis, George Cornewall. *On Local Disturbances in Ireland and on the Irish Church Question*. London: Fellows, 1836.

Lloyd, David. "The Indigent Sublime: Specters of Irish Hunger." *Representations*, 92:1 (Fall 2005), 152–85.

Lyons, F. S. L. *Ireland since the Famine: 1850 to the Present*. London: Weidenfeld, Nicholson, 1971.

Mac Atasney, Gerard. "The Famine in County Armagh." In *The Famine in Ulster: The Regional Impact*, 35–58. Edited by Christine Kinealy and Trevor Parkhill. Belfast: Ulster Historical Foundation, 1997.

———. "In the Shadow of Sliabh Iarainn." In *Atlas of the Great Irish Famine*, 298–304. Edited by John Crowley, William J. Smyth and Mike Murphy. New York: New York University Press, 2012.

———. "Lurgan Workhouse." In *Atlas of the Great Irish Famine*, 164–67. Edited by John Crowley, William J. Smyth and Mike Murphy. New York: New York University Press, 2012.

———. "Mohill Union Workhouse." In *Atlas of the Great Irish Famine*, 305–7. Edited by John Crowley, William J. Smyth and Mike Murphy. New York: New York University Press, 2012.

———. "'A Picture of Famine and Wretchedness': The Women of County Leitrim during the Great Hunger." In *Women and the Great Hunger*, 57–69. Edited by Christine Kinealy, Jason King and Ciarán Reilly. Hamden, CT: Quinnipiac University Press, 2016.

———. *"This Dreadful Visitation:" The Famine; in Lurgan/Portadown*. Belfast: Beyond the Pale Publications, 1997.

———, and Christine Kinealy. "The Great Hunger in Belfast." In *Atlas of the Great Irish Famine*, 434–39. Edited by John Crowley, William J. Smyth and Mike Murphy. New York: New York University Press, 2012.

Mac Cárthaigh, Críostóir. "Clare Island Folklife." In *New Survey of Clare Island: Volume I, History and Cultural Landscape*, 41–72. Edited by Críostóir Mac Cárthaigh and Kevin Whelan. Dublin: Royal Irish Academy, 1999.

McCavery, Trevor. "The Famine in County Down." In *The Famine in Ulster: The Regional Impact*, 99–127. Edited by Christine Kinealy and Trevor Parkhill. Belfast: Ulster Historical Foundation, 1997.

McCulloch, J. R. *Statistical Account of the British Empire, Exhibiting Its Extent, Physical Capabilities, Population, Civil and Religious Institutions*. 2 vols. London: Charles Knight, 1837.

MacCurtain, Margaret. "Pre-Famine Peasantry in Ireland: Definition and Theme." In *Irish University Review: A Journal of Irish Studies*. 4:2 (Autumn 1974), 188–98.

MacDonagh, Oliver. "The Economy and Society, 1830–45." In *A New History of Ireland, v. Ireland Under the Union, I, 1801–1870*, 218–41. Edited by W. E. Vaughan. Oxford: Clarendon, 1989.

———. *The Emancipist: Daniel O'Connell, 1830–1847*. New York: St. Martin's, 1989.

———. "Irish Overseas Emigration during the Famine." In *The Great Famine: Studies in Irish History, 1845–1852*, 319–88. Edited by R. Dudley Edwards and T. Desmond. Dublin: Browne, Nolan, 1956.

McDowell, R. B. "Ireland on the Eve of the Famine." In *The Great Famine: Studies in Irish History, 1845–1852*, 3–88. Edited by R. Dudley Edwards and T. Desmond. Williams. Dublin: Browne, Nolan, 1956.

Mac Éirni, Piaras. "Famine and the Irish Diaspora." In *Atlas of the Great Irish Famine*, 589–99. Edited by John Crowley, William J. Smyth and Mike Murphy. New York: New York University Press, 2012.

McGowan, Mark G. "Black '47 and Toronto, Canada." In *Atlas of the Great Irish Famine*, 525-31. Edited by John Crowley, William J. Smyth and Mike Murphy. New York: New York University Press, 2012.

———. "Grosse Île Quebec" *Atlas of the Great Irish Famine*, 532–35. Edited by John Crowley, William J. Smyth and Mike Murphy. New York: New York University Press, 2012.

McGregor, Patrick P. L. "Demographic Pressure and the Irish Famine: Malthus after Mokyr." *Land Economics*, 65 (August 1989), 228–38.

McHugh, Roger J. "The Famine in Irish Oral Tradition." In *The Great Irish Famine: Studies in Irish History, 1845–52*, 391–436. Edited by R. Dudley Edwards and T. Desmond Williams. Dublin: Browne and Nolan, 1956.

Macintyre, Angus. *The Liberator: Daniel O'Connell and the Irish Party, 1830–47*. New York: Macmillan, 1965.

MacLaughlin, Jim. "The Management of Famine in Donegal in the Hungry Forties." In *Atlas of the Great Irish Famine*, 450–57. Edited by John Crowley, William J. Smyth and Mike Murphy. New York: New York University Press, 2012.

MacMahon, Bryan. *The Great Famine in Tralee and North Kerry*. Cork: Mercier, 2017.

MacManus, Rev. Henry. *Sketches of the Irish Highlands, Descriptive, Social and Religious, with Special Reference to Irish Missions in Connacht since 1840*. London: Hamilton, Adams, 1863.

McPartlin, Joseph. "Diet, Politics and Disaster: The Great Irish Famine." *Proceedings of the Nutrition Society*, 56 (1997), 211–23.

Mac Suibhne, Breandán. *The End of Outrage: Post-Famine Adjustment in Rural Ireland*. Oxford: Oxford University Press, 2017.

McVeagh, John. *Irish Travel Writing: A Bibliography*. Dublin: Wolfhound, 1996.

Mahoney, Paschal. *Grim Bastilles of Despair: The Poor Law Union Workhouses in Ireland*. Ireland's Great Hunger Museum. Hamden, CT: Quinnipiac University Press, 2016.

Manning, Richard. *Against the Grain: How Agriculture Changed Civilization*. New York: North Point, 2004.

Martin, Amy. "'The Skeleton at the Feast': Lady Wilde's Famine Poetry and Irish International Critiques of Food Scarcity." *Women and the Great Hunger*, 149–60. Edited by Christine Kinealy, Jason King and Ciarán Reilly. Hamden, CT: Quinnipiac University Press, 2016.

Martineau, Harriet. *Letters from Ireland* [1852]. Edited by Glenn Hooper. Dublin: Irish Academic Press, 2001.

Martinez, Vanesa. "How Your Diet Could Affect Generations to Come." *Irish Times*, January 13, 2017. https://www.irishtimes.com/news/science/how-your-diet-could-affect-the-generations-to-come-1.3118344

Mason, William Shaw. *A Statistical Account or Parochial Account of Ireland Drawn from the Communications with the Clergy*. 2 vols. Dublin: Printed by Graiseberry and Campbell, 1814.

Maxwell, Constantia. *The Stranger in Ireland: From the Reign of Elizabeth to the Great Famine*. London: Jonathan Cape, 1954.

Meloy, Elizabeth. "'Dawn of a Brighter Day': Re-presenting the Famine at the Irish International Exhibition of 1853." *New Hibernia Review*. 22:1 (Errach/Spring, 2018), 19–44.

Miller, Kerby A. "Emigration to North America in the Era of the Great Famine, 1845–55." In *Atlas of the Great Irish Famine*, 214–27. Edited by John Crowley, William J. Smyth and Mike Murphy. New York: New York University Press, 2012.

———. *Emigrants and Exiles: Ireland and the Irish Exodus to North America*. Oxford: Oxford University Press, 1985.

———, Brian Gurrin and Líam Kennedy. "The Great Famine and Religious Demography in Mid-Nineteenth Century Ulster." In *Atlas of the Great Irish Famine*, 426–33. Edited by John Crowley, William J. Smyth and Mike Murphy. New York: New York University Press, 2012.

Mitchel, John. *The Last Conquest of Ireland (Perhaps)*. Glasgow: R. & T. Washbourne, 1876.

Mitchell, Frank. *The Shell Guild to Reading the Irish Landscape (Incorporating the Irish Landscape)*. Dublin: Michael Joseph, Country House, 1986.

Mokyr, Joel. *Why Ireland Starved: A Quantitative and Analytical History of the Irish Economy, 1800–1850*. London: George Allen & Urwin, 1985.

Montaño, John Patrick. *The Roots of English Colonialism in Ireland*. Cambridge: Cambridge University Press, 2011.

Moran, Gerard. *Fleeing from Famine in Connemara: James Hack Tuke and His Assisted Emigration Scheme in the 1880s*. Maynooth Studies in Irish Local History Number 135. Edited by Raymond Gillespie. Dublin: Irish Academic Press, 2018.

———. "'Permanent Deadweight:' Female Pauper Emigration from Mountbellow Workhouse to Canada." In *Women and the Great Hunger*, 109–21. Edited by Christine Kinealy, Jason King and Ciarán Reilly. Hamden, CT: Quinnipiac University Press, 2016.

———. "'Shoveling out the Paupers': The Irish Poor Law and Assisted Emigration during the Great Famine." In *The Famine Irish: Emigration and the Great Hunger*, 22–40. Edited Ciarán Reilly. Dublin: The History Press Ireland, 2016.

———. "'Suffer Little Children,' Life in the Workhouse during the Famine." In *Children of the Great Hunger in Ireland*, 25–50. Edited by Christine Kinealy, Jason King and Gerard Moran. Hamden, CT: Quinnipiac, 2018.

Morash, Christopher [Chris]. "Literature, Memory, Atrocity." In *Fearful Realities: New Perspectives on the Famine*, 110–18. Edited by Chris Morash and Richard Hayes. Dublin: Irish Academic Press, 1996.

———. "Making Memories: The Literature of the Irish Famine." In *The Meaning of the Famine*, 40–55. The Irish World Wide: History, Heritage, Identity, v. 6. Edited by Patrick O'Sullivan. London: Leicester University Press, 2000.

———. *Writing the Irish Famine*. Oxford: Clarendon Press, 1995.

Murphy, Ignatius. *Before the Famine Struck: Life in West Clare, 1835–1845*. Dublin: Irish Academic Press, 1996.

———. *A People Starved: Life and Death in West Clare, 1845–51*. Dublin: Irish Academic Press, 1996.

Nally, David P. *Human Encumbrances: Political Violence and the Great Irish Famine*. Notre Dame, IN: University of Notre Dame Press, 2011.

National Archives Currency Converter: 1270-2017. http://www.nationalarchives.gov.uk/currency/results.asp#mid. (Accessed June 22, 2020).

Neal, Frank. "Black '47: Britain and the Irish Famine." In *The Famine Lectures/Léachtaí an Ghorta*, 329–56. Edited by Breandán Ó Conaire. Boyle, County Roscommon: Comhdháil an Chraoibhín, 1995–1997.

———. "Black '47: Liverpool and the Irish Famine." In *The Hungry Stream: Essays on Immigration and Famine*, 123–36. Edited by E. Margret Crawford. Belfast: Institute of Irish Studies, 1997.

———. "The Famine Irish in England and Wales." In *The Meaning of the Famine*, 56–80. The Irish World Wide: History, Heritage, Identity, v. 6. Edited by Patrick O'Sullivan. London: Leicester University Press, 2000.

Neave, Sir Digby, Bart. *Four Days in Connemara*. London: Richard Bentley, 1852.
Neeson, Eoin. *A History of Irish Forestry*. Dublin: Lilliput, 1991.
Newman, Gerald. *The Rise of English Nationalism, A Cultural History, 1740–1830*. London: Macmillan, 1997.
Nic Craith, Máiréad. "Legacy and Loss: The Great Silence and Its Aftermath." In *The Atlas of the Great Irish Famine*, 580–87. Edited by John Crowley, William J. Smyth and Mike Murphy. New York: New York University Press, 2012.
Nicholls, George. *A History of the Irish Poor Law: In Connexon with the Condition of the People*. London: John Murray, 1856.
Nicholson, Asenath. *Annals of the Famine in Ireland*. Edited by Maureen Murphy. Dublin: Lilliput, 1998.
———. *Ireland's Welcome to the Stranger*. Edited by Maureen Murphy. Dublin: Lilliput, 2002.
Ní Ghiobúin, Mealla. *Dugort, Achill Island, 1831–1861: The Rise and Fall of a Missionary Community*. Maynooth Studies in Irish Local History Number 39. Edited by Raymond Gillespie. Dublin: Irish Academic Press, 2001.
Nolan, Janet. "The Great Famine and Women's Immigration from Ireland." In *The Hungry Stream: Essays on Immigration and Famine*, 61–70. Edited by E. Margaret Crawford. Belfast: Queen's University Press, 1997.
Nolan, Willie. "Land Reform in Post-Famine Ireland." In *The Atlas of the Great Irish Famine*, 570–79. Edited by John Crowley, William J. Smyth and Mike Murphy. New York: New York University Press, 2012.
Norton, Desmond. "Communication: Lord Palmerston and the Famine Emigration: A Rejoinder." *The Historical Journal*, 46:1 (2003), 155–65.
Nowlan, Kevin B. "The Political Background." In *The Great Irish Famine: Studies in Irish History, 1845-52*, 131–206. Edited by R. Dudley Edwards and T. Desmond Williams. Dublin: Browne, Nolan, 1956.
———. *The Politics of Repeal: A Study in the Relations Between Britain and Ireland, 1841–1850*. Studies in Irish History, vol. 3. Edited by T. W. Moody, J. C. Beckett and T. D. Williams. London: Routledge, Kegan Paul, 1965.
Nusteling, Hubert H. "How Many Irish Potato Famine Deaths? Toward Coherence of the Evidence?" *Historical Methods*, 42: 2 (Spring 2009), 57–80.
Nye, Eric. "Pounds Sterling to Dollars: Historical Conversion of Currency." Department of English, University of Wyoming. https://www.uwyo.edu/numimage/currency.htm
Ó Cathaoir, Brendan. "Ireland in the First Year of the Famine." *The Famine Lectures/Léachtaí an Ghorta*, 189–203. Edited by Brendan Ó Conaire. Boyle, County Roscommon: Comhdháil an Chraoibhín, 1995–97.
Ó Cathaoir, Eva. "The Workhouse during the Great Famine." *The Famine Lectures/Léachtaí an Ghorta*, 218–37. Edited by Breandán Ó Conaire. Boyle, County Roscommon: Comhdháil an Chraoibhín, 1995–97.
O'Connor, Patrick J. *Living in a Coded Land*. Landscape Series No. 1. Limerick: Oireacht na Mumhan Books, 1992.
Ó Crualaoich, Gearóid. "The 'Merry Wake'" *Irish Popular Culture, 1650–1850*, 173–200. Edited by James S. Donnelly, Jr. and Kerby A. Miller. Dublin: Academic Press, 1998.
Ó Cuív, Brian, editor. *A View of the Irish Language*. Dublin: Stationary Office, 1969.
Ó Giolláin, Diarmuid, "The Pattern." *Irish Popular Culture, 1650–1850*, 201–21. Edited by James S. Donnelly, Jr. and Kerby A. Miller. Dublin: Irish Academic Press, 1998.
Ó Gráda, Cormac. *Black '47 and Beyond: The Great Irish Famine in History, Economy and Memory*. Princeton, NJ: Princeton University Press, 1999.
———. *Famine: A Short History*. Princeton, NJ: Princeton University Press, 2009.
———. "The Great Famine and Other Famines." *Famine 150: Commemorative Lecture Series*, 129–57. Edited by Cormac Ó Gráda. Dublin: Teagasc, 1997.
———. *The Great Irish Famine*. New Studies in Economic and Social History. Cambridge: Cambridge University Press, 1995.

———. "Industry and Communications, 1801–1845." *A New History of Ireland, v. Ireland Under the Union, I, 1801–1870*. Edited by W. E. Vaughan. Oxford: Clarendon Press, 1989.

———. *Ireland: Before and After the Famine: Explorations in Economic History, 1800–1925*. 2nd ed. New York: Manchester University Press, 1993.

———. *Ireland: A New Economic History, 1780–1939*. New York: Oxford University Press, 1994.

———. "Poverty, Population and Agriculture, 1801–1845." *A New History of Ireland, v. Ireland Under the Union, I, 1801–1870*, 108–36. Edited by W. E. Vaughan. New York: Oxford University Press, 1994.

———, and Kevin H. O'Rourke. "Migration as Disaster Relief: Lessons from the Great Irish Famine." *European Review of Economic History*, 1:1 (April 1997), 3–25.

Ó hAllmhuráin, Gearóid. "The Great Famine: A Catalyst in Irish Traditional Music Making." *The Great Famine and the Irish Diaspora in America*, 104–32. Edited by Arthur Gribben. Amherst: University of Massachusetts Press, 1999.

O'Mahony, Michelle. "The Cork Workhouse." In *Atlas of the Great Irish Famine*, 150–55. Edited by John Crowley, William J. Smyth and Mike Murphy. New York: New York University Press, 2012, 150–55.

Ó Murchadha, Ciarán. *The Great Famine: Ireland's Agony, 1845–52*. New York: Continuum International, 2011.

———. *Sable Wings Over the Land: Ennis, County Clare and Its Wider Community during the Great Famine*. Ennis, County Clare: Clasp Press, 1998.

O'Neill, T. Patrick. "The Organization and Administration of Relief, 1849–52." *The Great Irish Famine: Studies in Irish History, 1845–52*, 209–59. Edited by R. Dudley Edwards and T. Desmond Williams. Dublin: Browne, Nolan, 1956.

O'Neill, Tim P. "Famine Evictions." In *Famine, Land and Culture in Ireland*, 29–70. Edited by Carla King. Dublin: University College Dublin Press, 2000.

O'Rourke, Kevin. "Did the Great Famine Matter?" *The Journal of Economic History*, 51:1 (March 1991), 1–22.

O'Sullivan, Niamh. *The Tombs of the Departed: Illustrations of Ireland's Great Hunger*. Ireland's Great Hunger Museum. Hamden, CT: Quinnipiac University Press, 2014.

O'Sullivan, Patrick, and Robert Lucking. "The Famine World Wide: The Irish Famine and the Development of Famine Policy and Famine Theory." *The Meaning of the Famine*, 195–232. The Irish World Wide: History, Heritage, Identity, v. 6. Edited by Patrick O'Sullivan. London: Leicester University Press, 2000.

Ó Tuathaigh, Gearóid. *I mBéal an Bháis: The Great Famine and the Language Shift in Nineteenth-Century Ireland*. Ireland's Great Hunger Museum. Hamden, CT: Quinnipiac University Press, 2015.

———. *Ireland before the Famine: 1798–1848*. The Gill History of Ireland. Dublin: Gill, Macmillan, 1972.

Orser, Jr., Charles E. "The People's Pottery: Irish Course Earthenwares and their Cultural Significance." In *Unearthing Hidden Ireland: Historical Archaeology at Ballykilcline, County Roscommon*, 72–96. Edited by Charles E. Orser, Jr. Bray: County. Wicklow: Worldwell, 2006.

Osborn, Sidney Godolphin, *Gleanings in the West of Ireland*. London: T. & W. Bonne, 1850.

Osner, Jr., Charles E. "Ballykilcline, County Roscommon." In *Atlas of the Great Irish Famine*, 318–23. Edited by John Crowley, William J. Smyth and Mike Murphy. New York: New York University Press, 2012,

Otway, Caesar. *Sketches in Erris and Tyrawly*. Dublin: William Curry, June 1841.

———. *Sketches in Ireland. Descriptive of Interesting and Hitherto Unnoticed Districts in the North and South*. Dublin: William Curry, June 1827.

———. *A Tour of Connaught, Comprising Sketches of Clonmacnoise* [sic], *Joyce Country and Achill, By the Author of Sketches in Ireland. With Illustrations Engraved in Wood*. Dublin: William Curry, June 1839.

Overton, Mark. *Agricultural Revolution in England: The Transformation of the Agrarian Economy, 1500–1850*. Cambridge: Cambridge University Press, 1996.

Parkhill, Trevor. "The Famine in County Londonderry." In *The Famine in Ulster: The Regional Impact*, 147–68. Edited by Christine Kinealy and Trevor Parkhill, Belfast: Ulster Historical Foundation, 1997.
Pim, Jonathan. *The Conditions and Prospects of Ireland and the Evils Arising from the Present Distribution of Landed Property: With Suggestions for a Remedy*. Dublin: Hodges Smith, 1848.
Pittock, Murry G. H. *Celtic Identity and the British Image*. New York: Manchester University Press, 1999.
Plumptre, Anne. *Narrative of a Residence in Ireland during the Summer of 1814 and that of 1815*. London: H. Colburn, 1817.
Póirtéir, Cathal. "Folk Memory and the Famine." In *The Great Irish Famine*, 219–31. The Thomas Davis Lecture Series. Edited by Cathal Póirtéir. Dublin: Mercier, 1995.
Quigley, Michael. "Grosse Île: Canada's Famine Memorial." In *The Great Famine and the Irish Diaspora in America*, 133–54. Edited by Arthur Gribben. Amherst: University of Massachusetts Press, 1999.
Quinn, Eileen Moore. "Externalizing Famine, Reconstituting Self: Testimonial Narrative from Ireland." *Anthropological Quarterly*, 74:2 (April 2001), 72–88.
Reader, John. *Potato: A History of the Propitious Esculent*, New Haven, CT: Yale University Press, 2009.
Rees, Jim. "The Surplus People." *Beaver*, Oct/Nov 1998, Vol. 78, Issue 5 (online version, no pages).
———. *The Surplus People: The Fitzwilliam Clearances, 1854–1856*. Cork: Collins Press, 2000.
Reid, Thomas. *Travels in Ireland in the Year 1822, Exhibiting Brief Sketches of the Moral, Physical and Political State of the Country: With Reflections on the Best Means of Improving its Condition*. London: Longman, Hurst Rees, Orme, Brown, 1823.
Reilly, Ciarán. *The Irish Land Agent, 1830–60: The Case of King's County*. Dublin: Four Courts, 2014.
———. "King's County During the Great Famine: 'Poverty and Plenty.'" In *The Atlas of the Great Irish Famine*, 349–53. Edited by John Crowley, William J. Smyth and Mike Murphy. New York: New York University Press, 2012.
———. "'Nearly Starved to Death': The Female Petition during the Great Hunger." In *Women and the Great Hunger*, 47–56. Edited by Christine Kinealy, Jason King and Ciarán Reilly. Hamden, CT: Quinnipiac University Press, 2016.
Richardson, Joseph. "Political Anglicanism in Ireland, 1692–1801: From the Language of Liberty to the Language of Union." In *The Irish Act of Union, 1800: Bicentennial Essays*, 58-67. Edited by Michael Brown, Patrick M. Geoghegan, James Kelly. Dublin: Irish Academic Press, 2003.
Ristaino, J. B., and Chia-Hui Hu. "DNA Sequence Analysis of the Late-Blight Pathogen Gives Clues to the World-wide Migration." https://ristainolab.cals.ncsu.edu/files/2015/07/Ristaino-Hu-DNA-Sequence-Analysis-of-the-Late-Blight-Pathogen-Gives-Clues-to-the-World-wide-Migration.pdf (accessed on 6/22/2020).
Ritchie, Leitch. *Ireland, Picturesque and Romantic, with Nineteen Engravings from Drawings by D. M'Clise, A. R. A. Ritchie, and T. Creswick*. 2 vols. London: Longman, Orme, Browne, Green and Longmans, 1837.
Roberts, Paul E. W. "Caravats and Shanavests: Whiteboyism and Faction Fighting in East Munster, 1801–1811." In *Irish Peasants: Violence & Political Unrest, 1780–1914*. 64–101. Edited by Samuel Clark and James S. Donnelly, Jr. Madison: University of Wisconsin Press, 1983.
Robinson, Marilynne. "Which Way to the City on the Hill." *New York Review of Books*, 66:12 (July 18, 2019), 43.
Rogers, William B. "The Great Hunger: Act of God or Acts of Man?" In *Ireland's Great Hunger: Silence, Memory and Commemoration*, 235–56. Quinnipiac University Studies in the Great Hunger. Edited by David A. Valone and Christine Kinealy. New York: University Press of America, 2002.
Romani, Robert. "British Views on Irish National Character, 1800–1845: An Intellectual History," *European History of Ideas*, 23:5–6 (1997), 193–219.
Ryder, David, and Charles E. Orser, Jr. "From Farmers to Defendants: Ballykilcline and Its Historical Context." In *Unearthing Hidden Ireland: Historical Archaeology at Ballykilcline, County Roscommon*, 18–36. Edited by Charles E. Orser, Jr. Bray: County Wicklow: Worldwell, 2006.

Ryder, Sean. "Reading Lessons: Famine and the *Nation*." In *Fearful Realities: New Perspectives on the Irish Famine*, 151–63. Edited by Chris Morash and Richard Hayes. Dublin: Irish Academic Press, 1996.

Rynne, Colin. *Industrial Ireland, 1750–1930: An Archaeology*. Cork: Collins Press, 2006.

Salaman, Redcliffe N. *The History and Social Influence of the Potato*. Cambridge: Cambridge University Press, 1949/1970.

Scally, Robert James. *The End of Hidden Ireland: Rebellion, Famine and Emigration*. Oxford: Oxford University Press, 1995.

Schrier, Arnold. *Ireland and the American Emigration*. Chester, PA: Dufour Editions [1958] 1997.

Schulz, Kathryn. "Annals of Seismology: The Really Big One." *New Yorker*, July 20, 2015, 52–59.

Scott, Thomas. *Ireland Estimated as a Field of Investment*. London: Thomas Harrison, 1854.

Scott, Thomas Colville. *Connemara after the Famine: A Journal of the Survey of the Martin Estate, 1853*. Edited with introduction by Tim Robinson. Dublin: Lilliput, 1995.

Searle, Geoffrey Russell. *Morality and the Market in Victorian Britain*. New York: Oxford University Press, 1998.

Sen, Amartya. *Poverty and Famine: An Essay on Entitlement and Deprivation*. Oxford: Oxford University Press, 1981.

Senior, Nassau William. "Relief of Irish Distress in 1847 and 1848." In *Journals, Conversations and Essays Relating to Ireland in Two Volumes*. Vol. 1, 208–82. London: Longman, Greene, 1868.

Sexton, Regina. "Diet in Pre-Famine Ireland." *Atlas of the Great Irish Famine*, 41–43. Edited John Crowley, William J. Smyth and Mike Murphy. New York: New York University Press, 2012.

Shaw, Fr. Francis. "The Canon of Irish History: A Challenge." *Studies: An Irish Quarterly Review*, 61:242 (Summer 1972), 117–53.

Sheil, Helen. *Falling into Wretchedness: Ferbane in the Late 1830s*. Maynooth Studies in Irish Local History Number 15. Edited by Raymond Gillespie. Dublin: Irish Academic Press, 1998.

Smith, Henry Nash. *Virgin Land: The American West as Symbol and Myth*. Cambridge, MA: Harvard University Press, 1973.

Smith, Rev. Joseph Denham Smith. *Connemara: Past and Present*. Dublin: Robertson, 1853.

Smyth, William J. "Classify, Confine, Discipline and Punish—The Roscrea Union: A Microgeography of the Workhouse System during the Famine." In *Atlas of the Great Irish Famine*, 128–44. Edited by John Crowley, William J. Smyth and Mike Murphy. New York: New York University Press, 2012.

———. "Exodus from Ireland—Patterns of Emigration." In *Atlas of the Great Irish Famine*, 494–504. Edited by John Crowley, William J. Smyth and Mike Murphy. New York: New York University Press, 2012.

———. "'Mapping the People,' The Growth and Distribution of the People." In *Atlas of the Great Irish Famine*, 13–22. Edited by John Crowley, William J. Smyth and Mike Murphy. New York: New York University Press, 2012.

———. "The Province of Connacht and the Great Famine." In *Atlas of the Great Irish Famine*, 281–90. Edited by John Crowley, William J. Smyth and Mike Murphy. New York: New York University Press, 2012.

———. "The Province of Munster and the Great Famine." In *Atlas of the Great Irish Famine*, 359–70. Edited by John Crowley, William J. Smyth and Mike Murphy. New York: New York University Press, 2012.

———. "The Province of Ulster and the Great Famine." In *Atlas of the Great Irish Famine*, 417–25. Edited by John Crowley, William J. Smyth and Mike Murphy. New York: New York University Press, 2012.

Society of Friends. *Transactions of the Central Relief Committee of the Society of Friends during the Famine in Ireland in 1846 and 1847*. Dublin: Hodges, Smith, 1852.

Solar, Peter M. "The Potato Famine in Europe." In *Famine 150: Commemorative Lecture Series*, 113–127. Edited by Cormac Ó Gráda. Dublin: Teagasc, 1997.

Somerville, Alexander. *Letters from Ireland During the Famine of 1847*. Edited by K. D. M. Snell. Blackrock, County Dublin: Irish Academic Press, 1994.

Spurr, David. *Rhetoric of Empire: Colonial Discourse in Journalism, Travel Writing and Imperial Administration*. Durham, NC: Duke University Press, 1993.

Stout, Mathew. "The Geography and Implications of Post-Famine Population Decline in Baltyboys, County Wicklow." In *Fearful Realities: New Perspectives on the Irish Famine*, 11–34. Edited by Chris Morash and Richard Hayes. Dublin: Irish Academic Press, 1996.

Strang, Jillian, Joyce Toomre, "Alexis Soyer and the Irish Famine: Splendid Promises and Abortive Measures." In *The Great Famine and the Irish Diaspora in America*, 66–84. Edited by Arthur Gribben. Amherst: University of Massachusetts Press, 1999.

Thackeray, William Makepeace. *The Irish Sketchbook*. New York: P. F. Collier & Son, 1911.

Thomas, Liz. "Ulster Workhouses—Ideological Geometry and Conflict." In *Atlas of the Great Irish Famine*, 156–63. Edited by John Crowley, William J. Smyth and Mike Murphy. New York: New York University Press, 2012.

Thompson, Spurgeon. "Famine Travel: Irish Tourism from the Great Famine to Decolonization." In *Travel Writing and Tourism in Britain and Ireland*, 164–80. Edited by Benjamin Colbert. New York: Palgrave, Macmillan, 2012.

Tóibín, Colm. *The Irish Famine*. London: Profile Books/London Review of Books, 1999.

Trant, Kathy. *The Blessington Estate: 1667–1908*. Dublin: Anvil Books, 2004.

Trench, William Steuart. *Realities of Irish Life*. 3rd edition. London: Longman, Green, 1869.

Trevelyan, Charles. *The Irish Crisis*. London: Longman, Brown, Green, Longmans, 1848.

Tunney, Carmen, and Pat Nugent, "Liverpool and the Great Irish Famine." In *Atlas of the Great Irish Famine*, 504–10. Edited by John Crowley, William J. Smyth and Mike Murphy. New York: New York University Press, 2012.

Turner, Michael. *After the Famine: Irish Agriculture, 1850–1914*. Cambridge: Cambridge University Press, 1996.

Tymoczko, Maria, and Colin Ireland. "Language and Tradition in Ireland: Prolegomena." In *Language and Tradition in Ireland: Communities and Displacements*, 1–27. Edited by Maria Tymoczko and Colin Ireland. Amherst, Boston: University of Massachusetts Press, 2003.

Vandermeer, John. *The Ecology of Agroecosystems*. Boston, MA: Jones, Bartlett, 2011.

Villers-Tuthill, Kathleen. *Beyond the Twelve Bens: A History of Clifden and District, 1860–1923*. Dublin: Connemara Girl Publications, 1986,

———. "Clifden Union, Connemara, County Galway." In *Atlas of the Great Irish Famine*. 291–97. Edited by John Crowley, William J. Smyth and Mike Murphy. New York: New York University Press, 2012.

———. *History of Clifden, 1810–1860*. County Galway: Connacht Tribune, 1982.

W. T. H. See Hamilton, William Tighe.

Wall, Maureen. "The Decline of the Irish Language." In *A View of the Irish Language*, 81–90. Edited by Brian Ó Cuív. Dublin: Stationary Office, 1969.

Walsh, Oonagh. "'An Invisible but Unescapable Trauma': Epigenetics and the Great Famine." In *Women and the Great Hunger*,173–83. Edited by Christine Kinealy, Jason King and Ciarán Reilly. Hamden, CT: Quinnipiac University Press, 2016.

Watts, Ben. "The Dangers of Monoculture Farming." https://www.challenge.org/knowledgeitems/the-dangers-of-monoculture-farming/#:~:text=The%20continued%20degradation%20of%20soil%20is%20making%20it%20unusable%20for%20agriculture.&text=Monoculture%20farming%2C%20however%2C%20has%20some,soil%20fertility%20and%20environmental%20pollution. (accessed June 22, 2020).

Webster, William Bullock. *Ireland Considered as a Field for Investment and Residence*. 2 vols. Dublin: Hodges, Smith, 1852.

Weld, Isaac. *Illustrations of the Scenery of Killarney and the Surrounding Country*. London: Longmans, Hurst, Rees, Orme, Brown, 1807.

Whelan, Irene. *The Bible War in Ireland: The "Second Reformation" and the Polarization of Protestant-Catholic Relations, 1800–1840*. Dublin: Lilliput, 2005.

———. "The Stigma of Souperism." *The Great Irish Famine*. 134–54. The Thomas Davis Lecture Series. Edited by Cathal Póirtéir. Dublin: Mercier, 1995.

Whelan, Kevin. "Born Astride a Grave: The Cultural Effects of the Great Irish Famine." *The Famine Lectures/Léachtaí an Ghorta*, 204–17. Edited by Brendan Ó Conaire. Boyle, County Roscommon: Comhdáil an Chraoibhín, 1995–97.

———. "The Cultural Effects of the Famine." Academe, PDF. https://www.academia.edu/34933948/Cultural_effects_of_the_Irish_Famine_pdf

———. "Landscape and Society on Clare Island, 1700–1900." In *New Survey of Clare Island, Volume I: History and Cultural Landscape*, 73–98. Edited by Críostóir Mac Cárthaigh and Kevin Whelan. Dublin: Royal Irish Academy, 1999.

———. "The Modern Landscape: From Plantation to Present." In *The Atlas of the Irish Rural Landscape*, 67–103. Edited by F. H. A. Aalen, Kevin Whelan and Mathew Stout. Cork: Cork University Press, 1997.

———. "Pre and Post-Famine Landscape Change." In *The Great Irish Famine*, 19–33. Thomas Davis Lecture. Edited by Cathal Póirtíer. Cork: Mercier, 1995.

———. "Settlement Patterns in the West of Ireland in the Pre-Famine Period." In *Decoding the Landscape*, 60–78. Edited by Timothy Collins. Galway: Centre for Landscape Studies, 1994.

———. *The Tree of Liberty: Radicalism, Catholicism and the Construction of Irish Identity, 1760–1830*. Field Day Essays and Monographs, 7. Notre Dame, IN: University of Notre Dame Press, 1996.

White, George Preston. *A Tour of Connemara, with Remarks on Its Great Physical Capabilities*. London: W. H. Smith, 1849, 1851.

Williams, Leslie A. "Bad Press: Thomas Campbell Foster and British Reportage on the Irish Famine, 1845–1849." *Nineteenth-Century Media and the Construction of Identities*, 295–309. Edited by Laurel Blake, Bill Bell and David Finkelstein. Basingstoke: Palgrave, 2000.

———. *Daniel O'Connell, the British Press and the Irish Famine: Killing Remarks*. Burlington, VT: Ashgate/Routledge, 2003.

———. "Irish Identity and the *Illustrated London News*, 1846–1851: Famine to Depopulation," 59–93. In *Representing Ireland: Gender, Class and Nationality*. Edited by Susan Shaw Sailer. Gainesville: University Press of Florida, 1997.

Williams, William H. A. *Creating Irish Tourism: The First Century, 1750–1850*. London: Anthem Press, 2010.

———. "The Irish Tour, 1800–50." *Travel Writing and Tourism in Britain and Ireland*, 97-113. Edited by Benjamin Colbert. New York: Palgrave Macmillan, 2012.

———. *Tourism, Landscape, and the Irish Character: British Travel Writers in Pre-Famine Ireland*. Madison: University of Wisconsin Press, 2008.

Wolf, Daphne. "'Nearly Naked:' Clothing and the Great Hunger in Ireland," 83–93. In *Women and the Great Hunger*. Edited by Christine Kinealy, Jason King and Ciarán Reilly. Hamden, CT: Quinnipiac University Press, 2016.

Wood, Gillen D'arcy. *Tambora: The Eruption that Changed the World*. Princeton, NJ: Princeton University Press, 2004.

Woodham-Smith, Cecil. *The Great Hunger: Ireland, 1845–49*. New York: Old Town Books, [1962] 1989.

Woods, C. J. *Travellers' Accounts as Source-Material for Irish Historians*. Maynooth Research Guides for Irish Local History. Dublin: Four Courts, 2009.

Yates, Nigel. *The Religious Condition of Ireland, 1770–1850*. Oxford: Oxford University Press, 2006.

Young, Arthur. *A Tour in Ireland with General Observations on the Present State of that Kingdom 1776, 1777, and 1778*. Edited by Constantia Maxwell. London: Cambridge University Press, 1925.

INDEX

Aalen, F. H. A. 78, 85
Achill Island, Protestant colony 29, 83, 159, 160, 234–35. *See also* Nangle, Edward
Act of Union 23, 25, 27, 30, 31, 47, 48, 53, 115, 186, 211
agrarian resistance 54–57, 65, 141, 171
agricultural exports as "surplus" 62, 93, 141
agricultural holdings, size of 151, 173
agriculture, pre-Famine 51–54, 72–87
Ainsworth Magazine 245
Akenson, Donald Harmon 288
Altick, Richard D. 37
Amended Poor Law Act of 1847 150, 157, 165, 199, 229, 282, 283
American letters 286
Anglican Church 27, 29, 159
Anglo-Irish aristocracy 10–14, 27, 53, 63–64
Anglo-Saxon. *See* Saxon
anti-Catholic sentiment 25, 26, 30. *See also* Bible Wars, Manooth Grant, Penal Laws
Anti-Corn Law League 35, 105, 109–10
anti-Protestantism 28, 55. *See also* Prophecies of Pastorini
arable land 52, 61, 69, 83, 246
Ashworth, John Harvey 239, 240, 241–43
assisted emigration 177–80
Atthill, Lombe 136
Australian orphan scheme 178
averted births 250

Ballinasloe Star 123
Barrow, John 237 157
Bayley, Frederick 129, 217
begging 68, 129, 131, 173
    seasonal 78
Belfast 20–21, 47–51, 57
Bennett, William 130–31, 172–73
Benthamite principles 36, 39, 42
Bessborough, 4th Earl of 119, 123, 135
Bible Wars 30, 233–36. *See also* Second Reformation

Binns, Jonathan 43, 89
Blackwood, Frederick Temple. *See* Dufferin, Lord
Blair, Tony 3
Blake family of Renvyle 67, 237
Blessington estate 71
bluestone. *See* copper sulfate
Board of Health 153
Board of Works 133, 134
booleying 82
Bourke, Austin 70–71, 74, 78, 93, 96, 99, 141, 142, 144
Boylan, Ciara 286
British Association 158, 159, 183, 199, 203
British national identity 22–23
British press. *See also* individual publications
    and the blight 103–6
    and Daniel O'Connell 33–34, 106–7
    and Famine reporting 126–32
British public opinion 111–12, 118, 187, 211, 217
    and donor fatigue 183–85
    and Evangelicalism 35
British taxpayers 112, 124, 157, 158, 183, 217
Burritt, Elihu 130
Butt, Isaac 190
Butterly, John R. 2, 74, 92, 94, 117
Byron, Reginald 261

Caird, James 239
Carlyle, Thomas 21, 173
Cascadian subduction zone 97
Catholic Association 26, 30
Catholic Emancipation 12–13, 22, 25–27, 28, 69, 255
Catholic Rent 26
Caufield, Rev. C. 157
Céide Fields 76
Celts, Celtic 17, 20–21, 22, 210, 240–41, 247
Census of 1851 228, 229, 237, 249, 266
Central Relief Committee. *See* Society of Friends

310 INDEX

charitable giving. *See also* donor fatigue
  American 159, 162
  British 157–59
Chatterton, Lady Henrietta 18
cheap labor. *See* potato and cheap labor
children 130, 132, 135, 137, 147–48, 158–59,
  172, 176, 234, 250
Choctaw Nation 159, 162
Christian Economics 37, 110
clachans. *See* rundale system
Clanricarde, 1st Marquis of 98, 120, 156, 178,
  188, 221
Clare Journal 103
Clarendon, Lord 188, 189, 204, 283
  on harvest of 1849 215
Clarkson, L. A. 74, 75, 91, 92, 93
class structure in Ireland. *See* middleclass, Irish,
  British perceptions of
class tensions
  post-Famine 255, 270–72
  pre-Famine 56 0
Clontarf, meeting at 32
Coercion Acts 56, 117, 188
coffin ships 175
Coghlan, John 105
Colley, Linda 22, 25
conacre farmers 54, 66–68, 70, 118
confessional landscapes. *See* landscape and
  religion
Congested Districts Board 253
Connacht District Lunatic Asylum 274
Connemara
  and post-Famine imperial designs 237–48
  and Second Reformation 233–36
Connolly, S. J. 35, 263
Connor, Brian 206
Consolidated Annuities Act of 1850 226
copper sulfate 91, 112
Cork Examiner 162
Cork Southern Reporter 128
Corn Laws 35, 36, 52, 105, 108–13, 116–17,
  119, 143, 144, 246
cottiers 52, 66–68, 78, 118, 124, 167, 195,
  209, 228, 272–73
cotton manufacturing. *See* textiles,
  manufacturing of
Coulter, Henry 246
Crawford, E. Margaret 74, 75, 91, 92, 93, 114
Croker, T. Crofton 81
Cromwell, Thomas 68
crop rotation 74

Cullen, Louis M. 16, 52, 73, 92, 94, 95
Curti, Merle 185

D'Arcys of Clifden 235
Dallas, Alexander 233, 235
Dargen, William 243
Darwin, Charles 241
Davy, Humphry 238
de Fréine, Seán 267
de Nie, Michael 21, 23, 211
dehumanizing Famine victims 132, 172, 279
deindustrialization. *See* Irish economy,
  pre-Famine
Devon Commission 71, 128, 210
Devotional Revolution 265, 182
diaspora 260–62, 274
Dickson, M. F. 62
Dingle Peninsula, Protestant colony 29
Donnelly, Jr., James S. 55, 71, 185, 188, 201,
  208, 210, 217, 228, 247, 253, 255, 259
donor fatigue 183–86
Donovan, Dr. David 128
Dooley, Terence 55, 69
Dorian, Hugh 137
Downpatrick Recorder 229
drumlins 19–20, 49, 60–61, 83, 182
Dublin Botanical Gardens 103
Dublin Castle 14
Dublin Statistical Society 210
dúchas 258
Dufferin, Lord 130–31, 198
Duffy, Gavin 127, 132
Duffy, Patrick 89
Dugor. *See* Achill Island

East, Rev. John 18–19, 68, 168, 171, 172–73
Economist 125, 167, 169, 183, 226, 278
Edinburgh Review 191
Eiríksson, Andrés 142, 143, 187
Ejection Act of 1815 71
Elgee, Jane Francesca. *See* Wilde, Lady
emigration
  assisted 41, 57, 126, 177, 178–80, 201, 229
  as "exile" 183, 259
  Famine era 115, 172, 173–83
  and geographical patterns 123
  to Great Britain 175–77
  and the Irish language 182–83, 267
  and mortality 123
  post-Famine 255, 257–60
  pre-Famine 51, 53, 60, 86

and religion 123
transatlantic 173–75
emigrants
   as economic migrants 261
   economic status of 115, 122–23, 181–83
enclosure movement 19, 47, 192
Encumbered Estates Act 211, 217, 225, 235, 237, 238, 240, 248, 257, 283, 284
entitlements to food 279–80
epigenetics 274
Evangelicals, British 27–28, 35–38, 106, 110, 124, 159, 233, 278
Evangelicals, Irish 27–30, 106, 234–36. *See also* Second Reformation
Evans, E. Estyn 82
Evening Mail 103, 104, 164
evictions
   Famine era 115, 127, 171, 179, 182, 205–9, 216–25, 243–44, 271, 285
   pre-Famine 44, 53, 54–55, 56, 71, 94

faction fights 17
family structure 253–56
Famine Walks 288
famines, general
   as a contested term 2
   and poverty 2
   and seasonal migration 92
   warning signs 117
Farrell, James M. 162
fertility rates 250
fevers. *See* workhouses, diseases
financial crisis of 1847 145, 156, 183
Fitzgerald, Patrick 91, 92
Fitzpatrick, David 255, 258
Fitzwilliam estate 64–65, 70, 179
fixity of tenure 72. *See also* tenants' rights. Ulster rights
Flanagan, Catherine 91
food bias, British 15–16, 108, 113
food crises. *See* subsistence crises
Forbes, John 244
Foster, R. F. 27, 32
Foster, Thomas Campbell 108, 124, 184
Foster, William Edward 131, 161
free trade, British commitment to 139
Freeman, T. W. 51, 60, 62
Freeman's Journal 112
Funnell, Warwick 280

Gaelic. *See* Irish language
Galway Vindicator 170

Gardiner's Chronicle 103, 195
General Election of 1847 163, 183
General Relief Committee of New York 159
Gibbons, Luke 18, 280
gothic tropes 18, 132, 221
Graham, Sir James 110, 116
Graham, Robert 20
grain exports
   during the Famine 140–44
   Pre-Famine 51–52, 62
grain imports 137–40, 142, 144, 152, 153
grain prices
   Famine era 121, 137–38, 142, 144–45, 181
   pre-Famine 51–54, 108, 109, 113
Gray, Peter 37, 125
grazing. *See* pasturage
Gregg, Tresham 106
Gregory Clause. *See* Quarter Acre Clause
Gregory, William 156 04
Grey, 3rd Earl 120, 179
Grey, Sir George 120, 164, 203
Grosse-Île 174
Guinnane, Timothy W. 87

Haines, Robin 158, 190
Hall, Anna and Samuel Carter 15, 20
Hall, Spencer T. 131, 172
Hamilton, William Tighe 239
Hancock, William Neilson 210
Handlin, Oscar 260–61
hanging gale 208
harvest cycle 4, 100, 164
harvests, failures, Pre-Famine 52, 90
Head, Francis Bond 244
Henry II 10
Henry VII 10
Henry VIII 10–11
Hibernian Bible Society 28
high farming 57, 80, 239, 247
Hill, George 71
Hilton, Boyd 36, 37
Hole, Samuel Reynolds 240, 247
Hooper, Glenn 240, 242
hungry months 68, 78, 92

Illustrated London News 129–30, 150, 195, 205–8, 209, 212, 217–24, 236, 283
immigrants in the United States. *See* diaspora
Indian meal. *See* maize
Inglis, Henry D. 20, 81, 237
Irish as the Other 15–18, 21–23
Irish character 16, 21, 30, 37, 136, 186, 191, 242

Irish Confederation 189
Irish Crisis. See Trevelyan, Charles
Irish economy
  agriculture 51–57. *See also* pasturage, tillage
  manufacturing and
    deindustrialization 47–51
  post-Famine 255–57, 259
  post-war depression 51, 52, 55
  pre-Famine 47–57, 95
Irish Famine
  and altered landscape 227, 243–45
  as ambiguous concept 2
  and class 277–79
  and conflicting priorities 281–84
  cost to British Government 157, 227, 285
  as genocide 286–89
  and nationalist memory 271, 278
  as "opportunity" 42, 111, 113, 159, 192
  and the oral tradition 269–70
  poor as victims of 2, 87, 271, 278
  and traditional culture 272–74
  as "textual creation" 103
  and violence 187–90
Irish Famine and religion 264–66. *See also*
  Second Reformation, providentialism
Irish famines pre-1840 90–91, 93
Irish Folklore Commission 269
Irish language
  and evangelical proselytization 29, 233, 234
  and the Famine 182, 266–69
Irish narrative 15–23, 26, 30, 34, 51, 57,
  106–8, 128, 136, 154, 186–87, 190–91,
  241, 277–78. *See also* Irish stereotypes
Irish nationalism 26, 30, 31, 263
Irish poverty 15–17, 22, 30, 40–44, 52, 57,
  62–63, 78, 83, 85, 92–95, 203, 242, 258
Irish stereotypes 15–23. *See also* Irish character,
  Irish narrative
  and agrarian landscape 19
  and agriculture 18–19
  and Irish Catholicism 18
  and the potato 15–16, 108
  and poverty 15–23
Irish Tourist's Illustrated Handbook 243

James I 11
James II 11
Johnson, Dr. James 20
Jordan, Donald E. 82

Keane, John B. 255
Kennedy, Arthur 272, 279, 288, 170, 200, 208

Kennedy, Liam 187, 193, 199
Kenny, Kevin 260
Kerr, Donald 213
Kerry Examiner 104, 121
Kildare Place Society 28
Kinealy, Christine 144, 157, 195, 264
Kingsley, Charles 241
Knight, Patrick 16–17
Knox, Robert 241

Labouchere, Henry 157
Labour Rate Act of 1846 132–33
laissez-faire principles 33, 36, 91, 124, 125,
  163, 209, 211, 225, 277–80, 282
Lalor, James Fintan 127, 190
Lambert, H. 126–27
Lancet 151
Land League 263
  land management 59, 85, 251. *See also*
    rundale system and subdivision,
    subletting 68–72
  pyramid structure 63, 65, 69–70, 85, 126
Land Question 263
land transfer to tenants 243–48
landlords 29, 41, 55. *See also* evictions
  and agrarian unrest 54–57
  British opinions of 111, 124
  and conacre farmers 66–67
  and cottiers 66–67
  debt and bankruptcy 209–12
  definition of 69
  and improvements 54, 57, 70, 71–72, 218,
    244, 245
  and linin production 49
  and Quater Acre Clause 156
  and resistance to government policy 126–27
  and rundale system 84
  and subdivision 66–67, 69–70
  and taxes 132, 155, 205, 209, 224
  as tenants 126
landowners. *See* proprietors
landscape
  and agriculture 19
  and culture 258
  and religion 18
Larkin, Emmet 265
Law Life Insurance Company 245, 246
lazy bed. *See* potato cultivation, raised beds
Lengel, Edward G. 17, 186, #241
Lewis, George Cornewall 41, 56
liberalism 37
Lindley, John 103

linen production 19–20, 48–51, 60, 156, 182, 201, 254
Litchfield House Compact 30, 119
Liverpool
  as embarkation point 173
  and Irish migration 176, 260
living standards, post-Famine 256, 176
Lloyd, David 86, 131–32, 279
loan funds 66
London Companies 179
Lucan, third Earl 208
Lumpers 78, 79, 98, 100, 108, 196, 202, 218. *See* also potato varieties
Lyons, F. S. L. 252, 264

Mac Atasney, Gerard 50
McCulloch, J. R. 239, 247 158, 163
MacDonagh, Oliver 67, 71, 81
McDowell, R. B. 69
Mac Éirni, Piaras 269
McGregor, Patrick P. L. 63
MacHale, Archbishop John 209, 212, 235, 267
MacLaughlin, Jim 148
MacManus, Henry 235, 246, 248
McNamara, Justin 52
Mac Suibhne, Breandán 83, 92, 265
Mackay, Charles 217
Mahon, Major Denis 180, 187
Mahony, James 129–30
maize 78, 134, 137–38, 140, 153, 197
  Peel's purchase of 113–14, 117
Major, John 3
making the pattern 17.
Malthus, Thomas 39, 59, 87
Malthusian principles 36, 39, 59–63, 87, 93
Manchester Examiner 167
Manchester Guardian 168
Mansion House Committee 116
marriage rates 60, 86, 86, 91, 250–51, 254
Martin estate 239, 254, 256
Martineau, Harriet 244, 246, 247
Maynooth College Grant 106
meal months. *See* hungry months
meitheal tradition 82, 253, 273
middleclass, British 35, 163, 277, 279
middleclass, Irish
  perceptions of 16, 42
  post-Famine 262
  underground gentry 64–65
middlemen 55–56, 64–65, 67, 68, 70, 71–73, 179

migration
  internal 172–73
  to Great Britain 175–77
Mill, John Stuart 127, 257
Miller, Kerby A. 70, 174, 182, 258, 261, 267
Miller, Thomas 245
Mitchel, John 2, 127, 189, 271, 286
Mokyr, Joel 57, 63, 95, 250
Molly Maguires 175
monoculture. *See* potato monoculture
Moore, David 103
moralism 36, 37, 38, 40, 115, 143, 184, 279
Morash, Christopher 1, 103, 271, 287–88
Morning Chronicle 103–4, 105, 108, 123, 124, 127
mortality rates. *See also* workhouses mortality
  1848 199
  1849 216
  1851 228
  compared to emigration rates 182
  and farm size 71
  post-Famine 249–50, 171–72
  and poverty 180
  by province 250
  and subsistence crises 90

Nally, David P. 267
Nangle, Edward 159, 234, 235
Nation 32–33, 115, 116, 127, 286
Neal, Frank 176
Neave, Digby 228, 244
Nemo, Alexander 238
Newman,, Gerald 36
News of the World 21, 83, 105, 106, 109, 111, 116
Nicholls, George 41–44, 178, 200, 202
Nicholson, Asenath 131, 234, 273
Northern Standard 140
Nowlan, Kevin B. 120, 17
nutritional transition 94

O'Brien, William Smith 189
O'Connell, Daniel 22, 28, 42, 64, 69, 163, 261
  and British politics 26, 31–34, 108
  and Catholic Emancipation 25–27
  and the Famine 110, 115–16, 163, 164, 116
  and liberalism 33, 35, 42, 116
  and Mansion House Committee 115–16
  and Peel 116–17
  and *Punch* 33–34, 106–7
  and Repeal 30–34
  and the state trial 32
  and the Whigs 25, 26, 28, 30–34, 117, 119, 163
  and Young Ireland 32–33, 119, 163

O'Donnell, Bridget 147
O'Gorman, Richard 116
Ó Gráda, Cormac 53, 60, 90, 91, 93, 95, 103, 134, 142, 147, 159, 175, 196, 198, 209–10, 257, 269
Ó hAllmhuráin, Gearóid 273
Ó Murchadha, Ciarán 117, 223, 224, 246
O'Rourke, Kevin 254, 257
Ó Tuathaigh, Gearóid 268
Oath of Supremacy 26 14
oats 49, 52, 61, 74, 75, 78, 105, 137, 138, 139, 141–42, 167, 168
Observer 104, 111
Orange Order 106
orphaned girls. *See* Australian orphan scheme
Orser, Jr, Charles E. 65, 67, 42, 43, 54, 83
Osborne, Bernal 126
Osborne, Sidney Godolphin 233
Otway, Caesar 18, 59–60, 62, 89
outdoor relief 149, 155–56, 169–71, 199–201, 100, 103–4, 114–15, 135–36

Palmerston, Lord 179
Parliament, Irish 10, 11–14, 30 32, 265, 282
Parliament, United Kingdom 13, 14, 17, 26, 27, 30, 48, 51, 116, 149, 163–64, 201, 203, 204, 209, 226, 283–84
Parnell, Charles Stewart 190
partible inheritance 70–71
pasturage 19, 51–54, 80, 82, 85, 86, 205, 246–47, 251–52, 257, 259
peasant proprietor. *See* tenant ownership
Peel, Robert 26, 27, 30, 32, 277, 281
 and the Corn Laws 106, 109–10, 116–18
 and Encumbered Estates Act 211, 214, 237
 and Famine as opportunity 115, 211
 and Famine relief policies 112–16, 117, 121, 124, 136, 142
 and Maynooth Grant 106
 and providentialism 110–11
 and purchase of maize 113–14
Penal Laws 12, 18, 25, 26
people's crop 78–79, 105–6
Phytophthora infestans. *See* potato blight
pigs 80–81, 85, 117, 251
Pim Johnathan 210
Pitt, William, the Younger 25
Pittock, Murry G. H. 17, 22, 23.
Póirtéir, Cathal 270
Political Economy 35, 38, 86, 110, 115, 125, 132, 136, 143, 165, 244, 279, 283, 285

Ponsonby, John William. *See* Bessborough, Fourth Earl of
Poor Law Commission 43, 114, 170, 196, 199–200, 202, 203, 282
Poor Law Extension Act of 1847 154–57, 199, 103–5, 135
Poor Law of 1838, Irish 40–44
Poor Law of 1834, New English 39–40, 44
Poor Law, Old English 38–39
Poor Law Unions. *See* workhouses
Poor Law workhouse test 41, 42–44, 115, 200, 226
population
 density 19, 61, 84
 disequilibrium 60, 85
 growth 49, 50–51, 59–63, 75, 85–86
 post-Famine 249–51, 252–53, 255, 257, 25, 264
 pre-Famine 51, 59–63
post-war depression. *See* Irish economy
potato
 and agricultural exports 74
 and cheap labor 51, 53, 59, 85–86, 240, 246, 251–52
 dependency 50, 51, 74–75, 92, 93, 127, 154, 249, 253, 257, 281
 disadvantages of 79–80
 as fodder 73, 74, 79
 and human fertility 75
 introduced into Ireland 72–73
 as invasive species 2, 85
 and Irish stereotypes 15–16
 and linen production 49
 and "nutritional transition" 74, 94
 nutritional value of 15–16, 62, 75, 142, 197
 and population growth 75, 85
 as substitute food 73–74
 surplus of 80, 269–70
potato blight. *See also* potato harvests
 arrival in Europe 99–100
 arrival in Ireland 103–6
 cumulative effect of 100, 229
 and inevitability 89–95, 97–100
 and monoculture 97–99
 origins of 98–99
 and politics 106–12
 post-Famine return 257
 and providentialism 110–11
 and question of exports 111
potato cultivation 76–78. *See also* potato monoculture
 acreage 80, 118, 169

adapted to Ireland 72–73
and contour levels 89
crop yields 76, 77, 79, 100, 168, 195, 216, 251, 257
and the pig 80–81
and plaggen soil 77, 245
and raised beds 15, 76–77
and role of manure 15, 57, 61, 87, 75–77, 79, 80, 82, 168, 251, 252
use in crop rotation 73, 74
potato economy 59, 80–81, 84–87, 191
collapse of 84, 87, 89–90, 95, 99, 117–18, 126, 128, 167, 216, 257
as cybernetic trap 84–87
sustainability of 86–87, 90, 94
two-tiers 95
potato harvests
1845 100, 103–4, 117
1846 121, 123
1847 167–69
1848 195
1849 215
1850–1852 227
over abundance 80
potato monoculture 3, 84–87, 97–99, 169, 196, 277, 281
potato varieties 73, 78–79, 98. *See also* Lumpers
potato wage 66, 72, 113
poverty trap 258–59
Poynings, Edward 10, 12
price shocks 251
"Prophecies of Pastorini" 28, 55
proprietors 44, 48, 52, 63–65, 70, 71–72, 78, 87, 126, 133, 138, 156, 205, 210–11, 213, 218, 224, 245, 246, 247, 257, 284
absentee 64
and assisted emigration 178–80
Protestant Ascendancy. *See* Anglo-Irish aristocracy
Protestant colonies, missions 29, 233, 235. *See also* Dingle, Achill Island
Protestant Colonization Society 29
Protestant gaze 18–19
Protestant proselytism 28–29, 55, 159, 233–35
Protestantism in Ulster 20–21
Protestants and Famine relief 158
Protestants, British 11, 18, 23, 25–27
Protestants, Irish 11–12, 13, 20–21, 25, 27–30
providentialism 36, 37, 110, 159, 192, 211, 234, 269, 278
public works
under Peel 113, 115, 117, 118, 119, 120–21

under Russell 132–37, 141, 143, 149, 151–52, 155, 161, 167–69, 187, 278, 282, 284
Punch 33–34, 106–7, 188, 201, 211, 212, 213

Quakers. *See* Society of Friends
Quarter Acre Clause 156, 171, 205
Quarterly Review 242
Queen's Letter
first appeal 158
second appeal 183, 184

racial concepts 18–22, 118, 241. *See also* Celts, Saxons
racial depictions of the Irish 34, 241–43
rack-renting 64, 71
Raleigh, Sir Walter 73
Rate-in-Aid 202, 226
rates. *See* taxes
Reform Bill of 1832 35
Reid, Thomas 16, 22
Rein, M. 278
Relief Commission 114
remittances 254, 261
rent. *See also* rack-renting
and conacre farming 67
and cottiers 66
and improvements 72
and middlemen 64
and population pressure 62–63
and subdivision 69–70
rent farming 69, 85
Repeal Association 30, 33, 119
Repeal Campaign 30–34
restructuring Irish agriculture 3, 42, 113, 118, 124, 125, 157, 164, 186, 191–92, 202, 210, 213, 226, 237–40, 247–48, 283–84, 289
rice 114
Rider, David 82
Ritchie, Leitch 20, 42, 78
roads in Ireland 47
Roberts, Paul E. W. 68
Robinson, Marilynne 22
Roebuck, John Arthur 54
Rogers, William B. 287
Rossa, Jeremiah O'Donovan 140
Routh, Randolph 113, 114, 121, 124, 138
rundale system 81–84, 86, 216, 252, 273
Russell, Lord John 41, 100, 109, 117, 120, 128, 134, 179, 189, 191, 201–2, 211, 215, 277, 286
on evictions 209
and General Election 1847 163–64

Russell, Lord John (*cont.*)
  on Irish landlords 188
  on limits to relief 149, 225
  on Peel's relief policies 136
  on public works 136
  takes office 1846 118–21
  on Trevelyan 225
Ryder, David 65, 67

Saxon 17, 21, 240–42, 243, 248
Sayers, Peig 270
scailp (scalp, scalpeen) 68, 205–6
Scally, Robert James 82, 94, 241
Schrier, Arnold 259
Scotsman 103, 104, 115, 132, 168, 176, 196, 200, 215
Scott, Thomas Colville 245
Scrope, George Poulett 54–55, 127, 217, 224, 225, 226
Searle, Geoffrey Russell 37
Second Reformation 28–30, 233–36. *See also* Bible Wars
Sen, Amartya 279
Senior, Nassau 157
Shepherd, Jack 2, 74, 92, 94, 117
Sligo Champion 105, 109
Smith, Adam 35, 36, 37, 39
Smith, Elizabeth 16, 114, 141, 156, 163
Smith, Joseph Denham 155, 162
Smyth, William J. 225
Society for the Irish Church Missions 233
Society of Friends 130, 131, 153, 160–62, 168, 172, 264
  Central Relief Committee 67, 87, 132–33, 152, 160–62, 168
  soup kitchen 130
Solar, Peter 49, 87
Somerville, Alexander 64, 67–68, 134, 167–68
Soup Act 149–54, 284
souperism 30, 234, 236
Soyer, Alexis 151
spailpíní (spalpeens) 68
Spurr, David 241–43
squatters 68, 84
Standard 109
starvation gap 142, 144
Strzelecki, Paul 153
subdivision, subletting 64, 69–72, 253, 281, 283
subsistence crises, pre-Famine 23, 29, 44, 57, 60, 62, 90–91, 94, 113

taxes. *See also* landlords and taxes, British taxpayers
  versus charity 157
  collecting 169
  and Government policy 283
  and Rate-in-Aid 202
  striking the rates 43, 148
Temporary Relief Act 1847. *See* Soup Act
tenant farmers, pre-Famine 63–66
tenant ownership 127, 190–91, 229, 253, 257, 263, 281, 285
tenant rights 64, 72, 127–28, 163, 190, 263, 261, 281.*See also* Ulster rights
tenant-at-will 68
textiles, manufacturing 48–51, 55. *See also* linin production
Thackeray, William Makepeace 20, 21, 34, 49, 238
Three Fs. *See* tenant rights
throughotherness 82
tillage. *See also* potato cultivation
  and grain cultivation 12, 51–54, 62, 73–74, 76, 85, 94
  shift to pasturage 53 54, 56, 85, 246, 251, 259
Times 44, 104, 106, 108, 109, 110, 111, 115, 118, 124, 126, 134, 155, 157, 171, 182, 186, 212, 213, 217, 247, 280
  on administration of the Poor Law 213
  on Irish character 186
  on Irish "mendicity" 158
  on Irish in Britain 175, 177
  on the Mahon assassination 187–88
  on opposition to public works 134
  on property rights 280
  on the Rising of 1848 190
Titanic, RMS 95 97, 99
Tithe Wars 29–30
Tóibín, Colm 271
  post-Famine 243, 248
tourism 16–18, 76, 78, 89, 130, 238
tourist gaze 16.
Townsend, Rev. R. 157
Tralee Chronicle 112, 121, 216
Trench. William Stuart 180
Trevelyan, Charles 114, 124, 132, 135, 136, 139, 140, 151, 171, 178, 183, 199, 203–5, 225, 226, 237, 278, 280
  as administrator 171
  on agricultural restructuring 169, 229, 230
  background 120

and the British Association 158–59, 183, 199, 105
and grain merchants 143
and high price of food 140
on the Irish character 170, 191
on Irish landlords 126
on preventing starvation 125
and support of second Queen's letter 183
and "this great opportunity" 3, 124, 192, 130
The Irish Crisis 190–93
Turner, Michael 246
Twining, Frederick 243
Twistleton, Edward 170, 203–4

Ulster 19–21, 47, 45–50, 54, 61, 74, 63, 70.
   See also Belfast
   and the Famine 202–3, 137–38, 182
   and population 61
   and racial concepts 20–22
   and textiles 48–50
   as moral model 20
   the two Ulsters 18
Ulster "rights" 72
underground gentry. *See* middleclass, Irish
United Irishman, Rising of 1798 13

Victoria, Queen 158, 212–13. *See also* Queen's letters

wages, agricultural 86
wages fund theory 124–25
Wall, Maureen 268
Walmsley, Charles. *See* Prophecies of Pastorini
Walsh, Oonagh 274
Webster, William Bulloch 239
Weld, Isaac 18
Wellington, Duke of 26
west of Ireland. *See* Connemara
Whately, Archbishop Richard 40–41, 43, 185, 210
Whelan, Irene 30, 236
Whelan, Kevin 17, 53, 65, 76, 81, 83, 84, 85, 93, 94, 265, 288

Whig radicals 163–64
Whigs 30, 33, 36, 40, 109, 116–17, 118–21, 149, 154, 163–64, 192
White, George Preston 238
Whiteboys, etc. *See* agrarian unrest
Wilberforce, William 36
Wilde, Lady 140, 286
Wilde, Dr. William 91, 198, 246
Wilkinson, George 43
Williams, Leslie A., xiii–xiv 23, 168, 185
Wilson, James 125, 167, 223, 226, 238
   on moralism 278
   on restructuring Irish agriculture 169
   on second Queen's letter 183–84
women
   and agriculture 76
   and linin production 49, 50
   in post-Famine economy 254
   on public works 135, 137
   and remittances 254
   in workhouses 147, 161, 196
Wood, Sir Charles 120, 124, 133, 151, 154, 164, 179, 203, 227
   on importance of the Poor Law 154–55
Woodham-Smith, Cecil 2
workhouse graveyards 146, 196
workhouses 39–41, 43–44
   debt and bankruptcy 200, 201
   diseases 197–99
   expansion 196, 199
   mortality 146, 154, 197
   occupants, children 147–48
   occupants, gender 147
   overcrowding 145, 196–97, 216
   rations 148, 197 99
   workhouse test. *See* Poor Law
workhouse test

Yates, Neil 27
Young, Arthur 64–65
Young Ireland 33, 116, 119, 127, 163, 189–90, 263
   and the Rising of 1848 189–90

www.ingramcontent.com/pod-product-compliance
Lightning Source LLC
Chambersburg PA
CBHW021135230426
43667CB00005B/128